RECENT ADVANCES IN COMPUTER SCIENCE

RECENT ADVANCES IN COMPUTER SCIENCE

Prof. Akshaya Kumar Nayak
Dr. Avinash Chiranjeev

JNANADA PRAKASHAN (P&D)
in association with
THE GLOBAL OPEN UNIVERSITY
NAGALAND (INDIA)

Published by :
JNANADA PRAKASHAN (P&D)
4837/2, 24, Ansari Road, Daryaganj
New Delhi-110 002, India
Phone : +91-11-23272047
Mobile : +91-9212137080

Assisted by :
Text Book Promotion Society of India
4837/2, 24, Ansari Road, Daryaganj
New Delhi-110 002, India
Phone : +91-11-23272047
Mobile : +91-9212137080

First Edition : 2025

Pages: viii+454

Paper Quality: 80 gsm whtie

Recent Advances in Computer Science

ISBN: 978-81-7139-360-2

Typesetting by :
Vardhman Computers
New Delhi-110 017, India

Published by Mrs. S. Chowdhary for M/s. Jnanada Prakashan (P&D) Daryaganj, Ansari Road, New Delhi-110002, India and printed at Balaji Offset, Navin Shahdara, Delhi-110032, India.

FOREWORD

The first devices that resemble modern computers date to the mid-20th century (around 1940-1945), although the computer concept and various machines similar to computers existed earlier. Early electronic computers were the size of a large room, consuming as much power as several hundred modern personal computers. Modern computers are based on tiny integrated circuits and are millions to billions of times more capable while occupying a fraction of the space. Today, simple computers may be made small enough to fit into a wristwatch and be powered from a watch battery. Personal computers, in various forms, are icons of the Information Age and are what most people think of as "a computer"; however, the most common form of computer in use today is the embedded computer. Embedded computers are small, simple devices that are used to control other devices—for example, they may be found in machines ranging from fighter aircraft to industrial robots, digital cameras, and children's toys.

The ability to store and execute lists of instructions called programs makes computers extremely versatile and distinguishes them from calculators. The Church—Turing thesis is a mathematical statement of this versatility: any computer with a certain minimum capability is, in principle, capable of performing the same tasks that any other computer can perform. Therefore, computers with capability and complexity ranging from that of a personal digital assistant to a super-computer are all able to perform the same computational tasks given enough time and storage capacity.

The history of computing hardware encompasses the hardware, its architecture, and its impact on software. The elements of computing hardware have undergone significant improvement over their history. This improvement has triggered world-wide use of the technology, performance has improved and the price has declined. Computers have become commodities accessible to ever-increasing sectors of the world's population. Computing hardware has become a platform for uses other than computation, such as automation, communication, control, entertainment, and education. Each field in turn has imposed its own requirements on the hardware, which has evolved in response to those requirements.

The von Neumann architecture unifies our current computing hardware implementations. Since digital computers rely on digital storage, and tend to be limited by the size and speed of memory, the history of computer data storage is tied to the development of computers. The major elements of computing hardware implement abstractions: input, output, memory, and processor. A processor is composed of control and datapath. In the von Neumann architecture, control of the datapath is stored in memory. This allowed control to become an automatic process; the datapath could be under software control, perhaps in response to events. Beginning with mechanical datapaths such as the abacus and astrolabe, the hardware first started using analogs for a computation, including water and even air as the analog quantities: analog computers have used lengths, pressures, voltages, and currents to represent the results of calculations. Eventually the voltages or currents were standardized, and then digitized.

This Book titled "Recent Advances in Computer Science" discusses different aspects of service oriented modelling, wi-fi, artificial intelligence, bluetooth, thinkpad, windowsXP, computer recycling, green computing etc.

This Book will be of immense use to all those interested in the art and science of information technology in general and software technologies in particular. Suggestions are welcome for improving the next edition of this Book.

PR Trivedi

15 August 2009
Independence Day

Dr. Priya Ranjan Trivedi
Pro Chancellor and Plenipotentiary
The Global Open University, Nagaland

CONTENTS

	Foreword	(*v*)
1.	Computer	1
2.	Software	47
3.	Service Oriented Modelling	89
4.	Disk Enclosure	149
5.	Wi-Fi	191
6.	Artificial Intelligence	254
7.	Personal Digital Assistant	296
8.	Tablet PC	309
9.	IEEE 802.11	321
10.	Bluetooth	330
11.	Thinkpad	353
12.	Windows XP Editions	366
13.	Computer Recycling	399
14.	Green Computing	409
15.	Computer Security	429
	Bibliography	443
	Index	448

1

COMPUTER

Introduction

A computer is a machine that manipulates data according to a list of instructions. The first devices that resemble modern computers date to the mid-20th century (around 1940-1945), although the computer concept and various machines similar to computers existed earlier. Early electronic computers were the size of a large room, consuming as much power as several hundred modern personal computers. Modern computers are based on tiny integrated circuits and are millions to billions of times more capable while occupying a fraction of the space.

Today, simple computers may be made small enough to fit into a wristwatch and be powered from a watch battery. Personal computers, in various forms, are icons of the Information Age and are what most people think of as "a computer"; however, the most common form of computer in use today is the embedded computer. Embedded computers are small, simple devices that are used to control other devices—for example, they may be found in machines ranging from fighter aircraft to industrial robots, digital cameras, and children's toys.

The ability to store and execute lists of instructions called *programmes* makes computers extremely versatile and distinguishes them from calculators. The Church–Turing thesis is a mathematical statement of this versatility: any computer with a certain minimum capability is, in principle, capable of performing the same tasks that any other computer can perform. Therefore, computers with capability and complexity ranging from that of a personal digital assistant to a super-computer are all able to perform the same computational tasks given enough time and storage capacity.

The Columbia Supercomputer at NASA's Advanced Supercomputing Facility at Ames Research Center

History of Computing Hardware

The history of computing hardware encompasses the hardware, its architecture, and its impact on software. The elements of computing hardware have undergone significant improvement over their history. This improvement has triggered world-wide use of the technology, performance has improved and the price has declined. Computers have become commodities accessible to ever-increasing sectors of the world's population. Computing hardware has become a platform for uses other than computation, such as automation, communication, control, entertainment, and education. Each field in turn has imposed its own requirements on the hardware, which has evolved in response to those requirements.

The von Neumann architecture unifies our current computing hardware implementations. Since digital computers rely on digital storage, and tend to be limited by the size and speed of memory, the history of computer data storage is tied to the development of computers. The major elements of computing hardware implement abstractions: input, output, memory, and processor. A processor is composed of control and datapath. In the von Neumann architecture, control of the datapath is stored in memory. This allowed control to become an automatic process; the datapath could be under software control, perhaps in response to events. Beginning with mechanical datapaths such as the abacus and astrolabe, the hardware first started using analogs for a computation, including water and even air as the analog quantities: analog computers have used lengths, pressures, voltages, and currents to represent the results of calculations. Eventually the voltages or currents were standardised, and then digitised. Digital computing elements have ranged from mechanical gears, to electromechanical relays, to vacuum tubes, to transistors, and to integrated circuits, all of which are currently implementing the von Neumann architecture.

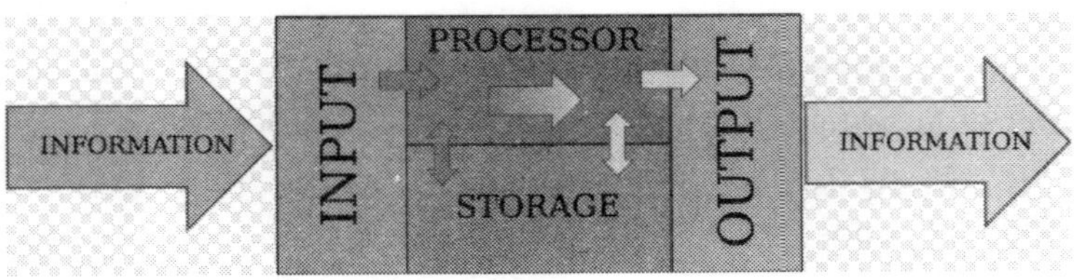

Before Computer Hardware

Originally calculations were computed by humans, whose job title was computers. These human computers were typically engaged in the calculation of a mathematical expression, say for astronomical ephemerides, for artillery firing tables, or for nautical navigation. The calculations of this period were specialised and expensive, requiring years of training in mathematics.

Earliest Calculators

Devices have been used to aid computation for thousands of years, using one-to-one correspondence with our fingers. The earliest counting device was probably a form of tally stick. Later record keeping aids throughout the Fertile Crescent included clay shapes, which represented counts of items, probably livestock or grains, sealed in containers. The abacus was used for arithmetic tasks. The Roman abacus was used in Babylonia as early as 2400 BC. Since then, many other forms of reckoning boards or tables have been invented. In a medieval counting house, a checkered cloth would be placed on a table, and markers moved around on it according to certain rules, as an aid to calculating sums of money.

A number of analog computers were constructed in ancient and medieval times to perform astronomical calculations. These include the Antikythera mechanism and the astrolabe from ancient Greece (c. 150–100 BC), which are generally regarded as the first mechanical analog computers. Other early versions of mechanical devices used to perform some type of calculations include the planisphere and other mechanical computing devices invented by Abû Rayhân al-Bîrûnî (c. AD 1000); the equatorium and universal latitude-independent astrolabe by Abû Ishâq Ibrâhîm al-Zarqâlî (c. AD 1015); the astronomical analog computers of other medieval Muslim astronomers and engineers; and the astronomical clock tower of Su Song (c. AD 1090) during the Song Dynasty.

Suanpan (the number represented on this abacus is 6,302,715,408).

Scottish mathematician and physicist John Napier noted multiplication and division of numbers could be performed by addition and subtraction, respectively, of logarithms of those numbers. While producing the first logarithmic tables Napier needed to perform many multiplications, and it was at this point that he designed Napier's bones, an abacus-like device used for multiplication and division. Since real numbers can be represented as distances or intervals on a line, the slide rule was invented in the 1620s to allow multiplication and division operations to be carried out significantly faster than was previously possible. Slide rules were used by generations of engineers and other mathematically inclined professional workers, until the invention of the pocket calculator. The engineers in the Apollo programme to send a man to the moon made many of their calculations on slide rules, which were accurate to three or four significant figures.

A mechanical calculator from 1914. Note the lever used to rotate the gears.

German polymath Wilhelm Schickard built the first digital mechanical calculator in 1623, and thus became the father of the computing era. Since his calculator used techniques such as cogs and gears first developed for clocks, it was also called a 'calculating clock'. It was put to practical use by his friend Johannes Kepler, who revolutionised astronomy when he condensed decades of astronomical observations into algebraic expressions. An original calculator by Pascal (1640) is preserved in the Zwinger Museum. Machines by Blaise Pascal (the Pascaline, 1642) and Gottfried Wilhelm von Leibniz (1671) followed. Leibniz once said "It is unworthy of excellent men to lose hours like slaves in the labour of calculation which could safely be relegated to anyone else if machines were used."

Around 1820, Charles Xavier Thomas created the first successful, mass-produced mechanical calculator, the Thomas Arithmometer, that could add, subtract, multiply, and divide. It was mainly based on Leibniz' work. Mechanical calculators, like the base-ten addiator, the comptometer, the Monroe, the Curta and the Addo-X remained in use until the 1970s. Leibniz also described the binary numeral system, a central ingredient of all modern computers. However, up to the 1940s, many subsequent designs (including Charles Babbage's machines of the 1800s and even ENIAC of 1945) were based on the decimal system; ENIAC's ring counters emulated the operation of the digit wheels of a mechanical adding machine.

1801: Punched Card Technology

As early as 1725 Basile Bouchon used a perforated paper loop in a loom to establish the pattern to be reproduced on cloth, and in 1726 his co-worker Jean-Baptiste Falcon improved on his design by using perforated paper cards attached to one another for efficiency in adapting and changing the programme. The Bouchon-Falcon loom was semi-automatic and required manual feed of the programme. In 1801, Joseph-Marie Jacquard developed a loom in which the pattern being woven was controlled by punched cards. The series of cards could be changed without changing the mechanical design of the loom. This was a landmark point in programmability.

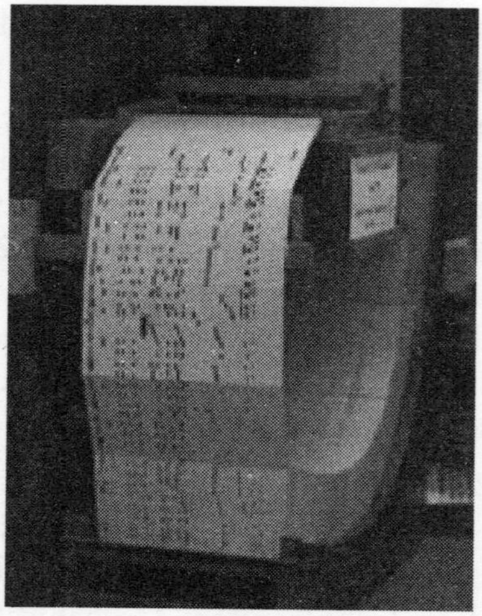

Punched card system of a music machine, also referred to as Book music, a one-stop European medium for organs

In 1833, Charles Babbage moved on from developing his difference engine to developing a more complete design, the analytical engine, which would draw directly on Jacquard's punched cards for its programming. In 1835, Babbage described his analytical engine. It was the plan of a general-purpose programmable computer, employing punch cards for input and a steam engine for power. One crucial invention was to use gears for the function served by the beads of an abacus. In a real sense, computers all contain automatic abacuses (the *datapath*, arithmetic logic unit, or floating-point unit). His initial idea was to use punch-cards to control a machine that could calculate and print logarithmic tables with huge precision (a specific purpose machine). Babbage's idea soon developed into a general-purpose programmable computer, his analytical engine. While his design was sound and the plans were probably correct, or at least debuggable, the project was slowed by various problems. Babbage was a difficult man to work with and argued with anyone who didn't respect his ideas. All the parts for his machine had to be made by hand. Small errors in each item can sometimes sum up to large discrepancies in a machine with thousands of parts, which required these parts to be much better than the usual tolerances needed at the time. The project dissolved in disputes with the artisan who built parts and was ended with the depletion of government funding. Ada Lovelace, Lord Byron's daughter, translated and added notes to the "*Sketch of the Analytical Engine*" by Federico Luigi, Conte Menabrea.

IBM 407 tabulating machine (1961)

A reconstruction of the Difference Engine II, an earlier, more limited design, has been operational since 1991 at the London Science Museum. With a few trivial changes, it works as Babbage designed it and shows that Babbage was right in theory. The museum used computer-operated machine tools to construct the necessary parts, following tolerances which a machinist of the period would have been able to achieve. The failure of Babbage to complete the engine can be chiefly attributed to difficulties not only related to politics and financing, but also to his desire to develop an increasingly sophisticated computer. Following in the footsteps of Babbage, although unaware of his earlier work, was Percy Ludgate, an accountant from Dublin, Ireland. He independently designed a programmable mechanical computer, which he described in a work that was published in 1909.

In 1890, the United States Census Bureau used punched cards, sorting machines, and tabulating machines designed by Herman Hollerith to handle the flood of data from the decennial census mandated by the Constitution. Hollerith's company eventually became the core of IBM. IBM developed punch card technology into a powerful tool for business data-processing and produced an extensive line of specialised unit record equipment. By 1950, the IBM card had become ubiquitous in industry and government. The warning printed on most cards intended for circulation as documents (checks, for example), "Do not fold, spindle or mutilate," became a motto for the post-World War II era.

Punched Card with the Extended Alphabet

Leslie Comrie's articles on punched card methods and W.J. Eckert's publication of *Punched Card Methods in Scientific Computation* in 1940, described techniques which were sufficiently advanced to solve differential equations or perform multiplication and division using floating point representations, all on punched cards and unit record machines. In the image of the tabulator (see left), note the patch panel, which is visible on the right side of the tabulator. A row of toggle switches is above the patch panel. The Thomas J. Watson Astronomical Computing Bureau, Columbia University performed astronomical calculations representing the state of the art in computing.

Computer programming in the punch card era revolved around the computer center. The computer users, for example, science and engineering students at universities, would submit their programming assignments to their local computer center. in the form of a stack of cards, one card per programme line. They then had to wait for the programme to be queued for processing, compiled, and executed. In due course a printout of any results, marked with the submitter's identification, would be placed in an output tray outside the computer center. In many cases these results would comprise solely a printout of error messages regarding programme syntax *etc.*, necessitating another edit-compile-run cycle. Punched cards are still used and manufactured to this day, and their distinctive dimensions (and 80-column capacity) can still be recognised in forms, records, and programmes around the world.

1930s–1960s: Desktop Calculators

The Curta calculator can also do multiplication and division

By the 1900s, earlier mechanical calculators, cash registers, accounting machines, and so on were redesigned to use electric motors, with gear position as the representation for the state of a variable. The word "computer" was a job title assigned to people who used these calculators to perform mathematical calculations. By the 1920s Lewis Fry Richardson's interest in weather prediction led him to propose human computers and numerical analysis to model the weather; to this day, the most powerful computers on Earth are needed to adequately model its weather using the Navier-Stokes equations.

Companies like Friden, Marchant Calculator and Monroe made desktop mechanical calculators from the 1930s that could add, subtract, multiply and divide. During the Manhattan project, future Nobel laureate Richard Feynman was the supervisor of the roomful of human computers, many of them women mathematicians, who understood the differential equations which were being solved for the war effort. Even the renowned Stanis³aw Ulam was pressed into service to translate the mathematics into computable approximations for the hydrogen bomb, after the war.

In 1948, the Curta was introduced. This was a small, portable, mechanical calculator that was about the size of a pepper grinder. Over time, during the 1950s and 1960s a variety of different brands of mechanical calculator appeared on the market. The first all-electronic desktop calculator was the British ANITA Mk.VII, which used a Nixie tube display and 177 subminiature thyratron tubes. In June 1963, Friden introduced the four-function EC-130. It had an all-transistor design, 13-digit capacity on a 5-inch (130 mm) CRT, and introduced reverse Polish notation (RPN) to the calculator market at a price of $2200. The model EC-132 added square root and reciprocal functions. In 1965, Wang Laboratories produced the LOCI-2, a 10-digit transistorised desktop calculator that used a Nixie tube display and could compute logarithms.

Advanced Analog Computers

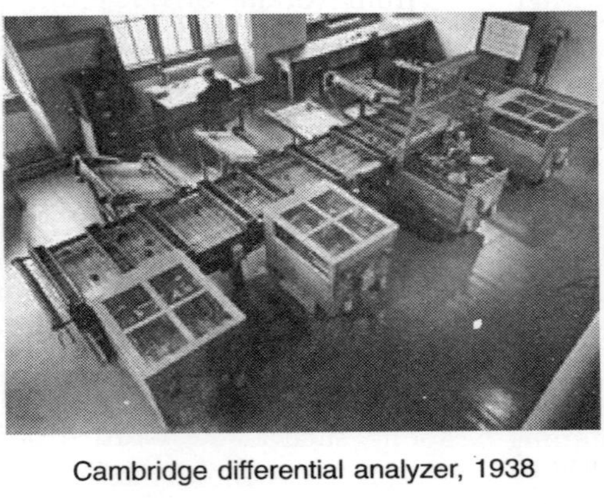

Cambridge differential analyzer, 1938

Before World War II, mechanical and electrical analog computers were considered the "state of the art", and many thought they were the future of computing. Analog computers take advantage of the strong similarities between the mathematics of small-scale properties—the position and motion of wheels or the voltage and current of electronic components—and the mathematics of other physical phenomena, e.g. ballistic trajectories, inertia, resonance, energy transfer, momentum, etc. They model physical phenomena with electrical voltages and currents as the analog quantities.

Centrally, these analog systems work by creating electrical *analogs* of other systems, allowing users to predict behaviour of the systems of interest by observing the electrical analogs. The most useful of the analogies was the way the small-scale behaviour could be represented with integral and differential equations, and could be thus used to solve those equations. An ingenious example of such a machine, using water as the analog quantity, was the water integrator built in 1928; an electrical example is the Mallock machine built in 1941. A planimeter is a device which does integrals, using distance as the analog quantity. Until the 1980's, HVAC systems used air both as the analog quantity and the controlling element. Unlike modern digital computers, analog computers are not very flexible, and need to be reconfigured (i.e., reprogrammed) manually to switch them from working on one problem to another. Analog computers had an advantage over early digital computers in that they could be used to solve complex problems using behavioural analogues while the earliest attempts at digital computers were quite limited.

Since computers were rare in this era, the solutions were often *hard-coded* into paper forms such as graphs and nomograms, which could then produce analog solutions to these problems, such as the distribution of pressures and temperatures in a heating system. Some of the most widely deployed analog computers included devices for aiming weapons, such as the Norden bombsight and the fire-control systems, such as Arthur Pollen's Argo system for naval vessels. Some stayed in use for decades after WWII; the Mark I Fire Control Computer was deployed by the United States Navy on a variety of ships from destroyers to battleships. Other analog computers included the Heathkit EC-1, and the hydraulic MONIAC Computer which modeled econometric flows.

The art of analog computing reached its zenith with the differential analyzer, invented in 1876 by James Thomson and built by H.W. Nieman and Vannevar Bush at MIT starting in 1927. Fewer than a dozen of these devices were ever built; the most powerful was constructed at the University of Pennsylvania's Moore School of Electrical Engineering, where the ENIAC was built. Digital electronic computers like the ENIAC spelled the end for most analog computing machines, but hybrid analog computers, controlled by digital electronics, remained in substantial use into the 1950s and 1960s, and later in some specialised applications. But like all digital devices, the decimal precision of a digital device is a limitation, as compared to an analog device, in which the accuracy is a limitation. As electronics progressed during the twentieth century, its problems of operation at low voltages whil maintaining high signal-to-noise ratios were steadily addressed, a shown below, for a digital circuit is a specialised form of analo circuit, intended to operate at standardised settings (continuing i the same vein, logic gates can be realised as forms of digital circuits But as digital computers have become faster and use larger memo (e.g., RAM or internal storage), they have almost entirely displac analog computers. Computer programming, or coding, has aris as another human profession.

Early Digital Computers

The era of modern computing began with a flurry development before and during World War II, as electronic circ elements replaced mechanical equivalents and digital calculati replaced analog calculations. Machines such as the Z3, Atanasoff–Berry Computer, the Colossus computers, and ENIAC were built by hand using circuits containing relay valves (vacuum tubes), and often used punched cards or punched paper tape for input and as the main (non-volatile) storage medium.

Punched tape programmes would be much longer than the short fragment shown.

In this era, a number of different machines were produced with steadily advancing capabilities. At the beginning of this period, nothing remotely resembling a modern computer existed, except in the long-lost plans of Charles Babbage and the mathematical musings of Alan Turing and others. At the end of the era, devices like the EDSAC had been built, and are universally agreed to be digital computers. Defining a single point in the series as the "first computer" misses many subtleties (see the table "Defining characteristics of some early digital computers of the 1940s" below).

Alan Turing's 1936 paper proved enormously influential in computing and computer science in two ways. Its main purpose was to prove that there were problems (namely the halting problem) that could not be solved by any sequential process. In doing so, Turing provided a definition of a universal computer which executes a programme stored on tape. This construct came to be called a Turing machine; it replaces Kurt Gödel's more cumbersome universal language based on arithmetics. Except for the limitations imposed by their finite memory stores, modern computers are said to be Turing-complete, which is to say, they have algorithm execution capability equivalent to a universal Turing machine.

For a computing machine to be a practical general-purpose computer, there must be some convenient read-write mechanism, punched tape, for example. With a knowledge of Alan Turing's theoretical 'universal computing machine' John von Neumann defined an architecture which uses the same memory both to store programmes and data: virtually all contemporary computers use this architecture (or some variant). While it is theoretically possible to implement a full computer entirely mechanically (as Babbage's design showed), electronics made possible the speed and later the miniaturisation that characterise modern computers.

There were three parallel streams of computer development in the World War II era; the first stream largely ignored, and the second stream deliberately kept secret. The first was the German work of Konrad Zuse. The second was the secret development of the Colossus computers in the UK. Neither of these had much influence on the various computing projects in the United States. The third stream of computer development, Eckert and Mauchly's ENIAC and EDVAC, was widely publicised.

Programme-controlled Computers

Working in isolation in Germany, Konrad Zuse starte construction in 1936 of his first Z-series calculators featurin memory and (initially limited) programmability. Zuse's pure mechanical, but already binary Z1, finished in 1938, never work reliably due to problems with the precision of parts.

A reproduction of Zuse's Z1 computer.

Zuse's subsequent machine, the Z3, was finished in 1941. It was based on telephone relays and did work satisfactorily. The Z3 thus became the first functional programme-controlled, all-purpose, digital computer. In many ways it was quite similar to modern machines, pioneering numerous advances, such as floating point numbers. Replacement of the hard-to-implement decimal system (used in Charles Babbage's earlier design) by the simpler binary system meant that Zuse's machines were easier to build and potentially more reliable, given the technologies available at that time.

Programmes were fed into Z3 on punched films. Conditional jumps were missing, but since the 1990s it has been proved theoretically that Z3 was still a universal computer (ignoring its physical storage size limitations). In two 1936 patent applications, Konrad Zuse also anticipated that machine instructions could be stored in the same storage used for data – the key insight of what became known as the von Neumann architecture and was first implemented in the later British EDSAC design (1949). Zuse also claimed to have designed the first higher-level programming language, (Plankalkül), in 1945 (which was published in 1948) although it was implemented for the first time in 2000 by a team around Raúl Rojas at the Free University of Berlin – five years after Zuse died.

Zuse suffered setbacks during World War II when some of his machines were destroyed in the course of Allied bombing campaigns. Apparently his work remained largely unknown to engineers in the UK and US until much later, although at least

IBM was aware of it as it financed his post-war startup company in 1946 in return for an option on Zuse's patents.

Colossus

During World War II, the British at Bletchley Park (40 miles north of London) achieved a number of successes at breaking encrypted German military communications. The German encryption machine, Enigma, was attacked with the help of electro-mechanical machines called *bombes*. The bombe, designed by Alan Turing and Gordon Welchman, after the Polish cryptographic *bomba* by Marian Rejewski (1938) came into use in 1941. They ruled out possible Enigma settings by performing chains of logical deductions implemented electrically. Most possibilities led to a contradiction, and the few remaining could be tested by hand.

Colossus was used to break German ciphers during World War II.

The Germans also developed a series of teleprinter encryption systems, quite different from Enigma. The Lorenz SZ 40/42 machine was used for high-level Army communications, termed "Tunny" by the British. The first intercepts of Lorenz messages began in 1941. As part of an attack on Tunny, Professor Max Newman and his colleagues helped specify the Colossus. The Mk I Colossus was built between March and December 1943 by Tommy Flowers and his colleagues at the Post Office Research Station at Dollis Hill in London and then shipped to Bletchley Park in January 1944.

Colossus was the first totally *electronic* computing device. The Colossus used a large number of valves (vacuum tubes). It had paper-tape input and was capable of being configured to perform a variety of boolean logical operations on its data, but it was not

Turing-complete. Nine Mk II Colossi were built (The Mk I was converted to a Mk II making ten machines in total). Details of their existence, design, and use were kept secret well into the 1970s. Winston Churchill personally issued an order for their destruction into pieces no larger than a man's hand. Due to this secrecy the Colossi were not included in many histories of computing. A reconstructed copy of one of the Colossus machines is now on display at Bletchley Park.

American Developments

In 1937, Shannon produced his master's thesis at MIT that implemented Boolean algebra using electronic relays and switches for the first time in history. Entitled *A Symbolic Analysis of Relay and Switching Circuits*, Shannon's thesis essentially founded practical digital circuit design. George Stibitz completed a relay-based computer he dubbed the "Model K" at Bell Labs in November 1937. Bell Labs authorised a full research programme in late 1938 with Stibitz at the helm. Their *Complex Number Calculator*, completed January 8, 1940, was able to calculate complex numbers. In a demonstration to the American Mathematical Society conference at Dartmouth College on September 11, 1940, Stibitz was able to send the Complex Number Calculator remote commands over telephone lines by a teletype. It was the first computing machine ever used remotely, in this case over a phone line. Some participants in the conference who witnessed the demonstration were John von Neumann, John Mauchly, and Norbert Wiener, who wrote about it in their memoirs.

Atanasoff–Berry Computer replica at 1st floor of Durham Center, Iowa State University

In 1939, John Vincent Atanasoff and Clifford E. Berry of Iowa State University developed the Atanasoff–Berry Computer (ABC), a special purpose digital electronic calculator for solving systems of linear equations. The design used over 300 vacuum tubes for high speed and employed capacitors fixed in a mechanically rotating drum for memory. Though the ABC machine was not programmable, it was the first to use electronic circuits. ENIAC co-inventor John Mauchly examined the ABC in June 1941, and its influence on the design of the later ENIAC machine is a matter of contention among computer historians. The ABC was largely forgotten until it became the focus of the lawsuit *Honeywell v. Sperry Rand*, the ruling of which invalidated the ENIAC patent (and several others) as, among many reasons, having been anticipated by Atanasoff's work.

In 1939, development began at IBM's Endicott laboratories on the Harvard Mark I. Known officially as the Automatic Sequence Controlled Calculator, the Mark I was a general purpose electro-mechanical computer built with IBM financing and with assistance from IBM personnel, under the direction of Harvard mathematician Howard Aiken. Its design was influenced by Babbage's Analytical Engine, using decimal arithmetic and storage wheels and rotary switches in addition to electromagnetic relays. It was programmable via punched paper tape, and contained several calculation units working in parallel. Later versions contained several paper tape readers and the machine could switch between readers based on a condition. Nevertheless, the machine was not quite Turing-complete. The Mark I was moved to Harvard University and began operation in May 1944.

ENIAC

The US-built ENIAC (Electronic Numerical Integrator and Computer) was the first electronic general-purpose computer. Built under the direction of John Mauchly and J. Presper Eckert at the University of Pennsylvania, it was 1,000 times faster than the Harvard Mark I. ENIAC's development and construction lasted from 1943 to full operation at the end of 1945.

ENIAC performed ballistics trajectory calculations with 160 kW of power.

When its design was proposed, many researchers believed that the thousands of delicate valves (i.e. vacuum tubes) would burn out often enough that the ENIAC would be so frequently down for repairs as to be useless. It was, however, capable of up to thousands of operations per second for hours at a time between valve failures.

ENIAC was unambiguously a Turing-complete device. A "programme" on the ENIAC, however, was defined by the states of its patch cables and switches, a far cry from the stored programme electronic machines that evolved from it. To programme it meant to rewire it. (Improvements completed in 1948 made it possible to execute stored programmes set in function table memory, which made programming less a "one-off" effort, and more systematic.) It was possible to run operations in parallel, as it could be wired to operate multiple accumulators simultaneously. Thus the sequential operation which is the hallmark of a von Neumann machine occurred *after* ENIAC.

First-generation von Neumann Machines

Even before the ENIAC was finished, Eckert and Mauchly recognised its limitations and started the design of a stored-programme computer, EDVAC. John von Neumann was credited with a widely-circulated report describing the EDVAC design in which both the programmes and working data were stored in a single, unified store. This basic design, denoted the von Neumann architecture, would serve as the foundation for the world-wide development of ENIAC's successors.

Design of the von Neumann architecture (1947)

In this generation of equipment, temporary or working storage was provided by acoustic delay lines, which used the propagation time of sound through a medium such as liquid mercury (or through a wire) to briefly store data. As series of acoustic pulses is sent along a tube; after a time, as the pulse reached the end of the tube, the circuitry detected whether the pulse represented a 1 or 0 and caused the oscillator to re-send the pulse. Others used Williams tubes, which use the ability of a television picture tube to store and retrieve data. By 1954, magnetic core memory was rapidly displacing most other forms of temporary storage, and dominated the field through the mid-1970s.

Magnetic core memory. Each core is one bit.

The first working von Neumann machine was the Manchester "Baby" or Small-Scale Experimental Machine, developed by Frederic C. Williams and Tom Kilburn at University of Manchester in 1948; it was followed in 1949 by the Manchester Mark I computer, a complete system, using Williams tube and magnetic drum memory, and introducing index registers. The other contender for the title "first digital stored programme computer" had been EDSAC, designed and constructed at the University of Cambridge. Operational less than one year after the Manchester "Baby", it was also capable of tackling real problems. EDSAC was actually inspired by plans for EDVAC (Electronic Discrete Variable Automatic Computer), the successor to ENIAC; these plans were already in place by the time ENIAC was successfully operational. Unlike ENIAC, which used parallel processing, EDVAC used a single processing unit. This design was simpler and was the first to be implemented in each succeeding wave of miniaturisation, and increased reliability. Some view Manchester Mark I / EDSAC / EDVAC as the "Eves" from which nearly all current computers derive their architecture. Manchester University's machine became the prototype for the Ferranti Mark I. The first Ferranti Mark I machine was delivered to the University in February, 1951 and at least nine others were sold between 1951 and 1957.

The first universal programmable computer in the Soviet Union was created by a team of scientists under direction of Sergei Alekseyevich Lebedev from Kiev Institute of Electrotechnology, Soviet Union (now Ukraine). The computer MESM (МЭСМ, *Small Electronic Calculating Machine*) became operational in 1950. It had about 6,000 vacuum tubes and consumed 25 kW of power. It could perform approximately 3,000 operations per second. Another early machine was CSIRAC, an Australian design that ran its first test programme in 1949. CSIRAC is the oldest computer still in existence and the first to have been used to play digital music.

In October 1947, the directors of J. Lyons & Company, a British catering company famous for its teashops but with strong interests in new office management techniques, decided to take an active role in promoting the commercial development of computers. By 1951 the LEO I computer was operational and ran the world's first regular routine office computer job. On 17 November 1951, the J. Lyons company began weekly operation of a bakery valuations job on the LEO (Lyons Electronic Office). This was the first business application to go live on a stored programme computer.

Defining characteristics of some early digital computers of the 1940s **(In the history of computing hardware)**

Name	First operational	Numeral system	Computing mechanism	Programming	Turing complete
Zuse Z3 (Germany)	May 1941	Binary	Electro-mechanical	Program-controlled by punched film stock	Yes (1998)
Atanasoff–Berry Computer (USA)	Summer 1941	Binary	Electronic	Not programmable—single purpose	No
Colossus (UK)	January 1944	Binary	Electronic	Program-controlled by patch cables and switches	No
Harvard Mark I – IBM ASCC (USA)	1944	Decimal	Electro-mechanical	Program-controlled by 24-channel punched paper tape (but no conditional branch)	Yes (1998)
ENIAC (USA)	November 1945	Decimal	Electronic	Program-controlled by patch cables and switches	Yes
Manchester Small-Scale Experimental Machine (UK)	June 1948	Binary	Electronic	Stored-program in Williams cathode ray tube memory	Yes
Modified ENIAC (USA)	September 1948	Decimal	Electronic	Program-controlled by patch cables and switches plus a primitive read-only stored programming mechanism using the Function Tables as program ROM	Yes

EDSAC (UK)	May 1949	Binary	Electronic	Stored-program in mercury delay line memory	Yes
Manchester Mark I (UK)	October 1949	Binary	Electronic	Stored-program in Williams cathode ray tube memory and magnetic drum memory	Yes
CSIRAC (Australia)	November 1949	Binary	Electronic	Stored-program in mercury delay line memory	Yes

In June 1951, the UNIVAC I (Universal Automatic Computer) was delivered to the U.S. Census Bureau. Remington Rand eventually sold 46 machines at more than $1 million each. UNIVAC was the first 'mass produced' computer; all predecessors had been 'one-off' units. It used 5,200 vacuum tubes and consumed 125 kW of power. It used a mercury delay line capable of storing 1,000 words of 11 decimal digits plus sign (72-bit words) for memory. Unlike IBM machines it was not equipped with a punch card reader but 1930s style metal magnetic tape input, making it incompatible with some existing commercial data stores. High speed punched paper tape and modern-style magnetic tapes were used for input/output by other computers of the era.

In 1952, IBM publicly announced the IBM 701 Electronic Data Processing Machine, the first in its successful 700/7000 series and its first IBM mainframe computer. The IBM 704, introduced in 1954, used magnetic core memory, which became the standard for large machines. The first implemented high-level general purpose programming language, Fortran, was also being developed at IBM for the 704 during 1955 and 1956 and released in early 1957. (Konrad Zuse's 1945 design of the high-level language Plankalkül was not implemented at that time.) A volunteer user group was founded in 1955 to share their software and experiences with the IBM 701; this group, which exists to this day, was a progenitor of open source.

IBM 650 front panel wiring.

IBM introduced a smaller, more affordable computer in 1954 that proved very popular. The IBM 650 weighed over 900 kg, the attached power supply weighed around 1350 kg and both were held in separate cabinets of roughly 1.5 meters by 0.9 meters by 1.8 meters. It cost $500,000 or could be leased for $3,500 a month. Its drum memory was originally only 2000 ten-digit words, and required arcane programming for efficient computing. Memory limitations such as this were to dominate programming for decades afterward, until the evolution of hardware capabilities and a programming model that were more sympathetic to software development.

In 1955, Maurice Wilkes invented microprogramming, which allows the base instruction set to be defined or extended by built-in programmes (now called firmware or microcode). It was widely used in the CPUs and floating-point units of mainframe and other computers, such as the IBM 360 series.

In 1956, IBM sold its first magnetic disk system, RAMAC (Random Access Method of Accounting and Control). It used 50 24-inch (610 mm) metal disks, with 100 tracks per side. It could store 5 megabytes of data and cost $10,000 per megabyte. (As of 2008, magnetic storage, in the form of hard disks, costs less than one 50th of a cent per megabyte).

Second Generation: Transistors

In the second half of the 1950s bipolar junction transistors (BJTs) replaced vacuum tubes. Their use gave rise to the "second generation" computers. Initially, it was believed that very few computers would ever be produced or used. This was due in part to their size, cost, and the skill required to operate or interpret their results. Transistors greatly reduced computers' size, initial cost and operating cost.

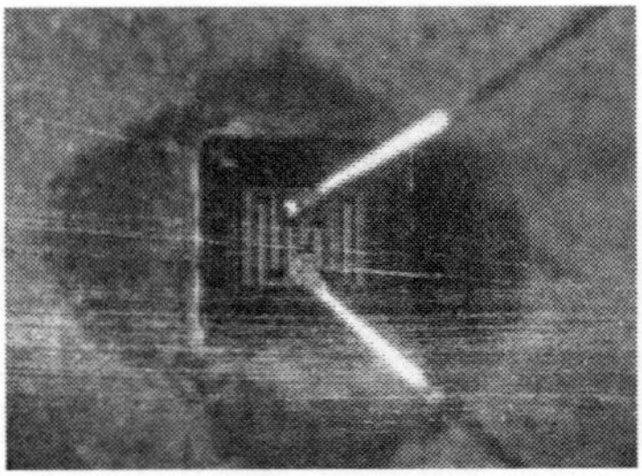

A bipolar junction transistor.

The bipolar junction transistor was invented in 1947. If no electrical current flows through the base-emitter path of a bipolar transistor, the transistor's collector-emitter path blocks electrical current (and the transistor is said to "turn full off"). If sufficient current flows through the base-emitter path of a transistor, that transistor's collector-emitter path also passes current (and the transistor is said to "turn full on"). Current flow or current blockage represent binary 1 (true) or 0 (false), respectively. Compared to vacuum tubes, transistors have many advantages: they are less expensive to manufacture and are ten times faster, switching from the condition 1 to 0 in millionths or billionths of a second. Transistor volume is measured in cubic millimeters compared to vacuum tubes' cubic centimeters. Transistors' lower operating temperature increased their reliability, compared to vacuum tubes. Transistorised computers could contain tens of thousands of binary logic circuits in a relatively compact space.

Typically, second-generation computers were composed of large numbers of printed circuit boards such as the IBM Standard Modular System each carrying one to four logic gates or flip-flops. A second generation computer, the IBM 1401, captured about one third of the world market. IBM installed more than one hundred thousand 1401s between 1960 and 1964— This period saw the only Italian attempt: the ELEA by Olivetti, produced in 110 units.

This RAMAC DASD is being restored at the Computer History Museum.

Transistorised electronics improved not only the CPU (Central Processing Unit), but also the peripheral devices. The IBM 350 RAMAC was introduced in 1956 and was the world's first disk drive. The second generation disk data storage units were able to store tens of millions of letters and digits. Multiple Peripherals can be connected to the CPU, increasing the total memory capacity to hundreds of millions of characters. Next to the fixed disk storage units, connected to the CPU via high-speed data transmission, were removable disk data storage units. A removable disk stack can be easily exchanged with another stack in a few seconds. Even if the removable disks' capacity is smaller than fixed disks,' their interchangeability guarantees an nearly unlimited quantity of data close at hand. But magnetic tape provided archival capability fo this data, at a lower cost than disk.

Many second generation CPUs delegated peripheral device communications to a secondary processor. For example, while the communication processor controlled card reading and punching, the main CPU executed calculations and binary branch instructions. One databus would bear data between the main CPU and core memory at the CPU's fetch-execute cycle rate, and other databusses would typically serve the peripheral devices. On the PDP-1, the core memory's cycle time was 5 microseconds; consequently most arithmetic instructions took 10 microseconds (100,000 operations per second) because most operations took at least two memory cycles; one for the instruction, one for the operand data fetch.

During the second generation remote terminal units (often in the form of teletype machines like a Friden Flexowriter) saw greatly increased use. Telephone connections provided sufficient speed for early remote terminals and allowed hundreds of kilometers separation between remote-terminals and the computing center. Eventually these stand-alone computer networks would be generalised into an interconnected *network of networks* — the Internet.

Post-1960: Third generation and beyond

The explosion in the use of computers began with 'Third Generation' computers. These relied on Jack St. Clair Kilby's and

Intel 8742 eight-bit microcontroller IC.

Robert Noyce's independent invention of the integrated circuit (or microchip), which later led to the invention of the microprocessor, by Ted Hoff, Federico Faggin, and Stanley Mazor at Intel. The integrated circuit in the image on the right, for example, an Intel 8742, is an 8-bit microcontroller that includes a CPU running at 12 MHz, 128 bytes of RAM, 2048 bytes of EPROM, and I/O in the same chip.

During the 1960s there was considerable overlap between second and third generation technologies. IBM implemented its IBM Solid Logic Technology modules in hybrid circuits for the IBM System/360 in 1964. As late as 1975, Sperry Univac continued the manufacture of second-generation machines such as the UNIVAC 494. The Burroughs large systems such as the B5000 were stack machines which allowed for simpler programming. These pushdown automatons were also implemented in minicomputers and microprocessors later, which influenced programming language design. Minicomputers served as low-cost computer centers for industry, business and universities. It became possible to simulate analog circuits with the *simulation programme with integrated circuit emphasis*, or SPICE (1971) on minicomputers, one of the programmes for electronic design automation (EDA). The microprocessor led to the development of the microcomputer, small, low-cost computers that could be owned by individuals and small businesses. Microcomputers, the first of which appeared in the 1970s, became ubiquitous in the 1980s and beyond. Steve Wozniak, co-founder of Apple Computer, is credited with developing the first mass-market home computers. However, his first computer the Apple I, came out some time after the KIM-1 and Altair 8800 and the first Apple computer with graphic and sound capabilities came out well after the Commodore PET. Computing has evolved with microcomputer architectures, with features added from their larger brethren, now dominant in most market segments.

Systems as complicated as computers require very high reliability. ENIAC remained on, in continuous operation from 1947 to 1955, for eight years before being shut down. Although vacuum tube might fail, it would be replaced without bringing down the system. By the simple strategy of never shutting down ENIAC, the failures were dramatically reduced. Hot-pluggable hard disks, like the hot-pluggable vacuum tubes of yesteryear, continue the tradition of repair during continuous operation. Semiconductor memories routinely have no errors when they operate, although operating systems like Unix have employed memory tests on start-up to detect failing hardware. Today, the requirement of reliable performance is made even more stringent when server farms are the delivery platform. Google has managed this by using fault-tolerant software to recover from hardware failures, and is even working on the concept of replacing entire server farms on-the-fly, during a service event.

In the twenty-first century, multi-core CPUs became commercially available. Content-addressable memory (CAM) has become inexpensive enough to be used in networking, although no computer system has yet implemented hardware CAMs for use in programming languages. Currently, CAMs (or associative arrays) in software are programming-language-specific. Semiconductor memory cell arrays are very regular structures, and manufacturers prove their processes on them; this allows price reductions on memory products. After semiconductor memories became commodities, computer software became less labour-intensive; programming codes became less arcane, more understandable. When the CMOS field effect transistor-based logic gates supplanted bipolar transistors, computer power consumption could decrease dramatically (A CMOS FET draws current during the 'transition' between logic states, unlike the higher current draw of a BJT). This has allowed computing to become a commodity which is now ubiquitous, embedded in many forms, from greeting cards and telephones to satellites. Computing hardware and its software have even become a metaphor for the operation of the universe.

An indication of the rapidity of development of this field can be inferred by the history of the seminal article. By the time that anyone had time to write anything down, it was obsolete. After

1945, others read John von Neumann's *First Draft of a Report on the EDVAC*, and immediately started implementing their own systems. To this day, the pace of development has continued, worldwide.

The term hardware covers all of those parts of a computer that are tangible objects. Circuits, displays, power supplies, cables, keyboards, printers and mice are all hardware.

History of Computing Hardware

<table>
<tr><td rowspan="2">First Generation (Mechanical/Electromechanical)</td><td>Calculators</td><td>Antikythera mechanism, Difference Engine, Norden bombsight</td></tr>
<tr><td>Programmable Devices</td><td>Jacquard loom, Analytical Engine, Harvard Mark I, Z3</td></tr>
<tr><td rowspan="2">Second Generation (Vacuum Tubes)</td><td>Calculators</td><td>Atanasoff–Berry Computer, IBM 604, UNIVAC 60, UNIVAC 120</td></tr>
<tr><td>Programmable Devices</td><td>Colossus, ENIAC, Manchester Small-Scale Experimental Machine, EDSAC, Manchester Mark I, CSIRAC, EDVAC, UNIVAC I, IBM 701, IBM 702, IBM 650, Z22</td></tr>
<tr><td rowspan="2">Third Generation (Discrete transistors and SSI, MSI, LSI Integrated circuits)</td><td>Mainframes</td><td>IBM 7090, IBM 7080, System/360, BUNCH</td></tr>
<tr><td>Minicomputer</td><td>PDP-8, PDP-11, System/32, System/3</td></tr>
<tr><td rowspan="2">Fourth Generation (VLSI integrated circuits)</td><td>Minicomputer</td><td>VAX, IBM System i</td></tr>
<tr><td>4-bit microcomputer</td><td>Intel 4004, Intel 404</td></tr>
</table>

Fourth Generation (VLSI integrated circuits)	8-bit microcomputer	Intel 8008, Intel 8080, Motorola 6800, Motorola 6809, MOS Technology 6502, Zilog Z80
	16-bit microcomputer	Intel 8088, Zilog Z8000, WDC 65816/65802
	32-bit microcomputer	Intel 80386, Pentium, Motorola 68000, ARM architecture
	64-bit microcomputer	x86-64, PowerPC, MIPS, SPARC
	Embedded computer	Intel 8048, Intel 8051
	Personal computer	Desktop computer, Home computer, Laptop computer, Personal digital assistant (PDA), Portable computer, Tablet computer, Wearable computer
Theoretical/experimental	Quantum computer, Chemical computer, DNA computing, Optical computer, Spintronics based computer	

Other Hardware Topics

Peripheral device (Input/output)	Input	Mouse, Keyboard, Joystick, Image scanner
	Output	Monitor, Printer
	Both	Floppy disk drive, Hard disk, Optical disc drive, Teleprinter
Computer busses	Short range	RS-232, SCSI, PCI, USB
	Long range (Computer networking)	Ethernet, ATM, FDDI

Stored Programme Architecture

The defining feature of modern computers which distinguishes them from all other machines is that they can be programmed. That is to say that a list of instructions (the programme) can be given to the computer and it will store them and carry them out at some time in the future.

In most cases, computer instructions are simple: add one number to another, move some data from one location to another, send a message to some external device, etc. These instructions are read from the computer's memory and are generally carried out (executed) in the order they were given. However, there are usually specialised instructions to tell the computer to jump ahead or backwards to some other place in the programme and to carry on executing from there. These are called "jump" instructions (or branches). Furthermore, jump instructions may be made to happen conditionally so that different sequences of instructions may be used depending on the result of some previous calculation or some external event. Many computers directly support subroutines by providing a type of jump that "remembers" the location it jumped from and another instruction to return to the instruction following that jump instruction.

Programme execution might be likened to reading a book. While a person will normally read each word and line in sequence, they may at times jump back to an earlier place in the text or skip sections that are not of interest. Similarly, a computer may sometimes go back and repeat the instructions in some section of the programme over and over again until some internal condition is met. This is called the flow of control within the programme and it is what allows the computer to perform tasks repeatedly without human intervention.

Comparatively, a person using a pocket calculator can perform a basic arithmetic operation such as adding two numbers with just a few button presses. But to add together all of the numbers from 1 to 1,000 would take thousands of button presses and a lot of time—with a near certainty of making a mistake. On the other hand, a computer may be programmed to do this with just a few simple instructions. For example:

```
mov     #0,sum     ; set sum to 0
mov     #1,num     ; set num to 1
loop:   add num, sum     ; add num to sum
add     #1, num     ; add 1 to num
cmp     num,#1000     ; compare num to 1000
ble loop     ; if num <= 1000, go back to 'loop'
halt     ; end of programme. stop running
```

Once told to run this programme, the computer will perform the repetitive addition task without further human intervention. It will almost never make a mistake and a modern PC can complete the task in about a millionth of a second.

However, computers cannot "think" for themselves in the sense that they only solve problems in exactly the way they are programmed to. An intelligent human faced with the above addition task might soon realise that instead of actually adding up all the numbers one can simply use the equation

$$1 + 2 + 3 + \ldots + n = \frac{n(n+1)}{2}$$

and arrive at the correct answer (500,500) with little work. In other words, a computer programmed to add up the numbers one by one as in the example above would do exactly that without regard to efficiency or alternative solutions.

Programmes

A 1970s punched card containing one line from a FORTRAN programme. The card reads: “Z(1) = Y+W(1)” and is labelled “PROJ039” for identification purposes.

In practical terms, a computer programme may run from just a few instructions to many millions of instructions, as in a programme for a word processor or a web browser. A typical modern computer can execute billions of instructions per second (gigahertz or GHz) and rarely make a mistake over many years of operation. Large computer programmes comprising several million instructions may take teams of programmers years to write, thus the probability of the entire programme having been written without error is highly unlikely.

Errors in computer programmes are called “bugs”. Bugs may be benign and not affect the usefulness of the programme, or have only subtle effects. But in some cases they may cause the programme to “hang”—become unresponsive to input such as mouse clicks or keystrokes, or to completely fail or “crash”. Otherwise benign bugs may sometimes may be harnessed for malicious intent by an unscrupulous user writing an “exploit”—code designed to take advantage of a bug and disrupt a program's proper execution. Bugs are usually not the fault of the computer. Since computers merely execute the instructions they are given, bugs are nearly always the result of programmer error or an oversight made in the program's design.

In most computers, individual instructions are stored as machine code with each instruction being given a unique number (its operation code or opcode for short). The command to add two numbers together would have one opcode, the command to multiply them would have a different opcode and so on. The simplest computers are able to perform any of a handful of different instructions; the more complex computers have several hundred to choose from—each with a unique numerical code. Since the computer's memory is able to store numbers, it can also store the instruction codes. This leads to the important fact that entire programmes (which are just lists of instructions) can be represented as lists of numbers and can themselves be manipulated inside the computer just as if they were numeric data. The fundamental concept of storing programmes in the computer's memory alongside the data they operate on is the crux of the von Neumann, or stored programme, architecture. In some cases, a computer might store some or all of its programme in memory that is kept separate from the data it operates on. This is called the Harvard architecture after the Harvard Mark I computer. Modern von Neumann computers display some traits of the Harvard architecture in their designs, such as in CPU caches.

While it is possible to write computer programmes as long lists of numbers (machine language) and this technique was used with many early computers, it is extremely tedious to do so in practice, especially for complicated programmes. Instead, each basic instruction can be given a short name that is indicative of its function and easy to remember—a mnemonic such as ADD, SUB, MULT or JUMP. These mnemonics are collectively known as a computer's assembly language. Converting programmes written in assembly language into something the computer can actually understand (machine language) is usually done by a computer programme called an assembler. Machine languages and the assembly languages that represent them (collectively termed low-level programming languages) tend to be unique to a particular type of computer. For instance, an ARM architecture computer (such as may be found in a PDA or a hand-held videogame) cannot understand the machine language of an Intel Pentium or the AMD Athlon 64 computer that might be in a PC.

Though considerably easier than in machine language, writing long programmes in assembly language is often difficult and error prone. Therefore, most complicated programmes are written in more abstract high-level programming languages that are able to express the needs of the computer programmer more conveniently (and thereby help reduce programmer error). High level languages are usually "compiled" into machine language (or sometimes into assembly language and then into machine language) using another computer programme called a compiler. Since high level languages are more abstract than assembly language, it is possible to use different compilers to translate the same high level language programme into the machine language of many different types of computer. This is part of the means by which software like video games may be made available for different computer architectures such as personal computers and various video game consoles.

The task of developing large software systems is an immense intellectual effort. Producing software with an acceptably high reliability on a predictable schedule and budget has proved historically to be a great challenge; the academic and professional discipline of software engineering concentrates specifically on this problem.

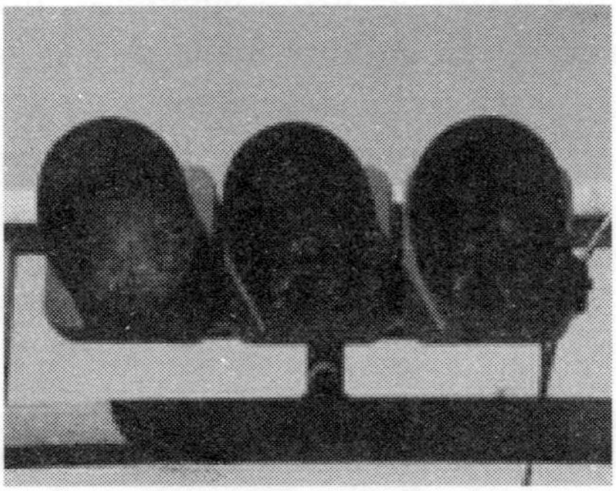

A traffic light showing red.

Example

Suppose a computer is being employed to drive a traffic light. A simple stored programme might say:

1. Turn off all of the lights
2. Turn on the red light
3. Wait for sixty seconds
4. Turn off the red light
5. Turn on the green light

6. Wait for sixty seconds
7. Turn off the green light
8. Turn on the yellow light
9. Wait for two seconds
10. Turn off the yellow light
11. Jump to instruction number (2)

With this set of instructions, the computer would cycle the light continually through red, green, yellow and back to red again until told to stop running the programme.

However, suppose there is a simple on/off switch connected to the computer that is intended to be used to make the light flash red while some maintenance operation is being performed. The programme might then instruct the computer to:

1. Turn off all of the lights
2. Turn on the red light
3. Wait for sixty seconds
4. Turn off the red light
5. Turn on the green light
6. Wait for sixty seconds
7. Turn off the green light
8. Turn on the yellow light
9. Wait for two seconds
10. Turn off the yellow light
11. If the maintenance switch is NOT turned on then jump to instruction number 2
12. Turn on the red light
13. Wait for one second
14. Turn off the red light
15. Wait for one second
16. Jump to instruction number 11

In this manner, the computer is either running the instructions from number (2) to (11) over and over or its running the instructions from (11) down to (16) over and over, depending on the position of the switch.

How Computers Work

A general purpose computer has four main sections: the arithmetic and logic unit (ALU), the control unit, the memory, and the input and output devices (collectively termed I/O). These parts are interconnected by busses, often made of groups of wires.

The control unit, ALU, registers, and basic I/O (and often other hardware closely linked with these) are collectively known as a central processing unit (CPU). Early CPUs were composed of many separate components but since the mid-1970s CPUs have typically been constructed on a single integrated circuit called a *microprocessor*.

Control Unit

The control unit (often called a control system or central controller) directs the various components of a computer. It reads and interprets (decodes) instructions in the programme one by one. The control system decodes each instruction and turns it into a series of control signals that operate the other parts of the computer. Control systems in advanced computers may change the order of some instructions so as to improve performance.

MIPS32 Add Immediate Instruction

001000	00001	00010	0000000101011110
OP Code	Addr 1	Addr 2	Immediate value

Equivalent mnemonic: **addi $r1, $r2, 350**

A key component common to all CPUs is the programme counter, a special memory cell (a register) that keeps track of which location in memory the next instruction is to be read from.

Diagram showing how a particular MIPS architecture instruction would be decoded by the control system.

The control system's function is as follows—note that this is a simplified description, and some of these steps may be performed concurrently or in a different order depending on the type of CPU:

1. Read the code for the next instruction from the cell indicated by the programme counter.
2. Decode the numerical code for the instruction into a set of commands or signals for each of the other systems.
3. Increment the programme counter so it points to the next instruction.
4. Read whatever data the instruction requires from cells in memory (or perhaps from an input device). The location of this required data is typically stored within the instruction code.
5. Provide the necessary data to an ALU or register.
6. If the instruction requires an ALU or specialised hardware to complete, instruct the hardware to perform the requested operation.
7. Write the result from the ALU back to a memory location or to a register or perhaps an output device.
8. Jump back to step (1).

Since the programme counter is (conceptually) just another set of memory cells, it can be changed by calculations done in the ALU. Adding 100 to the programme counter would cause the next instruction to be read from a place 100 locations further down the programme. Instructions that modify the programme counter are often known as "jumps" and allow for loops (instructions that are repeated by the computer) and often conditional instruction execution (both examples of control flow).

It is noticeable that the sequence of operations that the control unit goes through to process an instruction is in itself like a short computer programme—and indeed, in some more complex CPU designs, there is another yet smaller computer called a microsequencer that runs a microcode programme that causes all of these events to happen.

Arithmetic/logic Unit (ALU)

The ALU is capable of performing two classes of operations: arithmetic and logic.

The set of arithmetic operations that a particular ALU supports may be limited to adding and subtracting or might include multiplying or dividing, trigonometry functions (sine, cosine, etc) and square roots. Some can only operate on whole numbers (integers) whilst others use floating point to represent real numbers—albeit with limited precision. However, any computer that is capable of performing just the simplest operations can be programmed to break down the more complex operations into simple steps that it can perform. Therefore, any computer can be programmed to perform any arithmetic operation—although it will take more time to do so if its ALU does not directly support the operation. An ALU may also compare numbers and return boolean truth values (true or false) depending on whether one is equal to, greater than or less than the other ("is 64 greater than 65?").

Logic operations involve Boolean logic: AND, OR, XOR and NOT. These can be useful both for creating complicated conditional statements and processing boolean logic.

Superscalar computers contain multiple ALUs so that they can process several instructions at the same time. Graphics processors and computers with SIMD and MIMD features often provide ALUs that can perform arithmetic on vectors and matrices.

Memory

Magnetic core memory was popular main memory for computers through the 1960s until it was completely replaced by semiconductor memory.

A computer's memory can be viewed as a list of cells into which numbers can be placed or read. Each cell has a numbered "address" and can store a single number. The computer can be instructed to "put the number 123 into the cell numbered 1357" or to "add the number that is in cell 1357 to the number that is in cell 2468 and put the answer into cell 1595". The information stored in memory may represent practically anything. Letters, numbers, even computer instructions can be placed into memory with equal ease. Since the CPU does not differentiate between different types of information, it is up to the software to give significance to what the memory sees as nothing but a series of numbers.

In almost all modern computers, each memory cell is set up to store binary numbers in groups of eight bits (called a byte). Each byte is able to represent 256 different numbers; either from 0 to 255 or -128 to +127. To store larger numbers, several consecutive bytes may be used (typically, two, four or eight). When negative numbers are required, they are usually stored in two's complement notation. Other arrangements are possible, but are usually not seen outside of specialised applications or historical contexts. A computer can store any kind of information in memory as long as it can be somehow represented in numerical form. Modern computers have billions or even trillions of bytes of memory.

The CPU contains a special set of memory cells called registers that can be read and written to much more rapidly than the main memory area. There are typically between two and one hundred registers depending on the type of CPU. Registers are used for the most frequently needed data items to avoid having to access main memory every time data is needed. Since data is constantly being worked on, reducing the need to access main memory (which is often slow compared to the ALU and control units) greatly increases the computer's speed.

Computer main memory comes in two principal varieties: random access memory or RAM and read-only memory or ROM. RAM can be read and written to anytime the CPU commands it, but ROM is pre-loaded with data and software that never changes, so the CPU can only read from it. ROM is typically used to store the computer's initial start-up instructions. In general, the contents of RAM is erased when the power to the computer is turned off while ROM retains its data indefinitely. In a PC, the ROM contains a specialised programme called the BIOS that orchestrates loading the computer's operating system from the hard disk drive into RAM whenever the computer is turned on or reset. In embedded computers, which frequently do not have disk drives, all of the software required to perform the task may be stored in ROM. Software that is stored in ROM is often called firmware because it is notionally more like hardware than software. Flash memory blurs the distinction between ROM and RAM by retaining data when turned off but being rewritable like RAM. However, flash memory is typically much slower than conventional ROM and RAM sc its use is restricted to applications where high speeds are no required.

In more sophisticated computers there may be one or mor RAM cache memories which are slower than registers but faste than main memory. Generally computers with this sort of cach are designed to move frequently needed data into the cach automatically, often without the need for any intervention on th programmer's part.

Input/Output (I/O)

I/O is the means by which a computer receives information from the outside world and sends results back. Devices that provide input or output to the computer are called peripherals. On a typical personal computer, peripherals include input devices like the keyboard and mouse, and output devices such as the display and printer. Hard disk drives, floppy disk drives and optical disc drives serve as both input and output devices. Computer networking is another form of I/O.

Hard disks are common I/O devices used with computers.

Often, I/O devices are complex computers in their own right with their own CPU and memory. A graphics processing unit might contain fifty or more tiny computers that perform the calculations necessary to display 3D graphics. Modern desktop computers contain many smaller computers that assist the main CPU in performing I/O.

Multitasking

While a computer may be viewed as running one gigantic programme stored in its main memory, in some systems it is necessary to give the appearance of running several programmes simultaneously. This is achieved by having the computer switch rapidly between running each programme in turn. One means by which this is done is with a special signal called an interrupt which can periodically cause the computer to stop executing instructions where it was and do something else instead. By remembering where it was executing prior to the interrupt, the computer can return to that task later. If several programmes are running "at the same time", then the interrupt generator might be causing several hundred interrupts per second, causing a programme switch each time. Since modern computers typically execute instructions several orders of magnitude faster than human perception, it may appear that many programmes are running at the same time even though only one is ever executing in any given instant. This method of multitasking is sometimes termed "time-sharing" since each programme is allocated a "slice" of time in turn.

Before the era of cheap computers, the principle use for multitasking was to allow many people to share the same computer.

Seemingly, multitasking would cause a computer that is switching between several programmes to run more slowly—in direct proportion to the number of programmes it is running. However, most programmes spend much of their time waiting for slow input/output devices to complete their tasks. If a programme is waiting for the user to click on the mouse or press a key on the keyboard, then it will not take a "time slice" until the event it is waiting for has occurred. This frees up time for other programmes to execute so that many programmes may be run at the same time without unacceptable speed loss.

Multiprocessing

Some computers may divide their work between one or more separate CPUs, creating a multiprocessing configuration.

Cray designed many supercomputers that used multiprocessing heavily

Traditionally, this technique was utilised only in large and powerful computers such as supercomputers, mainframe computers and servers. However, multiprocessor and multi-core (multiple CPUs on a single integrated circuit) personal and laptop computers have become widely available and are beginning to see increased usage in lower-end markets as a result.

Supercomputers in particular often have highly unique architectures that differ significantly from the basic stored-programme architecture and from general purpose computers. They often feature thousands of CPUs, customised high-speed interconnects, and specialised computing hardware. Such designs tend to be useful only for specialised tasks due to the large scale of programme organisation required to successfully utilise most of the available resources at once. Supercomputers usually see usage in large-scale simulation, graphics rendering, and cryptography applications, as well as with other so-called "embarrassingly parallel" tasks.

Networking and the Internet

Computers have been used to coordinate information between multiple locations since the 1950s. The U.S. military's SAGE system was the first large-scale example of such a system, which led to a number of special-purpose commercial systems like Sabre.

In the 1970s, computer engineers at research institutions throughout the United States began to link their computers together using telecommunications technology. This effort was funded by ARPA (now DARPA), and the computer network that it produced was called the ARPANET. The technologies that made the Arpanet possible spread and evolved. In time, the network spread beyond academic and military institutions and became known as the Internet. The emergence of networking involved a redefinition of the nature and boundaries of the computer. Computer operating systems and applications were modified to include the ability to define and access the resources of other computers on the network, such as peripheral devices, stored information, and the like, as

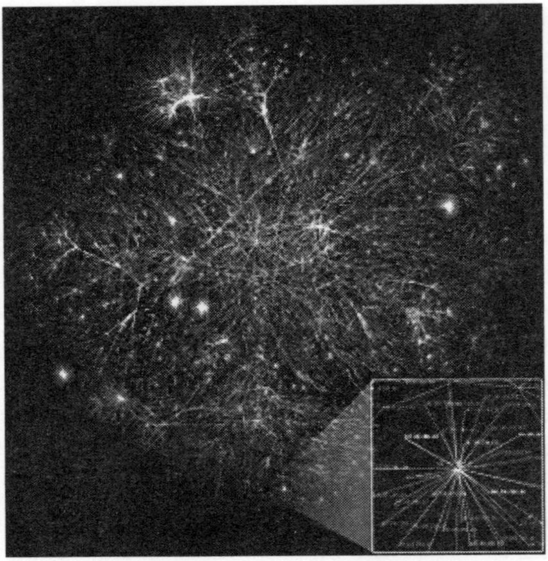

Visualisation of a portion of the routes on the Internet.

extensions of the resources of an individual computer. Initially these facilities were available primarily to people working in high-tech environments, but in the 1990s the spread of applications like e-mail and the World Wide Web, combined with the development of cheap, fast networking technologies like Ethernet and ADSL saw computer networking become almost ubiquitous. In fact, the number of computers that are networked is growing phenomenally. A very large proportion of personal computers regularly connect to the Internet to communicate and receive information. "Wireless" networking, often utilising mobile phone networks, has meant networking is becoming increasingly ubiquitous even in mobile computing environments.

2

SOFTWARE

Software refers to parts of the computer which do not have a material form, such as programmes, data, protocols, etc. When software is stored in hardware that cannot easily be modified (such as BIOS ROM in an IBM PC compatible), it is sometimes called "firmware" to indicate that it falls into an uncertain area somewhere between hardware and software.

Computer Software

Operating system	Unix/BSD	UNIX System V, AIX, HP-UX, Solaris (SunOS), IRIX, List of BSD operating systems
	GNU/Linux	List of Linux distributions, Comparison of Linux distributions
	Microsoft Windows	Windows 95, Windows 98, Windows NT, Windows 2000, Windows XP, Windows Vista, Windows CE
	DOS	86-DOS (QDOS), PC-DOS, MS-DOS, FreeDOS
	Mac OS	Mac OS classic, Mac OS X
	Embedded and real-time	List of embedded operating systems
	Experimental	Amoeba, Oberon/Bluebottle, Plan 9 from Bell Labs

Library	Multimedia	DirectX, OpenGL, OpenAL
	Programming library	C standard library, Standard template library
Data	Protocol	TCP/IP, Kermit, FTP, HTTP, SMTP
	File format	HTML, XML, JPEG, MPEG, PNG
User interface	Graphical user interface (WIMP)	Microsoft Windows, GNOME, KDE, QNX Photon, CDE, GEM
	Text user interface	Command line interface, shells
Application	Office suite	Word processing, Desktop publishing, Presentation program, Database management system, Scheduling & Time management, Spreadsheet, Accounting software
	Internet Access	Browser, E-mail client, Web server, Mail transfer agent, Instant messaging
	Design and manufacturing	Computer-aided design, Computer-aided manufacturing, Plant management, Robotic manufacturing, Supply chain management
	Graphics	Raster graphics editor, Vector graphics editor, 3D modeler, Animation editor, 3D computer graphics, Video editing, Image processing
	Audio	Digital audio editor, Audio playback, Mixing, Audio synthesis, Computer music
		Compiler, Assembler, Interpreter, Debugger, Text Editor, Integrated

	Software Engineering	development environment, Performance analysis, Revision control, Software configuration management
	Educational	Edutainment, Educational game, Serious game, Flight simulator
	Games	Strategy, Arcade, Puzzle, Simulation, First-person shooter, Platform, Massively multiplayer, Interactive fiction
	Misc	Artificial intelligence, Antivirus software, Malware scanner, Installer/Package management systems, File manager

Programming Languages

Programming languages provide various ways of specifying programmes for computers to run. Unlike natural languages, programming languages are designed to permit no ambiguity and to be concise. They are purely written languages and are often difficult to read aloud. They are generally either translated into machine language by a compiler or an assembler before being run, or translated directly at run time by an interpreter. Sometimes programmes are executed by a hybrid method of the two techniques. There are thousands of different programming languages—some intended to be general purpose, others useful only for highly specialised applications.

Programming Languages

Commonly used Assembly languages	ARM, MIPS, x86
Commonly used High level languages	BASIC, C, C++, C#, COBOL, Fortran, Java, Lisp, Pascal
Commonly used Scripting languages	Bourne script, JavaScript, Python, Ruby, PHP, Perl

Major Achievements

German military used the Enigma machine during World War II for communication they thought to be secret. The large-scale decryption of Enigma traffic at Bletchley Park was an important factor that contributed to Allied victory in WWII.

Despite its relatively short history as a formal academic discipline, computer science has made a number of fundamental contributions to science and society. These include:

Applications within computer science

- A formal definition of computation and computability, and proof that there are computationally unsolvable and intractable problems.
- The concept of a programming language, a tool for the precise expression of methodological information at various levels of abstraction.

Applications outside of computing

- Sparked the Digital Revolution which led to the current Information Age and the Internet.

- In cryptography, breaking the Enigma machine was an important factor contributing to the Allied victory in World War II.
- Scientific computing enabled advanced study of the mind and mapping the human genome was possible with Human Genome Project. Distributed computing projects like Folding@home explore protein folding.
- Algorithmic trading has increased the efficiency and liquidity of financial markets by using artificial intelligence, machine learning and other statistical and numerical techniques on a large scale.

Relationship with other Fields

Despite its name, a significant amount of computer science does not involve the study of computers themselves. Because of this, several alternative names have been proposed. Danish scientist Peter Naur suggested the term *datalogy*, to reflect the fact that the scientific discipline revolves around data and data treatment, while not necessarily involving computers. The first scientific institution to use the term was the Department of Datalogy at the University of Copenhagen, founded in 1969, with Peter Naur being the first professor in datalogy. The term is used mainly in the Scandinavian countries. Also, in the early days of computing, a number of terms for the and practitioners of the field of computing were suggested in the *Communications are of the ACM—turingineer, turologist, flow-charts-man, applied meta-mathematician*, and *applied epistemologist*. Three months later in the same journal, *comptologist* was suggested, followed next year by *hypologist*. Recently the term *computics* has been suggested. *Informatik* was a term used in Europe with more frequency.

The renowned computer scientist Edsger Dijkstra stated, "Computer science is no more about computers than astronomy is about telescopes." The design and deployment of computers and computer systems is generally considered the province of disciplines other than computer science. For example, the study of computer hardware is usually considered part of computer engineering, while the study of commercial computer systems and their deployment is often called information technology or information systems. Computer science is sometimes criticised as being insufficiently scientific, a view espoused in the statement "Science is to computer science as hydrodynamics is to plumbing", credited to Stan Kelly-Bootle and others. However, there has been much cross-fertilisation of ideas between the various computer-related disciplines. Computer science research has also often crossed into other disciplines, such as cognitive science, economics, mathematics, physics (see quantum computing), and linguistics.

Computer science is considered by some to have a much closer relationship with mathematics than many scientific disciplines. Early computer science was strongly influenced by the work of mathematicians such as Kurt Gödel and Alan Turing, and there continues to be a useful interchange of ideas between the two fields in areas such as mathematical logic, category theory, domain theory, and algebra.

The relationship between computer science and software engineering is a contentious issue, which is further muddied by disputes over what the term "software engineering" means, and how computer science is defined. David Parnas, taking a cue from the relationship between other engineering and science disciplines, has claimed that the principal focus of computer science is studying the properties of computation in general, while the principal focus of software engineering is the design of specific computations to achieve practical goals, making the two separate but complementary disciplines.

The academic, political, and funding aspects of computer science tend to have roots as to whether a department in the U.S. formed with either a mathematical emphasis or an engineering emphasis. In general, electrical engineering-based computer science departments have tended to succeed as computer science and/or engineering departments. Computer science departments with a mathematics emphasis and with a numerical orientation consider alignment computational science. Both types of departments tend to make efforts to bridge the field educationally if not across all research.

Fields of Computer Science

Computer science searches for concepts and formal proofs to explain and describe computational systems of interest. As with all sciences, these theories can then be utilised to synthesize practical engineering applications, which in turn may suggest new systems to be studied and analysed. While the ACM Computing Classification System can be used to split computer science up into different topics of fields, a more descriptive breakdown follows:

Mathematical Foundations

Mathematical logic

Boolean logic and other ways of modeling logical queries; the uses and limitations of formal proof methods.

Number theory

Theory of proofs and heuristics for finding proofs in the simple domain of integers. Used in cryptography as well as a test domain in artificial intelligence.

Graph theory

Foundations for data structures and searching algorithms.

Type theory

Formal analysis of the types of data, and the use of these types to understand properties of programmes, especially programme safety.

Category theory

Category theory provides a means of capturing all of math and computation in a single synthesis.

Computational geometry

The study of algorithms to solve problems stated in terms of geometry.

Numerical analysis

Foundations for algorithms in discrete mathematics, as well as the study of the limitations of floating point computation, including round-off errors.

Theory of Computation

Automata theory

Different logical structures for solving problems.

Computability theory

What is calculable with the current models of computers. Proofs developed by Alan Turing and others provide insight into the possibilities of what can be computed and what cannot.

Computational complexity theory

Fundamental bounds (especially time and storage space) on classes of computations; in practice, study of which problems a computer can solve with reasonable resources (while computability theory studies which problems can be solved at all).

Quantum computing theory

Representation and manipulation of data using the quantum properties of particles and quantum mechanism.

Algorithms and Data Structures

Analysis of algorithms

Time and space complexity of algorithms.

TESAlgorithms

Formal logical processes used for computation, and the efficiency of these processes.

Programming Languages and Compilers

Compilers

Ways of translating computer programmes, usually from higher level languages to lower level ones.

Interpreters

A programme that takes in as input a computer programme and executes it.

Programming languages

Formal language paradigms for expressing algorithms, and the properties of these languages (e.g., what problems they are suited to solve).

Concurrent, Parallel, and Distributed Systems

Concurrency

The theory and practice of simultaneous computation; data safety in any multitasking or multithreaded environment.

Distributed computing

Computing using multiple computing devices over a network to accomplish a common objective or task and thereby reducing the latency involved in single processor contributions for any task.

Parallel computing

Computing using multiple concurrent threads of execution.

Software Engineering

Algorithm design

Using ideas from algorithm theory to creatively design solutions to real tasks

Computer programming

The practice of using a programming language to implement algorithms

Formal methods

Mathematical approaches for describing and reasoning about software designs.

Reverse engineering

The application of the scientific method to the understanding of arbitrary existing software

Software development

The principles and practice of designing, developing, and testing programmes, as well as proper engineering practices.

System Architecture

Computer architecture

The design, organisation, optimisation and verification of a computer system, mostly about CPUs and memory subsystems (and the bus connecting them).

Computer organisation

The implementation of computer architectures, in terms of descriptions of their specific electrical circuitry

Operating systems

Systems for managing computer programmes and providing the basis of a useable system.

Communications

Computer audio

Algorithms and data structures for the creation, manipulation, storage, and transmission of digital audio recordings. Also important in voice recognition applications.

Networking

Algorithms and protocols for communicating data across different shared or dedicated media, often including error correction.

Cryptography

Applies results from complexity, probability and number theory to invent and break codes.

Databases

Data mining

Data mining is the extraction of relevant data from all sources of data.

Relational databases

Study of algorithms for searching and processing information in documents and databases; closely related to information retrieval.

OLAP

Online Analytical Processing, or OLAP, is an approach to quickly provide answers to analytical queries that are multi-dimensional in nature. OLAP is part of the broader category business intelligence, which also encompasses relational reporting and data mining.

Artificial intelligence

Artificial intelligence

The implementation and study of systems that exhibit an autonomous intelligence or behaviour of their own.

Artificial life

The study of digital organisms to learn about biological systems and evolution.

Automated reasoning

Solving engines, such as used in Prolog, which produce steps a result given a query on a fact and rule database.

Computer vision

Algorithms for identifying three dimensional objects from one or more two dimensional pictures.

Machine learning

Automated creation of a set of rules and axioms based on input.

Natural language processing/Computational linguistics

Automated understanding and generation of human language

Robotics

Algorithms for controlling the behaviour of robots.

Visual Rendering (or Computer Graphics)

Computer graphics

Algorithms both for generating visual images synthetically, and for integrating or altering visual and spatial information sampled from the real world.

Image processing

Determining information from an image through computation.

Human-Computer Interaction

Human computer interaction

The study of making computers and computations useful usable and universally accessible to people, including the stud and design of computer interfaces through which people us computers.

Scientific Computing

Bioinformatics

The use of computer science to maintain, analyse, and sto biological data, and to assist in solving biological problems such protein folding, function prediction and phylogeny.

Cognitive Science

Computational modelling of real minds.

Computational chemistry

Computational modelling of theoretical chemistry in order to determine chemical structures and properties

Computational neuroscience

Computational modelling of real brains

Computational physics

Numerical simulations of large non-analytic systems

Numerical algorithms

Algorithms for the numerical solution of mathematical problems such as root-finding, integration, the solution of ordinary differential equations and the approximation/evaluation of special functions.

Symbolic mathematics

Manipulation and solution of expressions in symbolic form, also known as Computer algebra.

Formal Methods

In computer science and software engineering, formal methods are particular kind of mathematically-based techniques for the specification, development and verification of software and hardware systems. The use of formal methods for software and hardware design is motivated by the expectation that, as in other engineering disciplines, performing appropriate mathematical analyses can contribute to the reliability and robustness of a design. However, the high cost of using formal methods means that they are usually only used in the development of high-integrity systems, where safety or security is important.

Uses

Formal methods can be applied at various points through the development process. (For convenience, we use terms common to the waterfall model, though any development process could be used.)

Specification

Formal methods may be used to give a description of the system to be developed, at whatever level(s) of detail desired. This formal description can be used to guide further development activities (see following sections); additionally, it can be used to verify that the requirements for the system being developed have been completely and accurately specified.

The need for formal specification systems has been noted for years. In the ALGOL 60 Report, John Backus presented a formal notation for describing programming language syntax (later named Backus normal form or Backus-Naur form (BNF)); Backus also described the need for a notation for describing programming language semantics. The report promised that a new notation, as definitive as BNF, would appear in the near future; it never appeared.

Development

Once a formal specification has been developed, the specification may be used as a guide while the concrete system i developed (i.e. realised in software and/or hardware). Examples:

- If the formal specification is in an operational semantic the observed behaviour of the concrete system can b compared with the behaviour of the specification (whic itself should be executable or simulateable). Additionall the operational commands of the specification may b amenable to direct translation into executable code.
- If the formal specification is in an axiomatic semantics, t preconditions and postconditions of the specification m become assertions in the executable code.

Verification

Once a formal specification has been developed, the specification may be used as the basis for proving properties of the specification (and hopefully by inference the developed system).

Human-directed Proof

Sometimes, the motivation for proving the correctness of a system is not the obvious need for re-assurance of the correctness of the system, but a desire to understand the system better. Consequently, some proofs of correctness are produced in the style of mathematical proof: handwritten (or typeset) using natural language, using a level of informality common to such proofs. A "good" proof is one which is readable and understandable by other human readers.

Critics of such approaches point out that the ambiguity inherent in natural language allows errors to be undetected in such proofs; often, subtle errors can be present in the low-level details typically overlooked by such proofs. Additionally, the work involved in producing such a good proof requires a high level of mathematical sophistication and expertise.

Automated Proof

In contrast, there is increasing interest in producing proofs of correctness of such systems by automated means. Automated techniques fall into two general categories:

- Automated theorem proving, in which a system attempts to produce a formal proof from scratch, given a description of the system, a set of logical axioms, and a set of inference rules.
- Model checking, in which a system verifies certain properties by means of an exhaustive search of all possible states that a system could enter during its execution.

Neither of these techniques work without human assistance. utomated theorem provers usually require guidance as to which properties are "interesting" enough to pursue; model checkers can quickly get bogged down in checking millions of uninteresting states if not given a sufficiently abstract model.

Proponents of such systems argue that the results have greater mathematical certainty than human-produced proofs, since all the tedious details have been algorithmically verified. The training required to use such systems is also less than that required to produce good mathematical proofs by hand, making the techniques accessible to a wider variety of practitioners.

Critics note that such systems are like oracles: they make a pronouncement of truth, yet give no explanation of that truth. There is also the problem of "verifying the verifier"; if the programme which aids in the verification is itself unproven, there may be reason to doubt the soundness of the produced results.

Criticisms

The field of formal methods has its critics. At the current state of the art, proofs of correctness, whether handwritten or computer-assisted, need significant time (and thus money) to produce, with limited utility other than assuring correctness. This makes formal methods more likely to be used in fields where the benefits of having such proofs, or the danger in having undetected errors, makes them worth the resources. Example: in aerospace engineering, undetected errors may cause death, so formal methods are more popular than in other application areas.

At times, proponents of formal methods have claimed tha their techniques would be the silver bullet to the software crisis Of course, it is widely believed that there is no silver bullet fo software development, and some have written off formal method due to those overstated, overreaching claims.

Formal Methods and Notations

There are a variety of formal methods and notations availabl including:

- Abstract State Machines (ASMs)
- Alloy
- B-Method
- Process calculi
  - CSP
  - LOTOS
  - π-calculus
- Actor model
- Esterel
- Lustre
- mCRL2
- Petri nets
- RAISE
- VDM
  - VDM-SL
  - VDM++
- Z notation
- Rebeca Modeling Language

Year 2038 Problem

The year 2038 problem (also known as "Unix Millennium bug", "Y2K38," "Y2K+38," or "Y2.038K" by analogy to the Y2K problem) may cause some computer software to fail before or in the year 2038. The problem affects Unix-like dating systems, which represent system time as the number of seconds (ignoring leap seconds) since 00:00:00 January 1, 1970. This representation also affects software written for most other operating systems because of the broad deployment of C. On most 32-bit systems, the time_t data type used to store this second count is a signed 32-bit integer. The latest time that can be represented in this format, following the POSIX standard, is 03:14:07 UTC on Tuesday, January 19, 2038. Times beyond this moment will "wrap around" and be represented internally as a negative number, and cause programmes to fail, since they will see these times as being not in 2038, but rather in 1901. Erroneous calculations and decisions may therefore result.

Binary : 10000000 00000000 00000000 00001001

Decimal : -2147483639

Date : 1901-12-13 20:46:01 (UTC)

Date : 2038-01-19 03:14:17 (UTC)

Example showing how the date would reset (at 03:14:08 UTC on 19 January 2038).

Known Problems

In May 2006, reports surfaced of an early Y2038 problem in the AOLserver software. The software would specify that a database request should "never" time out by specifying a timeout date one billion seconds in the future. One billion seconds (just over 31 years 251 days and 12 hours) after 21:27:28 on 12 May 2006 is beyond the 2038 cutoff date, so after this date, the timeout calculation overflowed and calculated a timeout date that was actually in the past, causing the software to crash.

Example

$ date

Su 6. Jul 00:32:27 CEST 2008

$ openssl req -x509 -in server.csr -key server.key -out server.crt -days 10789 && openssl x509 -in server.crt -text | grep After

Not After : Jan 18 22:32:32 2038 GMT

$ openssl req -x509 -in server.csr -key server.key -out server.crt days 10790 && openssl x509 -in server.crt -text | grep After

Not After : Dec 14 16:04:21 1901 GMT (32-Bit System)

```
$ openssl req -x509 -in server.csr -key server.key -out server.crt -
days 2918831 && openssl x509 -in server.crt -text | grep After
        Not After : Dec 31 22:41:18 9999 GMT (64-Bit System)
```

Solutions

There is no easy fix for this problem for existing CPU/OS/File System combinations. Changing the definition of time_t to use a 64-bit type would break binary compatibility for software, data storage, and generally anything dealing with the binary representation of time. Changing time_t to an unsigned 32-bit integer, effectively allowing timestamps to be accurate until the year 2106, would affect many programmes that deal with time differences, and thus also break binary compatibility in many cases.

Most operating systems for 64-bit architectures already use 64-bit integers in their time_t. The move to these architectures is already under way and many expect it to be complete before 2038. Using a (signed) 64-bit value introduces a new wraparound date in about 290 billion years, on Sunday, December 4, 292,277,026,596. This problem, however, is not widely regarded as a pressing issue. As of 2007, however, hundreds of millions of 32-bit systems are deployed, many in embedded systems, and it is far from certain they will all be replaced by 2038.

Despite the modern 18- to 24-month generational update in computer systems technology, embedded computers may operate unchanged for the life of the system they control. The use of 32-bit time_t has also been encoded into some file formats, which means it can live on for a long time beyond the life of the machines involved.

A variety of alternative proposals have been made, some of which are in use, including storing either milliseconds or microseconds since an epoch (typically either January 1, 1970 or January 1, 2000) in a signed-64 bit integer, providing a minimum of 300,000 years range. Other proposals for new time representations provide different precisions, ranges, and sizes (almost always wider than 32 bits), as well as solving other related problems, such as the handling of leap seconds.

Software Engineering Disasters

Software engineering is a process that is vulnerable to cost overruns, shifting targets, poor communication, and creeping complexity. Although those who study software engineering aim to mitigate these risks, engineers have not eliminated them completely, often leading to epic failures.

This page lists failures in software engineering, the study and application of principles that produce usable software products, as opposed to computer science, which is the study of more abstract principles.

Understanding past mistakes is an important part of systems engineering, and software engineering failures such as the Therac-25 are incorporated into engineering course curricula.

The Mythical Man-Month

The Mythical Man-Month: Essays on Software Engineering is a book on software project management by Fred Brooks, whose central theme is that "Adding manpower to a late software project makes it later." This idea is known as Brooks's law, and is presented along with the second-system effect and advocacy of prototyping. The work was first published in 1975, and republished as an anniversary edition in 1995 (ISBN 0-201-83595-9) with the essay "No Silver Bullet" and commentary by the author.

Brooks's observations are based on his experiences at IBM while managing the development of OS/360. He had mistakenly added more workers to a project falling behind schedule. He also made the mistake of asserting that one project — writing an Algol compiler — would require six months—regardless of the number of workers involved (it required longer). The tendency for managers to repeat such errors in project development led Brooks to quip that his book is called "The Bible of Software Engineering" because "everybody reads it but nobody does anything about it!"

IDEAS PRESENTED

The Mythical Man-Month

Assigning more programmers to a project running behind schedule will make it even later, due to the time required for the new programmers to learn about the project, as well as the increased communication overhead. When N people have to communicate among themselves (without a hierarchy), as N increases, their output M decreases and can even become negative (i.e. the total work remaining at the end of a day is greater than the total work that had been remaining at the beginning of that day, such as when many bugs are created).

- Group Intercommunication Formula: $n(n - 1) / 2$
- Example: 50 developers -> 50(50 – 1) / 2 = 1225 channels of communication

The Second-system Effect

The second system an engineer designs is the most dangerous system he will ever design, since he will tend to incorporate all of the additions he originated but did not add (due to the inherent time constraints) to the first system. Thus, when embarking upon a second system an engineer should be mindful that he is susceptible to over-engineering it.

Progress Tracking

Question: How does a large software project get to be one year late? Answer: One day at a time! Incremental slippages on many fronts eventually accumulate to produce a large overall delay. Continued attention to meeting small individual milestones is required at each level of management.

Conceptual Integrity

To make a user-friendly system, the system must have conceptual integrity, which can only be achieved by separating architecture from implementation. A single chief architect (or a small number of architects), acting on the user's behalf, decides what goes in the system and what stays out. A "super cool" idea by someone may not be included if it does not fit seamlessly with the overall system design. In fact, to ensure a user-friendly system, a system may deliberately provide *fewer* features than it is capable of. The point is that if a system is too complicated to use, then many of its features will go unused because no one has the time to learn how to use them.

The Manual

What the chief architect produces are written specifications for the system in the form of the manual. It should describe the external specifications of the system in detail, i.e., everything that the user sees. The manual should be altered as feedback comes in from the implementation teams and the users.

The Pilot System

When designing a new kind of system, a team *will* design a throw-away system (whether it intends to or not). This system acts as a *pilot plant* that reveals techniques that will subsequently cause a complete redesign of the system. This second *smarter* system should be the one delivered to the customer, since delivery of the pilot system would cause nothing but agony to the customer, and possibly ruin the system's reputation and maybe even the company's.

Formal Documents

Every project manager should create a small core set of *formal documents* which acts as the roadmap as to what the project objectives are, how they are to be achieved, who is going to achieve them, when they are going to be achieved, and how much they are going to cost. These documents may also reveal inconsistencies that are otherwise hard to see.

Project Estimation

When estimating project times, it should be remembered that programming products (which can be sold to paying customers) and programming systems are both three times as hard to write as in-house programmes. It should be kept in mind how much of the work-week will actually be spent on technical issues, as opposed to administrative or other non-technical tasks, such as meetings.

Communication

To avoid disaster, all the teams working on a project should remain in contact with each other in as many ways as possible (e-mail, phone, meetings, memos etc.) Instead of assuming something, the implementer should instead ask the architects to clarify their intent on a feature he is implementing, before proceeding with an assumption that might very well be completely incorrect.

The Surgical Team

Much as a surgical team during surgery is led by one surgeon performing the most critical work himself while directing his team to assist with or overtake less critical parts, it seems reasonable to have a "good" programmer develop critical system components while the rest of a team provides what is needed at the right time. Additionally, Brooks muses that "good" programmers are generally 5-10 times as productive as mediocre ones. See also Organisation and Team Patterns.

Code Freeze and System Versioning

Software is invisible. Therefore, many things only become apparent once a certain amount of work has been done on a new system, allowing a user to experience it. This experience will yield insights, which will change a user's needs or the perception of the user's needs. The system should, therefore, be changed to fulfill the changed requirements of the user. This can only occur up to a certain point, otherwise the system may never be completed. At a certain date, no more changes would be allowed to the system and the code would be frozen. All requests for changes should be delayed until the *next* version of the system.

Specialised Tools

Instead of every programmer having his own special set of tools, each team should have a designated tool-maker who may create tools that are highly customised for the job that team is doing, e.g., a code generator tool that spits out code based on a specification. In addition, system-wide tools should be built by a common tools team, overseen by the project manager.

Lowering Software Development Costs

There are two techniques for lowering software development costs that Brooks writes about:

- Implementers may be hired only after the architecture of the system has been completed (a step that may take several months, during which time prematurely-hired implementers may have nothing to do).
- Another technique Brooks mentions is not to develop software at all, but to simply buy it "off the shelf" when possible.

Reverse Engineering

Reverse engineering (RE) is the process of discovering the technological principles of a device, object or system through analysis of its structure, function and operation. It often involves taking something (e.g. a mechanical device, electronic component, or software programme) apart and analysing its workings in detail, usually to try to make a new device or programme that does the same thing without copying anything from the original.

Motivation

Reasons for reverse-engineering:

- interoperability.
- lost documentation: Reverse engineering often is done because the documentation of a particular device has been lost (or was never written), and the person who built the

widget is no longer available. Integrated circuits often seem to have been designed on obsolete, proprietary systems, which means that the only way to incorporate the functionality into new technology is to reverse-engineer the existing chip and then re-design it.

- product analysis. To examine how a product works, what components it consists of, estimate costs, identify potential patent infringement.
- security auditing
- removal of copy protection, circumvention of access restrictions.
- creation of unlicensed/unapproved duplicates
- fraud e.g. revealing secret keys from smart cards

Reverse Engineering of Mechanical Devices

As computer-aided design has become more popular, reverse engineering has become a viable method to create a 3D virtual model of an existing physical part for use in 3D CAD, CAM, CAE and other software. The reverse engineering process involves measuring an object and then reconstructing it as a 3D model. The physical object can be measured using 3D scanning technologies like CMMs, laser scanners, structured light digitizers or computed tomography. The measured data alone, usually represented as a point cloud, lacks topological information and is therefore often processed and modeled into a more usable format such as a triangular faced mesh, a set of NURBS surfaces or a CAD model. Applications like Imageware, PolyWorks, Rapidform or Geomagic are used to process the point clouds themselves into formats usable in other applications such as 3D CAD, CAM, CAE or visualisation.

Reverse engineering is also used by businesses to bring existing physical geometry into digital product development environments, to make a digital 3D record of their own products or assess competitors' products. It is used to analyze, for instance, how a product works, what it does, what components it consists of, estimate costs, identify potential patent infringement, etc. Value engineering is a related activity also used by business. It involves deconstructing and analysing products, but the objective is to find opportunities for cost cutting.

Reverse Engineering of Software

The term "reverse engineering" as applied to software means different things to different people, prompting Chikofsky and Cross to write a paper researching the various uses and defining a taxonomy. From their paper: Reverse engineering is the process of analysing a subject system to create representations of the system at a higher level of abstraction. It can also be seen as "going backwards through the development cycle". In this model, the output of the implementation phase (in source code form) is reverse engineered back to the analysis phase, in an inversion of the traditional waterfall model. Reverse engineering is a process of examination only: the software system under consideration is not modified (which would make it reengineering). Software anti-tamper technology is used to deter both reverse engineering and reengineering of proprietary software and software-powered systems. In practice, two main types of reverse engineering emerge. In the first case, source code is already available for the software, but higher level aspects of the programme, perhaps poorly documented or documented but no longer valid, are discovered. In the second case, there is no source code available for the software, and any efforts towards discovering one possible source code for the software are regarded as reverse engineering. This second usage of the term is the one most people are familiar with. Reverse engineering of software can make use of the clean room design technique to avoid infringing copyrights. The reverse engineering of software accounts for 95% of all instances of reverse engineering.

On a related note, black box testing in software engineering has a lot in common with reverse-engineering. The tester usually has the API, but their goals are to find bugs and undocumented features by bashing the product from outside.

Other purposes of reverse engineering include security auditing, removal of copy protection ("cracking"), circumvention of access restrictions often present in consumer electronics, customisation of embedded systems (such as engine management systems), in-house repairs or retrofits, enabling of additional features on low-cost "crippled" hardware (such as some graphics card chipsets), or even mere satisfaction of curiosity.

Binary Software

This process is sometimes termed *Reverse Code Engineering* or RCE. As an example, decompilation of binaries for the Java platform can be accomplished using Jad. One famous case of reverse engineering was the first non-IBM implementation of the PC BIOS which launched the historic IBM PC compatible industry that has been the overwhelmingly dominant computer hardware platform for many years. An example of a group that reverse engineers software for enjoyment is CORE which stands for "Challenge Of Reverse Engineering". In the United States, the Digital Millennium Copyright Act exempts from the circumvention ban some acts of reverse engineering aimed at interoperability of file formats and protocols, but judges in key cases have ignored this law, since it is acceptable to circumvent restrictions for use, but not for access. Aside from restrictions on circumvention, reverse engineering of software is protected in the U.S. by the fair use exception in copyright law. The Samba software, which allows systems that are not running Microsoft Windows systems to share files with systems that are, is a classic example of software reverse engineering, since the Samba project had to reverse-engineer unpublished information about how Windows file sharing worked, so that non-Windows computers could emulate it. The Wine project does the same thing for the Windows API, and OpenOffice.org is one party doing this for the Microsoft Office file formats. The ReactOS project is even more ambitious in its goals as it strives to provide binary (ABI and API) compatibility with the current Windows OSes of the NT branch, allowing software and drivers written for Windows to run on a clean room reverse engineered GPL open source counterpart.

Binary Software Techniques

Reverse engineering of software can be accomplished by various methods. The three main groups of software reverse engineering are

1. Analysis through observation of information exchange, most prevalent in protocol reverse engineering, which involves using bus analyzers and packet sniffers, for example, for accessing a computer bus or computer network connection and revealing the traffic data thereon. Bus or network behaviour can then be analysed to produce a stand-alone implementation that mimics that behaviour. This is especially useful for reverse engineering device drivers. Sometimes reverse-engineering on embedded systems is greatly assisted by tools deliberately introduced by the manufacturer, such as JTAG ports or other debugging means. In Microsoft Windows, low-level debuggers such as SoftICE are popular.
2. Disassembly using a disassembler, meaning the raw machine language of the programme is read and understood in its own terms, only with the aid of machine language mnemonics. This works on any computer programme but can take quite some time, especially for someone not used to machine code. The Interactive Disassembler is a particularly popular tool.
3. Decompilation using a decompiler, a process that tries, with varying results, to recreate the source code in some high level language for a programme only available in machine code or bytecode.

Source Code

A number of UML tools refer to the process of importing source code in order to generate UML diagrams, as "reverse engineering".

Reverse-Engineering of Integrated Circuits/Smart Cards

Reverse Engineering is an invasive and destructive form of analysing a smart card. The attacker grinds away layer by layer of the smart card and takes pictures with an elec ron-microscope. With this technique it is possible to reveal the complete hardware and software part of the smart card. The major problem for the attacker is to bring everything into the right order to find out how everything works. Engineers try to hide keys and operations by mixing up memory positions, for example busscrambling. In some cases it is even possible to attach a probe to direct measure voltages while the smart card is still operational. Engineers employ sensors to detect and prevent this attack. It takes very high effort to break a smart card used for payment e.g., and the technical equipment is only available to large chip-producers. Additionally the gain is low due to other security mechanisms like shadow accounts.

Code Morphing

Code morphing is one of the approaches to protect software pplications from reverse engineering, analysis, modifications, and racking used in obfuscating software. This technology protects itermediate level code such as compiled from Java and .NET nguages (C#, Visual Basic, etc.) rather than binary object code. ode morphing breaks up the protected code into several processor mmands or small command snippets and replaces them by others, iile maintaining the same end result. Thus the protector obfuscates e code at the intermediate level.

Code morphing is a multilevel technology containing hundreds unique code transformation patterns. In addition this technology nsforms some intermediate layer commands into Virtual Machine nmands (like P-Code). Code Morphing may also turn binary e into an undecipherable mess that is not similar to normal npiled code, and completely hides execution logic of the tected code.

Unlike other code protectors, there is no concept of code yption with this method. Protected code blocks are always in the executable state, and they are executed (interpreted) as transformed obfuscated code. The original intermediate code is completely absent.

"Code Morphing" is also used to refer to the Just-in-time compilation technology used in Transmeta processors such as the Crusoe and Efficeon to implement the X86 instruction set architecture.

Forensic Engineering

Forensic engineering is the investigation of materials, products, structures or components that fail or do not operate/function as intended, causing personal injury or damage to property. The consequences of failure are dealt by the law of product liability The subject is applied most commonly in civil law cases, althougl may be of use in criminal law cases. Generally the purpose of forensic engineering investigation is to locate cause or causes o failure with a view to improve performance or life of a componen or to assist a court in determining the facts of an accident. It ca also involve investigation of intellectual property claims, especial patents.

Methods

Methods used in forensic investigations include rever engineering, inspection of witness statements, a working knowled of current standards, as well as examination of the failed compone itself. The fracture surface of a failed product can reveal mu information on how the item failed and the loading pattern pr to failure. The study of fracture surfaces is known as fractograp Fatigue often produces a characteristic fracture surface for exam enabling diagnosis to be made of the cause of the failure. The task in many such investigations is to identify the failure mechan by examining the failed part using physical and chemical techniq This activity is sometimes called root cause analysis. Corrosio another common failure mode needing careful analysis to detern the active agents in the environment which initiated the corrc attack. Accidents caused by fire are especially challenging owir the frequent loss of critical evidence, although when halted early enough can usually lead to the cause. Fire investigation is a specialist skill where arson is suspected, but is also important in vehicular accident reconstruction where faulty fuel lines, for example, may be the cause of an accident.

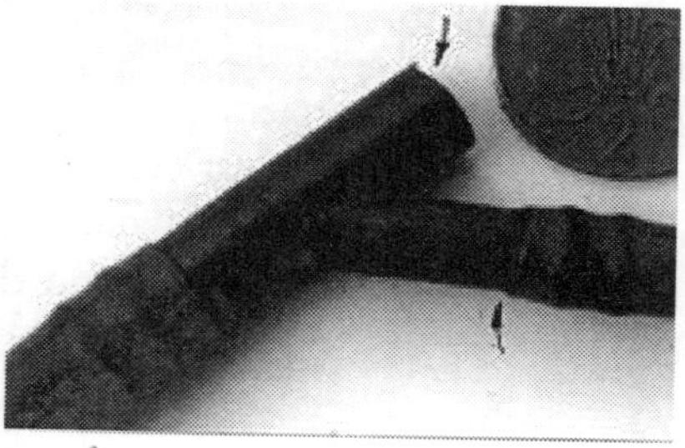

Close-up of broken fuel pipe from road traffic accident

Close-up of broken fuel pipe

amples

The broken fuel pipe shown at right caused a serious accident en diesel fuel poured out from a van onto the road. A following skidded and the driver was seriously injured when she collided ı an oncoming lorry. Scanning electron microscopy or SEM wed that the nylon connector had fractured by stress corrosion king due to a small leak of battery acid. Nylon is susceptible to rolysis in contact with sulfuric acid, and only a small leak of would have sufficed to start a brittle crack in the injection lded nylon 6,6 connector by a mechanism known as stress corrosion cracking, or SCC. The crack took about 7 days to grow across the diameter of the tube, hence the van driver should have seen the leak well before the crack grew to a critical size. He did not, therefore resulting in the accident. The fracture surface showed a mainly brittle surface with striations indicating progressive growth of the crack across the diameter of the pipe. Once the crack had penetrated the inner bore, fuel started leaking onto the road. Diesel is especially hazardous on road surfaces because it forms a thin oily film which cannot be seen easily by drivers. It is akin to black ice in lubricity, so skids are common when diesel leaks occur. The insurers of the van driver admitted liability and the injured driver was compensated.

Analysis

FMEA and fault tree analysis methods also examine produc or process failure in a structured and systematic way, in the gener context of safety engineering. However, all such techniques rely c accurate reporting of failure rates, and precise identification, of th failure modes involved.

There is some common ground between forensic science a forensic engineering, such as scene of crime and scene of accide analysis, integrity of the evidence and court appearances. Bo disciplines make extensive use of optical and scanning electr microscopes, for example. They also share common use spectroscopy (infra-red, ultra-violet and nuclear magnetic resonar to examine critical evidence. Radiography using X-rays or neutr is also very useful in examining thick products for their inte defects before destructive examination is attempted. Often, howe a simple hand lens suffices to reveal the cause of a partic problem.

Trace evidence is sometimes an important factor in rec tructing the sequence of events in an accident. For example burn marks on a road surface can enable vehicle speeds t estimated, when the brakes were applied and so on. Ladde often leave a trace of movement of the ladder during a slip and may show how the accident occurred. When a product fails for no obvious reason, SEM and Energy dispersive X-ray spectroscopy or EDX performed in the microscope can reveal the presence of aggressive chemicals which have left traces on the fracture or adjacent surfaces. Thus an acetal resin water pipe joint suddenly failed and caused substantial damages to a building in which it was situated. Analysis of the joint showed traces of chlorine, indicating a stress corrosion cracking failure mode. The failed fuel pipe junction mentioned above showed traces of sulfur on the fracture surface from the sulfuric acid which had initiated the crack.

Forensic materials engineering involves methods applied to specific materials, such as metals, glasses, ceramics, composites and polymers.

Applications

Most manufacturing models will have a forensic component that monitors early failures to improve quality or efficiencies. Insurance companies use forensic engineers to prove liability or alternatively non liability. Most engineering disasters (structural failures such as bridge and building collapses) are subject to forensic investigation by engineers experienced in forensic methods of investigation. Rail crashes, aviation accidents and some automobile accidents are investigated by forensic engineers particularly where component failure is suspected. Furthermore, appliances, consumer products, medical devices, structures, industrial machinery, and even simple hand tools such as hammers or chisels can warrant investigations upon incidents causing injury or property damages. The failure of medical devices is often safety-critical to the user, so reporting failures and analysing them is particularly important. The environment of the body is complex, and implants must both survive this environment, and not leach potentially toxic impurities. Problems have been reported with breast implants , heart valves, and catheters, for example.

Failures which occur early in the life of a new product are vital information for the manufacturer to improve the product. New product development aims to eliminate defects by testing in the factory before launch, but some may occur during its early life. Testing products to simulate their behaviour in the external environment is a difficult skill, and may involve accelerated life testing for example. The worst kind of defect to occur after launch is a safety-critical defect, a defect which can endanger life or limb. Their discovery usually leads to a product recall or even complete withdrawal of the product from the market. Product defects often follow the bath-tub curve, with high initial failures, a lower rate during regular life, followed by another rise due to wear-out. National standards, such as those of ASTM and the British Standards Institute, and International Standards can help the designer in increasing product integrity.

Interactive Disassembler

The Interactive Disassembler, more commonly known as simply **IDA**, is a commercial disassembler widely used for reverse engineering. It supports a variety of executable formats for different processors and operating systems. It also can be used as a debugger for Windows PE, Mac OS X Mach-O, and Linux ELF executables.

Although IDA performs a large degree of automatic code analysis to a certain extent, leveraging cross-references between code sections, knowledge of parameters of API calls, and other information, it is focused on being interactive. A typical IDA user will begin with an automatically generated disassembly listing and then rename, annotate, or otherwise add information to the listing, until it becomes clear what it does, creating an effective reverse-engineering.

Created as a shareware application by Ilfak Guilfanov, it was later turned into a commercial product by DataRescue, a Belgian company, who improved it and sold it under the name IDA Pro. In 2007, Guilfanov founded Hex-Rays to pursue the development of the Hex-Rays Decompiler IDA extension. In January 2008, Hex-Rays assumed the development and support of Datarescue's IDA Pro.

Ilfak is the main author of IDA (Interactive Disassembler Pro).

Scripting

"IDC scripts" make it possible to extend the operation of the disassembler. Some helpful scripts are provided, which can serve as the basis for user written scripts. Most frequently scripts are used for extra modification of the generated code. For example, external symbol tables can be loaded thereby using the function names of the original source code. There are websites devoted to IDA scripts and offer assistance for frequently arising problems.

Users have created plugins that allow other common scripting languages to be used instead of, or in addition to, IDC. IdaRUB supports Ruby and IDAPython adds support for Python.

Supported systems/processors/compilers

- Operating systems
  - x86 Windows GUI
  - x86 Windows console
  - x86 Linux console
  - x86 Mac OS X
  - ARM Windows CE
- Executable file formats
  - PE (Windows)
  - ELF (Linux, most *BSD)
  - Mach-O (Mac OS X)
  - Netware .exe
  - OS/2 .exe
  - Geos .exe
  - raw binary, such as a ROM image
- Processors
  - Intel 80x86 family
  - ARM, including thumb code
  - Motorola 68xxx/h8

- Zilog Z80
- MOS Technology 6502
- Intel i860
- DEC Alpha
- Analog Devices ADSP218x
- Angstrem KR1878
- Atmel AVR series
- DEC series PDP11
- Fujitsu F2MC16L/F2MC16LX
- Fujitsu FR 32-bit Family
- Hitachi SH3/SH3B/SH4/SH4B
- Hitachi H8: h8300/h8300a/h8s300/h8500
- Intel 196 series: 80196/80196NP
- Intel 51 series: 8051/80251b/80251s/80930b/80930s
- Intel i960 series
- Intel ia64 series
- Java virtual machine
- MIPS: mipsb/mipsl/mipsr/mipsrl/r5900b/r5900l
- Microchip PIC: PIC12Cxx/PIC16Cxx/PIC18Cxx
- MSIL
- Mitsubishi 7700 Family: m7700/m7750
- Mitsubishi m32/m32rx
- Mitsubishi m740
- Mitsubishi m7900
- Motorola DSP 5600x Family: dsp561xx/dsp5663xx/dsp566xx/dsp56k
- Motorola ColdFire
- Motorola HCS12
- NEC 78K0/78K0S
- PA-RISC
- PowerPC

  - o SGS-Thomson ST20/ST20c4/ST7
  - o SPARC Family
  - o Samsung SAM8
  - o Siemens C166 series
  - o TMS320Cxxx series
- Compiler/libraries (for automatic library function recognition)
  - o Borland C++ 5.x for DOS/Windows
  - o Borland C++ 3.1
  - o Borland C Builder v4 for DOS/Windows
  - o GNU C++ for Cygwin
  - o MS C (16 bit) for DOS/Windows
  - o MS Visual Studio .NET
  - o MS Visual C++ v6
  - o Watcom C++ (16/32 bit) for DOS/OS2
  - o ARM C v1.2
  - o GNU C++ for Unix/common

Knowledge Discovery Metamodel

Knowledge Discovery Metamodel (KDM) is publicly available specification from the Object Management Group (OMG). KDM is a common intermediate representation for existing software systems and their operating environments, that defines common metadata required for deep semantic integration of Application Lifecycle Management tools. KDM was designed as the OMG's foundation for software modernisation, IT portfolio management and software assurance. KDM uses OMG's Meta-Object Facility to define an XMI interchange format between tools that work with existing software as well as an abstract interface (API) for the next-generation assurance and modernisation tools. KDM standardises existing approaches to knowledge discovery in software engineering artifacts, also known as software mining.

History of KDM

- In November 2003, the OMG's Architecture-Driven Modernisation Task Force recommended, and the Platform Technical Committee issued, the Knowledge Discovery Metamodel (KDM) RFP. The objective of this RFP was to *provide a common repository structure to represent information about existing software assets and their operating environment.* The goal of KDM was defined as *exchanging information related to transformation of existing software assets.* The RFP stated that KDM shall provide *the ability to document existing systems, discover reusable components in existing software, support transformations to other languages and to MDA, or enable other potential transformations. The Knowledge Discovery Metamodel will also enable information about existing software artifacts to be exchanged among different tools. This will enable vendors that specialise on certain languages, platforms or types of transformations to deliver customer solutions in conjunction with other vendors.*
- The original KDM RFP is available to OMG members for download (document lt/03-11-04 (http://www.omg.org/cgi-bin/doc?lt/03-11-04).
- Throughout 2004 and 2005 12 companies collaborated to prepare a joint response to the KDM RFP. More than 30 organisations from 5 countries have contributed to the development and review of the KDM specification.
- In May 2006, the Team's submission—the Knowledge Discovery Metamodel (KDM)—moved into the finalisation stage of the OMG's standards adoption process. The OMG adopted Specification for KDM became publicly available (OMG document ptc/06-06-07).
- In March 2007 the KDM Finalisation Task Force finished the finalisation stage of the OMG's standards adoption process. The formal KDM specification KDM 1.0 is available from OMG (http://www.omg.org/spec/KDM/1.0/ KDM 1.0]).

- KDM Analytics maintains Open portal for KDM news, reference and education materials and tools

Overview of KDM

The goal of KDM is to ensure interoperability between tools for maintenance, evolution, assessment and modernisation. KDM is defined as a metamodel that can be also viewed as an ontology for describing the key aspects of knowledge related to the various facets of enterprise software. KDM support means investment into the KDM ecosystem—a growing open-standard based cohesive community of tool vendors, service providers, and commercial components.

KDM represents entire enterprise software systems, not just code. KDM is a wide-spectrum entity-relationship representation for describing existing software. KDM represents structural and behaviour elements of existing software systems. The key concept of KDM is a *container*: an entity that owns other entities. This allows KDM to represent existing systems at various degrees of granularity.

KDM defines precise semantic foundation for representing behaviour, the so-called *micro-KDM*. It provides a high-fidelity intermediate representation which can be used, for example, for performing static analysis of existing software systems. micro-KDM is similar in purpose to a Virtual machine for KDM, although KDM is not an executable model, or a constraint model, but a representation of existing artifacts for analysis purposes.

KDM facilitates incremental analysis of existing software systems, where the initial KDM representation is analysed and more pieces of knowledge are extracted and made explicit as KDM to KDM transformation performed entirely within the KDM technology space. The steps of the knowledge extraction process can be performed by tools, and may involve the analyst.

KDM is the uniform language- and platform- independent representation. Its extensibility mechanism allows addition of domain-, application- and implementation-specific knowledge.

Architecture of KDM

Knowledge Discovery Metamodel consists of 12 packages arranged into 4 layers.

KDM packages are arranged into the following four layers:

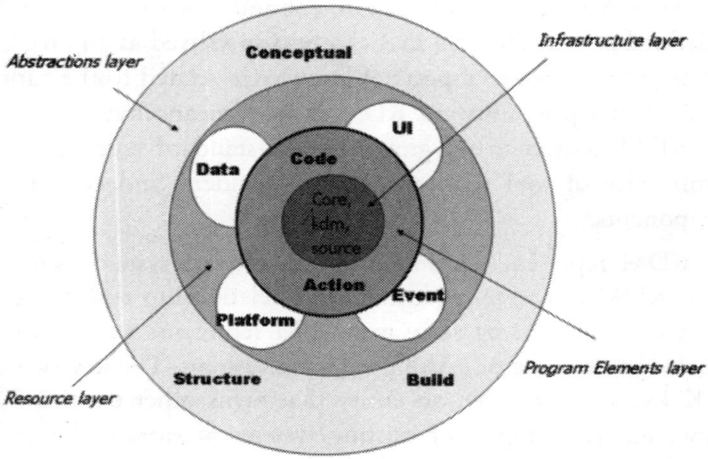

Infrastructure Layer

The KDM Infrastructure Layer consists of the **Core**, **kdm**, and **Source** packages which provide a small common core for all other packages, the inventory model of the artifacts of the existing system and full traceability between the meta-model elements as links back to the source code of the artifacts, as well as the uniform extensibility mechanism. The Core package determines several of patterns that are reused by other KDM packages. Although KDM is a meta-model that uses Meta-Object Facility, there is an alignment between the KDM Core and Resource Description Framework (RDF).

Programme Elements Layer

The Programme Elements Layer consists of the Code and Action packages.

- The **Code package** represents programming elements as determined by programming languages, for example data types, procedures, classes, methods, variables, etc. This package is similar in purpose to the Common Application Meta-model (CAM) from another OMG specification, called Enterprise Application Integration (EAI). KDM Code package provides greater level of detail and is seamlessly integrated with the architecturally significant views of the software system. Representation of datatypes in KDM is aligned with ISO standard ISO/IEC 11404.
- The **Action package** captures the low level behaviour elements of applications, including detailed control- and data flow between statements. Code and Action package in combination provide a high-fidelity intermediate representation of each component of the enterprise software system

Resource Layer

The Resource Layer represents the operational environment of the existing software system. it is related to the area of Enterprise Application Integration (EAI).

- **Platform package** represents the operating environment of the software, related to the operating system, middleware, etc. including the control flows between components as they are determined by the runtime platform
- **UI package** represents the knowledge related to the user interfaces of the existing software system
- **Event package** represents the knowledge related to events and state-transition behaviour of the existing software system
- **Data package** represents the artifacts related to persistent data, such as indexed files, relational databases, and other kinds of data storage. These assests are key to enterprise software as they represent the enterprise metadata. The KDM Data package is aligned with another OMG specification, called Common Warehouse Metamodel (CWM).

Abstractions Layer

The Abstraction Layer represents domain and application abstractions.

- **Conceptual package** represent business domain knowledge and business rules, insofar as this information can be mined from existing applications. These packages are aligned with another OMG specification, called Semantics of Business Vocabulary and Business Rules (SBVR)
- **Structure package** describes the meta-model elements for representing the logical organisation of the software system into subsystems, layers and components
- **Build** package represents the engineering view of the software system.

3

SERVICE ORIENTED MODELLING

Service-oriented modeling is a software development methodology that employs disciplines and a universal language to provide tactical and strategic solutions to enterprise problems. Service-oriented modeling takes an anthropomorphic view to the modeling process by striving to create models that can be understood by individuals with diverse levels of business and technical understanding. The service-oriented modeling paradigm advocates taking a holistic view of the analysis, design, and architecture of all 'Software Entities' in an Organisation. Service-oriented modeling encourages viewing software entities as 'assets' (service-oriented assets), and refers to these assets collectively as 'services'.

The service-oriented modeling methodology includes a modeling language that can be employed by both the 'problem domain organisation' (the Business), and 'solution domain organisation' (the Information Technology Department), whose unique perspectives typically influence the 'service' development life-cycle strategy and the projects implemented using that strategy.

The service-oriented modeling paradigm is based upon the following vision:

- Introduce a state-of-the-art and holistic modeling language that can facilitate an SOA implementation

- Introduce advanced service life cycle concepts and processes that can be employed to manage service-oriented projects
- Enable business and IT personnel to equally partner in service-oriented modeling efforts and to represent their unique perspectives

The service-oriented modeling practice employs the following disciplines that are widely utilised during service-oriented development life cycle:

- *Service-oriented conceptualisation*
- *Service-oriented discovery and analysis*
- *Service-oriented business integration*
- *Service-oriented design*
- *Service-oriented conceptual architecture*
- *Service-oriented logical architecture*

Service-oriented modeling framework (SOMF)

The service-oriented modeling framework (SOMF) that was devised by Michael Bell is a service-oriented development life cycle methodology. It offers a number of modeling practices and disciplines that contribute to a successful service-oriented life cycle management and modeling (see image on right).

It illustrates the major elements that identify the "what to do" aspects of a service development scheme. These are the modeling pillars that will enable practitioners to craft an effective project plan and to identify the milestones of a service-oriented initiative—either a small or large-scale business or a technological venture.

The provided image thumb (on the right hand side) depicts the four sections of the modeling framewoik that identify the general direction and the corresponding units of work that make up a service-oriented modeling strategy: practices, environments, disciplines, and artifacts. Remember, these elements uncover the context of a modeling occupation and do not necessarily describe the process or the sequence of activities needed to fulfill modeling goals. These should be ironed out during the project plan – th

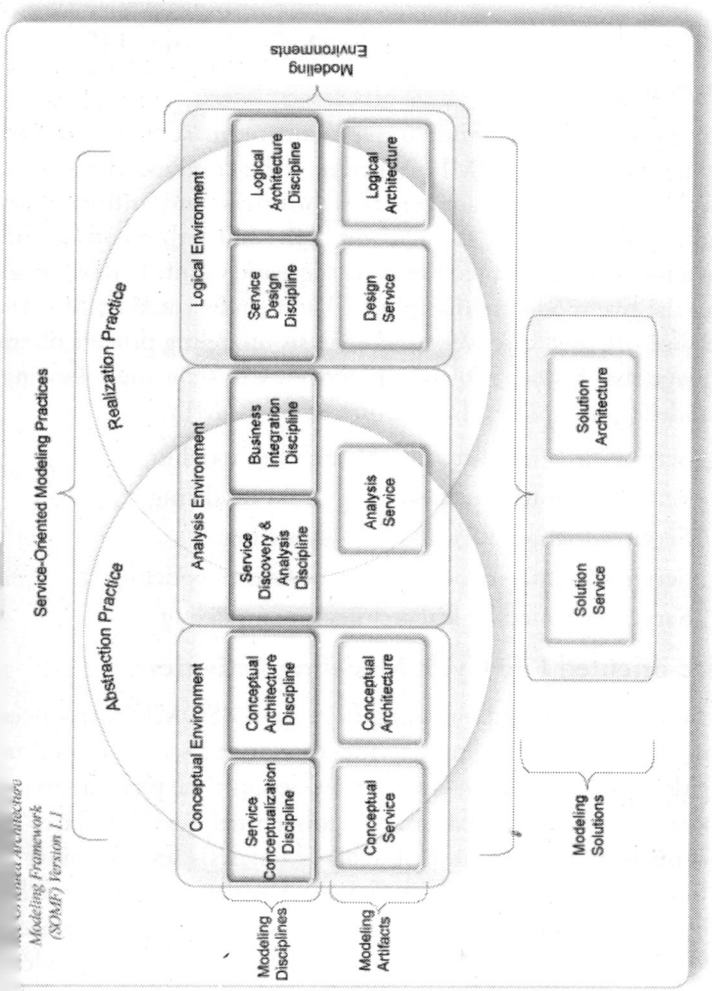

Service-oriented modeling framework (SOMF) Version 1.1

service-oriented development life cycle strategy – that typically sets initiative boundaries, timeframe, responsibilities and accountabilities, and achievable project milestones.

SOA Life Cycle Modeling: An SOA Governance Life Cycle Approach

Unlike any other modeling practice, the service-oriented modeling framework (SOMF) is driven by the development process of services. This approach enables business and information technology professionals to focus on deliverables that correspond to a specific service-oriented life cycle stage and event. For example, among the five modeling disciplines that are advocated by SOMF, the service-oriented discovery and analysis modeling process offers a language that fosters SOA best practices. Consider the following five modeling disciplines that are offered by SOMF:

- Service-oriented discovery & analysis modeling
- Service-oriented business integration modeling
- Service-oriented logical design modeling
- Service-oriented conceptual architecture modeling
- Service-oriented logical architecture modeling

Service-oriented Life Cycle Modeling Activities

The service-oriented modeling framework (SOMF) introduce five major life cycle modeling activities that drive a service evolutio during design-time and run-time. At the design-time phase a servic originates as a conceptual entity (conceptual service), later i transforms into an SOA unit of analysis (analysis service), next i transitions into a contractual and logical entity (design service and finally is established as a concrete service (solution service The following identify the major contributions of the servic oriented modeling activities:

- Service-oriented discovery & analysis modeling: Discov and analyse services for granularity, reusabilit interoperability, loose-coupling, and identify consolidati opportunities.

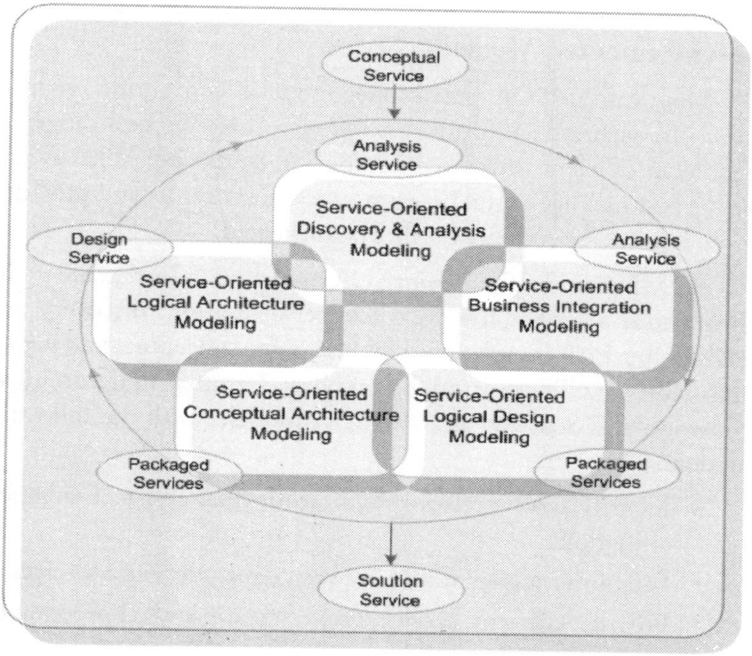

- Service-oriented business integration modeling: Identify service integration and alignment opportunities with business domains' processes (organisations, products, geographical locations)
- Service-oriented logical design modeling: Establish service relationships and message exchange paths. Address service visibility. Craft service logical compositions. Model service transactions
- Service-oriented conceptual architecture modeling: Establish an SOA architectural direction. Depict an SOA technological environment. Craft an SOA technological stack. Identify business ownership.
- Service-oriented logical architecture modeling: Integrate SOA software assets. Establish SOA logical environment dependencies. Foster service reuse, loose coupling, and consolidation.

Service-oriented Modeling Styles

How can an SOA practitioner model a computing environment? In what type of forms can a group of services be arranged to enable an efficient integrated computing landscape? What would be the best message routes between a service consumer and provider? How can interoperability hurdles be mitigated?

SOMF provides four major SOA modeling styles that are useful throughout a service life cycle (conceptualisation, discovery and analysis, business integration, logical design, conceptual and logical architecture). These modeling styles: Circular, Hierarchical, Network, and Star, can assist an SOA modeler with the following modeling aspects:

- Identify service relationships: contextual and technological affiliations
- Establish message routes between consumers and services
- Provide efficient service orchestration and choreography methods
- Create powerful service transaction and behavioural patterr
- Offer valuable service packaging solutions

In the below illustration you will find the major four servic oriented modeling styles that SOMF offers. Each pattern identifi the various approaches and strategies that one should consid employing when modeling an SOA environment.

- Circular Modeling Style: enables message exchange in circular fashion, rather than employing a controller to ca out the distribution of messages. The Circular Style a offers a conceptual method to affiliating services.
- Hierarchical Modeling Style: offers a relationship patt between services for the purpose of establishing transacti and message exchange routes between consumers services. The Hierarchical pattern founds parent/c associations between services.

- Network Modeling Style: this pattern establishes "many to many" relationship between services, their peer services, and consumers. The Network pattern accentuates on distributed environments and interoperable computing networks.
- Star Modeling Style: the Stare pattern advocates arranging services in a star formation, in which the central service passes messages to its extending arms. The Star modeling style is often used in "multi casting" or "publish and subscribe" instances, where "solicitation" or "fire and forget" message styles are involved.

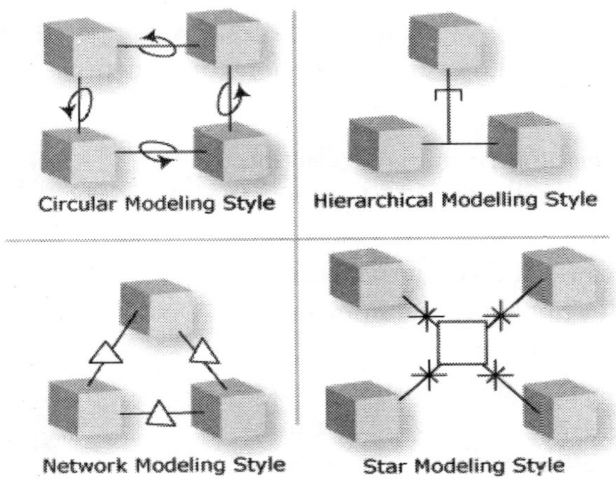

Service-oriented Modeling Assets

The service-oriented modeling framework (SOMF) introduces three major service formations. These structures are software entities that habitually exist in out computing environments:

- *Atomic service*: an indivisible software component that is too granular and executes fewer business or technical functionalities. An atomic formation is also a piece of software that typically is not subject to decomposition analysis activities and its business or technological functionality does not justify breakdown to smaller components.

Examples: customer address service and checking account balance service.

Atomic Service

- *Composite service*: a composite service structure aggregates smaller and fine-grained services. This hierarchical service formation is characteristically known as coarse-grained entity that encompasses more business or technical processes. A composite service may aggregate atomic or other composite services.

Examples: customer checking service that aggregates smaller checking account and savings account services. An application that is composed of sub-systems, an ESB that is composed of routing, orchestration, and data transformation components.

- *Service cluster*: this is a collection of distributed and related services that are gathered because of their mutual business or technological commonalities. A service cluster both affiliates services and combines their offerings to solve a business problem. A cluster structure can aggregate atomic as well as composite formations.

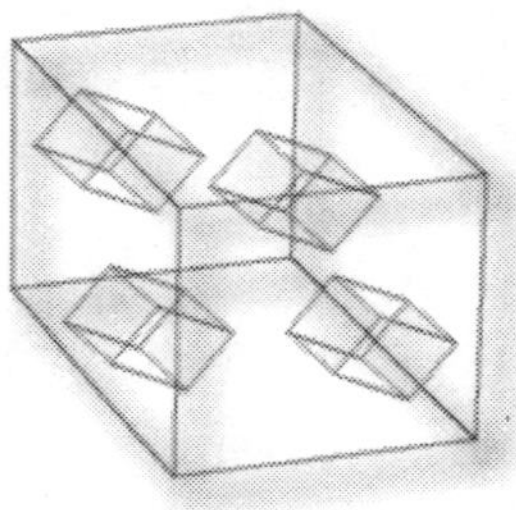

Composite Service

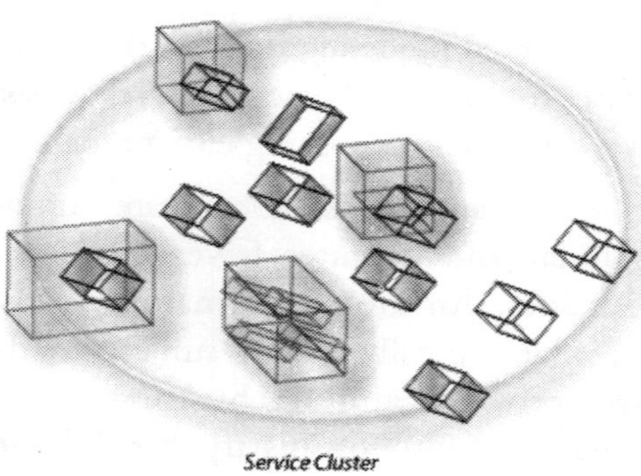

Service Cluster

Examples: A Mutual Funds service cluster that is composed of related and distributed mutual funds services. A Customer Support service cluster that offers automated bill payments, online account statements, and money transfer capabilities

The SOMF also introduces a simple notation to describe the three major service formations, as illustrated in the below image: Atomic Service, Composite Service, and Service Cluster.

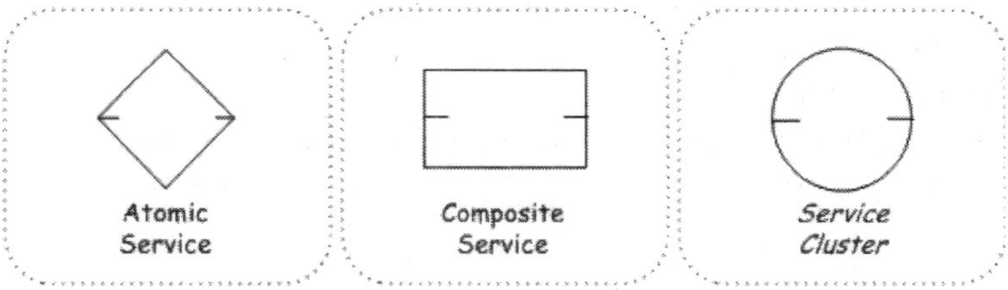

Service-oriented Discovery and Analysis Modeling Notation

The service-oriented discovery and analysis notation represents eight simple icons, each of which enables us to operate on a service (atomic or composite service) or on a group of services (service clusters) in different ways.

These operations promote core SOA best practices. Let us take a look at the below illustration to find out what these analysis operations mean and how they can be employed to draft an SOA analysis proposition diagram.

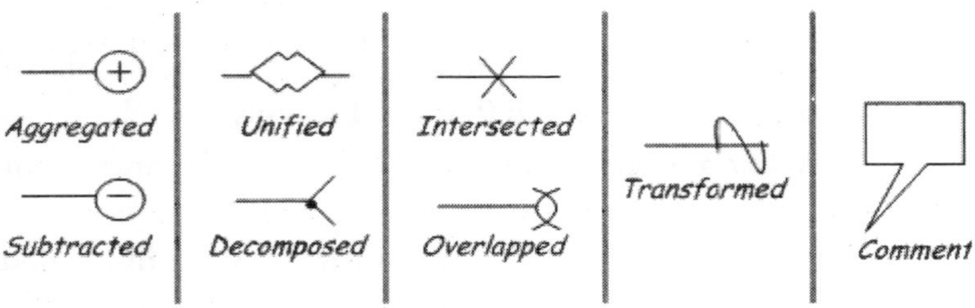

Here is a short description for these symbols:

- *Aggregated:* signifies service containment
- *Subtracted:* identifies service retirement or elimination
- *Unified:* indicates service consolidation

- *Decomposed:* depicts service decoupling
- *Intersected:* illustrates a junction point between two or more service groups (known as service clusters)
- *Overlapped:* describes common functionality and processes that services provide (typically between service clusters)
- *Transformed:* represents transformation of a service type to another (atomic to composite, etc)
- *Comment:* a place to put notes

Why Service-oriented Discovery & Analysis Modeling?

The SOMF model recommends that business and IT people share the responsibility of SOA modeling activities. This modeling language is simple enough that can be understood by all stakeholders in an SOA initiative.

Why are we required to "record" the service analysis activities? The service-oriented discovery and analysis phase is not only about the final state of a service structure and functionality; it is also about business and technological traceability. Meaning, we are mandated to answer the following questions when delivering an analysis proposition diagram:

- *Financial traceability:* How much it would cost (or what was the price) to transform a service from one state to another?
- *Historical traceability:* Capture the date/time when a software transformation occurred (historical reasons)
- *SOA best-practices traceability:* What were the architecture best practices that led to analysis decisions?
- *SOA analysis process tracking*: What are/were the various options and reasons for future/past implementation
- *Componentisation of Software Assets*: Service decomposition and segmentation
- And much more...

In other words, the analysis proposition diagram explains simple or complex transformation of software entities (services) that provide solutions, such as Substitution of services, Retirement of services, service Exchange, service Augmentation and other business patterns that can be illustrated by this process.

- "SOMF Examples" (Softcopy). Methodologies Corporation.
- "SOMF Examples & Language Notation" (Softcopy). Methodologies Corporation.

Service-oriented Discovery & Analysis Modeling Examples

Let us now view a number of SOA analysis modeling examples.

1. Use Case 1 depicts a simple aggregation case, in which atomic service A-1 is aggregated in composite service C-1 because of SOA best practice reasons.

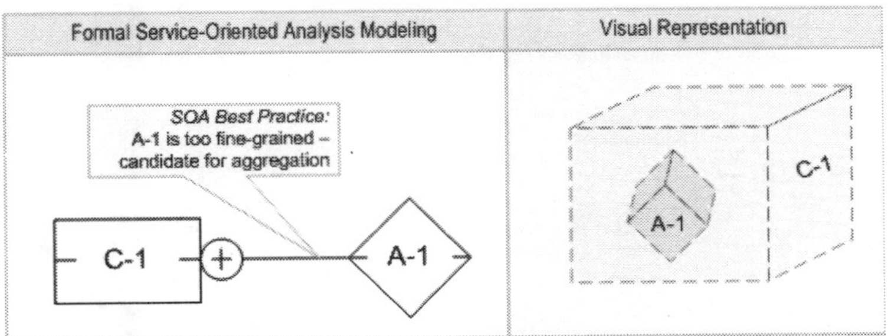

Use Case 1: SOA Best Practice Traceability – Aggregation

2. Use Case 2 describes service decomposition. Once again, this is because of an SOA best practice rule.

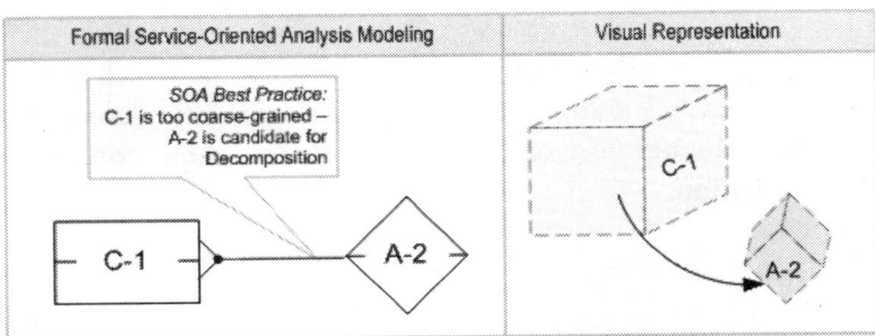

Use Case 2: SOA Best Practice Traceability - Decomposition

3. Use Case 3 illustrates a service retirement (elimination) employing the "subtracted" analysis operation.

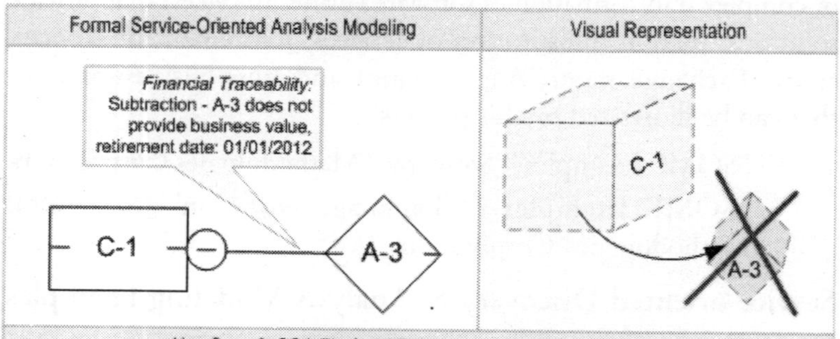

Use Case 3: SOA Financial Traceability – Service Retirement

4. Use Case 4 represents a common business substitution operation. Atomic service A-3 was retired and replaced with atomic service A-2.

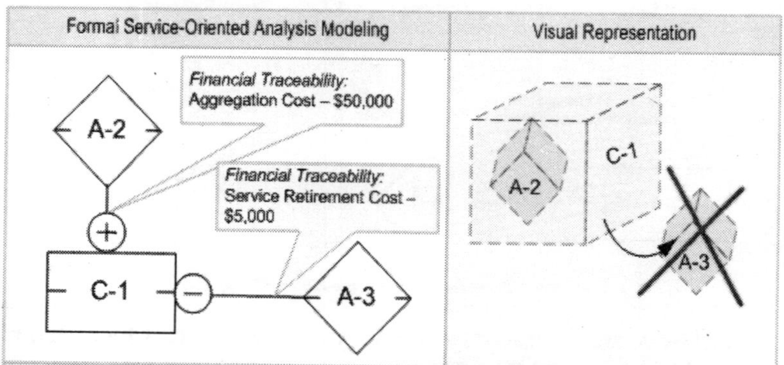

Use Case 4: Business & Financial Traceability – Service Substitution

5. Use Case 5 describes an analysis process, in which atomic services A-1 and A-2 exchange their aggregating composite services because of an adjustment to their contextual affiliation.

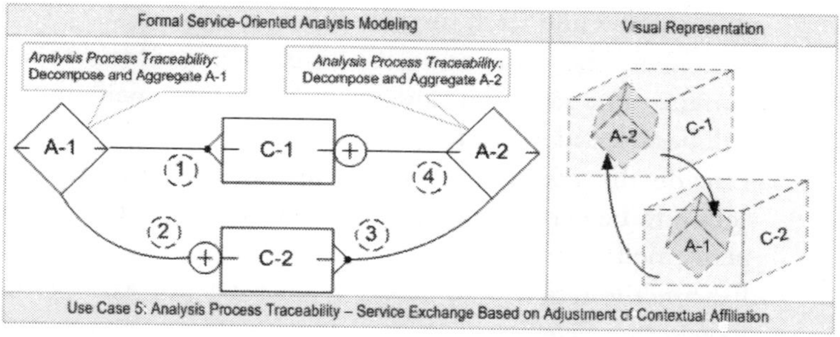

Little Man Computer

The Little Man Computer (LMC) was created by Dr. Stuart Madnick as an instructional model. The LMC models a simple von Neumann architecture computer, so it has all of the basic features of a modern computer. The LMC can be programmed in machine (albeit usually in decimal) or assembly code.

LMC Architecture

The LMC model is based on the concept of a little man locked in a small room. At one end of the room, there are 100 mailboxes (Memory), numbered 0 to 99, that can each contain a 3 digit instruction. Furthermore, there are two mailboxes at the other end labeled **INBOX** and **OUTBOX** which are used for receiving and outputting data. In the center of the room, there is a work area containing a simple 2 function (addition and subtraction) calculator known as the Accumulator and a resetable counter known as the Programme Counter. The Programme Counter is similar to what a doorperson uses to keep track of how many people have entered a facility—it can count up 1, or it can be reset to 0. As specified by the von Neumann architecture, memory contains both instructions and data. The user loads data into the mailboxes and then signals the little man to begin execution.

Execution Cycle

The little man performs the following steps to execute a programme:

1. Check the Programme Counter, go to the mailbox with that number and fetch the instruction
2. Increment the Programme Counter (i.e. add one to the current value so that it now refers to the next mailbox that will be accessed in the next cycle)
3. Decode the instruction (which includes determining the action to be performed and the mailbox on which it will be performed)
4. Execute the action
5. Repeat the cycle

LMC Commands: Numeric

While the LMC does reflect the actual workings of binary processors, the simplification of decimal numbers was made to minimise the complexity for students who may not be comfortable working in binary/hexadecimal.

Each LMC instruction is a 3 digit decimal number. The first digit represents the command to be performed and the final two digits represent the address of the mailbox affected by the command.

Instructions

- 1xx—ADD—Take the value stored in mailbox xx and add it to whatever value is currently on the accumulator.
- 2xx—SUBTRACT—Take the value stored in mailbox xx and subtract it from whatever value is currently on the accumulator.
- 3xx—STORE—Take the value from the accumulator (non-destructive) and store it in mailbox xx (destructive).
- 5xx—LOAD—Take the value from mailbox xx (non-destructive) and enter it in the accumulator (destructive).
- 6xx—BRANCH (unconditional)—Reset the programme counter to the value xx. That is, xx will be the next instruction executed.
- 7xx—BRANCH IF ZERO—If the accumulator contains the value 0, reset the programme counter to the value xx. Otherwise, do nothing.

- 8xx—BRANCH IF POSITIVE—If the accumulator is 0 or positive, reset the programme counter to the value xx. Otherwise, do nothing.
- 901—INPUT—Go to the INBOX, fetch the value from the user, and put it in the accumulator (destructive)
- 902—OUTPUT—Fetch the value from the accumulator (non-destructive), and put it in the OUTBOX for the user to read.
- 000—HALT—Stop working.

A Sample Programme

This programme takes two numbers as input and outputs the difference.

Mailbox	Instruction	Notes
00	901	INBOX —> ACCUMULATOR *fetch first number*
01	308	ACCUMULATOR —> MEMORY[08] *move it out of the way*
02	901	INBOX —> ACCUMULATOR *fetch second number*
03	309	ACCUMULATOR —> MEMORY[09] *move it out of the way*
04	508	MEMORY[08] —> ACCUMULATOR *now that both inputs are retrieved, move the first back to the accumulator*
05	209	ACCUMULATOR = ACCUMULATOR—MEMORY[09] *subtract second number*
06	902	ACCUMULATOR —> OUTBOX *output the result to the user*
07	000	HALT *We're Done!*

LMC Commands: mnemonic

LOAD mnemonic—LDA numerical/machine code—5

Load the contents of the given mailbox onto the accumulator (calculator). Note: the contents of the mailbox are not changed.

STORE mnemonic—STA numerical/machine code—3

Store the contents of the accumulator (calculator) to the mailbox of the given address. Note: the contents of the accumulator are not changed.

ADD mnemonic—ADD numerical/machine code—1

Add the contents of the given mailbox onto the accumulator (calculator). Note: the contents of the mailbox are not changed, and the actions of the accumulator are not defined for add instructions that cause sums larger than 3 digits.

SUBTRACT mnemonic—SUB numerical/machine code—2

Subtract the contents of the given mailbox from the accumulator (calculator). Note: the contents of the mailbox are not changed, and the actions of the accumulator are not defined for subtract instructions that cause negative results—however, a negative flag will be set so that BRP can be used properly (see below).

INPUT mnemonic—INP numerical/machine code—901

Copy the value from the "in box" onto the accumulator (calculator).

OUTPUT mnemonic—OUT numerical/machine code—902

Copy the value from the accumulator (calculator) to the "out box". Note: the contents of the accumlator are not changed.

END mnemonic—HLT numerical/machine code—000

Causes the Little Man Computer to stop executing your programme.

BRANCH IF ZERO mnemonic—BRZ numerical/machine code—7

If the contents of the accumulator (calculator) are 000, the PC (programme counter) will be set to the given address. Note: since the programme is stored in memory, data and programme instructions all have the same address/location format.

BRANCH IF ZERO OR POSITIVE mnemonic—BRP numerical/machine code—8

If the contents of the accumulator (calculator) are 000 or positive (i.e. the negative flag is not set), the PC (programme counter) will be set to the given address. Note: since the programme is stored in memory, data and programme instructions all have the same address/location format.

BRANCH ALWAYS mnemonic—BRA numerical/machine code—6

Set the contents of the programme counter to the given address.

DATA mnemonic—DAT numerical/machine code—none

This is an assembler instruction which simply loads the value into the next available mailbox. DAT can also be used in conjunction with labels to declare variables. For example, DAT 984 will store the value 984 into a mailbox.

Mnemonic Use Example and LMC Simulator

Using the above mnemonics, the assembly language version of the programme to subtract two numbers is given below. This programme can be compiled and run on the following LMC simulator. This java applet-based simulator includes full instructions and sample programmes, a compiler to convert the assembly into machine code, a control interface to execute and monitor programmes, and a step-by-step detailed description of each LMC instruction.

```
INP
STA FIRST
INP
STA SECOND
LDA FIRST
```

```
SUB SECOND
OUT
HLT
FIRST DAT
SECOND DAT
```

Using Labels

The convenience of assembled mnemonics is made apparent from this example—The programmer is no longer required to memorise a set of anonymous numeric codes, and can now programme with a set of more memorable instructions. However, the programmer is still required to manually keep track of mailbox locations. Furthermore, if an instruction was to be inserted somewhere in the programme, the final HLT instruction would move down to address 08. Suppose the user entered 600 as the first input. This value would overwrite the 000 (HLT) instruction. Since 600 means "Branch to mailbox 0" the programme, instead of halting, would get stuck in an endless loop.

To work around this difficulty, most assembly languages (including the LMC) allow the use of labels. A label is simply a word provided as a name to the left of a particular line in the programme text, which the assembler will convert to the appropriate address at the time of assembly. When seen to the right of the instruction, labels then take on the value of the address calculated.

Labels are commonly used to:

- identify a particular instruction as a target for a BRANCH instruction
- identify space as a named variable (using DAT)
- load data into the programme at assembly time for use by the programme.

This use is not obvious until one considers that there is no way of adding 1 to a counter. One could ask the user to input 1 at the beginning, but it would be better to have this loaded at the time of assembly

Label Use Example

This programme will take a user input, and count down to zero.

IN

LOOP SUB ONE // This address will be called LOOP, Subtract the value stored at ONE

OUT

BRZ QUIT //If we are at 0, then jump to the location QUIT

BRA LOOP //We are not at 0, go back to the start of LOOP

QUIT HLT

ONE DAT 1 //Put the value 1 in this mailbox, and call it ONE (variable declaration)

Interconnect Bottleneck

The interconnect bottleneck—the point where microchips reach their capacity—is expected sometime around 2010.

Improved performance of computer systems has been achieved, in large part, by downscaling the Integrated Circuit (IC) minimum feature size. This allows the basic IC building block, the transistor, to operate at a higher frequency, performing more computations per second. However, downscaling of the minimum feature size also results in tighter packing of the wires on a chip, which increases parasitic capacitance and signal propagation delay. Consequently, the delay due to the communication between the parts of a chip becomes comparable to the computation delay itself. This phenomenon, known as an "interconnect bottleneck", is becoming a major problem in high-performance computer systems.

This problem of "interconnect bottleneck" can be solved by utilising optical interconnects to replace the long metallic interconnects. Such hybrid optical/electronic interconnects promises better performance even with larger designs. Optics has widespread use in long-distance communications; still it has not yet been widely used in chip-to-chip or on-chip interconnections because they (in centimeter or micrometer range) are not yet industry-manufacturable owing to costlier technology and lack of fully mature technologies. As optical interconnections move from computer network applications to chip level interconnections, new requirements for high connection density and alignment reliability have become as critical for the effective utilisation of these links. There are still many materials, fabrication, and packaging challenges in integrating optic and electronic technologies.

Nanoscopy: Shedding Light on Life

Where traditional optical microscopy fails, a new tool, the nanoscope, overcomes the last barrier: the diffraction limit. It can explore the interior of cells in 3D, non-invasively, and with nanometric resolution.

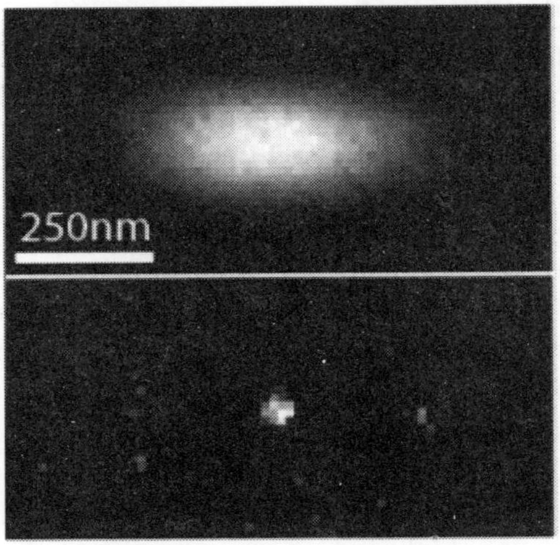

Microscope versus nanoscope. Diffraction-limited 3D foc spot in standard optical microscopy (*top*) compared to the 45 n spherical one now achieved in optical nanoscopy (*bottom*).

Nanoscopy! Remember this word: it is here to leave its ma Optical microscopy at the nanoscale is no longer science fictic

Indeed, researchers at the Max Planck Institute for Biophysical Chemistry in Göttingen (Germany), led by Stefan W. Hell, have significatively pushed the 3D resolution of optical microscopy down to the nanoscale, and have been able to non-invasively investigate the interior of cells.

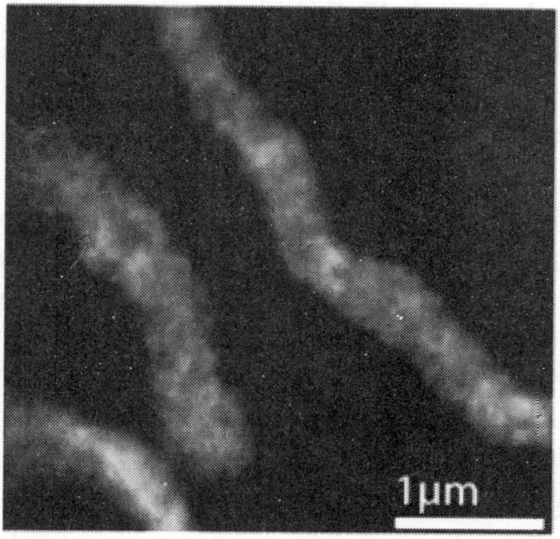

Cell nano-image. Distribution of membrane and matrix proteins in cellular mitochondria.

"The resolution of a microscope", Hell explains, "is given by he 3D size of the focal spot, which usually has an elliptical shape, imilar to a rugby ball—around 250 nm in the plane parallel to he sample and around 500 nm in the perpendicular plane. We ave shown that it is possible to squeeze this ellipsoid to a sphere, ownsizing the focus from a rugby ball to a tennis ball—around 5 nm in diameter. The squeezed spot leads to a substantial nprovement in resolution which we have used to map out the istribution of proteins in a cellular organelle without needing to op the cells into slices, as other techniques, such as electron icroscopy, would have required."

Since its dawn, mankind has always been fascinated by the known. Unluckily, only a tiny part of the much broader natural complexity can be experienced by our physiological perception, the five senses. Curiosity urged our ancestors to open the way to further information by developing dedicated tools, such as microscopes, to empower the sense of sight.

More than three hundred years ago, the Dutchman Antonie van Leeuwenhoek and the Englishman Robert Hooke separately observed the existence of tiny living organisms in drops of water using a rudimentary microscope. Since then giant steps have been taken in the field of optical microscopy.

Unfortunately, an optical microscope, even a perfect one, cannot be used to see objects that are smaller than half the wavelength of the illumination light, a few hundred nanometres. It is a fundamental physical law: the diffraction limit. Have you ever tried to pick up a very thin needle using your fingers alone? Standard microscopy makes use of rather clumsy fingers (the wavelength of light) to discern tiny objects: any object smaller than the diffraction limit is invisible.

We need a more refined tool to break the diffraction barrie and eventually pick up the aforementioned needle. For example electron microscopy has been widely employed in biology to gai resolution at the nanoscale. Indeed, the wavelength associated wit fast electrons is much smaller than that of light. However, thes unconventional microscopes have a major drawback: they ar typically incompatible with life. As a result, the clumsy fingers c focused light continue to provide us with the most promising wa to explore the 3D cell universe non-invasively. The challenge is t make them as little clumsy as possible.

One way to achieve this is by taking advantage of fluorescenc an optical property of some molecules. Fluorescent molecules abso light at a certain wavelength to emit it again at a longer one. Hi resolutions have been achieved through several fluorescence-bas approaches, but at most in 2D. Hell's group, for example, h previously studied the interaction between some fluoresc molecules and a focused laser beam in the shape of a doughnut. Even though the distribution of light is still diffraction limited, the interaction with the fluorescent molecule is not: instantly quenching the periphery, the excitation is effectively confined only to the hole of the doughnut, which is far below the diffraction limit. It is like placing ice on the rim of a hot plate to cool the edge down whilst leaving the centre hot.

Now Hell and coworkers have found the right recipe to place ice not only on a 2D plate, but in a whole 3D space. They have engineered the interference of laser beams in order to confine the fluorescence to a sphere of 45 nm in diameter. Hell affirms that "in theory this spot and hence the resolution can be squeezed down to the size of a molecule, a few nanometers.

However, practical issues will probably limit it to around 10-20 nm". Hell underlines that "the wavelength of light can be tuned so that it is not absorbed by the sample. Besides, the light intensity is almost three orders below that of multiphoton microscopy, which is nowadays broadly used for live cell imaging." Optical nanoscopy, therefore, would be a powerful tool to visualise and quantify molecular distributions in living cells without concern about biological damages.

At Harvard University (Massachusetts, USA), the group led by Xiaowei Zhuang had already achieved similar results with an alternative fluorescent-based method [1]. However, Lukas Novotny, from Rochester University (NY State, USA), explains that "Hell's technique has less stringent requirements and is faster in terms of video rate, since it can image many fluorescent molecules at once. This, I believe, will make it widely used in future." Bo Huang, from Zhuang's group, mostly agrees with Novotny's opinion, even though he adds that, regarding applications, "no approach will be more successful than others in full generality. Different problems will require different approaches."

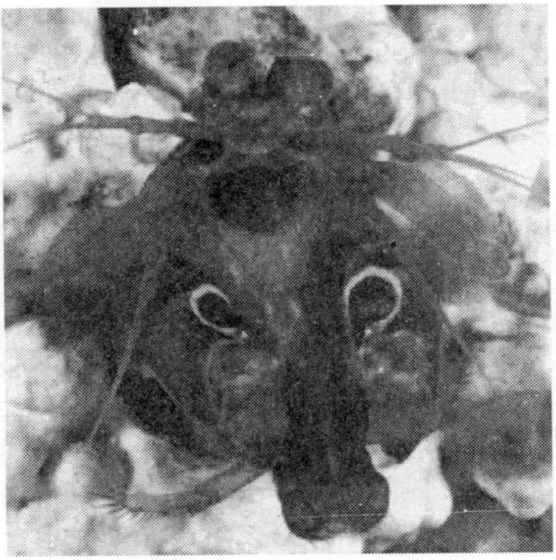

Super-Vision for Mr. Shrimp

There is an invisible world illuminated by polarised light. A world that has been disclosed to us only by the technological advances of the last decades. Surprisingly, various Australian shrimps can see it.

Mantis shrimp (Gonodactylus smithii). Each of its eyes measures the six polarisation components that are precisely required for perfect polarisation vision. Photograph: Roy Caldwell.

It is fascinating to realise how creative nature is. We invented photonic crystals, but they had been on butterfly wings for hundreds of millions of years. We came up with the idea of lasers, but giant lasers had been operating for billions of years in nebulae lost in deep interstellar space. However, until a few months ago we could still be proud to say that we had outpaced nature in mastering polarisation vision. Now Sonja Kleinlogel from Max Planck Institute for Biophysics in Frankfurt (Germany), Tsyr-Huei Chiou from the University of Maryland in Baltimore (USA), and coworkers have proved us wrong. Nature was there first—again! A stomatopod species, a crustacean similar to a shrimp, can distinguish circularly polarised light, and the mantis shrimp even has perfect polarisation vision. They can see a world invisible to all other animals, and disclosed to us only by the technological advances of the last decades. "It has been known since long ago that various animals can distinguish linear polarisation. For example, they exploit it in navigating. Ants and bees take advantage of the slight linear polarisation of the sky light to orient themselves," says Kleinlogel. "However, it was generally believed that animals were insensitive to circular polarisation."

Polarisation is a characteristic of waves, and light behaves as a wave. We can generate a linearly polarised wave by holding the end of a long stretched rope and waving it. A vertically polarised wave results from shaking it up and down in the vertical plane, and a horizontally polarised one from shaking it left and right in the horizontal plane. If we now move the end of the rope in a circle, a circularly polarised wave will result. Of course, it can be either left or right circularly polarised, depending on the sense of the rotation.

How is it possible to see linear polarisation? "Microvilli," explains Kleinlogel, "the part of the visual cells sensitive to light, naturally respond to linear polarisation." Indeed, they are an array of tubelike membranes, which respond to only one linear polarisation depending on how they are oriented. Somehow, light that is linearly polarised along a certain direction can only excite a microvillus with the same orientation. Ants, bees, and other animals have clusters of cells with such membranes all aligned in the same way to distinguish various polarisations; other animals, such as humans, have these membranes randomly oriented and, therefore, they are not sensitive to light polarisation. However, when it comes to circularly polarised light, microvilli are always responsive regardless of their orientation, since it is oscillating in all directions.

"The idea of circular polarisation vision in stomatopod crustacean was first published in 1991 by Justin Marshall and coworkers," Chiou notes, "based on the architecture of the photoreceptors in stomatopods." However, it is only in a recent article that Chiou, Kleinlogel, and collegues demonstrated that such structure behaves as a quarter wave plate, an optical element that transforms left and right circularly polarised light into perpendicularly oriented—for example, vertical and horizontal—linearly polarised light. After such transformation the microvilli can do their job—distinguishing the two linear polarisations—and the animal gains information about the original light polarisation state. Furthermore, they verified that these animals really use circularly polarised light by training them to associate either left or right circularly polarised light with a food reward. And indeed the crustaceans were responsive. The mantis shrimp studied by Kleinlogel and White goes a degree further: it combines circular and linear polarisation measurements to fully reconstruct the light polarisation state. Andrew White from the University of Queensland (Australia) explains, "each eye of the mantis shrimp measures the polarisation components that are precisely required for optimal polarisation vision."

So for what is perfect polarisation vision useful? Humans use polarised filters and imaging in everyday photography, medical photography, and object-detection in turbid environments. "Under water you have two problems: colours disappear, light is scattered." Kleinlogel points out, "additionally the reefs and waters that many stomatopods inhabit are often turbid. With polarising filters things look better, as fishermen well know. Furthermore, various animals reflect polarised light." "Currently we have found more than a dozen of stomatopod species with polarised light-reflecting body parts," explains Chiou, "by arranging a birefringent material above the polarised light reflector, some animals are able to generate circularly polarised light signals." "Some of the animals they like to eat are transparent," White notes, "and quite hard to see in sea-water—except they're packed full of polarising sugars—I suspect they light up like Christmas trees as far as these shrimps are concerned." "And of course," Kleinlogel concludes, "they can still flirt with each other using fancy polarisation cues!"

Flash Memory

Flash memory is non-volatile computer memory that can be electrically erased and reprogrammed. It is a technology that is primarily used in memory cards and USB flash drives for general storage and transfer of data between computers and other digital products. It is a specific type of EEPROM (Electrically Erasable Programmable Read-Only Memory) that is erased and programmed in large blocks; in early flash the entire chip had to be erased at once. Flash memory costs far less than byte-programmable EEPROM and therefore has become the dominant technology wherever a significant amount of non-volatile, solid-state storage is needed. Example applications include PDAs (personal digital assistants), laptop computers, digital audio players, digital cameras and mobile phones. It has also gained popularity in the game console market, where it is often used instead of EEPROMs or battery-powered SRAM for game save data.

Flash memory is non-volatile, which means that no power is needed to maintain the information stored in the chip. In addition, flash memory offers fast read access times (although not as fast as volatile DRAM memory used for main memory in PCs) and better kinetic shock resistance than hard disks. These characteristics explain the popularity of flash memory in portable devices. Another feature of flash memory is that when packaged in a "memory card," it is enormously durable, being able to withstand intense pressure, extremes of temperature, and even immersion in water.

Although technically a type of EEPROM, the term "EEPROM" is generally used to refer specifically to non-flash EEPROM which is erasable in small blocks, typically bytes. Because erase cycles are slow, the large block sizes used in flash memory erasing give it a significant speed advantage over old-style EEPROM when writing large amounts of data.

NOR Memories

Reading from NOR flash is similar to reading from random-access memory, provided the address and data bus are mapped correctly. Because of this, most microprocessors can use NOR flash memory as execute in place (XIP) memory, meaning that programmes stored in NOR flash can be executed directly without the need to copy them into RAM. NOR flash chips lack intrinsic bad block management, so when a flash block is worn out, the software or device driver controlling the device must handle this, or the device will cease to work reliably.

When unlocking, erasing or writing NOR memories, special commands are written to the first page of the mapped memory. These commands are defined by the *Common Flash memory Interface* (CFI) and the flash chips can provide a list of available commands to the physical driver.

Apart from being used as random-access ROM, NOR memories can also be used as storage devices. However, NOR flash chips typically have slow write speeds compared with NAND flash.

NAND Memories

NAND flash architecture was introduced by Toshiba in 1989. These memories are accessed much like block devices such as hard disks or memory cards. Each block consists of a number of pages. The pages are typically 512 or 2,048 or 4,096 bytes in size. Associated with each page are a few bytes (typically 12–16 bytes) that should be used for storage of an error detection and correction checksum.

Typical block sizes include:

32 pages of 512 bytes each for a block size of 16 kiB

64 pages of 2,048 bytes each for a block size of 128 kiB

64 pages of 4,096 bytes each for a block size of 256 kiB

128 pages of 4,096 bytes each for a block size of 512 kiB

While programming is performed on a page basis, erasure can only be performed on a block basis. Another limitation of NAND flash is data in a block can only be written sequentially. Number of Operations(NOPs) is the number of times the sectors can be programmed. So far this number for MLC flash is always one whereas for SLC flash it is 4.

NAND devices also require bad block management by the device driver software, or by a separate controller chip. SD cards, for example, include controller circuitry to perform bad block management and wear leveling. When a logical block is accessed by high-level software, it is mapped to a physical block by the device driver or controller, and a number of blocks on the flash chip are set aside for storing mapping tables to deal with bad blocks. The overall memory capacity gradually shrinks as more blocks are marked as bad.

The error-correcting and detecting checksum will typically correct an error where one bit per 256 bytes (2,048 bits) is incorrect. When this happens, the block is marked bad in a logical block allocation table, and its undamaged contents are copied to a new block and the logical block allocation table is altered accordingly. If more than one bit out of 2,048 is corrupted, the contents are partly lost, i.e. it is no longer possible to reconstruct the original contents. If this is detected when the block is written, the contents may still be available.

Most NAND devices are shipped from the factory with some bad blocks which are typically identified and marked according to a specified bad block marking strategy. By allowing some bad blocks, the manufacturers achieve far higher yields than would be possible if all blocks were tested good. This significantly reduces NAND flash costs and only slightly decreases the storage capacity of the parts.

The first physical block (block 0) is always guaranteed to be readable and free from errors. Hence, all vital pointers for partitioning and bad block management for the device must be located inside this block (typically a pointer to the bad block tables etc). If the device is used for booting a system, this block may contain the master boot record.

When executing software from NAND memories, virtual memory strategies are often used: memory contents must first be paged or copied into memory-mapped RAM and executed there. A memory management unit (MMU) in the system is helpful, but this can also be accomplished with overlays. For this reason, some systems will use a combination of NOR and NAND memories, where a smaller NOR memory is used as software ROM and a larger NAND memory is partitioned with a file system for use as a random access storage area. NAND is best suited to flash devices requiring high capacity data storage. This type of flash architecture combines higher storage space with faster erase, write, and read capabilities over the execute in place advantage of the NOR architecture.

Standardisation

A group called the Open NAND Flash Interface Working Group (ONFI) has developed a standardised low-level interface for NAND flash chips. This allows interoperability between conforming NAND devices from different vendors. The ONFI specification version 1.0 was released on December 28, 2006. It specifies:

- a standard physical interface (pinout) for NAND flash in TSOP-48, WSOP-48, LGA-52, and BGA-63 packages
- a standard command set for reading, writing, and erasing NAND flash chips
- a mechanism for self-identification (comparable to the Serial Presence Detection feature of SDRAM chips)

The ONFI group is supported by major NAND flash manufacturers, including Intel, Micron Technology, and Sony, as well as by major manufacturers of devices incorporating NAND flash chips.

A group of vendors, including Intel, Dell, and Microsoft formed a Non-Volatile Memory Host Controller Interface (NVMHCI) Working Group. The goal of the group is to provide standard software and hardware programming interfaces for nonvolatile memory subsystems, including the "flash cache" device connected to the PCI Express bus.

Flash file Systems

Because of the particular characteristics of flash memory, it is best used with either a controller to perform wear-levelling and error correction or specifically designed file systems which spread writes over the media and deal with the long erase times of NOR flash blocks. The basic concept behind flash file systems is: When the flash store is to be updated, the file system will write a new copy of the changed data over to a fresh block, remap the file pointers, then erase the old block later when it has time.

One of the earliest flash file systems was Microsoft's FFS2 (presumably preceded by FFS1), for use with MS-DOS in the early 1990s.

Around 1994, the PCMCIA, an industry group, approved the **Flash Translation Layer (FTL)** specification, which allowed a Linear Flash device to look like a FAT disk, but still have effective wear levelling. Other commercial systems such as FlashFX and FlashFX Pro by Datalight were created to avoid patent concerns with FTL.

ZFS by Sun Microsystems has been optimised to manage Flash SSD systems, both as cache as well as main storage facilities, available for OpenSolaris, Mac OSX, and the Linux operating system. Sun has announced a complete line of Flash enabled systems and storage devices.

JFFS was the first flash-specific file system for Linux, but it was quickly superseded by JFFS2, originally developed for NOR flash. Then YAFFS was released in 2002, dealing specifically with NAND flash, and JFFS2 was updated to support NAND flash too.

In practice, flash file systems are only used for "Memory Technology Devices" ("MTD"), which are embedded flash memories that do not have a controller. Removable flash memory cards and USB flash drives have built-in controllers to perform wear-levelling and error correction so use of a specific flash file system does not add any benefit. These removable flash memory devices use the FAT file system to allow universal compatibility with computers, cameras, PDAs and other portable devices with memory card slots or ports.

Capacity

Multiple chips are often arrayed to achieve higher capacities for use in consumer electronic devices such as multimedia player or GPS. The capacity of flash chips generally follows Moore's Law because they are manufactured with many of the same integrated circuits techniques and equipment.

Consumer flash drives typically have sizes measured in powers of two (e.g. 512 MB, 8 GB), but unlike DIMMs (and like hard drives) these sizes use decimal units.

In 2005, Toshiba and SanDisk developed a NAND flash chip capable of storing 1 GB of data using Multi-level Cell (MLC) technology, capable of storing 2 bits of data per cell. In September 2005, Samsung Electronics announced that it had developed the world's first 2 GB chip.

In March 2006, Samsung announced flash hard drives with a capacity of 4 GB, essentially the same order of magnitude as smaller laptop hard drives, and in September 2006, Samsung announced an 8 GB chip produced using a 40 nanometer manufacturing process.

In January 2008 Sandisk announced availability of their 12GB MicroSDHC and 32GB SDHC Plus cards.

Flash Memory as a Replacement for Hard Drives

An obvious extension of flash memory would be as a replacement for hard disks. Flash memory does not have the mechanical limitations and latencies of hard drives, so the idea of a solid-state drive, or SSD, is attractive when considering speed, noise, power consumption, and reliability.

There remain some aspects of flash-based SSDs that make the idea unattractive. Most importantly, the cost per gigabyte of flash memory remains significantly higher than that of platter-based hard drives. Although this ratio is decreasing rapidly for flash memory, it is not yet clear that flash memory will catch up to the capacities and affordability offered by platter-based storage. Still, research and development is sufficiently vigorous that it is not clear that it will not happen, either.

There is also some concern that the finite number of erase/write cycles of flash memory would render flash memory unable to support an operating system. This seems to be a decreasing issue as warranties on flash-based SSDs are approaching those of current hard drives.

As of May 24, 2006, South Korean consumer-electronics manufacturer Samsung Electronics had released the first flash-memory based PCs, the Q1-SSD and Q30-SSD, both of which have 32 GB SSDs. Dell Computer introduced the Latitude D430 laptop with 32 GB flash-memory storage in July 2007—at a price significantly above a hard-drive equipped version.

At the Las Vegas CES 2007 Summit Taiwanese memory company A-DATA showcased SSD hard disk drives based on Flash technology in capacities of 32 GB, 64 GB and 128 GB. Sandisk announced an OEM 32 GB 1.8" SSD drive at CES 2007. The XO-1, developed by the One Laptop Per Child (OLPC) association, uses flash memory rather than a hard drive. As of June 2007, a South Korean company called Mtron claims the fastest SSD with sequential read/write speeds of 100 MB/80 MB per second.

Rather than entirely replacing the hard drive, hybrid techniques such as hybrid drive and ReadyBoost attempt to combine the advantages of both technologies, using flash as a high-speed cache for files on the disk that are often referenced, but rarely modified, such as application and operating system executable files. Also, Addonics has a PCI adapter for 4 CF cards, creating a RAID-able array of solid-state storage that is much cheaper than the hardwired-chips PCI card kind.

The ASUS Eee PC uses a flash-based SSD of 2GB to 20GB, depending on model. The Apple Inc. Macbook Air has the option to upgrade the standard hard drive to a 64GB Solid State hard drive. The Lenovo ThinkPad X300 also features a built-in 64GB Solid State Drive.

Solid-state Drive

A solid-state drive (SSD) is a data storage device that uses solid-state memory to store persistent data. Unlike flash-based memory cards, an SSD emulates a hard disk drive, thus easily replacing it in most applications. An SSD using SRAM or DRAM (instead of flash memory) is often called a **RAM-drive.**

The original usage of the term *solid-state* (from solid-state physics) refers to the use of semiconductor devices rather than electron tubes, but has in this context been adopted to distinguish solid-state electronics from electromechanical devices as well. With no moving parts, solid-state drives are inherently less fragile than harddisks and therefore also silent (unless a cooling fan is used); as there are no mechanical delays, they usually enjoy low access time and latency.

SSDs have begun to appear in laptops, although they are at present substantially more expensive per unit of capacity than hard drives.

In 1995 M-Systems introduced flash-based solid-state drives. (SanDisk acquired M-Systems in November 2006). Since then, SSDs have been used successfully as hard disk drive replacements by the military and aerospace industries, as well as other mission-critical applications. These applications require the exceptional mean time between failures (MTBF) rates that solid-state drives achieve, by virtue of their ability to withstand extreme shock, vibration and temperature ranges.

The Gigabyte i-RAM uses standard DDR modules and connects to its host via Serial ATA. This card can use the system's standby power (also used for Wake-on-LAN and similar features) to maintain its RAM contents even with the system powered off and includes a battery that can retain the data when the system is completely disconnected from power.

An SSD is commonly composed of either NAND flash non-volatile memory or DRAM volatile memory.

Advantages

- Faster start-up (over 30 times faster)—as no spin-up is required. (RAM & Flash)
- Typically fast random access for reading—as there is no read/write head to move. (RAM & Flash)
- Extremely low read and write latency times—as SSD seek-times are orders of magnitude lower than the best current hard disk drives. (RAM) In applications where hard disk seeks are the limiting factor this results in faster boot and application launch times (see Amdahl's law). (RAM)
- No noise—a lack of moving parts makes SSDs completely silent, unless, as in the case of some high-end and high-capacity models, they have cooling fans attached. (RAM & Flash)
- For low-capacity SSDs, low power consumption and heat production—although high-end SSDs and DRAM-based SSDs may have significantly higher power requirements.
- High mechanical reliability – the lack of moving parts almost eliminates the risk of mechanical failure. (RAM & Flash)
  - Ability to endure extreme shock, high altitude, vibration and extremes of temperature – once again because there are no moving parts. This makes SSDs useful for laptops, mobile computers, and devices that operate in extreme conditions. (Flash)
- Relatively deterministic performance – unlike hard disk drives, performance of SSDs is almost constant and deterministic across the entire storage. This is because the seek time is almost constant and is not dependent on the physical location of the data, and so, file fragmentation has almost no impact on performance.

- For low-capacity SSDs, lower weight and size – although size and weight per unit storage are still better for traditional hard drives, and microdrives allow up to 20 GB storage in a CompactFlash 42.8×36.4×5 mm (1.7×1.4×.2 in) form-factor. Up to 256 GB, SSDs are currently lighter than hard drives of the same capacity.

Disadvantages

- Price—as of mid-2008, flash memory prices are still considerably more costly per gigabyte than are comparable conventional hard drives: around USD 3.50 per GB compared to typically less than USD 0.40 for mechanical drives.
- Capacity—although currently far lower than that of conventional hard drives, SSD capacity is predicted to increase rapidly, with experimental drives of up to 1 TB in test.
- Higher vulnerability to certain types of effects, including abrupt power loss (especially DRAM based SSDs), magnetic fields and electric/static charges, in comparison to normal HDDs (which store the data inside a Faraday cage).
- Limited write cycles—flash-memory storage will often wear out after 300,000-500,000 write cycles, while high endurance flash-memory storage may have an endurance of 1–5 million write cycles (many log files, file allocation tables and other commonly used parts of the file system exceed this over the lifetime of a computer. Special file systems or firmware designs can mitigate this problem by spreading writes over the entire device (so-called wear levelling), rather than rewriting files in place. This problem is being improved all the time, with consequent increases in expected lifespan. Today's drives can last up to 20 years with average usage. An example for the lifetime of SSD is explained in detail here. SSDs based on DRAM, however, do not suffer from this problem.

- Slower write speeds—as erase blocks on flash-based SSDs generally are quite large, they are far slower than conventional disks for random writes, and in some cases for sequential writes. SSDs based on DRAM do not suffer from this problem.
- Lower storage density—hard disks can store more data per unit volume than DRAM or flash SSDs, except for very low capacity/small devices. With the introduction of smaller technology node processes, the storage density of SSDs is expected to rapidly increase in the near future.
- Higher power consumption—at idle or under low workloads laptop battery runtimes decrease when using an SSD over a 7200 RPM 2.5" laptop hard drive, flash drives also take more power per gigabyte.

Availability

One of the first mainstream releases of SSD was the XO Laptop built under the 'One Laptop Per Child' project. Mass production of these computers built for children in developing countries begun in December 2007. These machines use 1024 MiB SLC NAND flash as primary storage solution which is considered more suitable for the harsher than normal conditions they are expected to be used in. Dell has begun shipping ultra-portable laptops with SanDisk SSDs on April 26, 2007. Asus released the Eee PC subnotebook on October 16 2007, and after a successful commercial start in 2007, expects to ship several million PCs in 2008, with 2, 4 or 8 gigabytes of flash memory. On January 31, 2008 Apple Inc. released the MacBook Air, a thin laptop with optional 64 GB SSD. The cost is $599 more for this option if configured in the Apple Store, as compared to that of an 80 GB 4200 RPM Hard Disk Drive. Another option—IBM Lenovo ThinkPad X300 with 64Gbyte SSD—was announced by Lenovo in February 2008, and is currently available to consumers in some countries.

Product Timeline

- Mtron announces flash memory solid-state drive, performing 100 MB/s Read, 80 MB/s Write, 72,000 Max IOPS in December 2005.
- SanDisk released a 32 GB 2.5-inch solid-state drive on March 13, 2007. The SSD SATA 5000 is being sold to computer manufacturers for $350.
- Taiwanese A-DATA introduced at the Las Vegas CES 2007 (January 2007) SSD drives at capacities of 32 GB, 64 GB (1.8" model) and 128 GB (2.5" model). It is expected to be commercially available by mid-2007.
- Hyperdrive release the rev.4 designed to use 8 standard DDR ECC Registered memory modules on a native SATA and IDE interface. February 2007.
- On February 26, 2007, SMART Modular Technologies launched its first line of XceedUltra solid-state drives (SSDs). SMART's XceedUltra U100 is the industry's first SSD with a serial ATA (SATA) interface that achieves sustained read speeds of 100 MB/s and write speeds of 60 MB/s.
- Super Talent Technology announced a 3.5-inch 128 GB solid-state drive in April 2007.
- STEC, Inc. has announced a 64 GB SSD that is only 9.5 mm thick, half the size of competing SSDs. On April 18, 2007, STEC announced 256 GB enterprise-level drives available immediately, and 512 GB drives available late 2007.
- Lexar ExpressCard SSD is shipping in 4 GB, 8 GB, and 16 GB capacities, as of May 2007.
- PNY announces SSD lineup targeting OEM customers in 1.8" and 2.5" form-factors, PATA and SATA, capacities reaching 128 GB in May 24, 2007.
- Power Quotient International (PQI) Announces 256 GB SSD on 28 May 2007.
- SanDisk announces 64 GB SSDs of 1.8 UATA 5000 and 2.5 SATA 5000 on June 4, 2007.

- Violin Memory announces 1010 memory appliance on August 2, 2007. The DRAM version of their appliance is capable of supporting 504 GB of memory and the expected flash version will scale to a little over 5 TB. This 2U appliance is capable of over 3 Million random I/O per Second (IOPS). It is attached to a server through a 20 Gbit/s PCI Express connection (8 lanes) and has demonstrated 1400 MB/s read rate and 1000 MB/s write rate with 3ìs latency.
- SMART On August 7, 2007, SMART Modular Technologies launched the XceedLite SATA SSD product line.
- Fusion-io announces ioDrive 640 GB 100,000 IOPS 800 MB/s NAND Flash PCI Card on September 24, 2007.
- Trident Space & Defense in October 2007 introduces highly rugged Triton Series Drives (shock, vibration, splash resistant) for military and industrial applications in a standard 2.5-inch form factor with 9.4 mm height.
- BiTMICRO launches SSD 3.5" with a capacity of 1.6 TB in November 2007. Will mostly be used for the army.
- SanDisk released a 32 GB 1.8-inch solid-state drive on January 4, 2008.
- Texas Memory Systems achieved the highest number of IOPS (291,208.58) and the lowest Price Performance ($0.67/IOPS) when they took part in the Storage Performance Council's SPC-1 IOPS test in January 2008.
- Imation announces Pro7000 SSD drive with 120 MB/s read and 90MB/s write performance [IOPS:81000/18000] and 0,1ms avg access time on March 10, 2008.
- ROMEDIA announced a 3.5-inch 128 GB solid-state drive on stock for sale on March 2008.
- Memoright announces SSD drives with 115 MB/s read and write performance confirmed on May 9, 2008.
- Samsung announces increase in capacity of its flash-based SSD line to 256 GB on May 25, 2008. This drive has reported speeds of 200MB/sec read and 160MB/sec write.

- Toshiba introduced a notebook that the vendor claims is the lightest laptop (2.4-pound) with a 128-GB Solid-State Drive, June 17, 2008.
- Fusion-io and Hewlett Packard announce working together to adapt the ioDrive flash SSD to provide acceleration in HP's BladeSystem and Enterprise Servers, June 18, 2008.

USB Flash Drive

A USB flash drive is a NAND-type flash memory data storage device integrated with a USB (universal serial bus) connector. USB flash drives are typically removable and rewritable, much shorter than a floppy disk (1 to 4 inches or 2.5 to 10 cm), and weigh less than 2 ounces (60 g). Storage capacities typically range from 64 MB to 32 GB or more. Some allow 1 million write or erase cycles and have 10-year data retention, connected by USB 1.1 or USB 2.0. USB Memory card readers are also available, whereby rather than being built-in, the memory is a removable flash memory card housed in what is otherwise a regular USB flash drive, as described below.

USB flash drives offer potential advantages over other portable storage devices, particularly the floppy disk. They are more compact, faster, hold much more data, have a more durable design, and are more reliable for lack of moving parts. Additionally, it has become increasingly common for computers to ship without floppy disk drives. USB ports, on the other hand, appear on almost every current mainstream PC and laptop. These types of drives use the USB mass storage standard, supported natively by modern operating systems such as Windows, Mac OS X, Linux, and other Unix-like systems. USB drives with USB 2.0 support can also be faster than an optical disc drive, while storing a larger amount of data in a much smaller space.

With nothing being mechanically driven in a flash drive, th name is something of a misnomer. It is called a "drive" because i appears to the computer operating system (and the user) in a manne identical to a mechanical disk drive, and is accessed in the same way.

A flash drive consists of a small printed circuit board typically in a plastic or metal casing and more recently in rubber casings to increase their robustness. This makes the drive sturdy enough to be carried about in a pocket, for example as a key fob, or on a lanyard. Only the USB connector protrudes, and it is typically protected either by a removable cap or by retracting into the body of the drive. Most flash drives use a standard type-A USB connection allowing them to be connected directly to a port on a personal computer.

To access the data stored in a flash drive, the drive must be connected to a USB port through either a host controller built into a computer, a USB hub, or some other device designed to access the data, such as an mp3 player with a USB-in port. Flash drives are active only when plugged into a USB connection and draw all necessary power from the supply provided by that connection. Some flash drives, however, especially high-speed drives, may require more power than the limited amount provided by a bus-powered USB hub, such as those built into some computer keyboards or monitors. These drives will not work properly unless plugged directly into a host controller (i.e., the ports found on the computer itself) or a self-powered hub.

Technology

Flash memory is actually a combination of a number of older technologies, with the low cost, low power consumption and small size being made possible by recent advances in microprocessor technology. The memory storage is based on earlier EPROM and EEPROM technologies. These had very limited capacity, were very slow for both reading and writing, required complex high-voltage drive circuitry, and could only be re-written after erasing the entire contents of the chip.

Later EEPROMS were developed where the erasure region was broken up into smaller "fields" that could be erased individually without affecting the others. Altering the contents of a particular memory location involved first copying the entire field into an off-chip buffer memory, erasing the field, and then re-writing the data back into the same field, making the necessary alteration to the relevant memory location while doing so. This required considerable computer support, and PC-Based EEPROM flash memory systems often carried their own dedicated microprocessor system. Flash drives are more or less a miniaturised version of this.

The development of high-speed serial data interfaces such as USB for the first time made serially accessed storage memory systems viable, and the simultaneous development of small, high-speed, low-power microprocessor systems allowed this to be incorporated into extremely compact systems. Serial access also greatly reduced the number of electrical connections required for the memory chips, which has allowed the successful manufacture of multi-gigabyte capacities. (Every external electrical connection is a potential source of manufacturing failure, and with traditional manufacturing, a point is rapidly reached where the successful yield approaches zero).

Modern flash memory systems are accessed very much like hard disk drives, where the controller system has full control over where information is actually stored. The actual EEPROM writing and erasure processes are, however, still very similar to the earlier systems described above.

Many low-cost MP3 Players simply add extra software to a standard flash memory control microprocessor so it can also serve as a music playback decoder. Most of these players can also be used as a conventional flash drive.

First Commercial Product

Trek Technology and IBM began selling the first USB flash drives commercially in 2000. Singaporean company Trek Technology sold a model dubbed the "ThumbDrive," and IBM marketed the first such drives in North America, with its product the "DiskOnKey" (which was manufactured by M-Systems). IBM's USB flash drive became available December 15, 2000, and had a storage capacity of 8 MiB, more than five times the capacity of the (at the time) commonly used floppy disks.

Flash drive with retractable USB connector

Lexar can also lay claim to a pioneering USB flash drive product. In 2000, it introduced a Compact Flash (CF) card with a USB connection. Lexar also offered a companion card reader and USB cable that eliminated the need for a USB hub.

In 2004, Trek Technology brought several lawsuits against other USB flash drive manufacturers and distributors in an attempt to assert its patent rights to the USB flash drive. A court in Singapore ordered competitors to cease selling similar products that would be covered by Trek's patent, but a court in the United Kingdom revoked one of Trek's patents in that country.

Second Generation

Toshiba TransMemory Flash Drive with cover on. Comes pre-installed with U3, allowing users to take their applications, fully installed and operational, to any desktop.

Modern flash drives have USB 2.0 connectivity. However, they do not currently use the full 480 Mbit/s the specification supports due to technical limitations inherent in NAND flash. The fastest drives currently available use a dual channel controller, although they still fall considerably short of the transfer rate possible from a current generation hard disk, or the maximum high speed USB throughput.

Typical overall file transfer speeds are about 3 MB/s. The highest current overall file transfer speeds are about 10-60 MB/s. Older, "full speed" 12 Mbit/s devices are limited to a maximum of about 1 MB/s.

Design and Implementation

One end of the device is fitted with a single male type-A USB connector. Inside the plastic casing is a small printed circuit board. Mounted on this board is some simple power circuitry and a small number of surface-mounted integrated circuits (ICs). Typically, one of these ICs provides an interface to the USB port, another drives the onboard memory, and the other is the flash memory.

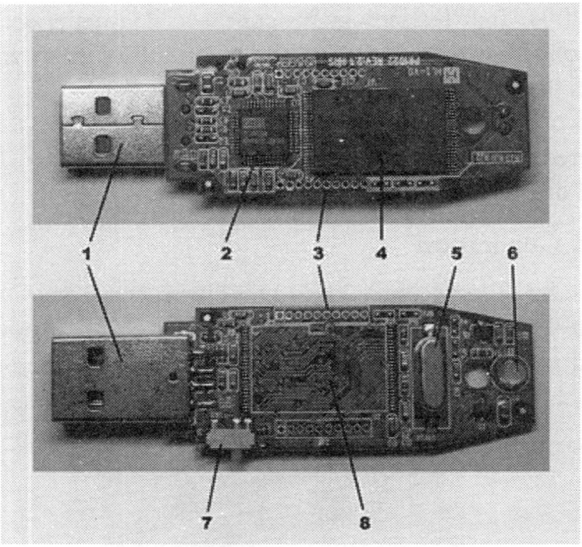

Internals of a typical USB flash drive

1. USB connector
2. USB mass storage controller device
3. Test points
4. Flash memory chip
5. Crystal oscillator
6. LED

7. Write-protect switch
8. Space for second flash memory chip

Essential Components

There are typically four parts to a flash drive:

- Male type-A USB connector—provides an interface to the host computer.
- USB mass storage controller—implements the USB host controller. The controller contains a small RISC microprocessor and a small amount of on-chip ROM and RAM.
- NAND flash memory chip—stores data. NAND flash is typically also used in digital cameras.
- Crystal oscillator—produces the device's main 12 MHz clock signal and controls the device's data output through a phase-locked loop.

Additional Components

The typical device may also include:

- Jumpers and test pins — for testing during the flash drive's manufacturing or loading code into the microprocessor.
- LEDs — indicate data transfers or data reads and writes.
- Write-protect switches — indicate whether the device should be in "write-protection" mode.
- Unpopulated space — provides space to include a second memory chip. Having this second space allows the manufacturer to develop only one printed circuit board that can be used for more than one storage size device, to meet the needs of the market.
- USB connector cover or cap — reduces the risk of damage due to static electricity, and improves overall device appearance. Some flash drives do not feature a cap, but instead have retractable USB connectors. Other flash drives have a "swivel" cap that is permanently connected to the drive itself and eliminates the chance of losing the cap.

- Transport aid — In some cases, the cap or the main body contains a hole suitable for connection to a key chain or lanyard.

Size and Style of Packaging

Some manufacturers differentiate their products by using elaborate housings, which are often bulky and make the drive difficult to connect to the USB port. Because the USB port connectors on a computer housing are often closely spaced, plugging a flash drive into a USB port may block an adjacent port. Such devices may only carry the USB logo if sold with a separate extension cable.

Flash drives come in various, sometimes bulky or novelty, shapes and sizes, in this case ikura sushi

USB flash drives have been integrated into other tools commonly carried on one's person such as watches, pens, and even the Swiss Army Knife; others have been fitted with novelty cases such as toy cars or LEGO bricks. The small size, robust nature and relatively low price of USB flash drives makes them an increasingly popular peripheral for case modding.

Overweight or ill-fitting flash drive packaging can cause disconnection from the host computer. This can be overcome by using a short USB to USB (male to female) extension cable to relieve tension on the port. Such cables are USB-compatible, but do not conform to the USB 1.0 standard.

File System

Most flash drives ship preformatted with the FAT or FAT 32 file system. The ubiquity of this file system allows the drive to be accessed on virtually any host device with USB support. Also, standard FAT maintenance utilities (e.g. ScanDisk) can be used to repair or retrieve corrupted data. However, because a flash drive appears as a USB-connected hard drive to the host system, the drive can be reformatted to any file system supported by the host operating system.

It is worth noting that while defragmentation utilities can be run against a flash drive, there is no point in doing so. Defragmentation is a process intended to optimise access to data on a drive with spinning platters and moving heads; however, since flash memory is truly random-access (a read to an adjacent cell is no faster than a read from any other cell), there is no performance gain. Further, the flash controller abstracts the physical memory location used for a given "sector", so that the host machine doesn't really know the layout of the data. Finally, as the defragmentation process moves data around, attempting to optimise it, a small portion of the flash memory's wear life is consumed.

USES

Personal data transport

The most common use of flash drives is to transport and store personal files such as documents, pictures and videos. Individuals also store medical alert information on MedicTag flash drives for use in emergencies and for disaster preparation.

Secure storage of data, application and software files

With wide deployment(s) of flash drives being used in various environments (secured or otherwise), the issue of data and information security remains of the utmost importance. The use of biometrics and encryption is becoming the norm with the need for increased security for data; OTFE systems such as FreeOTFE and TrueCrypt are particularly useful in this regard, as they can transparently encrypt large amounts of data.

System Administration

Flash drives are particularly popular among system and network administrators, who load them with configuration information and software used for system maintenance, troubleshooting, and recovery.

Computer Repair

Flash drives enjoy notable success in the PC repair field as a means to transfer recovery and antivirus software to infected PCs, while allowing a portion of the host machine's data to be archived in case of emergency. As the drives have increased in storage space, they have also replaced the need to carry a number of CD ROMs and installers which were needed when reinstalling or updating a system.

Application Carriers

Flash drives are used to carry applications that run on the host computer without requiring installation. While any standalone application can be used this way, the U3 company, works with drive makers (parent company SanDisk as well as others) to deliver Windows applications from a flash drive custom-tuned for this purpose. U3 also provides a software framework for ISVs interested in their platform. Ceedo is an alternative product with the key difference that it does not require Windows applications to be modified in order for them to be carried and run on the drive.

Computer Forensics—Law Enforcement

A recent development for the use of a USB Flash Drive as an application carrier is to carry the Computer Online Forensic Evidence Extractor (COFEE) application, developed by Microsoft. COFEE is a set of applications designed to search for and extract digital evidence on computers confiscated from suspects.

To Boot Operating Systems

Most current PC firmware permits booting from a USB drive, allowing the launch of an operating system from a bootable flash drive. Such a configuration is known as a Live USB.

While a Live USB could be used for general-purpose applications, size and memory wear make them poor choices compared to alternatives. They are more suited to special-purpose or temporary tasks, such as:

- Loading a minimal, hardened kernel for embedded applications (e.g. network router, firewall).
- Bootstrapping an operating system install or disk cloning operation, often across a network.
- Maintenance tasks, such as virus scanning or low-level data repair, without the primary host operating system loaded.

Windows Vista ReadyBoost

In Windows Vista, the ReadyBoost feature allows use of some flash drives to augment operating system memory.

Audio Players

Many companies make solid-state digital audio players in a small form factor, essentially producing flash drives with sound output and a simple user interface. Examples include the Creative MuVo and the iPod shuffle. While a few of these players fit the accepted definition of a "true" USB flash drive (including the ability to plug directly into a USB A socket), the majority require a separate cable.

Many of the smallest players also contain a rechargeable battery, charged from the USB interface.

Music Storage

Digital audio files can be transported from one computer to another like any other document, and played on a compatible media player (with caveats for DRM-locked files). In addition, many home Hi-Fi and car stereo head units are now equipped with a USB port. This allows a USB flash drive, loaded with media files (usually MP3 or WMA, although sometimes other formats such as Ogg/Vorbis may be used), to be played directly.

Most often, these files will be from the user's personal collection (e.g. ripped from CD or purchased online), although there have been some examples of pre-encoded music sold or given away for promotion on USB flash drives:

- In 2004, the German band WIZO made a recording industry first of releasing the "Stick EP", an album available only as a USB drive. In addition to five high-bitrate MP3s, it also included a video, pictures, lyrics, and guitar tablature.
- *Third* album by Portishead in the limited edition box set.
- *Not Here to Please You* EP by Hadouken!
- *Icky Thump* single by White Stripes
- *Good Life* single by Kanye West
- *X* album by Kylie Minogue
- Nine Inch Nails promoted their album *Year Zero* by hiding USB drives at concerts, usually with content like select songs contained on them.
- *Nothing In My Way* single by Keane The 512MiB drive was loaded with the audio track, music video, and several extras.
- *The Bedlam in Goliath* album by The Mars Volta was released on a USB drive shaped like a ouija planchette to coincide with the album's concept. In addition to the music files, the drive can be used to unlock exclusive material on the band's website.
- In 2007, a product known as the MU-STIK appeared in the market, offering a means of packaging music albums by containing all relevant digital audio/video data and a customizable player interface within a USB key.
- *The I Heart Revolution: With Hearts as One* album by Hillsong United was released in 2008 on a flash drive

embedded in a black rubber wristband. In addition to the music files, the drive included the lyrical overhead master sheets, a PDF copy of the liner sleeve, and the two versions of the album cover.

In Arcades

In the arcade game *In the Groove* and more commonly *In The Groove 2*, flash drives are used to transfer high scores, screenshots, dance edits, and combos throughout sessions. As of software revision 21 (R21), players can also store custom songs and play them on any machine on which this feature is enabled. While use of flash drives is common, the drive must be Linux compatible, causing problems for some players.

Brand/product promotion

The availability of inexpensive flash drives has enabled them to be used for promotional and marketing purposes, particularly within technical and computer-industry circles (e.g. technology trade shows). These may be given away for free, sold at less than wholesale price, or included as a bonus with another purchased product.

Usually, such drives will be custom-stamped with a company's logo, as a form of advertising to increase mind share and brand awareness. Sometimes, the drive is simply an ordinary blank drive for the customer's use, and simple advertising is the only purpose. Often, however, the drive's storage may be preloaded with graphics, documentation, web links, Flash animation or other multimedia, and even free or demonstration software.

In some cases, such preloaded drives may have had an internal wiring trace severed to disable writing (rendering the drive as read-only to the end-user). This serves the dual-purposes of ensuring that the original promotional data remains intact (and isn't simply deleted to free up capacity), as well as reducing the possibility that drives will become infected with a virus or other malware before reaching the customer. An alternative is that some drives can be configured with two separate partitions: one read-only (preloaded with the promotional data), and another writable and blank for the end-user's use. However, such dual-purpose drives tend to be more expensive, thus reducing their suitability as promotional items.

USB Flash Drives can also be set up with an autorun feature to display or start up preloaded presentations, websites and articles immediately on insertion of the drive. This can be accomplished by saving a file called autorun.inf in the root directory of the drive. This file needs to contain appropriate shell script telling the operating system which files to execute. The auto run feature is often used on promotional flash drives to increase the probability that the recipient reads the preloaded promotional material or visits a particular website.

Backup

Some value-added resellers are now using a flash drive as part of small-business turnkey solutions (e.g. point-of-sale systems). The drive is used as a backup medium: at the close of business each night, the drive is inserted, and a database backup is saved to the drive. Alternatively, the drive can be left inserted through the business day, and data is regularly updated. In either case, the drive is removed at night and taken offsite.

This strategy has several advantages. First, it can be made relatively simple for the end-user. This increases the likelihood tha backups will be performed regularly (one of the most commo reasons for a failure to backup is the complexity of the process) Second, because the drive is small, it is easy to carry by the manage or proprietor, thus ensuring that the data is offsite for disaste recovery. Third, flash drives are very robust and reliable, particular compared to other backup media (e.g. tape, optical media). Fourt the availability of large drives often permits the storage of sever backup images on a single medium, facilitating a GFS or oth hierarchical backup strategy (multiple flash drives are anoth option, but this increases the backup complexity). Finally, the fla solution is often far cheaper than alternatives, which may requ additional hardware or recurring media costs (e.g. tape drive, blank DVDs).

ADVANTAGES AND DISADVANTAGES

Advantages

Flash drives are nearly impervious to the scratches and dust that were problematic for previous forms of portable storage, such as compact discs, ZIP disks, and floppy disks, and their durable solid-state design means they often survive casual abuse. This makes them ideal for transporting personal data or work files from one location to another, such as from home to school or office or for carrying around personal data that the user typically wants to access in a variety of places. The near-ubiquity of USB support on modern computers means that such a drive will work in most places.

Flash drives are also a relatively dense form of storage, where even the cheapest will store dozens of floppy disks worth of data. Many can hold more data than a CD (703 MB). Top of the line flash drives can store more data than a DVD (4.7 GB), and flash drives with 64 GB storage are now available.

The power consumption of a typical flash drive is very low; the common alternative, the portable hard disk, might take 3 to 4 times the power for 10 to 100 times the capacity. Flash drives have no moving parts, hard disks, on the other hand, require several motors or actuators to rotate the disk platter, and move the read / write head. Consequently, the USB flash drive need not be as heavy, allowing greater portability.

Flash drives implement the USB mass storage device class, meaning that most modern operating systems can read and write to flash drives without any additional device drivers. The flash drives present a simple block-structured logical unit to the host operating system, hiding the individual complex implementation details of the various underlying flash memory devices. The operating system can use whatever type of file system or block addressing scheme it wants. Some computers have the ability to boot up from flash drives.

Flash drives are much more tolerant of abuse than mechanical drives, but can still be damaged or have data corrupted by severe physical impacts. Improperly wired USB ports can also destroy the circuitry of a flash drive, a danger in home-built desktop PCs.

Some flash drives can retain their memory after being submerged in water, even through a machine wash. Leaving the flash drive out to dry completely before allowing current to run through it has been known to result in a working drive with no future problems. Channel Five's Gadget Show cooked a flash drive with propane, froze it with dry ice, submerged it in various acidic liquids, ran over it with a jeep and fired it against a wall with a mortar. A company specialising in recovering lost data from computer drives managed to recover all the data on the drive. All the other removal storage devices, using optical or magnetic discs or semiconductor (Secure Digital) were completely destroyed.

Disadvantages

Like all flash memory devices, flash drives can sustain only a limited number of write and erase cycles before failure. Mid-range flash drives under normal conditions will support several hundred thousand cycles, although write operations will gradually slow as the device ages. This should be a consideration when using a flash drive to run application software or an operating system. To address this, as well as space limitations, some developers have produced special versions of operating systems (such as Linux in Live USB) or commonplace applications (such as Mozilla Firefox) designed to run from flash drives. These are typically optimised for size and configured to place temporary or intermediate files in the computer's main RAM rather than store them temporarily on the flash drive.

Most USB flash drives do not include a write-protect mechanism, although some have a switch on the housing of the drive itself to keep the host computer from writing or modifying data on the drive. Write-protection makes a device suitable for repairing virus-contaminated host computers without risk of infecting the USB flash drive itself.

A drawback to the small size is that they are easily misplaced, left behind, or otherwise lost. This is a particular problem if the data they contain are sensitive (see data security). As a consequence, some manufacturers have added encryption hardware to their drives—although software encryption systems achieve the same thing, and are universally available for all USB flash drives. Others just have the possibility of being attached to keychains, necklaces and lanyards.

Compared to other portable storage, particularly external hard drives, USB flash drives have a high price per unit storage and are only available in comparatively small capacities.

Comparison with other Portable Memory Forms

Flash storage devices are often compared to other common, portable, swappable data storage devices, such as floppy disks, Zip disks, miniCD /miniDVD, CD-R/CD-RW and DVD-RW discs.

Floppy Disk

Following magnetic tape, the floppy disk was the first popular method of file transport; but floppies have been almost completely phased out due to their low capacity, low speed, and low durability. Virtually no new computers include floppy drives, but they do include USB ports.

However, floppy disks are still being used because of their low cost, are often the easiest or only way to share files with older systems, are easily bootable, and because floppy drives can be added to new systems in external or internal forms. In addition, office workplaces have often disabled high volume writable media such as optical drivers and USB ports to prevent employees from taking large amounts of data, so the small capacity of the floppy limits the information compromised.

Zip Drive

Attempts to extend the floppy standard (such as the Imation SuperDisk) were not successful because of a reputation for unreliability and the lack of a single standard for PC vendors to adopt. The Iomega Zip drive enjoyed some popularity, but never reached the point of ubiquity in computers. Also, the larger sizes of Zip—now up to 750 MB—cannot be read on older drives. Unless one were to carry an external drive, their usefulness as a means of moving data was rather limited. The cost per megabyte was fairly high, with individual disks often costing US$10 or more.

Because moving parts are involved and the material used for creating the storage medium in Zip disks is similar to that used in floppy disks, Zip disks have a high risk of failure and data loss compared to flash drives. Larger removable storage media, like Iomega's Jaz drive, had even higher costs for both drives and media, and as such were not pervasively adopted as a floppy alternative.

Optical Media

CD-R and CD-RW are swappable storage media alternatives. Unlike Zip and floppy drives, DVD and CD recorders are now common in personal computer systems. CD-Rs can be written to only once. But CD-RWs are rated at up to 1,000 erase/write cycles, and modern NAND-based flash drives often last for 500,000 or more erase/write cycles.

Optical storage devices are generally among the cheapest methods of mass data storage after the hard drive. However, optical devices are slower than their flash-based counterparts. In addition, optical discs with a 12 cm diameter can be inconveniently large and, unlike flash drives, cannot fit into a pocket or hang from a key chain. Smaller optical media do exist, such as business card CD-Rs which have the same dimensions as a credit card, and the slightly less convenient but higher capacity 8 cm recordable CD/DVDs. But these are harder to obtain and generally more expensive than the standard 12 cm version. The small discs also require a tray-loading drive (or a ring adapter, but these are rare); they can cause damage if inserted directly into a slot-loading drive.

Universal Disk Format versions 1.50 and above have facilities to support rewritable discs like sparing tables and virtual allocation tables, but many older operating systems do not understand these versions or facilities. Packet-writing utilities like DirectCD and InCD exist but produce discs that are not universally readable (despite claims to be based on the UDF standard). The Mount Rainier standard addresses this shortcoming in CD-RW media by running the older file systems on top of it and performing defect management for those standards, but it requires support from both the CD/DVD burner and from the operating system. Many drives made today do not support Mount Rainier, and many older operating systems like Windows XP and below, and the Linux kernel versions below 2.6.2 do not support it. Windows Vista and Linux kernels 2.6.2 and newer support Mount Rainier. As a result, CDs/DVDs are a good way to record a great deal of information cheaply and have the advantage of being readable by most standalone players, but they are poor at making ongoing small changes to a large collection of information; flash drives' ability to do this is their major advantage.

External Hard Disk

Particularly with the advent of USB, external hard disks have become common and relatively inexpensive. External hard disk drives cost less than flash memories of the comparable capacity, and are available in the much larger capacities. For the host-to-drive connection, hard disks frequently offer multiple interfaces and/or faster interfaces than USB (e.g. IEEE 1394). For consecutive sector reads (for example, from an unfragmented file), most hard drives can provide a much higher sustained data rate than current NAND flash memory.

However, hard drives are far more fragile than flash drives: they are less resistant to shock, have limitations on use at high altitude, and (like all magnetic media) are vulnerable when exposed to electromagnetic fields. Hard drives are usually larger and heavier than flash drives, although not necessarily when compared per unit storage. Hard disks also suffer from file fragmentation (some filesystems are resistant to fragmentation, but no filesystem is completely immune), which can significantly reduce performance.

Security

Some flash drives feature encryption of the data stored on them, generally using full disk encryption below the file system. This prevents an unauthorised person from accessing the data stored on it. The disadvantage is that the drive is accessible only in the minority of computers which have compatible encryption software, for which no portable standard is widely deployed.

Some encryption applications allow running without installation. The executable files can be stored on the USB drive, together with the encrypted file image. The encrypted partition can be accessed on any computer running the correct operating system. Other flash drives allow the user to configure secure and public partitions of different sizes. Executable files for Windows, Macintosh, and Linux may be on the drive, depending on manufacturer support. Some security software may require administrative rights on the host PC to access data.

Newer flash drives support biometric fingerprinting to confirm the user's identity. As of mid-2005, this was a relatively costly alternative to standard password protection offered on many new USB flash storage devices. Most fingerprint scanning drives rely upon the host operating system to validate the fingerprint via a software driver, often restricting the drive to Microsoft Windows computers. However, there are USB drives with fingerprint scanners use controllers that allow access to protected data without any authentication.

Some manufacturers deploy physical authentication tokens in the form of a flash drive. These are used to control access to a sensitive system by containing encryption keys or, more commonly, communicating with security software on the target machine. The system is designed so the target machine will not operate except when the flash drive device is plugged into it. Some of these "PC lock" devices also function as normal flash drives when plugged into other machines.

All such forms of data protection security involve an increased risk of loss of access to the data by the legitimate owner/user.

Flash drives present a significant security challenge for large organisations. Their small size and ease of use allows unsupervised visitors or unscrupulous employees to smuggle confidential data out with little chance of detection. Equally, corporate and public computers alike are vulnerable to attackers connecting a flash drive to a free USB port and using malicious software such as rootkits or packet sniffers. To prevent this, some organisations forbid the use of flash drives, and some computers are configured to disable the mounting of USB mass storage devices by ordinary users, a feature introduced in Windows XP Service Pack 2; others use third-party software to control USB usage. In a lower-tech security solution, some organisations disconnect USB ports inside the computer or fill the USB sockets with epoxy.

Naming

Recently, "USB flash drive" or simply "UFD" has emerged as the de facto standard term for these devices, although potentially confusing alternatives (such as memory stick) are still prevalent. The myriad different brand names and terminology used, in the past and currently, make UFDs more difficult for manufacturers to market and for consumers to research. Some commonly used names are actually trademarks of particular companies, such as Cruzer, TravelDrive, ThumbDrive, and Disgo.

Future Developments

Semiconductor corporations have worked to reduce the cost of the components in a flash drive by integrating various flash drive functions in a single chip, thereby reducing the part-count and overall package cost.

Flash drive capacities on the market are continuously increasing. As of 2008, 256 MB and smaller capacity flash memory has been largely discontinued, and 512 MB capacity flash memory is being phased out. High-speed is now a standard for modern flash drives and capacities of up to 64 GB are available.

Lexar is attempting to introduce a USB FlashCard, which would be a compact USB flash drive intended to replace various kinds of flash memory cards. Pretec introduced a similar card, which also plugs into every USB port, but is just one quarter the thickness of the Lexar model SanDisk has a product called SD Plus, which is a SecureDigital card with a USB connector.

SanDisk has also introduced a new technology to allow controlled storage and usage of copyrighted materials on flash drives, primarily for use by students. This technology is termed FlashCP.

4

DISK ENCLOSURE

Disk Enclosure

A disk enclosure is essentially a specialised chassis designed to hold and power disk drives while providing a mechanism to allow them to communicate to one or more separate computers. Drive enclosures provide power to the drives therein and convert the data sent across their native data bus into a format usable by an external connection on the computers to which it is connected. In some cases, the conversion is as trivial as carrying a signal between different connector types. In others, it is so complicated as to require a separate embedded system to retransmit data over connector and signal of a different standard. Factory-assembled external hard disk drives, external DVD-ROM drives, and others are all built around disk enclosures. Bulkier models built around 2.5" & 3.5" hard drives and full-height 5.25" DVD-ROM drives use enclosures that are often nearly identical to OEM enclosures.

Factory-assembled Buffalo external hard drive in a disk enclosure

Benefits

Key benefits to using external disk enclosures include:

- Adding additional storage space and media types to small form factor and laptop computers, as well as sealed embedded systems, such as digital video recorders.
- Adding more drives to any given server or workstation than their chassis can hold.
- Transferring data between non-networked computers, jokingly known as sneakernet.
- Adding a backup source with a separate power supply from the connected computer.
- Sharing the data on a drive in a network-aware enclosure.
- Preventing the heat from a disk drive from increasing the heat inside an operating computer case.
- Simple and cheap approach to hot swapping.
- Recovering the data from a broken or damaged computer.
- Lower the cost of removable storage by reusing hardware designed for internal use.
- More memory than CDs, DVDs, and Flash Drives.
- Better protection of files from damage, age, weathering, and corruption, than CDs, DVDs, and Flash Drives.

Consumer Enclosures

In the consumer market, commonly used configurations of drive enclosures utilise magnetic hard drives or optical disc drives inside of USB, FireWire, or Serial ATA enclosures. External 3.5" floppy drive are also fairly common, following a trend to not integrate floppy drives into compact and laptop computers, started by Apple Computer with their iMac. Pre-built external drives are available through all major manufacturers of hard drives, as well as several third-parties.

Form Factors

- **"5.25 inch" drive:** (5.75 in x 1.63 in x 8 in = 146.1 mm x 41.4 mm x 203 mm).

  Most desktop models of drives for optical 120-mm disks (DVD-ROM or CD-ROM drives, CD or DVD burners), are designed to be mounted into a so-called "5.25-inch slot", which obtained its nickname because this slot size was initially used by drives for 5.25-inch diameter floppy disks in the IBM PC AT. (The original "5.25-inch slot" in the IBM PC was with 3.25 in (82.6 mm) twice as high as the one commonly used today.)
- **"3.5 inch" drive:** (1 in x 4 in x 5.75 in = 25.4 mm x 101.6 mm x 146.05 mm).

  This smaller, 4-inch wide disk-drive form factor was introduced with the IBM PS/2 series in 1987, which included drives of this size for 90-mm ("3.5-inch") floppy disks. This form factor is today used by most desktop hard drives. They usually have 10 mounting holes with American 6-32 UNC 2B threads: three on each side and four on the bottom.
- **"2.5 inch" drive:** (0.374 in x 2.75 in x 3.945 in = 9.5 mm x 69.85 mm x 100.2 mm)

  This even smaller, 2.75-inch wide form factor is widely used today for hard disks in many mobile devices (laptops, music players, etc.)
- **"1.8 inch" drive:** These are used in Apple's iPod Classic. There are several USB enclosures with such hard drives (eg. by LaCie).

A range of other form factors has emerged for mobile devices. While laptop hard drives are today generally of the 9.5 mm high variant of the "2.5 inch" drive form factor, older laptops and notebooks had hard drives that varied in height, which can make it difficult to find a well-fitting chassis. Laptop optical drives require "slim" 5.25" enclosures, since they have approximately half the thickness of their desktop counterparts, and most models use a special 50-pin connector that differs from the 40-pin connectors used on desktop ATA drives.

While they are less common now than they once were, it is also possible to purchase a drive chassis and mount that will convert a 3.5" hard drive into a removable hard disk that can be plugged into and removed from a mounting bracket permanently installed in a desktop PC case. The mounting bracket carries the data bus and power connections over a proprietary connector, and converts back into the drive's native data bus format and power connections inside the drive's chassis.

Enterprise Enclosures

In enterprise storage the term disk enclosure may refer to:

- The physical chassis of a more complex storage array either in a Network-attached storage or Storage area network environment.
- The entire set of components used to attach drives directly to a server. These may include a backplane, temperature sensors, enclosure management devices, and power supplies.

CONNECTIONS

Native Drive Protocols

SCSI, SAS, Fibre Channel, and eSATA protocols can be used to directly connect the external hard drive to an internal host adapter, without the need for any intervening controller. These native external drive protocols are extremely similar to the internal protocols, but expanded to carry power. This is the case with eSATA and the SCSI Single Connector Attachment standard. A host adapter with external port may be necessary to connect a drive, if a computer lacks an available external port.

Direct Attach Serial Protocols

USB or FireWire connections are typically used to attach consumer class external hard drives to a computer. Unlike SCSI, eSATA, or SAS these require circuitry to convert the hard disk's native signal to the appropriate protocol. Parallel ATA and internal Serial ATA hard disks are frequently connected to such chassis because nearly all computers on the market today have USB or FireWire ports, and these chassis are inexpensive and easy to find.

Network Protocols

iSCSI, NFS, or Windows File Sharing are all commonly used protocols that are used to allow an external hard drive to use a network to send data to a computer system. This type of external hard drive is also known as Network-attached storage or NAS. Often, such drives are embedded computers running operating systems such as Linux or VxWorks that use their NFS daemons and SAMBA to provide a networked file system. A newer technology, Network-Attached Storage (NAS), has been applied to some disk enclosures, which allows network ability, direct connection (e.g. USB) and even RAID features.

USB Mass Storage Device Class

The USB mass storage device class or USB MSC or UMS is a set of computing communications protocols defined by the USB Implementers Forum that run on the Universal Serial Bus. The standard provides an interface to a variety of storage devices.

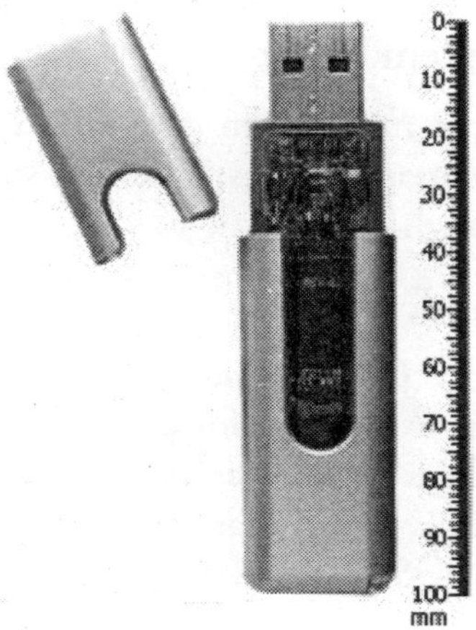

A USB flash drive like this one, will typically implement the USB mass storage device class.

Some of the devices which are connected to computers via this standard are:

- external magnetic hard drives
- external optical drives, including CD and DVD reader and writer drives
- portable flash memory devices
- adapters bridging between standard flash memory cards and a USB connection
- digital cameras
- various digital audio players & portable media players
- Card readers
- Portable Gaming systems (Nokia N-GAGE/Sony PSP)
- personal data assistants and handheld computers
- some newer mobile phones, such as the Sony Ericsson K800 and K510, Nokia N73, Nokia E61.

Devices which support this standard are referred to as MSC (Mass Storage Class) devices. While MSC is the official acronym, UMS (Universal Mass Storage) has become common as an online jargon.

Operating System Support

Most current mainstream operating systems include support for USB mass storage devices, although support on older systems is available through patches.

Microsoft Windows

Windows 95 OSR2.1, an update to the operating system, featured very limited support for USB. During that time, no generic USB mass storage driver was produced by Microsoft, even for Windows 98. This meant that a device-specific driver was needed for each type of USB storage device. Today, generic drivers which support USB flash drives even in Windows 98 are available as freedownloads. By 2000, the problem was almost solved. Products designed for Windows Me and Windows 2000 (where a specific driver was required only for rare devices) are only fully corrected in subsequent OSes. On Windows Server 2003, however, a drive letter has to be assigned to it in order to access it. This can be done in Disk Management (under Computer Management (local)).

There is no native (supplied by Microsoft) support for USB in Windows NT, earlier versions of Windows, or MS-DOS, although some third-party solutions exist for each OS. A third party driver for Windows 98 and Windows 98SE is also now available. There is also a USB UMS driver for Windows NT 4.FreeDOS supports USB mass storage as ASPI devices.

Windows Mobile supports accessing of the most USB mass storage devices formatted with FAT on devices with USB Host, although portable devices typically cannot provide enough power for disk enclosures containing hard drives (a 2.5" hard drive typically requires the maximum 2.5 W provided by the USB specification). On the other way around, Windows Mobile devices can not show their file systems as a mass storage device unless the device implementer explicitly decides to add such functionality. However, third party applications exist to add MSC emulation to most WM devices (commercial "Softick CardExport" and free "WM5torage"). Generally only memory cards can be exported, and not internal storage memory, due to the complications outlined below.

Mac OS

Apple Computer's Mac OS 8.5.1 supports USB mass storage through an optional driver. Mac OS 9 and Mac OS X support USB mass storage natively.

Unix-like

The Linux kernel has supported USB mass storage devices via generic driver since kernel version 2.4 (year 2001); kernel 2.2 has also been back-patched to support it. Solaris also supports devices since the 2.8 release and up (year 1998), NetBSD since the 1.5 release and up (year 2000), FreeBSD since the 4.0 release and up (year 2000), and OpenBSD since the 2.7 release and up (year 2000).

AmigaOS

AmigaOS supports UMASS storage devices through Poseidon, a third-party USB stack which has become a de facto standard. It supports various USB device types through a modular system of Hardware Independent Device Driver (HIDD) classes. Poseidon as used in AmigaOS Classic up to version 4.0, and in the MorphOS operating system. The supposedly final AmigaOS version of the Poseidon stack is released OEM licensed with the Deneb USB card in May 2008. AmigaOS 4.0 has its own USB stack called Sirion, though it can still use Poseidon. A new USB stack called ANAIIS (Another Native Amiga IO Interface Stack) is available for all Amiga platforms with Highway or Subway hardware, but does not yet support UMASS.

FAT16 and FAT32 filesystems are supported by the FAT95 filesystem.

AROS, an Open Source AmigaOS clone for Intel based PCs, does support UHCI and OHCI USB root hubs (since May 2007) but does not yet support USB mass storage class.

Game consoles

The Xbox 360 and PlayStation 3 support most mass storage devices.

Graphing Calculators

Independent developers have released drivers for the TI-84 Plus and TI-84 Plus Silver Edition in order to access USB mass storage devices. usb8x contains the driver for this access, while msd8x handles the user interface.

Device Access

A USB Card reader like this one, will typically implement the USB mass storage device class.

The USB mass storage specification does not require any particular file system to be used on conforming devices. Instead, it provides a simple interface to read and write sectors of data—much like the low-level interface used to access any hard drive—using the "SCSI transparent command set." Operating systems may treat the USB drive like a hard drive, and can format it with any file system they like.

Because of its ubiquity and relative simplicity, the most common file system on embedded devices such as USB flash drives, cameras, or digital audio players is Microsoft's FAT or FAT32 file system with (optional) support for long names. Large USB-based hard disks may come formatted with NTFS, which is much less supported outside Microsoft Windows. However, a keydrive or any other device may be formatted using another file system (for example HFS Plus on an Apple Macintosh, or Ext2 under Linux, or Unix File System under Solaris or BSD). Of course, this choice may limit other operating systems' ability to access the contents of the device.

In cameras, MP3 players, and similar gadgets which must access the file system independently from an external host, the FAT file system is typically preferred by device manufacturers.

Complications of the Mass-storage Device Class

The mass storage interface is an attractive option for many devices, such as cameras and media players, which are nonetheless capable of more functionality than being simple data repositories. By presenting themselves as simple data stores, these devices can take advantage of the high degree of support for the USB mass-storage device class in current operating systems' USB driver stacks and allow easy read and write access to their internal memories. The downside of doing so is that it prevents the device from easily presenting its actual functional behaviour across the USB interface too. For example, the makers of a digital still camera would also like it to implement the USB still-image device class, allowing it to be controlled by image capture software.

Some USB digital cameras feature a switch allowing them to appear either as a mass-storage device or as a still-picture device (PictBridge or PTP), but they cannot be both at the same time because file system layers in operating systems usually assume that they are the only user. However, the PTP implementation in the device would change the underlying filesystem without being able to notify the host's operating system about the changed sectors.

Flash-based Devices

Disk file systems were not devised with flash memory in mind. Flash-specific concerns like limited number of writes per cell can be affected by a write-heavy file system, causing flash memory manufacturers to reserve about 5 per cent of each medium's capacity for wear leveling. On the other hand, issues such as fragmentation or contiguity which affect magnetic disk performance are irrelevant in flash, because they impose no appreciable I/O seeking delays. However, fragmentation may lead to reduced performance with file systems that use extents.

Hard Drive-based Devices

Many modern hard drives support additional advanced commands, such as Native Command Queuing, which may increase performance, and S.M.A.R.T., which allows a computer to measure various indicators of drive reliability. These exist as extensions to the basic low-level command sets used by hard drives, such as SCSI, SATA, or PATA.

These features do not work when hard drives are encapsulated in a disk enclosure supporting the USB mass storage interface. USB mass storage provides a *generic* interface which only provides basic read/write commands, as outlined above. This works perfectly well for basic data transfer using hard drive-based devices, however it means that there is no simple way to send advanced, device-specific commands to USB mass storage devices (although devices may create their own communication protocols over the USB-standard "control interface").

The new eSATA standard for external drives promises to address this issue, since it extends the internal SATA bus to external disks without any intermediate translation layer.

ExpressCard

ExpressCard® technology provides users with the ability to easily add features that aren't part of their computers when they purchase them. ExpressCard/34 modules fit in both ExpressCard/34 and ExpressCard/54 slots.

ExpressCard is a hardware standard replacing PC cards (also known as PCMCIA cards), both developed by the Personal Computer Memory Card International Association (PCMCIA). The host device supports both PCI Express and USB 2.0 connectivity through the ExpressCard slot, and each card uses whichever the designer feels most appropriate to the task. The cards are hot-pluggable. This is an open standard by ITU-T definition which can be obtained from the ExpressCard website. However, a US$2,500 fee is required to access the documentation for non-PCMCIA members.

Uses

These slots can accept Firewire 800 (1394B), Serial ATA external disk drives, Solid-state drives, Wireless network interface cards, TV tuner cards, soundcards, additional memory and memory card readers, among other things. Asus has recently revealed an external graphics card that can be connected to laptops through the interface, the XG Station.

Form Factors

ExpressCard supports two form factors, ExpressCard/34 (34 mm wide) and ExpressCard/54 (54 mm wide, in an L-shape) —the connector is the same on both (width 34 mm). Standard cards are 75 mm long (10.6 mm shorter than CardBus) and 5 mm thick, but may be thicker on sections that extend outside the standard form—for antennas, sockets, etc. The 34 mm form factor cards fit into both 34 mm and 54 mm card slots via a diagonal guide in the rear of the 54 mm slot that guides the card to the connector. The 54 mm card will only fit in a 54 mm slot.

Comparison to CardBus

The major benefit of ExpressCard technology over the previous PCMCIA CardBus PC card is a dramatic increase in bandwidth afforded by the fact that the ExpressCard has a direct connection to the system bus over a PCI Express x1 lane and USB 2.0, whereas CardBus utilises an interface controller that only interfaces with

PCI. The ExpressCard has a maximum throughput of 2.5 Gbit/s through PCI Express and 480 Mbit/s through USB 2.0 dedicated for each slot, versus CardBus's shared 1.06 Gbit/s bandwidth.

In addition, the ExpressCard standard uses lower voltages than the previous CardBus slots (1.5V and 3.3V versus 3.3V and 5.0V).

The ExpressCard FAQ also claims other advantages, including lower cost, better scalability, and better integration with motherboard chipset technology. The ExpressCard interface is not backwards-compatible with CardBus devices, which presents a problem for those who may purchase a new system only to find that their devices do not work with the new slot design.

Availability

ExpressCard has become quite prominent on most new or high-end laptops made since 2006. Hewlett-Packard began shipping

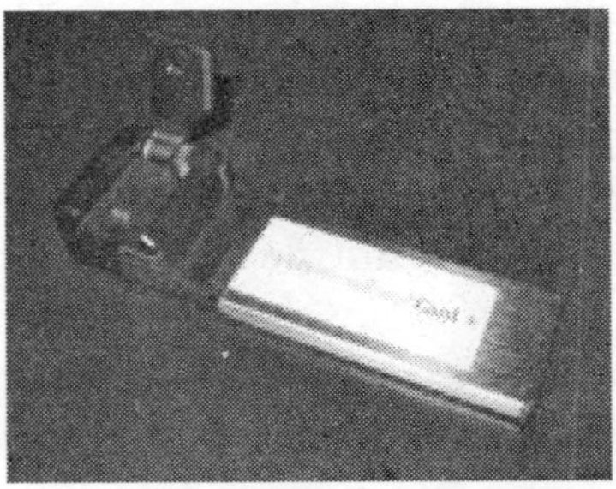

A mobile broadband antenna integrated into ExpressCard 34

An ExpressCard 34 mobile broadband modem slotted inside a PC Card adaptor.

A PC Card adaptor designed for ExpressCard 34

systems with ExpressCard in November of 2004, and Lenovo integrated the slot into their flagship ThinkPad T43 in May 2005. Dell Computer also incorporates this in their Precision (the 17" models have them exclusively, the 15" Precisions have both express card and PCMCIA Card slots), Inspiron, Latitude (Latitude D-series have PCMCIA card slots. The D820/D830 have both express card and PCMCIA card slots), Vostro and XPS Laptop product lines. Fujitsu-Siemens began shipping systems with ExpressCard in mid 2005. Apple Inc. included a single ExpressCard/34 slot in their MacBook Pro notebook computer in January 2006. ASUS has also replaced the PC Card slot with an ExpressCard slot on many of its new models. Sony also began shipping systems with ExpressCard with its new laptop VGN-SZ product line. The Acer Aspire laptop series also has a single ExpressCard/54 slot on most new models. Panasonic incorporates ExpressCard/54 slots in all the fully rugged and semi-rugged models of their Toughbook brand of portable computers. Gateway notebooks (ML3109 and later) also ship with ExpressCard 54 interfaces.

Because of the lack of backward compatibility, some laptop manufacturers have chosen to release models incorporating both CardBus (PCMCIA, PC Card) and ExpressCard slots. These include certain models of Acer Aspire, Dell Latitude, MSI S42x and Lenovo ThinkPad Z60m and T60.

A large number of ExpressCard devices were presented at the CeBit trade show in Germany in March 2005. In November 2006, Belkin announced that it is launching the first ExpressCard docking station, which uses the PCIe part of an ExpressCard connection to enable 1600x1200 video and the USB part to provide USB, audio and network ports. This points to the ability for ExpressCard to allow more capable non-OEM docking stations for laptop computers.

Recently Sony has introduced its Vaio TZ model, which incorporates ExpressCards. Also the Sony VAIO FZ series has the ExpressCard 34 Slot integrated in them. Sony also uses the ExpressCard/34 form factor for the flash memory modules in its XDCAM EX/SxS based camcorders, making the copying of video data between these cameras and ExpressCard-equipped laptops trivial. For this reason, Sony also offers a USB-based SxS reader for desktop computers.

The new Toshiba Satellite P and X 200/205 series of laptops and desktop replacements have an ExpressCard/34 slot since April 2007.

ExpressCard 2.0

ExpressCard 2.0 is said to be on track for a "second-half 2008/ early 2009" delivery.

MODEM

Modem (from modulator-demodulator) is a device that modulates an analog carrier signal to encode digital information, and also demodulates such a carrier signal to decode the transmitted information. The goal is to produce a signal that can be transmitted easily and decoded to reproduce the original digital data. Modems can be used over any means of transmitting analog signals, from driven diodes to radio.

The most familiar example is a voiceband modem that turns the digital 1s and 0s of a personal computer into sounds that can be transmitted over the telephone lines of Plain Old Telephone Systems (POTS), and once received on the other side, converts those 1s and 0s back into a form used by a USB, Serial, or Network connection. Modems are generally classified by the amount of data they can send in a given time, normally measured in bits per second, or "bps". They can also be classified by Baud, the number of times the modem changes its signal state per second.

Baud is NOT the modem's speed. The baud rate varies, depending on the modulation technique used. Original Bell 103 modems used a modulation technique that saw a change in state 300 times per second. They transmitted 1 bit for every baud, and so a 300 bit/s modem was also a 300-baud modem. However, casual computerists confused the two. A 300 bit/s modem is the only modem whose bit rate matches the baud rate. A 2400 bit/s modem changes state 600 times per second, but due to the fact that it transmits 4 bits for each baud, 2400 bits are transmitted by 600 baud, or changes in states.

Faster modems are used by Internet users every day, notably cable modems and ADSL modems. In telecommunications, "radio modems" transmit repeating frames of data at very high data rates over microwave radio links. Some microwave modems transmit more than a hundred million bits per second. Optical modems transmit data over optical fibers. Most intercontinental data links now use optical modems transmitting over undersea optical fibers. Optical modems routinely have data rates in excess of a billion ($1x10^9$) bits per second. One kilobit per second (kbit/s or kb/s or kbps) as used in this article means 1000 bits per second and not 1024 bits per second. For example, a 56k modem can transfer data at up to 56,000 bits per second over the phone line.

Increasing speeds (V.21 V.22 V.22bis)

The 300 bit/s modems used frequency-shift keying to send data. In this system the stream of 1s and 0s in computer data is translated into sounds which can be easily sent on the phone lines. In the Bell 103 system the *originating* modem sends 0s by playing a 1070 Hz tone, and 1s at 1270 Hz, with the *answering* modem putting its 0s on 2025 Hz and 1s on 2225 Hz. These frequencies were chosen carefully, they are in the range that suffer minimum distortion on the phone system, and also are not harmonics of each other.

In the 1200 bit/s and faster systems, phase-shift keying was used. In this system the two tones for any one side of the connection are sent at the similar frequencies as in the 300 bit/s systems, but slightly out of phase. By comparing the phase of the two signals, 1s and 0s could be pulled back out, for instance if the signals were 90 degrees out of phase, this represented two digits, "1,0", at 180 degrees it was "1,1". In this way each cycle of the signal represents two digits instead of one. 1200 bit/s modems were, in effect, 600 symbols per second modems (600 baud modems) with 2 bits per symbol.

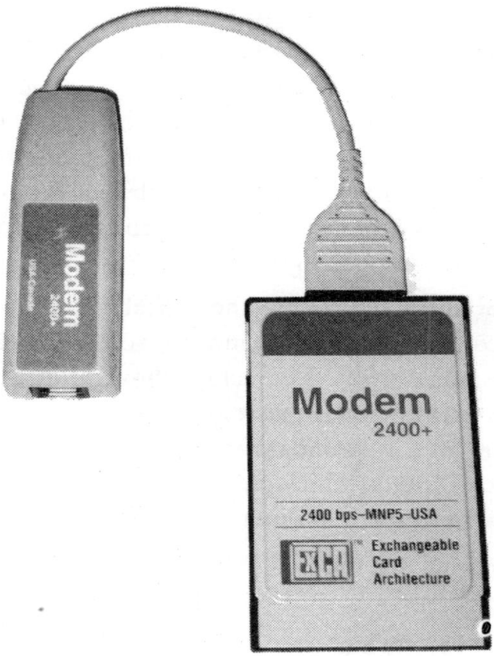

Voiceband modems generally remained at 300 and 1200 bit/s (V.21 and V.22) into the mid 1980s. A V.22bis 2400-bit/s system similar in concept to the 1200-bit/s Bell 212 signalling was introduced in the U.S., and a slightly different one in Europe. By the late 1980s, most modems could support all of these standards and 2400-bit/s operation was becoming common.

List of Device Bandwidths

This is a list of device bandwidths: the channel capacity (or, more informally, bandwidth) of some computer devices employing methods of data transport is quantified in units of kilobits per second (kbit/s), megabits per second (Mbit/s), or gigabits per second (Gbit/s) as appropriate. They are grouped by similar functionality, and then listed in order from lowest bandwidth to highest.

In addition, a common scale is used in order to better convey the magnitude of change to a non-technical person (for example: a 1.2 kbit/s telephone modem versus a 10,000 kbit/s DSL modem). Whether to use bit/s or byte/s (B/s) is often a matter of convention. The most commonly cited unit (bit/s or byte/s) is bolded. In general, parallel interfaces are quoted in byte/s (B/s), serial in bit/s. On devices like modems, bytes may be more than 8 bits long because they may be individually padded out with additional start and stop bits; the figures below will reflect this. Where channels use line codes, such as Ethernet, Serial ATA and PCI Express, quoted speeds are for the decoded signal.

Many of these figures are theoretical maxima, and various real-world considerations will generally keep the actual effective throughput much lower. The actual throughput achievable on Ethernet networks, for example (especially when heavily loaded or when running over substandard media), is debatable. The figures are also simplex speeds, which may conflict with the duplex speeds vendors sometimes use in promotional materials.

Note: All of the figures listed here use metric (base-10) abbreviations:

- 1 kbit = 1,000 bits
- 1 kB = 1,000 bytes
- 1 MB = 1,000,000 bytes
- 1 GB = 1,000,000,000 bytes
- 1 TB = 1,000,000,000,000 bytes

and so on.

Connection	Bit	Bytes
TTY/Teleprinter or Telecommunications device for the deaf		
TTY (V.18)	**0.045 kbit/s**	6 characters/sec
TTY (V.18)	**0.050 kbit/s**	6.6 characters/sec
NTSC Line 21 Closed Captioning	**1 kbit/s**	0.1 kB/s (~100 cps)

Modems/Home user connections

Note that the values given are maximum values, and actual values may be slower under certain conditions (for example, noisy phone lines). Where two values are listed, the first value is the downstream rate and the second value is the upstream rate.

Connection	Bit	Bytes
Modem 110 baud	**0.11 kbit/s**	0.010 kB/s (~10 cps)
Modem 300 (300 baud) (Bell 103 or V.21)	**0.3 kbit/s**	0.03 kB/s (~30 cps)
Modem 1200 (600 baud) (Bell 212A or V.22)	**1.2 kbit/s**	0.12 kB/s (~120 cps)
Modem 2400 (600 baud) (V.22bis)	**2.4 kbit/s**	0.24 kB/s
Modem 4800 (1600 baud) (V.27ter)	**4.8 kbit/s**	0.48 kB/s
Modem 9600 (2400 baud) (V.32)	**9.6 kbit/s**	0.96 kB/s
Modem 14.4 (2400 baud) (V.32bis)	**14.4 kbit/s**	1.44 kB/s
Modem 28.8 (3200 baud) (V.34)	**28.8 kbit/s**	2.88 kB/s
Modem 33.6 (3429 baud) (V.34)	**33.6 kbit/s**	3.38 kB/s
Modem 56k (8000/3429 baud) (V.90)	**56.0/33.6 kbit/s**	5.6/3.36 kB/s
Modem 56k (8000/8000 baud) (V.92)	**56.0/48.0 kbit/s**	5.6/4.8 kB/s
Hardware compression (variable) (V.90/V.42bis)	**56.0-220.0 kbit/s**	5.6-22 kB/s
Hardware compression (variable) (V.92/V.44)	**56.0-320.0 kbit/s**	5.6-32 kB/s
ISDN Basic Rate Interface & Primary Rate Interface data	**64/128 kbit/s**	8/16 kB/s
IDSL	**144 kbit/s**	18 kB/s
HDSL ITU G.991.1	**1544 kbit/s**	193 kB/s
MSDSL	**2000 kbit/s**	250 kB/s
SDSL	**2320 kbit/s**	290 KB/s
ADSL (typical)	**3000/768 kbit/s**	375/96 kB/s
SHDSL ITU G.991.2	**5690 kbit/s**	711 kB/s

ADSL	**8192/1024 kbit/s**	1024/128 kB/s
ADSL (G.DMT)	**12,288/1333 kbit/s**	1536/166 kB/s
ADSL2	**12,288/3584 kbit/s**	1536/448 kB/s
ADSL2+	**24,576/3584 kbit/s**	3072/448 kB/s
DOCSIS v1.0 (Cable modem)	**38,000/10,000 kbit/s**	4750/1250 kB/s
DOCSIS v2.0 (Cable modem)	**40,000/30,000 kbit/s**	5000/3750 kB/s
FiOS fiber optic service (typical)	**50,000/10,000 kbit/s**	6250/1250 kB/s
DOCSIS v3.0 (Cable modem)	**160,000/120,000 kbit/s**	20,000/15,000 kB/s
Uni-DSL	**200,000 kbit/s**	25,000 kB/s
VDSL ITU G.993.1	**200,000 kbit/s**	25,000 kB/s
VDSL2 ITU G.993.2	**250,000 kbit/s**	31,250 kB/s
BPON (G.983) fiber optic service	**622,000/155,000 kbit/s**	77,700/19,300 kB/s
GPON (G.984) fiber optic service	**2,488,000/1,244,000 kbit/s**	311,000/155,500 kB/s

Mobile telephone interfaces

Note that the values given are maximum values, and actual values may be slower under certain conditions (for example, noise). Where two values are listed, the first value is the downstream rate and the second value is the upstream rate.

GSM CSD	**14.4 kbit/s**	1.8 kB/s
HSCSD	**57.6/14.4 kbit/s**	5.4/1.8 kB/s
GPRS	**57.6/28.8 kbit/s**	7.2/3.6 kB/s
WiDEN	**100 kbit/s**	12.5 kB/s
CDMA2000 1xRTT	**153 kbit/s**	18 kB/s
EDGE (type 1 MS)	**236.8 kbit/s**	29.6 kB/s
UMTS	**384 kbit/s**	48 kB/s
EDGE (type 2 MS)	**473.6 kbit/s**	59.2 kB/s
EDGE Evolution (type 1 MS)	**1184/474 kbit/s**	148/59 kB/s
EDGE Evolution (type 2 MS)	**1894/947 kbit/s**	237/118 kB/s
1xEV-DO Rev. 0	**2457/153 kbit/s**	307.2/19 kB/s
1xEV-DO Rev. A	**3100/1800 kbit/s**	397/230 kB/s
3xEV-DO Rev. B	**9300/5400 kbit/s**	1162/675 kB/s
HSDPA/HSUPA	**14,400/5760 kbit/s**	1800/720 kB/s
4xEV-DO Enhancements (2X2 MIMO)	**34,400/12,400 kbit/s**	4300/1550 kB/s

HSPA+ (2X2 MIMO)	**42,000/11,500 kbit/s**	5250/ 1437 kB/s
15xEV-DO Rev. B	**73,500/27,000 kbit/s**	9200/ 3375 kB/s
UMB (2X2 MIMO)	**140,000/34,000 kbit/s**	17,500/ 4250 kB/s
LTE (2X2 MIMO)	**173,000/58,000 kbit/s**	21,625/ 7250 kB/s
UMB (4X4 MIMO)	**280,000/68,000 kbit/s**	35,000/ 8500 kB/s
EV-DO Rev. C	**280,000/75,000 kbit/s**	35,000/ 9000 kB/s
LTE (4X4 MIMO)	**326,000/86,000 kbit/s**	40,750/ 10,750 kB/s

Wide area network

Note that the values given are maximum values, and actual values may be slower under certain conditions (for example, noise). Where two values are listed, the first value is the downstream rate and the second value is the upstream rate.

DS0	**0.064 Mbit/s** (or 0.056 with robbed bit signaling)	0.008 MB/s
G.Lite (aka ADSL Lite)	**1.536/0.512 Mbit/s**	0.192/0.064 MB/s
DS1/T1	**1.544 Mbit/s**	0.192 MB/s
Frame Relay	**2 Mbit/s**	0.25 MB/s
E1	**2.048 Mbit/s**	0.256 MB/s
G.SHDSL	**2.304 Mbit/s**	0.288 MB/s
LR-VDSL2 (4 to 5 km [long-]range) (symmetry optional)	**4 Mbit/s**	0.512 MB/s
SDSL	**2.32 Mbit/s**	0.29 MB/s
T2	**6.312 Mbit/s**	0.789 MB/s
ADSL	**8.0/1.024 Mbit/s**	1/0.128 MB/s
E2	**8.448 Mbit/s**	1.056 MB/s
ADSL2	**12/3.5 Mbit/s**	1.5/0.448 MB/s
Satellite Internet	**16/1 Mbit/s**	2.0/0.128 MB/s
ADSL2+	**24/3.5 Mbit/s**	3.0/0.448 MB/s

E3	**34.368 Mbit/s**	4.296 MB/s
DOCSIS v1.0 (Cable modem)	**38.0/10.0 Mbit/s**	4.75/1.25 MB/s
DOCSIS v2.0 (Cable modem)	**40/30 Mbit/s**	5.0/3.75 MB/s
DS3/T3 ('45 Meg')	**44.736 Mbit/s**	5.5925 MB/s
STS-1/EC-1/OC-1/STM-0	**51.84 Mbit/s**	6.48 MB/s
OC-1	**51.84 Mbit/s**	6.48 MB/s
VDSL (symmetry optional)	**100 Mbit/s**	12.5 MB/s
DOCSIS v3.0 (Cable modem)	**160/120 Mbit/s**	20/15 MB/s
OC-3/STM-1	**155.52 Mbit/s**	19.44 MB/s
VDSL2 (symmetry optional)	**250 Mbit/s**	31.25 MB/s
T4	**274.176 Mbit/s**	34.272 MB/s
T5	**400.352 Mbit/s**	50.044 MB/s
OC-9	**466.56 Mbit/s**	58.32 MB/s
OC-12/STM-4	**622.08 Mbit/s**	77.76 MB/s
OC-18	**933.12 Mbit/s**	116.64 MB/s
OC-24	**1244 Mbit/s**	155.5 MB/s
OC-36	**1900 Mbit/s**	237.5 MB/s
OC-48/STM-16	**2488 Mbit/s**	311.04 MB/s
OC-96	**4976 Mbit/s**	622 MB/s
OC-192/STM-64	**9953 Mbit/s**	1244 MB/s
10 Gigabit Ethernet WAN PHY	**9953 Mbit/s**	1244 MB/s
10 Gigabit Ethernet LAN PHY	**10,000 Mbit/s**	1250 MB/s
OC-256	**13,271 Mbit/s**	1659 MB/s
OC-768/STM-256	**39,813 Mbit/s**	4976 MB/s
OC-1536/STM-512	**79,626 Mbit/s**	9953 MB/s
OC-3072/STM-1024	**159,252 Mbit/s**	19,907 MB/s

Local area networkNote:

Actual data throughput is much less than bandwidth of the data transmitted due to overhead and other factors, so do not mistake its speed as actual data transfer rate. "Typically one can expect about 1 3-2/3 of the actual speed based on several factors such as traffic Also, if there are problems in your physical layer causing retransmissions, your throughput will suffer as well."

LocalTalk	**0.230 Mbit/s**	0.0288 MB/s
Econet	**0.800 Mbit/s**	0.1 MB/s

PC-Network	2 Mbit/s	0.25 MB/s
ARCNET (Standard)	2.5 Mbit/s	0.3125 MB/s
Ethernet Experimental	3 Mbit/s	0.375 MB/s
Token Ring (Original)	4 Mbit/s	0.5 MB/s
Ethernet (10base-X)	10 Mbit/s	1.25 MB/s
Token Ring (Later)	16 Mbit/s	2 MB/s
ARCnet Plus	20 Mbit/s	2.5 MB/s
Token Ring IEEE 802.5t	100 Mbit/s	12.5 MB/s
Fast Ethernet (100base-X)	100 Mbit/s	12.5 MB/s
FDDI	100 Mbit/s	12.5 MB/s
HIPPI	800 Mbit/s	100 MB/s
Token Ring IEEE 802.5v (no known implementations)	1000 Mbit/s	125 MB/s
FireWire (IEEE 1394) 400	393.216 Mbit/s	49.152 MB/s
Gigabit Ethernet (1000base-X)	1000 Mbit/s	125 MB/s
Myrinet 2000	2000 Mbit/s	250 MB/s
Infiniband SDR 1X	2,000 Mbit/s	250 MB/s
Infiniband DDR 1X	4,000 Mbit/s	500 MB/s
Infiniband QDR 1X	8,000 Mbit/s	1,000 MB/s
Infiniband SDR 4X	8,000 Mbit/s	1,000 MB/s
10 gigabit Ethernet (10Gbase-X)	10,000 Mbit/s	1250 MB/s
Myri 10G	10,000 Mbit/s	1250 MB/s
Infiniband DDR 4X	16,000 Mbit/s	2,000 MB/s
Scalable Coherent Interface (SCI) Dual Channel SCI, x8 PCIe	20,000 Mbit/s	2500 MB/s
nfiniband SDR 12X	24,000 Mbit/s	3,000 MB/s
nfiniband QDR 4X	32,000 Mbit/s	4,000 MB/s
nfiniband DDR 12X	48,000 Mbit/s	6,000 MB/s
ıfiniband QDR 12X	96,000 Mbit/s	12,000 MB/s
00 gigabit Ethernet (100Gbase-X)	100,000 Mbit/s	12,500 MB/s

Vireless networking

Vote: 802.11 networks are half-duplex; all stations share the medium. ı access point mode, all traffic has to pass through the AP (Access oint). Two stations on the same AP which are communicating with ch other will have all traffic pass the medium twice: once sent by the sender to the AP, then from AP to receiver, thus approximately halving the effective bandwidth.

802.11 legacy 0.125	**2.0 Mbit/s**	0.25 MB/s
RONJA free space optical wireless	**10.0 Mbit/s**	1.25 MB/s
802.11b DSSS 0.125	**11.0 Mbit/s**	1.375 MB/s
802.11b+ non-standard DSSS 0.125	**44.0 Mbit/s**	5.5 MB/s
802.11a 0.75	**54.0 Mbit/s**	6.75 MB/s
802.11g OFDM 0.125	**54.0 Mbit/s**	6.75 MB/s
802.16 (WiMAX)	**70.0 Mbit/s**	8.75 MB/s
802.11gt DSSS 0.125 (aka Super G)	**108.0 Mbit/s**	13.5 MB/s
802.11n	**248.0 Mbit/s**	31 MB/s

Wireless device connection

IrDA-Control	**72 kbit/s**	9 kB/s
IrDA-SIR	**115.2 kbit/s**	14 kB/s
802.15.4 (2.4 GHz)	**250 kbit/s**	31.25 kB/s
Bluetooth 1.1	**1000 kbit/s**	125 kB/s
Bluetooth 2.0+EDR	**3000 kbit/s**	375 kB/s
IrDA-FIR	**4000 kbit/s**	510 kB/s
IrDA-VFIR	**16,000 kbit/s**	2000 kB/s
IrDA-UFIR	**100,000 kbit/s**	12,500 kB/s
WUSB-UWB	**480,000 kbit/s**	60,000 kB/s

Computer buses

I2c	3.4 Mbit/s	**425 KB/s**
ISA 8-Bit/4.77 MHz	9.6 Mbit/s	**1.2 MB/s**
Zorro II 16-Bit/7.14 MHz	28.56 Mbit/s	**3.56 MB/s**
ISA 16-Bit/8.33 MHz	42.4 Mbit/s	**5.3 MB/s**
Low Pin Count	133.33 Mbit/s	**16.67 MB/s**
HP-Precision Bus	184 Mbit/s	**23 MB/s**
EISA 8-16-32bits/8.33 MHz	320 Mbit/s	**32 MB/s**
VME64 32-64bits	400 Mbit/s	**40 MB/s**
NuBus 10 MHz	400 Mbit/s	**40 MB/s**
DEC TURBOchannel 32-bit/12.5 MHz	400 Mbit/s	**50 MB/s**
MCA 16-32bits/10 MHz	660 Mbit/s	**66 MB/s**
NuBus90 20 MHz	800 Mbit/s	**80 MB/s**

Sbus 32-bit/25 MHz	800 Mbit/s	**100 MB/s**
DEC TURBOchannel 32-bit/25 MHz	800 Mbit/s	**100 MB/s**
VLB 32-bit/33 MHz	1067 Mbit/s	**133.33 MB/s**
PCI 32-bit/33 MHz	1067 Mbit/s	**133.33 MB/s**
HP GSC-1X	1136 Mbit/s	**142 MB/s**
Zorro III 32-Bit/37.5 MHz	1200 Mbit/s	**150 MB/s**
Sbus 64-bit/25 MHz	1600 Mbit/s	**200 MB/s**
PCI Express (x1 link)	2000 Mbit/s	**250 MB/s**
HP GSC-2X	2048 Mbit/s	**256 MB/s**
PCI 64-bit/33 MHz	2133 Mbit/s	**266.7 MB/s**
PCI 32-bit/66 MHz	2133 Mbit/s	**266.7 MB/s**
AGP 1x	2133 Mbit/s	**266.7 MB/s**
HIO bus	2560 Mbit/s	**320 MB/s**
PCI Express (x2 link)	4000 Mbit/s	**500 MB/s**
AGP 2x	4266 Mbit/s	**533.3 MB/s**
PCI 64-bit/66 MHz	4266 Mbit/s	**533.3 MB/s**
PCI-X DDR 16-bit	4266 Mbit/s	**533.3 MB/s**
PCI 64-bit/100 MHz	6399 Mbit/s	**800 MB/s**
PCI Express (x4 link)	8000 Mbit/s	**1000 MB/s**
AGP 4x	8533 Mbit/s	**1067 MB/s**
PCI-X 133	8533 Mbit/s	**1067 MB/s**
PCI-X QDR 16-bit	8533 Mbit/s	**1067 MB/s**
nfiniBand single 4X	8000 Mbit/s	**1000 MB/s**
JPA	15,360 Mbit/s	**1920 MB/s**
CI Express (x8 link)	16,000 Mbit/s	**2000 MB/s**
GP 8x	17,066 Mbit/s	**2133 MB/s**
CI-X DDR	17,066 Mbit/s	**2133 MB/s**
yperTransport (800 MHz, 16-pair)	25,600 Mbit/s	**3200 MB/s**
yperTransport (1 GHz, 16-pair)	32,000 Mbit/s	**4000 MB/s**
CI Express (x16 link)	32,000 Mbit/s	**4000 MB/s**
CI Express 2.0 (x8 link)	32,000 Mbit/s	**4000 MB/s**
CI-X QDR	34,133 Mbit/s	**4266 MB/s**
GP 8x 64-bit	34,133 Mbit/s	**4266 MB/s**
CI Express (x32 link)	64,000 Mbit/s	**8000 MB/s**
CI Express 2.0 (x16 link)	64,000 Mbit/s	**8000 MB/s**

PCI Express 2.0 (x32 link)	128,000 Mbit/s	16,000 MB/s
HyperTransport (2.8 GHz, 32-pair)	179,200 Mbit/s	22,400 MB/s
Portable Computer buses		
PC Card 16 bit 255ns Byte mode	31.36 Mbit/s	3.92 MB/s
PC Card 16 bit 255ns Word mode	62.72 Mbit/s	7.84 MB/s
PC Card 16 bit 100ns Byte mode	80 Mbit/s	10 MB/s
PC Card 16 bit 100ns Word mode	160 Mbit/s	20 MB/s
PC Card 32 bit (CardBus) Byte mode	267 Mbit/s	33.33 MB/s
ExpressCard USB mode	480 Mbit/s	60 MB/s
PC Card 32 bit (CardBus) Word mode	533 Mbit/s	66.66 MB/s
PC Card 32 bit (CardBus) DWord mode	1067 Mbit/s	133.33 MB/s
ExpressCard PCI Express mode	2000 Mbit/s	250 MB/s
Computer buses (storage)		
PC Floppy Disk Controller (1.44MB)	0.5 Mbit/s	**0.062 MB/s**
CD Controller (1x)	1.4112 Mbit/s	**0.1764 MB/s**
MFM	5 Mbit/s	**0.625 MB/s**
RLL	7.5 Mbit/s	**0.9375 MB/s**
DVD Controller (1x)	11.1 Mbit/s	**1.32 MB/s**
ESDI	24 Mbit/s	**3 MB/s**
ATA PIO Mode 0	26.4 Mbit/s	**3.3 MB/s**
SCSI 1 (5 MHz)	40 Mbit/s	**5 MB/s**
ATA PIO Mode 1	41.6 Mbit/s	**5.2 MB/s**
ATA PIO Mode 2	66.4 Mbit/s	**8.3 MB/s**
Fast SCSI 2 (8 bits/10 MHz)	80 Mbit/s	**10 MB/s**
ATA PIO Mode 3	88.8 Mbit/s	**11.1 MB/s**
iSCSI over Fast Ethernet	100 Mbit/s	**12.5 MB/s**
ATA PIO Mode 4	133.3 Mbit/s	**16.7 MB/s**
Fast Wide SCSI 2 (16 bits/10 MHz)	160 Mbit/s	**20 MB/s**
Ultra DMA ATA 33	264 Mbit/s	**33 MB/s**
Ultra Wide SCSI 40 (16 bits/20 MHz)	320 Mbit/s	**40 MB/s**
Ultra DMA ATA 66	528 Mbit/s	**66 MB/s**
Ultra-2 wide SCSI 80 (16 bits/40 MHz)	640 Mbit/s	**80 MB/s**
Serial Storage Architecture SSA	640 Mbit/s	**80 MB/s**
Ultra DMA ATA 100	800 Mbit/s	**100 MB/s**
Fibre Channel 1GFC (1.0625 GHz)	850 Mbit/s	106.25 MB/s

iSCSI over Gigabit Ethernet	1000 Mbit/s	125 MB/s
Ultra DMA ATA 133	1064 Mbit/s	133 MB/s
Ultra-3 SCSI 160 (16 bits/40 MHz DDR)	1280 Mbit/s	160 MB/s
Serial ATA (SATA-150)	1500 Mbit/s	187.5 MB/s
Fibre Channel 2GFC (2.125 GHz)	1700 Mbit/s	212.5 MB/s
Ultra-320 SCSI (16 bits/ 80 MHz DDR)	2560 Mbit/s	320 MB/s
Serial ATA (SATA-300)	3000 Mbit/s	375 MB/s
Serial Attached SCSI (SAS)	3000 Mbit/s	375 MB/s
Fibre Channel 4GFC (4.25 GHz)	3400 Mbit/s	425 MB/s
Serial ATA (SATA-600)	4800 Mbit/s	600 MB/s
Ultra-640 SCSI (16 bits/ 160 MHz DDR)	5120 Mbit/s	640 MB/s
Serial Attached SCSI 2	6000 Mbit/s	750 MB/s
Fibre Channel 8GFC (8.50 GHz)	6800 Mbit/s	850 MB/s
iSCSI over 10G Ethernet (Very few products exist)	10000 Mbit/s	1250 MB/s
iSCSI over 100G Ethernet (Planned)	100000 Mbit/s	12500 MB/s

Computer buses (external)

Apple Desktop Bus	**0.010 Mbit/s**	0.00125 MB/s
MIDI	**0.0313 Mbit/s**	0.0039 MB/s
Serial RS-232 max	**0.2304 Mbit/s**	0.0288 MB/s
Parallel (Centronics) CPP ~133 kHz	1 Mbit/s	**0.133 MB/s**
Serial 16550 UART max	**1.5 Mbit/s**	0.15 MB/s
USB Low Speed (USB 1.0)	**1.536 Mbit/s**	0.192 MB/s
Serial UART max	**2.7648 Mbit/s**	0.3456 MB/s
Serial RS-422 max	**10 Mbit/s**	1.25 MB/s
USB Full Speed (USB 1.1)	**12 Mbit/s**	1.5 MB/s
Parallel (Centronics) EPP 2 MHz	16 Mbit/s	**2 MB/s**
Serial EIA-485 max	**35 Mbit/s**	3.5 MB/s
FireWire (IEEE 1394) 100	**98.304 Mbit/s**	12.288 MB/s
FireWire (IEEE 1394) 200	**196.608 Mbit/s**	24.576 MB/s
FireWire (IEEE 1394) 400	**393.216 Mbit/s**	49.152 MB/s
USB Hi-Speed (USB 2.0)	**480 Mbit/s**	60 MB/s
FireWire (IEEE 1394b) 800	**786.432 Mbit/s**	98.304 MB/s

Fibre Channel 1Gb SCSI	**1062.5 Mbit/s**	100 MB/s
FireWire (IEEE 1394b) 1600	**1573 Mbit/s**	196.6 MB/s
Camera Link Base (single) 24bit 85 MHz	**2040 Mbit/s**	261.12 MB/s
Fibre Channel 2Gb SCSI	**2125 Mbit/s**	200 MB/s
eSATA (SATA 300)	**2400 Mbit/s**	300 MB/s
FireWire (IEEE 1394b) 3200	**3145.7 Mbit/s**	393.216 MB/s
Fibre Channel 4Gb SCSI	**4250 Mbit/s**	531.25 MB/s
USB 3.0 (Planned)	**4800 Mbit/s**	600 MB/s
Camera Link Full (dual) 72bit 85 MHz	**6120 Mbit/s**	765 MB/s
Computer buses (MAC to PHY)		
MII (4 Lanes)	**100 Mbit/s**	12.5 MB/s
RMII (2 Lanes)	**100 Mbit/s**	12.5 MB/s
SMII (1 Lane)	**100 Mbit/s**	12.5 MB/s
GMII (8 Lanes)	**1.0 Gbit/s**	125 MB/s
RGMII (4 Lanes)	**1.0 Gbit/s**	125 MB/s
SGMII (2 Lanes)	**1.0 Gbit/s**	125 MB/s
XGMII (32 Lanes)	**10.0 Gbit/s**	1.25 GB/s
XAUI (4 Lanes)	**10.0 Gbit/s**	1.25 GB/s
Computer buses (PHY to XPDR)		
XSBI (16 Lanes)	**0.995 Gbit/s**	0.124 GB/s

Memory Interconnect Buses/RAM

NOTE: Dual channel bandwidths are theoretical maximums and do not always reflect real world performance. In many cases, performance may be closer to single channel operation (half the bandwidth).

FPM DRAM	1.408 Gbit/s	**0.176 GB/s**
EDO DRAM	2.112 Gbit/s	**0.264 GB/s**
SPARC MBus	2.55 Gbit/s	**0.32 GB/s**
PC66 SDRAM	4.264 Gbit/s	**0.533 GB/s**
PC100 SDRAM	6.4 Gbit/s	**0.8 GB/s**
HP Runway bus 125 MHz 64-bit	6.4 Gbit/s	**0.8 GB/s**
PC133 SDRAM	8.528 Gbit/s	**1.066 GB/s**
PC800 RDRAM (single-channel)	12.8 Gbit/s	**1.6 GB/s**
PC1600 DDR-SDRAM (single channel)	12.8 Gbit/s	**1.6 GB/s**

HP Runway bus 125 MHz 64-bit DDR	16 Gbit/s	**2 GB/s**
PC1066 RDRAM (single-channel)	16.8 Gbit/s	**2.1 GB/s**
PC2100 DDR-SDRAM (single channel)	16.8 Gbit/s	**2.1 GB/s**
PC1200 RDRAM (single-channel)	19.2 Gbit/s	**2.4 GB/s**
PC2700 DDR-SDRAM (single channel)	21.6 Gbit/s	**2.7 GB/s**
PC800 RDRAM (dual-channel)	25.6 Gbit/s	**3.2 GB/s**
PC1600 DDR-SDRAM (dual channel)	25.6 Gbit/s	**3.2 GB/s**
PC3200 DDR-SDRAM (single channel)	25.6 Gbit/s	**3.2 GB/s**
PC2-3200 DDR2-SDRAM (single channel)	25.6 Gbit/s	**3.2 GB/s**
PC1066 RDRAM (dual-channel)	33 6 Gbit/s	**4.2 GB/s**
PC2100 DDR-SDRAM (dual channel)	33.6 Gbit/s	**4.2 GB/s**
PC2-4200 DDR2-SDRAM (single channel)	34.136 Gbit/s	**4.267 GB/s**
PC4000 DDR-SDRAM (single channel)	34.3 Gbit/s	**4.287 GB/s**
PC1200 RDRAM (dual-channel)	38.4 Gbit/s	**4.8 GB/s**
PC2-5300 DDR2-SDRAM (single channel)	42.4 Gbit/s	**5.3 GB/s**
PC2-5400 DDR2-SDRAM (single channel)	42.664 Gbit/s	**5.333 GB/s**
PC2700 DDR-SDRAM (dual channel)	43.2 Gbit/s	**5.4 GB/s**
PC3200 DDR-SDRAM (dual channel)	51.2 Gbit/s	**6.4 GB/s**
PC2-3200 DDR2-SDRAM (dual channel)	51.2 Gbit/s	**6.4 GB/s**
PC2-6400 DDR2-SDRAM (single channel)	51.2 Gbit/s	**6.4 GB/s**
Itanium zx1 bus	51.2 Gbit/s	**6.4 GB/s**
PC4000 DDR-SDRAM (dual channel)	67.2 Gbit/s	**8.4 GB/s**
PC2-4200 DDR2-SDRAM (dual channel)	67.2 Gbit/s	**8.4 GB/s**

PC2-5300 DDR2-SDRAM (dual channel)	84.8 Gbit/s	10.6 GB/s
PC2-5400 DDR2-SDRAM (dual channel)	85.328 Gbit/s	10.666 GB/s
PC2-6400 DDR2-SDRAM (dual channel)	102.4 Gbit/s	12.8 GB/s
PC2-8000 DDR2-SDRAM (dual channel)	128.0 Gbit/s	16.0 GB/s
PC2-8500 DDR2-SDRAM (dual channel)	136.0 Gbit/s	17 GB/s
PC3-8500 DDR3-SDRAM (dual channel)	136.0 Gbit/s	17 GB/s
PC3-10600 DDR3-SDRAM (dual channel)	165.6 Gbit/s	21.2 GB/s
PC3-12800 DDR3-SDRAM (dual channel)	204.8 Gbit/s	25.6 GB/s

Increasing Speeds (one-way proprietary standards)

Many other standards were also introduced for special purposes, commonly using a high-speed channel for receiving, and a lower-speed channel for sending. One typical example was used in the French Minitel system, in which the user's terminals spent the majority of their time receiving information. The modem in the Minitel terminal thus operated at 1200 bit/s for reception, and 75 bit/s for sending commands back to the servers.

Three U.S. companies became famous for high-speed versions of the same concept. Telebit introduced its Trailblazer modem in 1984, which used a large number of 36 bit/s channels to send data one-way at rates up to 18,400 bit/s. A single additional channel in the reverse direction allowed the two modems to communicate how much data was waiting at either end of the link, and the modems could change direction on the fly. The Trailblazer modems also supported a feature that allowed them to "spoof" the UUCP "g" protocol, commonly used on Unix systems to send e-mail, and thereby speed UUCP up by a tremendous amount. Trailblazers thus became extremely common on Unix systems, and maintained their dominance in this market well into the 1990s.

U.S. Robotics (USR) introduced a similar system, known as HST, although this supplied only 9600 bit/s (in early versions at least) and provided for a larger backchannel. Rather than offer spoofing, USR instead created a large market among Fidonet users by offering its modems to BBS sysops at a much lower price, resulting in sales to end users who wanted faster file transfers. Hayes was forced to compete, and introduced its own 9600-bit/s standard, Express 96 (also known as "Ping-Pong"), which was generally similar to Telebit's PEP. Hayes, however, offered neither protocol spoofing nor sysop discounts, and its high-speed modems remained rare.

4800 and 9600 (V.27ter, V.32)

Echo cancellation was the next major advance in modem design. Local telephone lines use the same wires to send and receive, which results in a small amount of the outgoing signal bouncing back. This signal can confuse the modem. Is the signal it is "hearing" a data transmission from the remote modem, or its own transmission bouncing back? This was why earlier modems split the signal frequencies into answer and originate; each modem simply didn't listen to its own transmitting frequencies. Even with improvements to the phone system allowing higher speeds, this splitting of available phone signal bandwidth still imposed a half-speed limit on modems.

Echo cancellation got around this problem. Measuring the echo delays and magnitudes allowed the modem to tell if the received signal was from itself or the remote modem, and create an equal and opposite signal to cancel its own. Modems were then able to send at "full speed" in both directions at the same time, leading to the development of 4800 and 9600 bit/s modems.

Increases in speed have used increasingly complicated communications theory. 1200 and 2400 bit/s modems used the phase shift key (PSK) concept. This could transmit two or three bits per symbol. The next major advance encoded four bits into a combination of amplitude and phase, known as Quadrature Amplitude Modulation (QAM). Best visualised as a constellation diagram, the bits are mapped onto points on a graph with the x (real) and y (quadrature) coordinates transmitted over a single carrier.

The new V.27ter and V.32 standards were able to transmit 4 bits per symbol, at a rate of 1200 or 2400 baud, giving an effective bit rate of 4800 or 9600 bits per second. The carrier frequency was 1650 Hz. For many years, most engineers considered this rate to be the limit of data communications over telephone networks.

Error correction and compression

Operations at these speeds pushed the limits of the phone lines, resulting in high error rates. This led to the introduction of error-correction systems built into the modems, made most famous with Microcom's MNP systems. A string of MNP standards came out in the 1980s, each increasing the effective data rate by minimising overhead, from about 75% theoretical maximum in MNP 1, to 95% in MNP 4. The new method called MNP 5 took this a step further, adding data compression to the system, thereby increasing the data rate above the modem's rating. Generally the user could expect an MNP5 modem to transfer at about 130% the normal data rate of the modem. MNP was later "opened" and became popular on a series of 2400-bit/s modems, and ultimately led to the development of V.42 and V.42bis ITU standards. V.42 and V.42bis were non-compatible with MNP but were similar in concept: Error correction and compression.

Another common feature of these high-speed modems was the concept of fallback, allowing them to talk to less-capable modems. During the call initiation the modem would play a series of signals into the line and wait for the remote modem to "answer" them. They would start at high speeds and progressively get slower and slower until they heard an answer. Thus, two USR modems would be able to connect at 9600 bit/s, but, when a user with a 2400-bit/s modem called in, the USR would "fall back" to the common 2400-bit/s speed. This would also happen if a V.32 modem and a HST modem were connected. Because they used a different standard at 9600 bit/s, they would fall back to their highest commonly supported standard at 2400 bit/s. The same applies to V.32bis and 14400 bit/s HST modem, which would still be able to communicate with each other at only 2400 bit/s.

Breaking the 9.6k barrier

In 1980 Gottfried Ungerboeck from IBM Zurich Research Laboratory applied powerful channel coding techniques to search for new ways to increase the speed of modems. His results were astonishing but only conveyed to a few colleagues. Finally in 1982, he agreed to publish what is now a landmark paper in the theory of information coding. By applying powerful parity check coding to the bits in each symbol, and mapping the encoded bits into a two dimensional "diamond pattern", Ungerboeck showed that it was possible to increase the speed by a factor of two with the same error rate. The new technique was called "mapping by set partitions" (now known as trellis modulation). This new view was an extension of the "penny packing" problem and the related and more general problem of how to pack points into an N-dimension sphere such that they are far away from their neighbours. The greater two bit sequences are from one another, the easier it is to correct minor errors.

The industry was galvanised into new research and development. More powerful coding techniques were developed, commercial firms rolled out new product lines, and the standards organisations rapidly adopted to new technology. The "tipping point" occurred with the introduction of the SupraFAXModem 14400 in 1991. Rockwell had introduced a new chipset supporting not only V.32 and MNP, but the newer 14,400 bit/s V.32bis and the higher-compression V.42bis as well, and even included 9600 bit/s fax capability. Supra, then known primarily for their hard drive systems, used this chip set to build a low-priced 14,400 bit/s modem which cost the same as a 2400 bit/s modem from a year or two earlier (about US$300). The product was a runaway best-seller, and it was months before the company could keep up with demand.

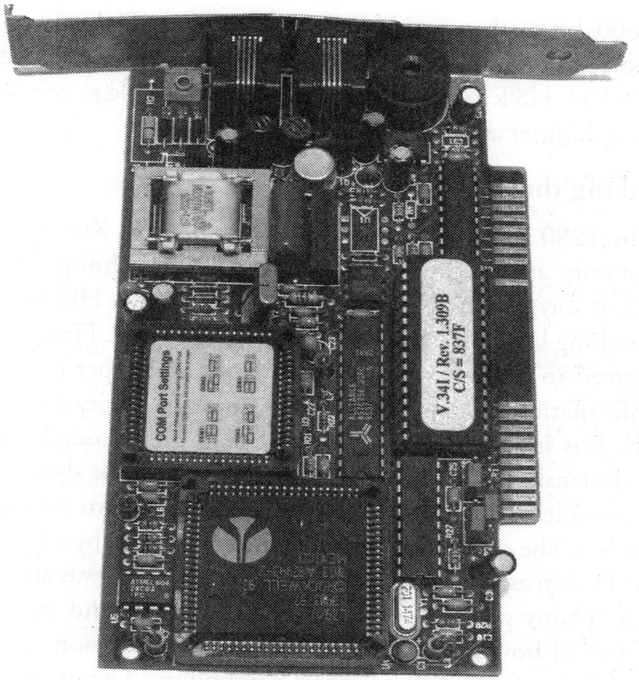

V.32bis was so successful that the older high-speed standards had little to recommend them. USR fought back with a 16,800 bit/s version of HST, while AT&T introduced a one-off 19,200 bit/s method they referred to as V.32ter (also known as V.32 terbo), but neither non-standard modem sold well.

V.34 /28.8k and 33.8k

Any interest in these systems was destroyed during the lengthy introduction of the 28,800 bit/s V.34 standard. While waiting, several companies decided to "jump the gun" and introduced modems they referred to as "V.FAST". In order to guarantee compatibility with V.34 modems once the standard was ratified (1994), the manufacturers were forced to use more "flexible" parts, generally a DSP and microcontroller, as opposed to purpose-designed "modem chips".

Today the ITU standard V.34 represents the culmination of the joint efforts. It employs the most powerful coding techniques including channel encoding and shape encoding. From the mere 4 bits per symbol (9.6 kbit/s), the new standards used the functional equivalent of 6 to 10 bits per symbol, plus increasing baud rates from 2400 to 3429, to create 14.4, 28.8, and 33.8 kbit/s modems. (See Tables 8 and 10 of the specification; maximum speed listed as "33 800".) This rate is near the theoretical Shannon limit. When calculated, the Shannon capacity of a narrowband line is *Bandwidth* * $log_2(1 + P_u / P_n)$, with P_u / P_n the signal-to-noise ratio. Narrowband phone lines have a bandwidth from 300-3100 Hz, so using $P_u / P_n = 100{,}000$: capacity is approximately 35 kbit/s.

Without the discovery and eventual application of trellis modulation, maximum telephone rates would have been limited to 3429 baud * 4 bits/symbol == approximately 14 kilobits per second using traditional QAM.

Using Digital Lines and PCM (V.90/92)

In the late 1990s Rockwell and U.S. Robotics introduced new technology based upon the digital transmission used in modern telephony networks. The standard digital transmission in modern networks is 64 kbit/s but some networks use a part of the bandwidth for remote office signaling (eg to hang up the phone), limiting the effective rate to 56 kbit/s DS0. This new technology was adopted into ITU standards V.90 and is common in modern computers. The 56 kbit/s rate is only possible from the central office to the user site (downlink) and in the United States, government regulation limits the maximum power output to only 53.3 kbit/s. The uplink (from the user to the central office) still uses V.34 technology at 33.6k.

Later in V.92, the digital PCM technique was applied to increase the upload speed to a maximum of 48 kbit/s, but at the expense of download rates. For example a 48 kbit/s upstream rate would reduce the downstream as low as 40 kbit/s, due to echo on the telephone line. To avoid this problem, V.92 modems offer the option to turn off the digital upstream and instead use a 33.6 kbit/s analog connection, in order to maintain a high digital downstream of 50 kbit/s or higher. (See November and October 2000 update at http://www.modemsite.com/56k/v92s.asp) V.92 also adds two other features. The first is the ability for users who have call waiting to put their dial-up Internet connection on hold for extended periods of time while they answer a call. The second feature is the ability to "quick connect" to one's ISP. This is achieved by remembering the analog and digital characteristics of the telephone line, and using this saved information to reconnect at a fast pace.

Using Compression to Exceed 56k

Today's V.42, V.42bis and V.44 standards allow the modem to transmit data faster than its basic rate would imply. For instance, a 53.3 kbit/s connection with V.44 can transmit up to 53.3*6 == 320 kbit/s using pure text. However, the compression ratio tends to vary due to noise on the line, or due to the transfer of already-compressed files (ZIP files, JPEG images, MP3 audio, MPEG video). At some points the modem will be sending compressed files at approximately 50 kbit/s, uncompressed files at 160 kbit/s, and pure text at 320 kbit/s, or any value in between.

In such situations a small amount of memory in the modem, a buffer, is used to hold the data while it is being compressed and sent across the phone line, but in order to prevent overflow of the buffer, it sometimes becomes necessary to tell the computer to pause the datastream. This is accomplished through *hardware flow control* using extra lines on the modem–computer connection. The computer is then set to supply the modem at some higher rate, such as 320 kbit/s, and the modem will tell the computer when to start or stop sending data.

Compression by the ISP

As telephone-based 56k modems began losing popularity, some Internet Service Providers such as Netzero and Juno started using pre-compression to increase the throughput and maintain their customer base. As example, the Netscape ISP uses a compression programme that squeezes images, text, and other objects at the server, just prior to sending them across the phone line. The server-side compression operates much more efficiently than the "on-the-fly" compression of V.44-enabled modems. Typically website text is compacted to 4% thus increasing effective throughput to approximately 1300 kbit/s. The accelerator also precompresses Flash executables and images to approximately 30% and 12%, respectively.

The drawback of this approach is a loss in quality, where the graphics become heavily compacted and smeared, but the speed is dramatically improved such that webpages load in less than 5 seconds, and the user can manually choose to view the uncompressed images at any time. The ISPs employing this approach advertise it as "DSL speeds over regular phone lines" or simply "high speed dialup".

List of Dialup Speeds

Note that the values given are maximum values, and actual values may be slower under certain conditions (for example, noisy phone lines). For a complete list see the companion article List of device bandwidths.

Connection	Bitrate
Modem 110 baud	0.1 kbit/s
Modem 300 (300 baud) (Bell 103 or V.21)	0.3 kbit/s
Modem 1200 (600 baud) (Bell 212A or V.22)	1.2 kbit/s
Modem 2400 (600 baud) (V.22bis)	2.4 kbit/s
Modem 2400 (1200 baud) (V.26bis)	2.4 kbit/s
Modem 4800 (1600 baud) (V.27ter)	4.8 kbit/s
Modem 9600 (2400 baud) (V.32)	9.6 kbit/s
Modem 14.4 (2400 baud) (V.32bis)	14.4 kbit/s
Modem 28.8 (3200 baud) (V.34)	28.8 kbit/s
Modem 33.6 (3429 baud) (V.34)	33.8 kbit/s
Modem 56k (8000/3429 baud) (V.90)	56.0/33.6 kbit/s

Modem 56k (8000/8000 baud) (V.92)	56.0/48.0 kbit/s
Bonding Modem (two 56k modems)) (V.92)	112.0/96.0 kbit/s
Hardware compression (variable) (V.90/V.42bis)	56.0-220.0 kbit/s
Hardware compression (variable) (V.92/V.44)	56.0-320.0 kbit/s
Server-side web compression (variable) (Netscape ISP)	100.0-1000.0 kbit/s

Radio Modems

Direct broadcast satellite, WiFi, and mobile phones all use modems to communicate, as do most other wireless services today. Modern telecommunications and data networks also make extensive use of radio modems where long distance data links are required. Such systems are an important part of the PSTN, and are also in common use for high-speed computer network links to outlying areas where fibre is not economical.

Even where a cable is installed, it is often possible to get better performance or make other parts of the system simpler by using radio frequencies and modulation techniques through a cable. Coaxial cable has a very large bandwidth, however signal attenuation becomes a major problem at high data rates if a digital signal is used. By using a modem, a much larger amount of digital data can be transmitted through a single piece of wire. Digital cable television and cable Internet services use radio frequency modems to provide the increasing bandwidth needs of modern households. Using a modem also allows for frequency-division multiple access to be used, making full-duplex digital communication with many users possible using a single wire.

Wireless modems come in a variety of types, bandwidths, and speeds. Wireless modems are often referred to as transparent or smart. They transmit information that is modulated onto a carrier frequency to allow many simultaneous wireless communication links to work simultaneously on different frequencies.

Transparent modems operate in a manner similar to their phone line modem cousins. Typically, they were half duplex, meaning that they could not send and receive data at the same time. Typically transparent modems are polled in a round robin manner to collect small amounts of data from scattered locations that do not have easy access to wired infrastructure. Transparent modems are most commonly used by utility companies for data collection.

Smart modems come with a media access controller inside which prevents random data from colliding and resends data that is not correctly received. Smart modems typically require more bandwidth than transparent modems, and typically achieve higher data rates. The IEEE 802.11 standard defines a short range modulation scheme that is used on a large scale throughout the world.

Broadband

ADSL modems, a more recent development, are not limited to the telephone's "voiceband" audio frequencies. Some ADSL modems use coded orthogonal frequency division modulation (DMT).

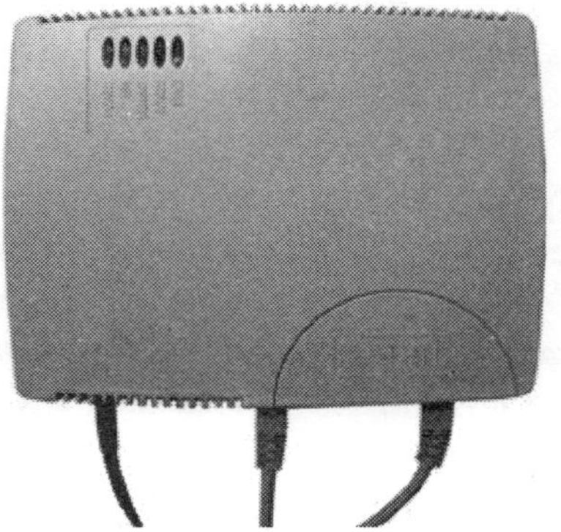

DSL Modem

Cable modems use a range of frequencies originally intended to carry RF television channels. Multiple cable modems attached to a single cable can use the same frequency band, using a low-level media access protocol to allow them to work together within the same channel. Typically, 'up' and 'down' signals are kept separate using frequency division multiple access.

New types of broadband modems are beginning to appear, such as doubleway satellite and powerline modems.

Broadband modems should still be classed as modems, since they use complex waveforms to carry digital data. They are more advanced devices than traditional dial-up modems as they are capable of modulating/demodulating hundreds of channels simultaneously.

Many broadband modems include the functions of a router (with Ethernet and WiFi ports) and other features such as DHCP, NAT and firewall features.

When broadband technology was introduced, networking and routers were unfamiliar to consumers. However, many people knew what a modem was as most internet access was through dialup. Due to this familiarity, companies started selling broadband modems using the familiar term "modem" rather than vaguer ones like "adapter" or "transceiver".

Most modems must be configured properly before they can use a router. This configuration is known as bridge mode.

Popularity

A CEA study in 2006 found that dial-up Internet access is on a notable decline in the U.S. In 2000, dial-up Internet connections accounted for 74% of all U.S. residential Internet connections. The US demographic pattern for (dialup modem users per capita) has been more or less mirrored in Canada and Australia for the past 20 years.

Dialup modem use in the US had dropped to 60% by 2003, and currently (2006) stands at 36%. Voiceband modems were once the most popular means of Internet access in the U.S., but with the advent of new ways of accessing the Internet, the traditional 56K modem is losing popularity.

Asymmetric Digital Subscriber Line

Asymmetric Digital Subscriber Line (**ADSL**) is a form of DSL a data communications technology that enables faster dat transmission over copper telephone lines than a conventional voiceband modem can provide. It does this by utilising frequencies that are not used by a voice telephone call. A splitter—or microfilter—allows a single telephone connection to be used for both ADSL service and voice calls at the same time. Because phone lines vary in quality and were not originally engineered with DSL in mind, it can generally only be used over short distances, typically less than 4km [William Stallings' book].

At the telephone exchange the line generally terminates at a DSLAM where another frequency splitter separates the voice band signal for the conventional phone network. Data carried by the ADSL is typically routed over the telephone company's data network and eventually reaches a conventional internet network. In the UK under British Telecom the data network in question is its ATM network which in turn sends it to its IP network IP Colossus.

ADSL Max

ADSL Max is a broad product set title given to a range of BT Wholesale ADSL products that are rate-adaptive, and are deployed over IPStream and Datastream. ADSL MAX was launched nationally in the UK in March 2006 and offers the best possible speed using existing ADSL standards.

A gateway is commonly used to make an ADSL connection. The modem in the picture is also a wireless access point, hence the antenna.

The services enabled customers to get up to 8 Mbit speeds downstream, and 832 kbit speeds upstream along a standard telephone line. The average customer will actually receive 5-6 Mb depending on their distance along the exchange loop. Customers can be directly next to the exchange but as it loops they can be at the end of the loop and receive 512 k broadband or even qualify for none at all.

During the first 10 days after the service has been provided a piece of equipment known as the DLM (Dynamic Line management) unit is constantly assessing the characteristics of the line in order to provide the end user with the maximum achievable speed for their line. In this period the DLM can make adjustments to the DSLAM output power, SNR and bit rate and even apply a form of error correction known as interleaving. Several factors dictate the maximum available speed, such as the presence of noise within the frequency spectrum used by ADSL but chiefly it is the distance from the Central Office (Telephone Exchange) which has the largest influence on the lines performance.

WiFi and WiMax

Wireless data modems are used in the WiFi and WiMax standards, operating at microwave frequencies.

WiFi is principally used in laptops for Internet connections (wireless access point) and wireless application protocol (WAP).

5

Wi-Fi

Wi-Fi is the trade name for a popular wireless technology used in home networks, mobile phones, video games and more. Wi-Fi is supported by nearly every modern personal computer operating system and most advanced game consoles, printers, and other peripherals.

Purpose

The purpose of Wi-Fi is to hide complexity by enabling wireless access to applications and data, media and streams. The main aims of Wi-Fi are the following:

- make access to information easier
- ensure compatibility and co-existence
- eliminate cabling and wiring
- eliminate switches, adapters, plugs and connectors.

Uses

A Wi-Fi enabled device such as a PC, game console, cell phone, MP3 player or PDA can connect to the Internet when within range of a wireless network connected to the Internet. The coverage of one or more interconnected access points—called a hotspot—can comprise an area as small as a single room with wireless-opaque walls or as large as many square miles covered by overlapping access points. Wi-Fi technology has served to set up mesh networks, for example, in London. Both architectures can operate in community networks.

In addition to restricted use in homes and offices, Wi-Fi can make access publicly available at Wi-Fi hotspots provided either free of charge or to subscribers to various providers. Organisations and businesses such as airports, hotels and restaurants often provide free hotspots to attract or assist clients. Enthusiasts or authorities who wish to provide services or even to promote business in a given area sometimes provide free Wi-Fi access. Metropolitan-wide Wi-Fi (Muni-Fi) already has more than 300 projects in process. There were 879 Wi-Fi based Wireless Internet service providers in the Czech Republic as of May 2008.

Wi-Fi also allows connectivity in peer-to-peer (wireless ad-hoc network) mode, which enables devices to connect directly with each other. This connectivity mode can prove useful in consumer electronics and gaming applications.

When wireless networking technology first entered the market many problems ensued for consumers who could not rely on products from different vendors working together. The Wi-Fi Alliance began as a community to solve this issue—aiming to address the needs of the end-user and to allow the technology to mature. The Alliance created the branding *Wi-Fi CERTIFIED* to reassure consumers that products will interoperate with other products displaying the same branding.

Many consumer devices use Wi-Fi. Amongst others, personal computers can network to each other and connect to the Internet, mobile computers can connect to the Internet from any Wi-Fi hotspot, and digital cameras can transfer images wirelessly.

Routers which incorporate a DSL-modem or a cable-modem and a Wi-Fi access point, often set up in homes and other premises, provide Internet-access and internetworking to all devices connected (wirelessly or by cable) to them. One can also connect Wi-Fi devices in ad-hoc mode for client-to-client connections without a router.

As of 2007 Wi-Fi technology had spread widely within business and industrial sites. In business environments, just like other environments, increasing the number of Wi-Fi access-points provides redundancy, support for fast roaming and increased overall network-capacity by using more channels or by defining smaller cells. Wi-Fi enables wireless voice-applications (VoWLAN or WVOIP). Over the years, Wi-Fi implementations have moved toward "thin" access-points, with more of the network intelligence housed in a centralised network appliance, relegating individual access-points to the role of mere "dumb" radios. Outdoor applications may utilise true mesh topologies. As of 2007 Wi-Fi installations can provide a secure computer networking gateway, firewall, DHCP server, intrusion detection system, and other functions.

ADVANTAGES AND CHALLENGES

Operational Advantages

Wi-Fi allows LANs (Local Area Networks) to be deployed without cabling for client devices, typically reducing the costs of network deployment and expansion. Spaces where cables cannot be run, such as outdoor areas and historical buildings, can host wireless LANs.

A keychain size Wi-Fi detector.

As of 2008, wireless network adapters are built into most modern laptops. The price of chipsets for Wi-Fi continues to drop, making it an economical networking option included in ever more devices. Wi-Fi has become widespread in corporate infrastructures.

Different competitive brands of access points and client network interfaces are inter-operable at a basic level of service. Products designated as "Wi-Fi Certified" by the Wi-Fi Alliance are backwards compatible. Wi-Fi is a global set of standards. Unlike mobile telephones, any standard Wi-Fi device will work anywhere in the world.

Wi-Fi is widely available in more than 220,000 public hotspots and tens of millions of homes and corporate and university campuses worldwide. WPA is not easily cracked if strong passwords are used and WPA2 encryption has no known weaknesses. New protocols for Quality of Service (WMM) make Wi-Fi more suitable for latency-sensitive applications (such as voice and video), and power saving mechanisms (WMM Power Save) improve battery operation.

Limitations

Spectrum assignments and operational limitations are not consistent worldwide. Most of Europe allows for an additional 2 channels beyond those permitted in the U.S. for the 2.4 GHz band. (1–13 vs. 1–11); Japan has one more on top of that (1–14). Europe, as of 2007, was essentially homogeneous in this respect. A very confusing aspect is the fact that a Wi-Fi signal actually occupies five channels in the 2.4 GHz band resulting in only three non-overlapped channels in the U.S.: 1, 6, 11, and three or four in Europe: 1, 5, 9, 13 can be used if all the equipment on a specific area can be granted not to use 802.11b at all, even as fallback or beacon. Equivalent isotropically radiated power (EIRP) in the EU is limited to 20 dBm (0.1 W).

Reach

Due to reach requirements for wireless LAN applications, power consumption is fairly high compared to some other low-bandwidth standards. Especially Zigbee and Bluetooth supporting wireless PAN applications refer to much lesser propagation range of <10m (ref. e.g. IEEE Std. 802.15.4 section 1.2 scope). Range is always making battery life a concern.

Wi-Fi networks have limited range. A typical Wi-Fi home router using 802.11b or 802.11g with a stock antenna might have a range of 32 m (120 ft) indoors and 95 m (300 ft) outdoors. Range also varies with frequency band. Wi-Fi in the 2.4 GHz frequency block has slightly better range than Wi-Fi in the 5 GHz frequency block. Outdoor range with improved (directional) antennas can be several kilometres or more with line-of-sight.

Wi-Fi performance decreases roughly quadratically as the range increases at constant radiation levels.

Mobility

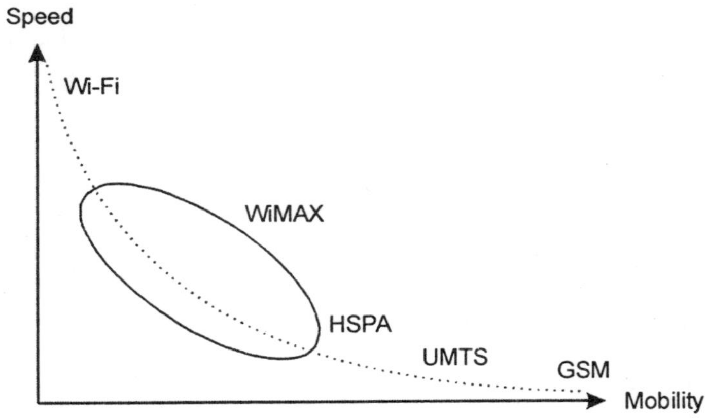

Speed vs. Mobility of wireless systems: **Wi-Fi**, HSPA, UMTS, GSM

Because of the very limited practical range of Wi-Fi, mobile use is essentially confined to such applications as inventory taking machines in warehouses or retail spaces, barcode reading devices at check-out stands or receiving/shipping stations. Mobile use of Wi-Fi over wider ranges is limited to move, use, move, as for instance in an automobile moving from one hotspot to another. Other wireless technologies are more suitable as illustrated in the graphic.

Threats to Security

The most common wireless encryption standard, Wired Equivalent Privacy or WEP, has been shown to be easily breakable even when correctly configured. Wi-Fi Protected Access (WPA and WPA2), which began shipping in 2003, aims to solve this problem and is now available on most products. Wi-Fi Access Points typically default to an "open" (encryption-free) mode. Novice users benefit from a zero-configuration device that works out of the box, but this default is without any wireless security enabled, providing open wireless access to their LAN. To turn security on requires the user to configure the device, usually via a software graphical user interface (GUI). Wi-Fi networks that are open (unencrypted) can be monitored and used to read and copy data (including personal information) transmitted over the network, unless another security method is used to secure the data, such as a VPN or a secure web page. (See HTTPS/Secure Socket Layer.)

Population

Many 2.4 GHz 802.11b and 802.11g Access points default to the same channel on initial startup, contributing to congestion on certain channels. To change the channel of operation for an access point requires the user to configure the device. Yet, this default use of channels 1, 6 and 11 gives better performance than "advanced" users choosing channels 2, 5, 7 and 9 as "unused, free".

Pollution

Standardisation is a process driven by market forces. Interoperability issues between non-Wi-Fi brands or proprietary deviations from the standard can still disrupt connections or lower throughput speeds on all user's devices that are within range, to include the non-Wi-Fi or proprietary product. Moreover, the usage of the ISM band in the 2.45 GHz range is also common to Bluetooth, WPAN-CSS, ZigBee and any new system will take its share.

Wi-Fi pollution, or an excessive number of access points in the area, especially on the same or neighbouring channel, can prevent access and interfere with the use of other access points by others, caused by overlapping channels in the 802.11g/b spectrum, as well as with decreased signal-to-noise ratio (SNR) between access points. This can be a problem in high-density areas, such as large apartment complexes or office buildings with many Wi-Fi access points. Additionally, other devices use the 2.4 GHz band: microwave ovens, security cameras, Bluetooth devices and (in some countries) Amateur radio, video senders, cordless phones and baby monitors, all of which can cause significant additional interference. General guidance to those who suffer these forms of interference or network crowding is to migrate to a Wi-Fi 5 GHz product, (802.11a, or the newer 802.11n if it has 5 GHz support) as the 5 GHz band is relatively unused and there are many more channels available. This also requires users to set up the 5 GHz band to be the preferred network in the client and to configure each network band to a different name (SSID). It is also an issue when municipalities, or other large entities such as universities, seek to provide large area coverage. This openness is also important to the success and widespread use of 2.4 GHz Wi-Fi.

HARDWARE

Standard Devices

A wireless access point connects a group of wireless devices to an adjacent wired LAN. An access point is similar to a network hub, relaying data between connected wireless devices in addition to a (usually) single connected wired device, most often an ethernet hub or switch, allowing wireless devices to communicate with other wired devices.

Wireless adapters allow devices to connect to a wireless network. These adapters connect to devices using various external or internal interconnects such as PCI, miniPCI, USB, ExpressCard, Cardbus and PC card. Most newer laptop computers are equipped with internal adapters. Internal cards are generally more difficult to install.

An embedded RouterBoard 112 with U.FL-RSMA pigtail and R52 mini PCI Wi-Fi card widely used by wireless Internet service providers (WISPs) in the Czech Republic.

Wireless routers integrate a WAP, ethernet switch, and internal Router firmware application that provides IP Routing, NAT, and DNS forwarding through an integrated WAN interface. A wireless router allows wired and wireless ethernet LAN devices to connect to a (usually) single WAN device such as cable modem or DSL modem. A wireless router allows all three devices (mainly the access point and router) to be configured through one central utility. This utility is most usually an integrated web server which serves web pages to wired and wireless LAN clients and often optionally to WAN clients. This utility may also be an application that is run on a desktop computer such as Apple's AirPort.

Wireless network bridges connect a wired network to a wireless network. This is different from an access point in the sense that an access point connects wireless devices to a wired network at the data-link layer. Two wireless bridges may be used to connect two wired networks over a wireless link, useful in situations where a wired connection may be unavailable, such as between two separate homes.

Wireless range extenders or wireless repeaters can extend the range of an existing wireless network. Range extenders can be strategically placed to elongate a signal area or allow for the signal area to reach around barriers such as those created in L-shaped corridors. Wireless devices connected through repeaters will suffer from an increased latency for each hop. Additionally, a wireless device connected to any of the repeaters in the chain will have a throughput that is limited by the weakest link between the two nodes in the chain from which the connection originates to where the connection ends.

Distance Records

Distance records (using non-standard devices) include 382 km (237 mi) in June 2007, held by Ermanno Pietrosemoli and EsLaRed of Venezuela, transferring about 3 MB of data between mountain tops of El Aguila and Platillon. The Swedish Space Agency transferred data 310 km (193 mi), using 6 watt amplifiers to reach an overhead stratospheric balloon.

Embedded Systems

Wi-Fi availability in the home is on the increase. This extension of the Internet into the home space will increasingly be used for remote monitoring. Examples of remote monitoring include security systems and tele-medicine. In all these kinds of implementation, if the Wi-Fi provision is provided using a system running one of operating systems mentioned above, then it becomes unfeasible due to weight, power consumption and cost issues.

Embedded serial-to-Wi-Fi module

Increasingly in the last few years (particularly as of early 2007), embedded Wi-Fi modules have become available which come with a real-time operating system and provide a simple means of wireless enabling any device which has and communicates via a serial port. This allows simple monitoring devices – for example, a portable ECG monitor hooked up to a patient in their home – to be created. This Wi-Fi enabled device effectively becomes part of the internet cloud and can communicate with any other node on the internet. The data collected can hop via the home's Wi-Fi access point to anywhere on the internet.

These Wi-Fi modules are designed so that designers need minimal Wi-Fi knowledge to wireless-enable their products.

Network Security

During the early popular adoption of 802.11, providing open access points for anyone within range to use was encouraged to cultivate wireless community networks; particularly since people on average use only a fraction of their upstream bandwidth at any given time. Later, equipment manufacturers and mass-media advocated isolating users to a predetermined whitelist of authorised users—referred to as "securing" the access point.

Measures to deter unauthorised users include suppressing the AP's SSID broadcast, allowing only computers with known MAC addresses to join the network, and various encryption standards. Suppressed SSID and MAC filtering are ineffective security methods as the SSID is broadcast in the open in response to a client SSID query and a MAC address can easily be spoofed. If the eavesdropper has the ability to change his MAC address, then he can potentially join the network by spoofing an authorised address.

WEP encryption can protect against casual snooping, but may also produce a misguided sense of security since freely available tools such as AirSnort or aircrack can quickly recover WEP encryption keys. Once it has seen 5-10 million encrypted packets, AirSnort can determine the encryption password in under a second; newer tools such as aircrack-ptw can use Klein's attack to crack a WEP key with a 50% success rate using only 40,000 packets. The newer Wi-Fi Protected Access (WPA) and IEEE 802.11i (WPA2) encryption standards do not have any of the serious weaknesses of WEP encryption.

One serious issue with wireless network security is not just encryption, but access to the network (signal reception). With wired networking it is necessary to get past either a firewall or the security guard & locked doors. With wireless it is only necessary to get reception and spend as long as you want, comfortably out of (easy) reach of the network owner. Most business networks protect sensitive data and systems by attempting to disallow external access. Thus being able to get wireless reception (and thus possibly break the encryption) becomes an attack vector on the network as well.

Recreational logging and mapping of other people's access points has become known as wardriving. It is also common for people to use open (unencrypted) Wi-Fi networks as a free service, termed piggybacking. Indeed, many access points are intentionally installed without security turned on so that they can be used as a free service. These activities do not result in sanctions in most jurisdictions, however legislation and case law differ considerably across the world. A proposal to leave graffiti describing available services was called warchalking. In a Florida court case, owner laziness was determined not to be a valid excuse.

Piggybacking is often unintentional. Most access points are configured without encryption by default, and operating systems such as Windows XP SP2 and Mac OS X may be configured to automatically connect to any available wireless network. A user who happens to start up a laptop in the vicinity of an access point may find the computer has joined the network without any visible indication. Moreover, a user intending to join one network may instead end up on another one if the latter's signal is stronger. In combination with automatic discovery of other network resources (see DHCP and Zeroconf) this could possibly lead wireless users to send sensitive data to the wrong middle man when seeking a destination. For example, a user could inadvertently use an insecure network to login to a website, thereby making the login credentials available to anyone listening, if the website is using an insecure protocol like HTTP, rather than a secure protocol like HTTPS.

Wi-Fi uses both single carrier direct-sequence spread spectrum radio technology (part of the larger family of spread spectrum systems) and multi-carrier OFDM (Orthogonal Frequency Division Multiplexing) radio technology. The regulations for unlicensed spread spectrum enabled the development of Wi-Fi, its onetime competitor HomeRF, Bluetooth, and many other products such as some types of cordless telephones.

Unlicensed spread spectrum was first made available in the US by the Federal Communications Commission in 1985 and these FCC regulations were later copied with some changes in many other countries enabling use of this technology in all major countries. The FCC action was proposed by Michael Marcus of the FCC staff in 1980 and the subsequent regulatory action took 5 more years. It was part of a broader proposal to allow civil use of spread spectrum technology and was opposed at the time by main stream equipment manufacturers and many radio system operators.

The precursor to Wi-Fi was invented in 1991 by NCR Corporation/AT&T (later Lucent & Agere Systems) in Nieuwegein, the Netherlands. It was initially intended for cashier systems; the first wireless products were brought on the market under the name WaveLAN with speeds of 1 Mbit/s to 2 Mbit/s. Vic Hayes, who held the chair of IEEE 802.11 for 10 years and has been named the 'father of Wi-Fi,' was involved in designing standards such as IEEE 802.11b, and 802.11a.

City wide Wi-Fi

Sunnyvale, California became the first city in the United States to offer city wide free Wi-Fi, Corpus Christi, Texas had offered free Wi-Fi until May 31, 2007 when the network was purchased by Earthlink. Philadelphia is also trying to save the Earthlink wifi for its city. New Orleans had free city wide Wi-Fi shortly after Hurricane Katrina. City wide Wi-Fi is available in nine cities in the UK, Newcastle Upon Tyne being the first UK city host, others include Leeds, Liverpool, Manchester, Norwich and London. Other cities, such as the Minneapolis metro area, have a large number of Wi-Fi hotspots so you can receive good signals anywhere, even if from different sources. In Europe, the City of Luxembourg has a city-wide Wi-Fi network.

In Latin America, Mexico City downtown has a public Wi-Fi network. Also, many public squares in towns of Puerto Rico are offering Wi-Fi Internet access.

As compared to Wireless Mesh, WiMax provides over 4 times the number of subcarriers over a variable bandwidth of 1 to 28 MHz. With more subcarriers and a variable length guard interval, the spectral efficiency has increased from 15% to 40% compared to Wireless Mesh. The error vector magnitude of Wireless Mesh is higher than WiMax. This makes WiMax have a longer range. Wireless Mesh transmits and receives functions on the same channel where as WiMax transmits and receives functions at a different channel and at a different time. In Wireless Mesh the output power is virtually fixed however in WiMax the devices closer to the base stations emit less output power whereas the ones further away emit maximum output power.

Wi-Fi can overpower WiMax if the city is meshed with hot spots. A very easy way to do it would be if mobile carriers integrate hot spots with their mobile base stations as WiMax chips are not as integrated as the Wi-Fi chips.

)rigin and meaning of the term "Wi-Fi"

The term "Wi-Fi" suggests "Wireless Fidelity", comparing with he long-established audio recording term "High Fidelity" or "Hi-i", and "Wireless Fidelity" has often been used in an informal ay, even by the Wi-Fi Alliance itself, but officially the term does ot mean anything.

"Wi-Fi" was coined by a brand consulting firm called nterbrand Corporation that had been hired by the Alliance to etermine a name that was "a little catchier than 'IEEE 802.11b irect Sequence'." Interbrand invented "Wi-Fi" as simply a *play--words* with "Hi-Fi", as well as creating the yin yang style Wi-Fi go.

The Wi-Fi Alliance initially complicated matters by stating at it *actually stood for* "Wireless Fidelity", as with the advertising gan "The Standard for Wireless Fidelity", but later removed the rase from their marketing. The Wi-Fi Alliance's early White pers still held in their knowledge base: "... a promising market wireless fidelity (Wi-Fi) network equipment." and "A Short

History of WLANs." The yin yang logo indicates that a product had been certified for interoperability.

The Alliance has since downplayed the connection to "Hi-Fi". Their official position is that it is merely a brand name that stands for nothing in particular, and they now discourage the use of the term "Wireless Fidelity".

Wi-Fi Alliance

The Alliance promotes standards with the aim of improving the interoperability of wireless local area network products based on the IEEE 802.11 standards. The Wi-Fi Alliance, a consortium of separate and independent companies, agrees on a set of common interoperable products based on the family of IEEE 802.11 standards. The Wi-Fi Alliance certifies products via a set of defined test-procedures to establish interoperability. Those manufacturers with membership of Wi-Fi Alliance and whose products pass these interoperability tests can mark their products and product packaging with the Wi-Fi logo.

Mobile Modems and Routers

External modems for mobile phone lines (GPRS and UMTS) are also known as datacards and cellular routers. The datacard is PC card, where a phone card is included, whereas a cellular router may or may not have an external datacard. Most cellular routers do, except for the WAAV CM3 mobile broadband cellular router.

Nowadays, there are USB modems with an integrated SIM cardholder (i.e, Huawei E220); that is, you only need a USB port and a modem to connect to the Internet.

Wireless Modem

Mobile phones can be employed as data modems to form wireless access point connecting a personal computer to the Internet (or some proprietary network). In this use the mobile phone providing a gateway between the cellular service provider's data network technology and Point-to-Point Protocol (PPP) spoken

PCs. Almost all current mobile phone models support the Hayes command set, a standard method of controlling modems. To the PC, the phone appears like an external modem when connected via serial cable, USB, IrDA infrared or Bluetooth wireless.

Wireless data modems are also used in the Wi-Fi and WiMAX standards, operating at microwave frequencies, to give a laptop, PDA or desktop computer an access point to a network. If combined with VoIP technology, these computing devices can achieve telephony capability to make and receive telephone calls.

While some analogue mobile phones provided a standard RJ11 telephone socket into which a normal landline modem could be plugged, this only provided slow dial-up connections, usually 2.4 kilobit per second (kbit/s) or less. The next generation of phones, known as 2G (for 'second generation'), were digital, and offered faster dial-up speeds of 9.6kbit/s or 14.4kbit/s without the need for a separate modem. A further evolution called HSCSD used multiple GSM channels (two or three in each direction) to support up to 43.2kbit/s. All of these technologies still required their users to have a dial-up ISP to connect to and provide the Internet access—t was not provided by the mobile phone network itself.

The release of 2.5G phones with support for packet data hanged this. The 2.5G networks break both digital voice and ata into small chunks, and mix both onto the network imultaneously in a process called packet switching. This allows he phone to have a voice connection and a data connection at the ame time, rather than a single channel that has to be used for one r the other. The network can link the data connection into a mpany network, but for most users the connection is to the nternet. This allows web browsing on the phone, but a PC can so tap in to this service if it connects to the phone. The PC needs send a special telephone number to the phone to get access to e packet data connection. From the PC's viewpoint, the nnection still looks like a normal PPP dial-up link, but it is all rminating on the phone, which then handles the exchange of data with the network. Speeds on 2.5G networks are usually in the 30-50kbit/s range.

3G networks have taken this approach to a higher level, using different underlying technology but the same principles. They routinely provide speeds over 300kbit/s. A further evolution is the 3.5G technology HSDPA, which has the capacity to provide speeds of multiple Megabits per second.

Service Providers

There are competing common carriers broadcasting signal in most nations of the earth. Some of these Cellular networks and the carrier's service plans are:

North America

- Canada providers
  - List of Canadian mobile phone companies
- United States providers
  - T-mobile
  - AT&T Mobility
  - Verizon Wireless
  - Sprint Nextel Corporation
  - Alltel

Europe

- United Kingdom providers
  - T-mobile
  - Vodafone
  - O2 plc
  - Orange SA
  - 3 (telecommunications)
- Spanish providers:
  - Movistar
  - Vodafone

- Orange
- Yoigo

Asia

- India providers
    - BSNL
    - VSNL
    - Airtel
    - Hutch
    - Reliance India Mobile

Oceania

- Australia providers
    - Telstra
    - Optus
    - 3 Mobile
    - Virgin Mobile

Device Manufacturers

- Danger
- Freewave Technologies
- HTC (includes Qtek and Dopod)
- Hewlett Packard (HP)
- Huawei
- LG Electronics
- Motorola
- Nokia
- Novatel Wireless
- Panasonic
- RIM (BlackBerry)
- Samsung
- Sony Ericsson
- Qualcomm

Technologies

- GPRS (2.5G)
- CDMA
- EDGE
- UMTS (3G)
- GPRS Core Network
- IP Multimedia Subsystem
- HSDPA (3.5G)

Residential Gateway

There are multiple devices that have been described as "residential gateways," each with a quite different function. Each type of device allows the connection of a LAN (used in the home) to a WAN (wide area network). The WAN can be the "Internet" or can merely be a larger LAN of which the home is a part (such as a municipal WAN that provides connectivity to the residences within the municipality).

A D-Link router/modem used as a residential gateway.

The term "residential gateway" was originally used to distinguish the inexpensive networking devices designated for use in the home from similar devices used in corporate LAN environments (which generally offered a greater array of capabilities). In recent years, however, the less expensive "residential gateways" have gained many of the capabilities of corporate gateways and the distinctions are fewer. Many home LANs now are able to provide most of the functions of small corporate LANs.

Therefore the term "residential gateway" is becoming obsolete and merely implies a less expensive, lower capability networking device.

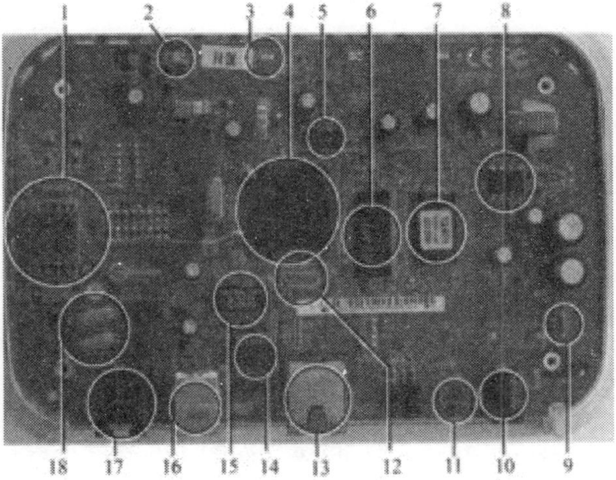

Multiple devices have been described as "residential gateways":

- Cable Modems
- DSL modems
- Routers or wireless routers
- Switch
- VoIP ATA
- Wireless access points
- Or, Any combination of the above

Types

A typical ADSL router.

- A router provides:
- IP address routing
- network address translation (NAT)
- DHCP functions
- firewall functions

- LAN connectivity like a network switch

Most routers are self-contained components, using internally-stored firmware. They are generally OS-independent (i.e. can be used with any operating system).

However, PCs can also provide the same functions as a router. A PC using the Linux OS, for example, is able to provide all the functions of a router (an external router is optional). (In fact some self-contained routers use a small version of Linux within their firmware.)

- Wireless routers perform the same functions as a router, but also allows connectivity for wireless devices with the LAN, or between the wireless router and another wireless router. (The wireless router-wireless router connection can be within the LAN or can be between the LAN and a WAN.)
- A modem (or ADSL modem) provides none of the functions of a router. It merely allows digital Ethernet data traffic to be modulated into analogue information suitable for transmission across telephone lines, cable wires, optical fibers, or wireless radio frequencies. On the receiving end is another modem that re-converts the transmission format back into digital data packets.

This allows network bridging using telephone, cable, optical, and radio connection methods. The modem also provides handshake protocols, so that the devices on each end of the connection are able to recognise each other. However, a modem generally provides few other network functions.

- A USB modem plugs into a single PC and allow connection of that single PC to a WAN. If that PC uses a Linux OS, then that PC can also function as the router for a home LAN.
- An internal modem can be installed on a single PC (e.g. on a PCI card), also allowing that single PC to connect to a WAN. Again, if that PC uses a Linux OS, then that PC can also function as the router for a home LAN.

- A wireless access point can function in a similar fashion to a modem. It can allow a direct connection from a home LAN to a WAN, if a wireless router or access point is present on the WAN as well.

Manufacturers

There are a number of manufacturers of networking devices that have been used as residential gateways:

- 3Com
- Apple Inc. (termed AirPort Base Stations)
- Asus
- AVM_GmbH
- Beetel
- Belkin
- Buffalo Technology
- Billion
- Check Point
- Draytek
- Enterasys Networks
- Huawei
- Lightning MultiCom
- Linksys
- Mikrotik
- Motorola
- NETGEAR
- Pivotal Networking
- Sagem Communications
- Siemens AG
- SMC Networks
- Speedtouch
- Tellabs
- U.S. Robotics

- Verizon
- Zoom Telephonics
- ZyXEL

WIRELESS ACCESS POINT

Introduction

In computer networking, a wireless access point (WAP or AP) is a device that allows wireless communication devices to connect to a wireless network. The WAP usually connects to a wired network, and can relay data between the wireless devices (such as computers or printers) and wired devices on the prior to wireless

Planet WsAP-4000 Wireless Access Point

Linksys WAP54G 802.11g Wireless Access Point

An embedded RouterBoard 112 with U.FL-RSMA pigtail and R52 mini PCI Wi-Fi card widely used by wireless Internet service providers (WISPs) in the Czech Republic.

networks, setting up a computer network in a business, home, or school often required running many cables through walls and ceilings in order to deliver network access to all of the network-enabled devices in the building. With the advent of the Wireless Access Point, network users are now able to add devices that access the network with few or no new cables. Today's WAPs are built to support a standard for sending and receiving data using radio frequencies rather than cabling. Those standards, and the frequencies they use are defined by the IEEE. A current popular IEEE standard for wireless networking is the IEEE 802.11.

Common WAP Applications

A typical corporate use involves attaching several WAPs to a wired network and then providing wireless access to the office LAN. Within the range of the WAPs, the wireless end user has a full network connection with the benefit of mobility. In this instance, the WAP functions as a gateway for clients to access the wired network.

Another wireless topology, a *lily-pad network*, consists of a series of access points spread over a large area, each connected to a different network. This provides hot spots where wireless clients can connect to the Internet without regard for the particular networks to which they have attached for the moment. The concept can become common in large cities, where a combination of coffeehouses, libraries, other public spaces offering wireless access, as well as privately owned open access points, allow clients to stay more or less continuously connected to a network (like hopping from lily pad to lilypad), while moving around.

Home wireless networks, the majority, generally have only one WAP to connect all the computers in a home. Most are wireless routers, meaning converged devices that include a WAP, Ethernet router, and often a switch in the same package. Many also converge a broadband modem. Most owners leave their encryption settings at default, hence neighbours can use them. In places where most homes have their own WAP within range of the neighbours' WAP, it's possible for technically savvy people to turn off their encryption and set up a wireless community network, creating an intra-city communication network without the need of wired networks.

A WAP may also act as the network's arbitrator, negotiating when each nearby client device can transmit. However, the vast majority of currently installed IEEE 802.11 networks do not implement this, using a distributed pseudo-random algorithm instead.

Access Point vs. Ad-Hoc Network

Some people prefer to use an ad-hoc network rather than an Access Point. This is because the stations can exchange data directly in the former. There is no need for a station to send data to the middle-man, i.e., the Access Point, and then have it resent to the destination station. Direct data transfer increases the bandwidth available.

However, it is generally advisable to use Access Points as opposed to Ad-Hoc Networks. This is because they provide a variety of benefits—they increase the range, provide better security, help in saving power, provide quality of service, allow roaming, and so on.

Limitations

One IEEE 802.11 WAP can typically communicate with 30 client systems located within a radius of 100 m. However, the actual range of communication can vary significantly, depending on such variables as indoor or outdoor placement, height above ground, nearby obstructions, other electronic devices that might actively interfere with the signal by broadcasting on the same frequency, type of antenna, the current weather, operating radio frequency, and the power output of devices. Network designers can extend the range of WAPs through the use of repeaters and reflectors, which can bounce or amplify radio signals that ordinarily would go un-received. In experimental conditions, wireless networking has operated over distances of several kilometers.

Most jurisdictions have only a limited number of frequencies legally available for use by wireless networks. Usually, adjacent WAPs will use different frequencies to communicate with their clients in order to avoid interference between the two nearby systems. But wireless devices can "listen" for data traffic on other frequencies, and can rapidly switch from one frequency to another to achieve better reception on a different frequency. However, the limited number of frequencies becomes problematic in crowded downtown areas with tall buildings housing multiple WAPs, when overlap causes interference.

Wireless networking lags behind wired networking in terms of increasing bandwidth and throughput. While (as of 2004) typical wireless devices for the consumer market can reach speeds of 11 Mbit/s (megabits per second) (IEEE 802.11b) or 54 Mbit/s (IEEE 802.11a, IEEE 802.11g), wired hardware of similar cost reaches 1000 Mbit/s (Gigabit Ethernet). One impediment to increasing the speed of wireless communications comes from Wi-Fi's use of a shared communications medium, so a WAP is only able to use somewhat less than half the actual over-the-air rate for data throughput. Thus a typical 54 MBit/s wireless connection actually carries TCP/IP data at 20 to 25 Mbit/s. Users of legacy wired networks expect the faster speeds, and people using wireless connections keenly want to see the wireless networks catch up.

As of 2006 a new standard for wireless, 802.11n is awaiting final certification from IEEE. This new standard operates at speeds up to 540 Mbit/s and at longer distances (~50 m) than 802.11g.

Use of legacy wired networks (especially in consumer applications) is expected to decline sharply as the common 100 Mbit/s speed is surpassed and users no longer need to worry about running wires to attain high bandwidth.

Interference can commonly cause problems with wireless networking reception, as many devices operate using the 2.4 GHz ISM band. A nearby wireless phone or anything with greater transmission power within close proximity can markedly reduce the perceived signal strength of a wireless access point. Microwave ovens are also known to interfere with wireless networks.

Wireless LAN Security

One issue with corporate wireless networks in general, and WLANs in particular, involves the need for security. Many early access points could not discern whether or not a particular user had authorisation to access the network. Although this problem reflects issues that have long troubled many types of wired networks (it has been possible in the past for individuals to plug computers into randomly available Ethernet jacks and get access to a local network), this did not usually pose a significant problem, since many organisations had reasonably good physical security. However, the fact that radio signals bleeds outside of buildings and across property lines makes physical security largely irrelevant to wardrivers. Such corporate issues are covered in wireless security.

Concerns

Anyone within the geographical network range of an open, unencrypted wireless network can sniff on all the traffic, gain unauthorised access to internal network resources as well as to the Internet, possibly sending spam or doing other illegal actions using the owner's IP address, all of which are rare for home routers but may be significant concerns for office networks.

If router security is not activated or if the owner deactivates it for convenience, it creates a free hotspot. Since most 21st century laptop PCs have wireless networking built in (cf. Intel 'Centrino' technology), they don't need a third-party adapter such as a PCMCIA Card or USB dongle. Built in wireless networking might be enabled by default, without the owner realising it, thus broadcasting the laptop's accessibility to any computer nearby.

Modern operating systems such as Linux, Mac OS, or Microsoft Windows as the 'standard' in home PCs make it very easy to set up a PC as a wireless LAN 'basestation' using Internet Connection Sharing, thus allowing all the PCs in the home to access the Internet via the 'base' PC. However, lack of knowledge about the security issues in setting up such systems often means that someone nearby, such as a next-door neighbour, may also use the Internet connection. Such "piggybacking" is typically done without the wireless network owner's knowledge; it may even be without the knowledge of the intruding user if his computer automatically selects a nearby unsecured wireless network to use as an access point.

Conversely, weak as the default encryption of most routers may be, it often defeats a user's attempt to use his own laptop wirelessly at home.

Security Options

There are three principal ways to secure a wireless network.

- For closed networks (like home users and organisations) the most common way is to configure access restrictions in the access points. Those restrictions may include encryption and checks on MAC address.
- For commercial providers, hotspots, and large organisations, the preferred solution is often to have an open and unencrypted, but completely isolated wireless network. The users will at first have no access to the Internet nor to any local network resources. Commercial providers usually forward all web traffic to a captive portal which provides for payment and/or authorisation. Another solution is to require the users to connect securely to a privileged network using VPN.

- Wireless networks are little more secure than wired ones; in many offices intruders can easily visit and hook up their own computer to the wired network without problems, gaining access to the network, and it's also often possible for remote intruders to gain access to the network through backdoors like Back Orifice. One general solution may be end-to-end encryption, with independent authentication on all resources that shouldn't be available to the public.

Access Control at the Access Point level

One of the simplest techniques is to only allow access from known, approved MAC addresses. However, this approach gives no security against sniffing, and client devices can easily spoof MAC addresses, leading to the need for more advanced security measures.

Another very simple technique is to have a secret ESSID (id/ name of the wireless network), though anyone who studies the method will be able to sniff the ESSID.

Today all (or almost all) access points incorporate Wired Equivalent Privacy (WEP) encryption and most wireless routers are sold with WEP turned on. However, security analysts have criticised WEP's inadequacies, and the U.S. FBI has demonstrated the ability to break WEP protection in only three minutes using tools available to the general public (see aircrack).

The Wi-Fi Protected Access (WPA and WPA2) security protocols were later created to address these problems. If a weak password, such as a dictionary word or short character string is used, WPA and WPA2 can be cracked. Using a long enough random password (e.g. 14 random letters) or passphrase (e.g. 5 randomly chosen words) makes pre-shared key WPA virtually uncrackable. The second generation of the WPA security protocol (WPA2) is based on the final IEEE 802.11i amendment to the 802.11 standard and is eligible for FIPS 140-2 compliance. With all those encryption schemes, any client in the network that knows the keys can read all the traffic.

Restricted Access Networks

Solutions include a newer system for authentication, IEEE 802.1x, that promises to enhance security on both wired and wireless networks. Wireless access points that incorporate technologies like these often also have routers built in, thus becoming wireless gateways.

End-to-End Encryption

One can argue that both layer 2 and layer 3 encryption methods are not good enough for protecting valuable data like passwords and personal emails. Those technologies add encryption only to parts of the communication path, still allowing people to spy on the traffic if they have gained access to the wired network somehow. The solution may be encryption and authorisation in the application layer, using technologies like SSL, SSH, GnuPG, PGP and similar.

The disadvantage with the end to end method is, it may fail to cover all traffic. With encryption on the router level or VPN, a single switch encrypts all traffic, even UDP and DNS lookups. With end-to-end encryption on the other hand, each service to be secured must have its encryption "turned on," and often every connection must also be "turned on" separately. For sending emails, every recipient must support the encryption method, and must exchange keys correctly. For Web, not all web sites offer https, and even if they do, the browser sends out IP addresses in clear text.

The most prised resource is often access to Internet. An office LAN owner seeking to restrict such access will face the non trivial enforcement task of having each user authenticate himself for the router.

Open Access Points

Today, there is almost full wireless network coverage in many urban areas—the infrastructure for the wireless community network which some consider to be the future of the internet) is already in place. One could roam around and always be connected to Internet if the nodes were open to the public, but due to security concerns, most nodes are encrypted and the users don't know how to disable encryption. Many people consider it proper etiquette to leave access points open to the public, allowing free access to Internet. Others think the default encryption provides substantial protection at small inconvenience, against dangers of open access that they fear may be substantial even on a home DSL router.

The density of access points can even be a problem—there are a limited number of channels available, and they partly overlap. Each channel can handle multiple networks, but places with many private wireless networks (for example, apartment complexes), the limited number of Wi-Fi radio channels might cause slowness and other problems.

According to the advocates of Open Access Points, it shouldn't involve any significant risks to open up wireless networks for the public:

- The wireless network is after all confined to a small geographical area. A computer connected to the Internet and having improper configurations or other security problems can be exploited by anyone from anywhere in the world, while only clients in a small geographical range can exploit an open wireless access point. Thus the exposure is low with an open wireless access point, and the risks with having an open wireless network are small. However, one should be aware that an open wireless router will give access to the local network, often including access to file shares and printers.
- The only way to keep communication truly secure is to use end-to-end encryption. For example, when accessing an internet bank, one would almost always use strong encryption from the web browser and all the way to the bank—thus it shouldn't be risky to do banking over an unencrypted wireless network. The argument is that anyone can sniff the traffic applies to wired networks too, where system administrators and possible crackers have access to the links and can read the traffic. Also, anyone knowing the

keys for an encrypted wireless network can gain access to the data being transferred over the network.

- If services like file shares, access to printers etc. are available on the local net, it is advisable to have authentication (i.e. by password) for accessing it (one should never assume that the private network is not accessible from the outside). Correctly set up, it should be safe to allow access to the local network to outsiders.
- With the most popular encryption algorithms today, a sniffer will usually be able to compute the network key in a few minutes.
- It is very common to pay a fixed monthly fee for the Internet connection, and not for the traffic—thus extra traffic will not hurt.
- Where Internet connections are plentiful and cheap, freeloaders will seldom be a prominent nuisance.

General Packet Radio Service

General Packet Radio Service (GPRS) is a packet oriented Mobile Data Service available to users of Global System for Mobile Communications (GSM) and IS-136 mobile phones. It provides data rates from 56 up to 114 kbit/s.

GPRS can be used for services such as Wireless Application Protocol (WAP) access, Short Message Service (SMS), Multimedia Messaging Service (MMS), and for Internet communication services such as email and World Wide Web access. GPRS data transfer is typically charged per megabyte of traffic transferred, while data communication via traditional circuit switching is billed per minute of connection time, independent of whether the user actually is using the capacity or is in an idle state. GPRS is a best-effort packet switched service, as opposed to circuit switching, where a certain Quality of Service (QoS) is guaranteed during the connection for non-mobile users.

2G cellular systems combined with GPRS are often described as "2.5G", that is, a technology between the second (2G) and third (3G) generations of mobile telephony. It provides moderate speed data transfer, by using unused Time division multiple access (TDMA) channels in, for example, the GSM system. Originally there was some thought to extend GPRS to cover other standards, but instead those networks are being converted to use the GSM standard, so that GSM is the only kind of network where GPRS is in use. GPRS is integrated into GSM Release 97 and newer releases. It was originally standardised by European Telecommunications Standards Institute (ETSI), but now by the 3rd Generation Partnership Project (3GPP).

Basics

WAP is just a gateway used to access Internet via mobile phone and vice-versa. Usually, GPRS data are billed per kilobyte of information transceived, while circuit-switched data connections are billed per minute. The latter is inefficient because even when no data are being transferred, the bandwidth is unavailable to other potential users.

The multiple access methods used in GSM with GPRS are based on frequency division duplex (FDD) and TDMA. During a session, a user is assigned to one pair of up-link and down-link frequency channels. This is combined with time domain statistical multiplexing, i.e. packet mode communication, which makes it possible for several users to share the same frequency channel. The packets have constant length, corresponding to a GSM time slot. The down-link uses first-come first-served packet scheduling, while the up-link uses a scheme very similar to reservation ALOHA. This means that slotted Aloha (S-ALOHA) is used for reservation inquiries during a contention phase, and then the actual data is transferred using dynamic TDMA with first-come first-served scheduling.

GPRS originally supported (in theory) Internet Protocol (IP) Point-to-Point Protocol (PPP) and X.25 connections. The last has been typically used for applications like wireless payment terminals although it has been removed from the standard. X.25 can still be supported over PPP, or even over IP, but doing this requires either a router to perform encapsulation or intelligence built in to the end-device/terminal e.g. UE(User Equipment). In practice, the mobile built-in browser uses IPv4. In this mode PPP is often not supported by the mobile phone operator, while IPv6 is not yet popular. But if the mobile is used as a modem to the connected computer, PPP is used to tunnel IP to the phone. This allows DHCP to assign an IP Address and then the use of IPv4 since IP addresses used by mobile equipment tend to be dynamic.

Class A

Can be connected to GPRS service and GSM service (voice, SMS), using both at the same time. Such devices are known to be available today.

Class B

Can be connected to GPRS service and GSM service (voice, SMS), but using only one or the other at a given time. During GSM service (voice call or SMS), GPRS service is suspended, and then resumed automatically after the GSM service (voice call or SMS) has concluded. Most GPRS mobile devices are Class B.

Class C

Are connected to either GPRS service or GSM service (voice, SMS). Must be switched manually between one or the other service.

A true Class A device may be required to transmit on two different frequencies at the same time, and thus will need two radios. To get around this expensive requirement, a GPRS mobile may implement the dual transfer mode (DTM) feature. A DTM-capable mobile may use simultaneous voice and packet data, with the network coordinating to ensure that it is not required to transmit on two different frequencies at the same time. Such mobiles are considered pseudo-Class A, sometimes referred to as "simple class A". Some networks are expected to support DTM in 2007.

GPRS is new technology in which speed is a direct function of the number of TDMA time slots assigned, which is the lesser of

(a) what the particular cell supports and (b) the maximum capability of the mobile device expressed as a **GPRS Multislot Class.**

Coding Scheme

Coding scheme	Speed (kbit/s)
CS-1	8.0
CS-2	12.0
CS-3	14.4
CS-4	20.0

Transfer speed depends also on the channel encoding used. The least robust, but fastest, coding scheme (CS-4) is available near a base transceiver station (BTS), while the most robust coding scheme (CS-1) is used when the mobile station (MS) is further away from a BTS.

Using the CS-4 it is possible to achieve a user speed of 20.0 kbit/s per time slot. However, using this scheme the cell coverage is 25% of normal. CS-1 can achieve a user speed of only 8.0 kbit/s per time slot, but has 98% of normal coverage. Newer network equipment can adapt the transfer speed automatically depending on the mobile location.

Like CSD, HSCSD establishes a circuit and is usually billed per minute. For an application such as downloading, HSCSD may be preferred, since circuit-switched data are usually given priority over packet-switched data on a mobile network, and there are relatively few seconds when no data are being transferred.

Technology	Download (kbit/s)	Upload (kbit/s)	Configuration
CSD	9.6	9.6	1+1
HSCSD	28.8	14.4	2+1
HSCSD	43.2	14.4	3+1
GPRS	80.0	20.0 (Class 8 & 10 and CS-4)	4+1
GPRS	60.0	40.0 (Class 10 and CS-4)	3+2

EGPRS (EDGE)	236.8	59.2 (Class 8, 10 and MCS-9)	4+1
EGPRS (EDGE)	177.6	118.4 (Class 10 and MCS-9)	3+2+10

GPRS is packet based. When TCP/IP is used, each phone can have one or more IP addresses allocated. GPRS will store and forward the IP packets to the phone during cell handover (when you move from one cell to another). A radio noise induced pause can be interpreted by TCP as packet loss, and cause a temporary throttling in transmission speed.

Services and Hardware

GPRS upgrades GSM data services providing:

- Multimedia Messaging Service (MMS)
- Push to talk over Cellular PoC / PTT
- Instant Messaging and Presence—Wireless Village
- Internet Applications for Smart Devices through Wireless Application Protocol (WAP)
- Point-to-point (PTP) service: internetworking with the Internet (IP protocols)
- Short Message Service (SMS)
- Future enhancements: flexible to add new functions, such as more capacity, more users, new accesses, new protocols, new radio networks.

USB GPRS Modem

USB GPRS modems use a terminal-like interface USB 2.0 and later, data formats V.42bis, and RFC 1144 and external antennas. Modems can be add in cards (for laptop) or external USB devices which are similar in shape and size to a computer mouse.

GPRS can be used as the bearer of SMS. If SMS over GPRS is used, an SMS transmission speed of about 30 SMS messages per minute may be achieved. This is much faster than using the ordinary SMS over GSM, whose SMS transmission speed is about 6 to 10 SMS messages per minute

The GPRS context 1 is set with +CGDCONT Hayes command.

Availability

In many areas, such as France, telephone operators have priced GPRS relatively cheaply (compared to older GSM data transfer, CSD and HSCSD). Some mobile phone operators offer flat rate access to the Internet, while others charge based on data transferred, usually rounded up to 100 kilobytes.

During the heyday of GPRS in the developed countries, around 2005, typical prices varied from EUR €0,24 per megabyte to over €20 per megabyte. In developing countries, prices vary widely, and change. Some operators gave free access while they decided pricing, for example in Togocel.tg in Togo, West Africa, others were over-priced, such as Tigo of Ghana at one US dollar per megabyte or Indonesia at $3 per megabyte. Mero Mobile of Nepal charges users up to a set amount and then has unlimited Internet access. AirTel of India charges $0.025 per megabyte. As of 2008, data access in Canada is still prohibitively expensive. For example, Fido charges $0.05 per kilobyte, or roughly $50 per megabyte. In Venezuela, Digitel charges about $20 per 100 Mb or $25 for unlimited access.

Pre-Paid SIM Cards allow travelers to buy short term internet access. The mean price in developing nations is US$1 per hour.

The maximum speed of a GPRS connection offered in 2003 was similar to a modem connection in an analog wire telephone network, about 32 to 40 kbit/s, depending on the phone used. Latency is very high; a round-trip ping is typically about 600 to 700 ms and often reaches 1s. GPRS is typically prioritised lower than speech, and thus the quality of connection varies greatly.

In order to set up a GPRS connection for a wireless modem, a user must specify an access point name (APN), optionally a user name and password, and very rarely an IP address, all provided by the network operator.

Devices with latency/RTT improvements (via e.g. the extended UL TBF mode feature) are generally available. Also, network upgrades of features are available with certain operators. With these enhancements the active round-trip time can be reduced, resulting in significant increase in application-level throughput speeds.

Code Division Multiple Access

Code division multiple access (CDMA) is a channel access method utilised by various radio communication technologies. It should not be confused with the mobile phone standards called cdmaOne and CDMA2000 (which are often referred to as simply "CDMA"), that use CDMA as their underlying channel access methods.

One of the basic concepts in data communication is the idea of allowing several transmitters to send information simultaneously over a single communication channel. This allows several users to share a bandwidth of frequencies. This concept is called multiplexing. CDMA employs spread-spectrum technology and a special coding scheme (where each transmitter is assigned a code) to allow multiple users to be multiplexed over the same physical channel. By contrast, time division multiple access (**TDMA**) divides access by time, while frequency-division multiple access (**FDMA**) divides it by frequency. CDMA is a form of "spread-spectrum" signaling, since the modulated coded signal has a much higher data bandwidth than the data being communicated.

An analogy to the problem of multiple access is a room (channel) in which people wish to communicate with each other. To avoid confusion, people could take turns speaking (time division), speak at different pitches (frequency division), or speak in different directions (spatial division). In CDMA, they would speak different languages. People speaking the same language can understand each other, but not other people. Similarly, in radio CDMA, each group of users is given a shared code. Many codes occupy the same channel, but only users associated with a particular code can understand each other.

Uses

- One of the early applications for code division multiplexing—predating, and distinct from cdmaOne—is in GPS.
- The Qualcomm standard IS-95, marketed as cdmaOne.
- The Qualcomm standard IS-2000, known as CDMA2000. This standard is used by several mobile phone companies, including the Globalstar satellite phone network.
- CDMA has been used in the OmniTRACS satellite system for transportation logistics.

Technical Details

CDMA is a spread spectrum multiple access technique. In CDMA a locally generated code runs at a much higher rate than the data to be transmitted. Data for transmission is simply logically XOR (exclusive OR) added with the faster code. The figure shows how spread spectrum signal is generated. The data signal with pulse duration of Tb is XOR added with the code signal with pulse duration of Tc. (Note: bandwidth is proportional to 1/T where T = bit time) Therefore, the bandwidth of the data signal is 1/Tb and the bandwidth of the spread spectrum signal is 1/Tc. Since Tc is much smaller than Tb, the bandwidth of the spread spectrum signal is much larger than the bandwidth of the original signal.

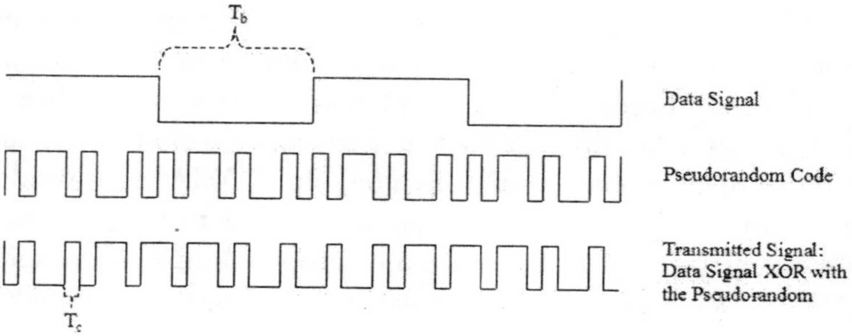

Each user in a CDMA system uses a different code to modulate their signal. Choosing the codes used to modulate the signal is very important in the performance of CDMA systems. The best performance will occur when there is good separation between the signal of a desired user and the signals of other users. The separation of the signals is made by correlating the received signal with the locally generated code of the desired user. If the signal matches the desired user's code then the correlation function will be high and the system can extract that signal. If the desired user's code has nothing in common with the signal the correlation should be as close to zero as possible (thus eliminating the signal); this is referred to as cross correlation. If the code is correlated with the signal at any time offset other than zero, the correlation should be as close to zero as possible. This is referred to as auto-correlation and is used to reject multi-path interference.

In general, CDMA belongs to two basic categories: synchronous (orthogonal codes) and asynchronous (pseudorandom codes).

Code Division Multiplexing (*Synchronous* CDMA)

Synchronous CDMA exploits mathematical properties of orthogonality between vectors representing the data strings. For example, binary string "1011" is represented by the vector (1, 0, 1, 1). Vectors can be multiplied by taking their dot product, by summing the products of their respective components. If the dot product is zero, the two vectors are said to be *orthogonal* to each other. (Note: If u=(a,b) and v=(c,d), the dot product u.v = a*c + b*d) Some properties of the dot product help to understand how WCDMA works. If vectors *a* and *b* are orthogonal, then

$$\mathbf{a} \cdot (\mathbf{a} + \mathbf{b}) = ||\mathbf{a}||^2 \quad \text{since} \quad \mathbf{a} \cdot \mathbf{a} + \mathbf{a} \cdot \mathbf{b} = ||a||^2 + 0.$$

$$\mathbf{a} \cdot (-\mathbf{a} + \mathbf{b}) = -||\mathbf{a}||^2 \quad \text{since} \quad -\mathbf{a} \cdot \mathbf{a} + \mathbf{a} \cdot \mathbf{b} = -||a||^2 + 0.$$

$$\mathbf{b} \cdot (\mathbf{a} + \mathbf{b}) = ||\mathbf{b}||^2 \quad \text{since} \quad \mathbf{b} \cdot \mathbf{a} + \mathbf{b} \cdot \mathbf{b} = 0 + ||b||^2.$$

Each user in synchronous CDMA uses an orthogonal codes to modulate their signal. An example of four mutually orthogonal digital signals is shown in the figure. Orthogonal codes have a cross-correlation equal to zero; in other words, they do not interfere with each other. In the case of IS-95 64 bit Walsh codes are used to encode the signal to separate different users. Since each of the 64 Walsh codes are orthogonal to one another, the signals are channelised into 64 orthogonal signals. The following example demonstrates how each users signal can be encoded and decoded.

Example

Start with a set of vectors that are mutually orthogonal. (Although mutual orthogonality is the only condition, these vectors are usually constructed for ease of decoding, for example columns or rows from Walsh matrices.) An example of orthogonal functions is shown in the picture on the left. These vectors will be assigned to individual users and are called the "code", "chipping code" or "chip code". In the interest of brevity, the rest of this example uses codes (v) with only 2 digits.

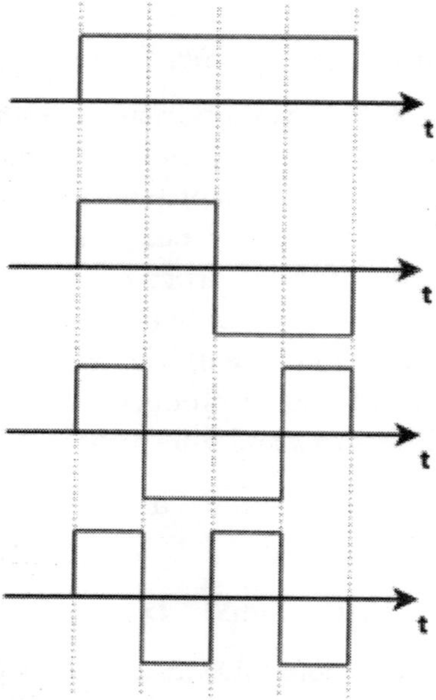

An example of four mutually orthogonal digital signals.

Each user is associated with a different code, say **v**. If the data to be transmitted is a digital zero, then the actual bits transmitted will be –**v**, and if the data to be transmitted is a digital one, then the actual bits transmitted will be **v**. For example, if **v**=(1,–1), and the data that the user wishes to transmit is (1, 0, 1, 1) this would correspond to (**v**, –**v**, **v**, **v**) which is then constructed in binary as ((1,–1),(–1,1),(1,–1),(1,–1)). For the purposes of this article, we call this constructed vector the *transmitted vector.*

Each sender has a different, unique vector **v** chosen from that set, but the construction method of the transmitted vector is identical.

Now, due to physical properties of interference, if two signals at a point are in phase, they add to give twice the amplitude of each signal, but if they are out of phase, they "subtract" and give a signal that is the difference of the amplitudes. Digitally, this behaviour can be modelled by the addition of the transmission vectors, component by component.

If sender0 has code (1,–1) and data (1,0,1,1), and sender1 has code (1,1) and data (0,0,1,1), and both senders transmit simultaneously, then this table describes the coding steps:

Step	Encode sender0	Encode sender1
0	vector0=(1,–1), data0=(1,0,1,1)=(1,–1,1,1)	vector1=(1,1), data1=(0,0,1,1)=(–1,–1,1,1)
1	encode0=vector0.data0	encode1=vector1.data1
2	encode0=(1,–1).(1,–1,1,1)	encode1=(1,1).(–1,–1,1,1)
3	encode0=((1,–1),(–1,1),(1,–1),(1,–1))	encode1=((–1,–1),(–1,–1),(1,1),(1,1))
4	signal0=(1,–1,–1,1,1,–1,1,–1)	signal1=(–1,–1,–1,–1,1,1,1,1)

Because signal0 and signal1 are transmitted at the same time into the air, they add to produce the raw signal:

(1,–1,–1,1,1,–1,1,–1) + (–1,–1,–1,–1,1,1,1,1) = (0,–2,–2,0,2,0,2,0)

This raw signal is called an interference pattern. The receiver then extracts an intelligible signal for any known sender by combining the sender's code with the interference pattern, the receiver combines it with the codes of the senders. The following table explains how this works and shows that the signals do not interfer with one another:

Step	Decode sender0	Decode sender1
0	vector0=(1,–1), pattern=(0,–2,–2,0,2,0,2,0)	vector1=(1,1), pattern=(0,–2,–2,0,2,0,2,0)
1	decode0=pattern.vector0	decode1=pattern.vector1
2	decode0=((0,–2),(–2,0),(2,0),(2,0)).(1,–1)	decode1=((0,–2),(–2,0),(2,0),(2,0)).(1,1)
3	decode0=((0+2),(–2+0),(2+0),(2+0))	decode1=((0–2),(–2+0),(2+0),(2+0))
4	data0=(2,–2,2,2)=(1,0,1,1)	data1=(–2,–2,2,2)=(0,0,1,1)

Further, after decoding, all values greater than 0 are interpreted as 1 while all values less than zero are interpreted as 0. For example, after decoding, data0 is (2,–2,2,2), but the receiver interprets this as (1,0,1,1).

We can also consider what would happen if a receiver tries to decode a signal when the user has not sent any information. Assume signal0=(1,-1,-1,1,1,-1,1,-1) is transmitted alone. The following table shows the decode at the receiver:

Step	Decode sender0	Decode sender1
0	vector0=(1,–1), pattern=(1,-1,-1,1,1,-1,1,-1)	vector1=(1,1), pattern=(1,-1,-1,1,1,-1,1,-1)
1	decode0=pattern.vector0	decode1=pattern.vector1
2	decode0=((1,–1),(–1,1),(1,-1),(1,-1)).(1,–1)	decode1=((1,–1),(–1,1),(1,-1),(1,-1)).(1,1)
3	decode0=((1+1),(–1-1),(1+1),(1+1))	decode1=((1–1),(–1+1),(1-1),(1-1))
4	data0=(2,–2,2,2)=(1,0,1,1)	data1=(0,0,0,0)

When the receiver attempts to decode the signal using sender1's code, the data is all zeros, therefore the cross correlation is equal to zero and it is clear that sender1 did not transmit any data.

Asynchronous CDMA

The previous example of orthogonal Walsh sequences describes how 2 users can be multiplexed together in a synchronous system, a technique that is commonly referred to as Code Division Multiplexing (CDM). The set of 4 Walsh sequences shown in the figure will afford up to 4 users, and in general, an NxN Walsh matrix can be used to multiplex N users. Multiplexing requires all of the users to be coordinated so that each transmits their assigned sequence **v** (or the complement, -**v**) starting at exactly the same time. Thus, this technique finds use in base-to-mobile links, where all of the transmissions originate from the same transmitter and can be perfectly coordinated.

On the other hand, the mobile-to-base links cannot be precisely coordinated, particularly due to the mobility of the handsets, and require a somewhat different approach. Since it is not mathematically possible to create signature sequences that are orthogonal for arbitrarily random starting points, unique "pseudo-random" or "pseudo-noise" (PN) sequences are used in *Asynchronous* CDMA systems. A PN code is a binary sequence that appears random but can be reproduced in a deterministic manner by intended receivers. These PN codes are used to encode and decode a users signal in Asynchronous CDMA in the same manner as the orthogonal codes in synchrous CDMA (shown in the example above). These PN sequences are statistically uncorrelated, and the sum of a large number of PN sequences results in Multiple Access Interference (MAI) that is approximated by a Gaussian noise process (following the "central limit theorem" in statistics). If all of the users are received with the same power level, then the variance (e.g., the noise power) of the MAI increases in direct proportion to the number of users. In other words, unlike synchronous CDMA, the signals of other users will appear as noise to the signal of interest and interfere slightly with the desired signal in proportion to number of users.

All forms of CDMA use spread spectrum process gain to allow receivers to partially discriminate against unwanted signals. Signals encoded with the specified PN sequence (code) are received, while signals with different codes (or the same code but a different timing offset) appear as wideband noise reduced by the process gain.

Since each user generates MAI, controlling the signal strength is an important issue with CDMA transmitters. A CDM (Synchronous CDMA), TDMA or FDMA receiver can in theory completely reject arbitrarily strong signals using different codes, time slots or frequency channels due to the orthogonality of these systems. This is not true for Asynchronous CDMA; rejection of unwanted signals is only partial. If any or all of the unwanted signals are much stronger than the desired signal, they will overwhelm it. This leads to a general requirement in any Asynchronous CDMA system to approximately match the various signal power levels as seen at the receiver. In CDMA cellular, the base station uses a fast closed-loop power control scheme to tightly control each mobile's transmit power. See Near-far problem for further information on this problem.

Advantages of Asynchronous CDMA over other Techniques

Asynchronous CDMA's main advantage over CDM (*Synchronous* CDMA), TDMA and FDMA is that it can use the spectrum more efficiently in mobile telephony applications. (*In theory, CDMA, TDMA and FDMA have exactly the same spectral efficiency but practically, each has its own challenges—power control in the case of CDMA, timing in the case of TDMA, and frequency generation/filtering in the case of FDMA.*) TDMA systems must carefully synchronise the transmission times of all the users to ensure that they are received in the correct timeslot and do not cause interference. Since this cannot be perfectly controlled in a mobile environment, each timeslot must have a guard-time, which reduces the probability that users will interfere, but decreases the spectral efficiency. Similarly, FDMA systems must use a guard-band between adjacent channels, due to the random doppler shift of the signal spectrum which occurs due to the user's mobility. The guard-bands will reduce the probability that adjacent channels will interfere, but decrease the utilisation of the spectrum.

Most importantly, Asynchronous CDMA offers a key advantage in the flexible allocation of resources. There are a fixed number of orthogonal codes, timeslots or frequency bands that can be allocated for CDM, TDMA and FDMA systems, which remain underutilised due to the bursty nature of telephony and packetised data transmissions. There is no strict limit to the number of users that can be supported in an *Asynchronous* CDMA system, only a practical limit governed by the desired bit error probability, since the SIR (Signal to Interference Ratio) varies inversely with the number of users. In a bursty traffic environment like mobile telephony, the advantage afforded by Asynchronous CDMA is that the performance (bit error rate) is allowed to fluctuate randomly, with an average value determined by the number of users times the percentage of utilisation. Suppose there are 2N users that only talk half of the time, then 2N users can be accommodated with the same *average* bit error probability as N users that talk all of the time. The key difference here is that the bit error probability for N users talking all of the time is constant, whereas it is a *random* quantity (with the same mean) for 2N users talking half of the time.

In other words, Asynchronous CDMA is ideally suited to a mobile network where large numbers of transmitters each generate a relatively small amount of traffic at irregular intervals. CDM (*Synchronous* CDMA), TDMA and FDMA systems cannot recover the underutilised resources inherent to bursty traffic due to the fixed number of orthogonal codes, time slots or frequency channels that can be assigned to individual transmitters. For instance, if there are N time slots in a TDMA system and 2N users that talk half of the time, then half of the time there will be more than N users needing to use more than N timeslots. Furthermore, it would require significant overhead to continually allocate and deallocate the orthogonal code, time-slot or frequency channel resources. By comparison, Asynchronous CDMA transmitters simply send when they have something to say, and go off the air when they don't, keeping the same PN signature sequence as long as they are connected to the system.

Spread Spectrum Characteristics of CDMA

Most modulation schemes try to minimise the bandwidth of this signal since bandwidth is a limited resource. However, spread spectrum techniques use a transmission bandwidth that is several orders of magnitude greater then the minimum required signal bandwidth. One of the initial reasons for doing this was military applications including guidance and communication systems. These systems were designed using spread spectrum because of its security and resistance to jamming. Asynchronous CDMA has some level of privacy built in because the signal is spread using a pseudorandom code; this code makes the spread spectrum signals appear random or have noise-like properties. A receiver cannot demodulate this transmission without knowledge of the pseudorandom sequence used to encode the data. CDMA is also resistant to jamming. A jamming signal only has a finite amount of power available to jam the signal. The jammer can either spread its energy over the entire bandwidth of the signal or jam only part of the entire signal.

CDMA can also effectively reject narrowband interference. Since narrowband interference affects only a small portion of the spread spectrum signal, it can easily be removed through notch filtering without much loss of information. Convolution encoding and interleaving can be used to assist in recovering this lost data. CDMA signals are also resistant to multipath fading. Since the spread spectrum signal occupies a large bandwidth only a small portion of this will undergo fading due to multipath at any given time. Like the narrowband interference this will result in only a small loss of data and can be overcome.

Another reason CDMA is resistant to multipath interference is because the delayed versions of the transmitted pseudorandom codes will have poor correlation with the original pseudorandom code, and will thus appear as another user, which is ignored at the receiver. In other words, as long as the multipath channel induces at least one chip of delay, the multipath signals will arrive at the receiver such that they are shifted in time by at least one chip from the intended signal. The correlation properties of the pseudorandom codes are such that this slight delay causes the multipath to appear uncorrelated with they intended signal, and it is thus ignored. However, spread spectrum signals can also exploit the multipath delay components to improve the performance of the system by using a Rake receiver which anticipates multipath propagation delays of the transmitted spread spectrum signal and combines the information obtained from several resolvable multipath components to produce a stronger version of the signal.

Frequency reuse is the ability to reuse the same radio channel frequency at other cell sites within a cellular system. In the FDMA and TDMA systems frequency planning is an important consideration. The frequencies used in different cells need to be planned carefully in order to ensure that the signals from different cells do not interfere with each other. In a CDMA system the same frequency can be used in every cell because channelisation is done using the pseudorandom codes. Reusing the same frequency in every cell eliminates the need for frequency planning in a CDMA system; however, planning of the different pseudorandom sequences must be done to ensure that the received signal from one cell does not correlate with the signal from a nearby cell.

Since adjacent cells use the same frequencies, CDMA systems have the ability to perform soft handoffs. Soft handoffs allow the mobile telephone to communicate simultaneously with two or more cells. The best signal quality is selected until the handoff is complete. This is different than hard handoffs utilised in other cellular systems. In a hard handoff situation, as the mobile telephone approaches a handoff, signal strength may vary abruptly. In contrast, CDMA systems use the soft handoff, which is undetectable and provides a more reliable and higher quality signal.

Cellular Router

Cellular routers (sometimes known as 3G Routers) are routers that provide shared Internet access by incorporating a cellular data modem as WAN interfaces (generally, Ethernet and WiFi).

They can be deployed as a primary WAN link to a location where wired connections are not cost-effective, and can also be used as a secondary or business continuity plan should the primary cabled link fail. Cellular routers range from simple SOHO network oriented devices through rugged industrial units with advanced features.

Types

There are two types:

- Compact : the cellular modem and the router are the same device.
- Modular: one can connect the cellular modem to the router.

Cellular Router Makers

DOVADO has introduced a low-cost router called the USB Mobile Broadband Router (UMR), specifically designed to host 3G USB modems from suppliers such as Huawei, Option and Novatel. The UMR offers WLAN and Ethernet connectivity within the home/office and DOVADO offers free firmware upgrades to support the latest USB and Express card modems.

CalAmp Corp. manufactures the Dataradio CiPHR Cellular Router that works with 3G cellular backhaul technologies such as CDMA EV-DO Rev. A or GSM HSDPA, backwards compatible to 2G cellular technologies like 1xRTT or GPRS / EDGE. Designed for public safety use, the unit offers extended temperature range, GPS tracking and I/O capabilities in a ruggedised enclosure.

CradlePoint Technology manufactures cellular routers that turn cellular data connections into Wi-Fi and Ethernet. CradlePoint supports of devices that can connect with 1xRTT, EV-DO, GPRS EDGE and HSPA connectivity as offered by carriers such as Sprint

AT&T and Verizon Wireless. Known for being innovative, CradlePoint routers showcase a number of unique features such as an integrated battery for true mobility and the first known ExpressCard 34 connection for a router. CradlePoint routers feature the trademarked "WiPipe" technology that streamlines and improves the user experience by simplifying connections and enhancing security.

NexAira Inc manufactures the NexConnect Cellular Router that works with 3G backhaul technologies such as CDMA or GSM and a traditional wired backhaul such as a DSL or Cable. Capable of handling continuous computing, allowing multiple users to share a Wi-Fi Hot Spot, supports VPN pass through, VOIP and media content storage.

Digi International manufactures a variety of 2.5G and 3G routers that can connect to electronics using a variety of communication protocols, including Wi-Fi, Ethernet, USB, ZigBee and serial devices.

Proxicast has been manufacturing the LAN-Cell family of "enterprise-grade" cellular routers since 2003. The LAN-Cell integrates a cellular modem, Ethernet switch, Wi-Fi access point, wired Ethernet WAN, firewall, full VPN end-point, and military grade encryption. The LAN-Cell has won several cdmA-List awards and their web site indicates many large customer deployments worldwide.

Nexus iSR manufactures the Nexus Hawk a cellular router with built in VPN, firewall, advanced routing functions, optional built in GPS, and optional built in Wi-Fi 802.11 a/b/g. In addition to ExpressCard 34 mm and PCMCIA cellular air cards, this router accepts PCMCIA air cards supporting 700 MHz public safety network in the United States National Capital Region (NCR). The Nexus Hawk has 2 PCMCIA card bus slots to support two simultaneous air cards supported with static routes and auto network failover and fail back.

Junxion is a manufacturer of a Wi-Fi router that allows a user to insert a cellular data card for an Internet connection. One of the original cellular router makers, Junxion has been around since 2004. Their website claims over 1000 customers.

WAAV Manufacturer of AirBox line of routers. WAAV, Inc. makes the AirBox X2 that has 2 cellular connections for additional bandwidth. One of the original cellular router manufacturers, WAAV has been around since 2004. Their website claims many prestigious customers.

Kyocera manufactures the KR1 cellular router. The entry level priced KR1 is very popular. It accepts a slide in cellular connection card. The Kyocera KR1 can be found through many online retailers.

Linksys manufactures the WRT54G3G cellular router. It accepts a slide in PCMCIA cellular connection card, a WAN RJ45 port, 4 client RJ45 ports . The Linksys WRT54G3G firmware is based on popular WRT54G/GL design supporting GPL code available on line from Linksys. Open-WRT port is available with open PCMCIA support .

Ericsson manufactures cellular router family W2x. All models have embedded RF HW. Models are W20e(Europe), W20a(America), W21 (worldwide capable), W25 (added Voip and Ipfax). The router software is based on Linux.

Improving data rates

Although advertised at 3.6 Mbit/s or even 7.2 Mbit/s download speeds, cellular routers often suffer from low data rates due to bad reception especially in fringe areas of network coverage and densely populated areas where base station masts are obstructed by buildings, trees etc. Signal strength can be improved by connecting external antennas or amplifiers to the Cellular router or Mobile USB modem.

Universal Serial Bus

Universal Serial Bus (USB) is a serial bus standard to interface devices. USB was designed to allow many peripherals to be connected using a single standardised interface socket and to improve the plug-and-play capabilities by allowing devices to be connected and disconnected without rebooting the computer (hot swapping). Other convenient features include providing power to low-consumption devices without the need for an external power supply and allowing many devices to be used without requiring manufacturer specific, individual device drivers to be installed.

USB *Universal Serial Bus*	
Original USB Logo	
Year created:	January 1996
Width:	1 bit
Number of devices:	127 per host controller
Capacity	12 or 480 Mbit/s (1.5 to 60 MByte/s)
Style:	Serial
Hotplugging?	Yes
External?	Yes

USB is intended to help retire all legacy varieties of serial and parallel ports. USB can connect computer peripherals such as computer mouse, keyboards, PDAs, gamepads and joysticks, scanners, digital cameras, printers, personal media players, and flash drives. For many of those devices USB has become the standard connection method. USB was originally designed for personal computers, but it has become commonplace on other devices such as PDAs and video game consoles. As of 2008, there are about 2 billion USB devices in the world.

The design of USB is standardised by the USB Implementers Forum (USB-IF), an industry standards body incorporating leading companies from the computer and electronics industries. Notable members have included Agere (now merged with LSI Corporation), Apple Inc., Hewlett-Packard, Intel, NEC, and Microsoft.

A USB Series "A" plug, the most common USB plug

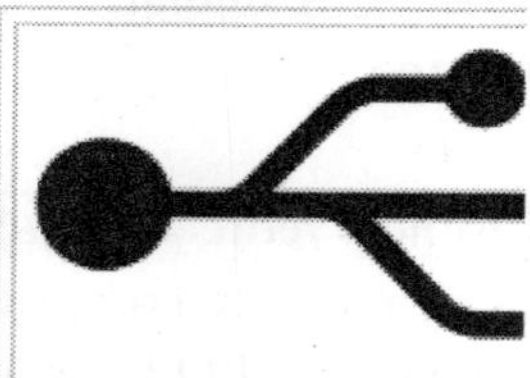

The USB "trident" Icon

The USB 1.0 specification was introduced in November 1995. USB was promoted by Intel (UHCI and open software stack), Microsoft (Windows software stack), Philips (Hub, USB-Audio), and US Robotics. Originally USB was intended to replace the multitude of connectors at the back of PCs, as well as to simplify software configuration of communication devices.

The original Apple "Bondi blue" iMac G3, introduced 6 May 1998, was the first computer to offer USB ports as standard, including the connector for its new keyboard and mouse. USB 1.1 came out in September 1998 to help rectify the adoption problems that occurred with earlier iterations of USB.

As of 2008, the USB specification is at version 2.0 (with revisions). Hewlett-Packard, Intel, Lucent (now Alcatel-Lucent), Microsoft, NEC, and Philips jointly led the initiative to develop a higher data transfer rate than the 1.1 specification. The USB 2.0 specification was released in April 2000 and was standardised by the USB-IF at the end of 2001. Equipment conforming with any version of the standard will also work with devices designed to any previous specification (known as backward compatibility).

Smaller USB plugs and receptacles for use in handheld and mobile devices, called **Mini-B**, were added to USB specification in the first engineering change notice. A new variant of smaller USB plugs and receptacles, Micro-USB, was announced by the USB Implementers Forum on January 4, 2007. Identifying USB Type A and B Plugs.

Human-interface Devices (HIDs)

Mice and keyboards are frequently fitted with USB connectors, but because most PC motherboards still retain PS/2 connectors for the keyboard and mouse as of 2007, they are often supplied with a small USB-to-PS/2 adaptor, allowing usage with either USB or PS/2 interface. There is no logic inside these adaptors: they make use of the fact that such HID interfaces are equipped with controllers that are capable of serving both the USB and the PS/2 protocol, and automatically detect which type of port they are plugged into. Joysticks, keypads, tablets and other human-interface devices are also progressively migrating from MIDI, PC game port, and PS/2 connectors to USB.

Apple Macintosh computers have been using USB exclusively for all external wired mice and keyboards since January 1999 (Powerbooks used ADB keyboards until 2005). The original iMac raised public awareness of USB considerably in August 1998, as it discarded legacy ports to use only USB. PCs had USB ports prior to the iMac's introduction, but they were included with a full complement of traditional ports which limited USB's adoption. The iMac's influence can be seen in the number of USB peripherals with matching translucent, coloured plastic enclosures that were available in the late '90s and early '00s.

USB Connector Properties

The connectors specified by the USB committee were designed to support a number of USB's underlying goals, and to reflect lessons learned from the varied menagerie of connectors then in service.

Series "A" plug and receptacle.

Usability

- It is difficult to incorrectly attach a USB connector. Connectors cannot be plugged-in upside down, and it is clear from the appearance and kinesthetic sensation of making a connection when the plug and socket are correctly mated. However, it is not obvious at a glance to the inexperienced user (or to a user without sight of the installation) which way around the connector goes, so it is often necessary to try both ways. More often than not, however, the side of the connector with the "trident" logo is the top.
- Only a moderate insertion/removal force is needed (by specification). USB cables and small USB devices are held in place by the gripping force from the receptacle (without the need for the screws, clips, or thumbturns that other connectors require). The force needed to make or break a connection is modest, allowing connections to be made in awkward circumstances or by those with motor disabilities.
- The connectors enforce the directed topology of a USB network. USB does not support cyclical networks, so the

connectors from incompatible USB devices are themselves incompatible. Unlike other communications systems (e.g. RJ-45 cabling) gender-changers are almost never used, making it difficult to create a cyclic USB network.

Types of USB Connector

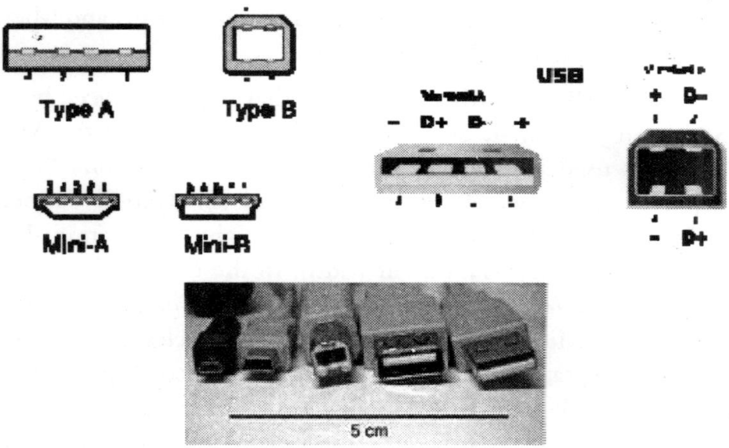

USB Connectors

Different types of USB connectors from left to right 8-pin mystery plug

Mini-B plug

B-type plug

A-type receptacle

A-type plug

Pin configuration of the USB connectors Standard A/B, viewed from face of plug.

There are several types of USB connectors, and some have been added as the specification has progressed. The original USB specification detailed Standard-A and Standard-B plugs and receptacles. The first engineering change notice to the USB 2.0 specification added Mini-B plugs and receptacles. The data slots in the A—Plug are actually farther in the plug than the outside power wires to prevent data errors by powering the device first, then transferring data.

The Mini-B, Micro-A, Micro-B , and Micro-AB connectors are used for smaller devices such as PDAs, mobile phones or digital cameras. The Standard-A plug is approximately 4 by 12 mm, the Standard-B approximately 7 by 8 mm, and the Micro-A and Micro-B plugs approximately 2 by 7 mm.

Micro-USB is a further connector, that was announced by the USB-IF on January 4, 2007. It is intended to replace the Mini-USB plugs used in many new smartphones and Personal digital assistants. This Micro-USB plug is rated for 10,000 connect-disconnect cycles. It is about half the height of the mini-USB connector, but features a similar width. In the *Universal Serial Bus Micro-USB Cables and Connectors Specification*, details have been laid down for Micro-A plugs, Micro-AB receptacles, and Micro-B plugs and receptacles, along with a Standard-A receptacle to Micro-A plug adapter. The carrier led group OMTP have recently endorsed micro-USB as the standard connector for data and power on mobile devices.

USB Cables

The maximum length of a standard USB cable is 5.0 meters (16.4 ft). The primary reason for this limit is the maximum allowed round-trip delay of about 1500 ns. If a USB device does not answer to host commands within the allowed time, the host considers the command to be lost. When USB device response time, delays from using the maximum number of hubs and delays from cables connecting the hubs, host and device are summed, the maximum delay caused by a single cable turns out to be 26 ns. The USB 2.0 specification states that the cable delay must be less than 5.2 ns per meter, which means that maximum length USB cable is 5 meters long. However, this is also very close to the maximum possible length when using a standard copper cable.

Pin	Name	Cable colour	Description
1	VCC	Red	+5V
2	D–	White	Data –
3	D+	Green	Data +
4	GND	Black	Ground

Miniplug/Microplug

Pin	Name	Colour	Description
1	VCC	Red	+5 V
2	D-	White	Data -
3	D+	Green	Data +
4	ID	none	Permits distinction of Micro-A- and Micro-B Plug Type A: connected to Ground Type B: not connected
5	GND	Black	Signal Ground

The data cables are a twisted pair to reduce noise and crosstalk.

Maximum Useful Signalling Distance

Although a single cable is limited to 5 meters, the USB specification permits up to five USB hubs in a long chain of cables and hubs. Consequently the maximum possible signalling distance is 30 meters, using six 5-meter cables and five hubs. In actual use, the last hub is a more convenient endpoint since some USB devices include built-in cables intended to directly connect to a hub, setting the maximum useful signalling distance at 25 meters.

Because USB is able to provide power for additional devices connected to the bus, a special type of USB extender cable was created which consists of a miniature one-port USB hub molded into one end of a 5 meter cable. These mini-hubs are fully self-contained within the cable, requiring no separate bulky hub device, and are as simple to use as plugging cables together, with each hub drawing power through all the previous single-port hubs in the chain. The bus power is limited however, so the most practical application is to use four single-port hub extender cables, one plain 5 meter cable, and then a powered multiport hub at the very end to support multiple additional USB devices.

Power

The USB specification provides a 5 V supply on a single wire from which connected USB devices may draw power. The specification provides for no more than 5.25 V and no less than 4.75 V (5 V±5%) between the positive and negative bus power lines. Initially, a device is only allowed to draw 100 mA. It may request more current from the upstream device in units of 2 mA up to a maximum of 500 mA.

If a bus-powered hub is used, the devices downstream may only use a total of four units — 400 mA — of current. This limits compliant bus-powered hubs to 4 ports. The host operating system typically keeps track of the power requirements of the USB network and may warn the computer's operator when a given segment requires more power than is available.

On-The-Go and *Battery Charging Specification* both add new powering modes to the USB specification. The latter specification allows USB devices to draw up to 1.5 A from hubs and hosts that follow the Battery Charging Specification.

As of June 14, 2007, all new mobile phones applying for a license in China are required to use the USB port as a power port.

In September, 2007 the Open Mobile Terminal Platform—a forum dominated by mobile network operators but including manufacturers such as Nokia, Samsung, Motorola, Sony Ericsson and LG—announced that its members had agreed on micro-USB as the future common connector for mobile devices.

Version History

Prereleases

Hi-Speed USB Logo

USB OTG Logo

- **USB 0.7**: Released in November 1994.
- **USB 0.8**: Released in December 1994.
- **USB 0.9**: Released in April 1995.
- **USB 0.99**: Released in August 1995.
- **USB 1.0 Release Candidate**: Released in November 1995.

USB 1.0

- **USB 1.0**: Released in January 1996. Specified data rates of **1.5 Mbit/s** (***Low-Speed***) and **12 Mbit/s** (***Full-Speed***). Did not anticipate or pass-through monitors. Few such devices actually made it to market.
- **USB 1.1**: Released in September 1998. Fixed problems identified in 1.0, mostly relating to hubs. Earliest revision to be widely adopted.

USB 2.0

- **USB 2.0**: Released in April 2000. Added higher maximum speed of **480 Mbit/s** (now called ***Hi-Speed***). Further modifications to the USB specification have been done via Engineering Change Notices (ECN). The most important of these ECNs are included into the USB 2.0 specification package available from USB.org:
    - o **Mini-B Connector ECN**: Released in October 2000. Specifications for Mini-B plug and receptacle. These should not be confused with Micro-B plug and receptacle.

- **Errata as of December 2000**: Released in December 2000.
- **Pull-up/Pull-down Resistors ECN**: Released in May 2002.
- **Errata as of May 2002**: Released in May 2002.
- **Interface Associations ECN**: Released in May 2003. New standard descriptor was added that allows multiple interfaces to be associated with a single device function.
- **Rounded Chamfer ECN**: Released in October 2003. A recommended, compatible change to Mini-B plugs that results in longer lasting connectors.
- **Unicode ECN**: Released in February 2005. This ECN specifies that strings are encoded using UTF-16LE. USB 2.0 did specify that Unicode is to be used but it did not specify the encoding.
- **Inter-Chip USB Supplement**: Released in March 2006.
- **On-The-Go Supplement 1.3**: Released in December 2006. USB On-The-Go makes it possible for two USB devices to communicate with each other without requiring a separate USB host. In practice, one of the USB devices acts as a host for the other device.
- **Battery Charging Specification 1.0**: Released in March 2007. Adds support for dedicated chargers (power supplies with USB connectors), host chargers (USB hosts that can act as chargers) and the No Dead Battery provision which allows devices to temporarily draw 100 mA current after they have been attached. If a USB device is connected to dedicated charger or host charger, maximum current drawn by the device may be as high as 1.5 A. (Note that this document is not distributed with USB 2.0 specification package.)
- **Micro-USB Cables and Connectors Specification 1.01** Released in April 2007.
- **Link Power Management Addendum ECN**: Released in July 2007. This adds a new power state between enabled

and suspended states. Device in this state is not required to reduce its power consumption. However, switching between enabled and sleep states is much faster than switching between enabled and suspended states, which allows devices to sleep while idle.

- o **High-Speed Inter-Chip USB Electrical Specification Revision 1.0:** Released in September 2007.

USB 3.0

- **USB 3.0 (Future version):** On September 18, 2007, Pat Gelsinger demonstrated USB 3.0 at the Intel Developer Forum. USB 3.0 is targeted at ten times the current bandwidth, reaching roughly 4.8 Gbit/s (600MB/s) by utilising two additional high-speed differential pairs for "Superspeed" mode, and with the possibility for optical interconnect. The USB 3.0 specification is planned to be released early in the second half of 2008, and commercial products are expected to arrive in 2009 or 2010.
- **Backwards-Compatibility and Efficiency:** USB 3.0 is designed to be backwards-compatible with USB 2.0 and USB 1.1 and employs more efficient protocols to conserve power.

Subscriber Identity Module

A Subscriber Identity Module (SIM) is part of a removable smart card ICC (Integrated Circuit Card), also known as SIM Cards, for mobile, telephony devices (such as computers) and mobile phones. SIM cards securely store the service-subscriber key (IMSI) used to identify a subscriber. The SIM card allows users to change phones by simply removing the SIM card from one mobile phone and inserting it into another mobile phone or broadband telephony device.

SIM cards are available in two standard sizes. The first is the size of a credit card (85.60 mm × 53.98 mm x 0.76 mm). The newer, more popular miniature-version has a width of 25 mm, a height of 15 mm, and a thickness of 0.76 mm. However most SIM cards are supplied as a full-sized card with the smaller card held in place by a few plastic links and can be easily broken off to be used in a phone that uses the smaller SIM.

The first SIM Card was made in 1991, with Munich smart card maker Giesecke & Devrient selling the first 300 SIM cards to Finnish wireless network operator Elisa Oyj (formerly Radiolinja).

W-SIM is a SIM card which also integrates core cellular technology into the card itself.

Usage in Mobile Phone Standards

The use of SIM cards is mandatory in GSM devices. The equivalent of a SIM in UMTS is called the Universal Subscriber Identity Module (USIM), whereas the Removable User Identity Module (RUIM) is more popular in CDMA-based devices. Many CDMA-based standards do not include any such card, and the service is bound to a unique identifier contained in the handset itself.

The Satellite phone networks Iridium, Thuraya and Inmarsat's BGAN also use SIM cards. Sometimes these SIM cards work in regular GSM phones and also allow GSM customers to roam in satellite networks by using their own SIM card in a satellite phone.

Japan

Japan's PDC system also specifies a SIM, but this has never been implemented commercially. The specification of the interface between the Mobile Equipment and the SIM is given in the RCR STD-27 annex 4. The Subscriber Identity Module Expert Group was a committee of specialists assembled by the European Telecommunications Standards Institute (ETSI) to draw up the specifications (GSM 11.11) for interfacing between smart cards and mobile telephones. In 1994, the name SIMEG was changed to SMG9.

Finland

In July 2005, the Finnish government announced that a *Citizen Certificate*—a government-guaranteed 'electronic identity' included in a SIM card—would be made available to every individual resident in Finland before the end of 2005, allowing mobile phone users to access e-services on the move. The Citizen Certificate has been described as "basically an e-ID card that will be compatible with several hardware devices, such as mobile phones, PDAs, personal computers, digital TV sets, and public web kiosks". It is based on open standards and secured Public Key Infrastructure (PKI).

KDDI's au IC-Card NTT DoCoMo's FOMA Card

6

ARTIFICIAL INTELLIGENCE

Artificial Intelligence (AI) is both the intelligence of machines and the branch of computer science which aims to create it. Major AI textbooks define artificial intelligence as "the study and design of intelligent agents," where an intelligent agent is a system that perceives its environment and takes actions which maximise its chances of success. John McCarthy, who coined the term in 1956, defines it as "the science and engineering of making intelligent machines."

Among the traits that researchers hope machines will exhibit are reasoning, knowledge, planning, learning, communication, perception and the ability to move and manipulate objects. General intelligence (or "strong AI") has not yet been achieved and is a long-term goal of AI research.

AI research uses tools and insights from many fields, including computer science, psychology, philosophy, neuroscience, cognitive science, linguistics, ontology, operations research, economics, control theory, probability, optimisation and logic. AI research also overlaps with tasks such as robotics, control systems, scheduling, data mining, logistics, speech recognition, facial recognition and many others.

Other names for the field have been proposed, such as computational intelligence, synthetic intelligence, intelligent systems, or computational rationality.

In the 90s and early 21st century AI achieved its greatest successes, albeit somewhat behind the scenes. Artificial intelligence was adopted throughout the technology industry, providing the heavy lifting for logistics, data mining, medical diagnosis and many other areas. The success was due to several factors: the incredible power of computers today, a greater emphasis on solving specific subproblems, the creation of new ties between AI and other fields working on similar problems, and above all a new commitment by researchers to solid mathematical methods and rigorous scientific standards.

Philosophy of Artificial Intelligence

The philosophy of artificial intelligence considers the relationship between *machines* and *thought* and attempts to answer such question as:

- Can a machine act intelligently? Can it solve *any* problem that a person would solve by thinking?
- Can a machine have a mind, mental states and consciousness in the same sense humans do? Can it *feel*?
- Are human intelligence and machine intelligence the same? Is the human brain essentially a computer?

These three questions reflect the divergent interests of AI researchers, philosophers and cognitive scientists respectively. The answers to these questions depend on how one defines "intelligence" or "consciousness" and exactly which "machines" are under discussion.

Important propositions in the philosophy of AI include:

- Turing's "polite convention": *If a machine acts as intelligently as a human being, then it is as intelligent as a human being.*
- The Dartmouth proposal: *Every aspect of learning or any other feature of intelligence can be so precisely described that a machine can be made to simulate it.*
- Newell and Simon's physical symbol system hypothesis: *A physical symbol system has the necessary and sufficient means of general intelligent action.*

- Searle's weak AI: *A physical symbol system can act intelligently.*
- Searle's strong AI: *A physical symbol system can have a mind and mental states.*
- Hobbes' mechanism: *Reason is nothing but reckoning.*

Can a machine display general intelligence?

Is it possible to create a machine that can solve *all* the problems humans solve using their intelligence? This is the question that AI researchers are most interested in answering. It defines the scope of what machines will be able to do in the future and guides the direction of AI research. It only concerns the *behaviour* of machines and ignores the issues of interest to psychologists, cognitive scientists and philosophers; to answer this question, it doesn't matter whether a machine is *really* thinking (as a person thinks) or is just *acting like* it is thinking.

The basic position of most AI researchers is summed up in this statement, which appeared in the proposal for the Dartmouth Conferences of 1956:

- *Every aspect of learning or any other feature of intelligence can be so precisely described that a machine can be made to simulate it.*

Arguments against the basic premise must show that building a working AI system is impossible, because there is some practical limit to the abilities of computers or that there is some special quality of the human mind that is necessary for thinking and yet can't be duplicated by a machine (or by the methods of current AI research). Arguments in favour of the basic premise must show that such a system is possible.

The first step to answering the question is to clearly define "intelligence."

INTELLIGENCE

Turing Test

Alan Turing, in a famous and seminal 1950 paper, reduced the problem of defining intelligence to a simple question about conversation. He suggests that: if a machine can answer *any* question put to it, using the same words that an ordinary person would, then we may call that machine intelligent. A modern version of his experimental design would use an online chat room, where one of the participants is a real person and one of the participants is a computer programme. The programme passes the test if no one can tell which of the two participants is human. Turing notes that no one (except philosophers) ever asks the question "can people think?" He writes "instead of arguing continually over this point, it is usual to have a polite convention that everyone thinks." Turing's test extends this polite convention to machines:

- *If a machine acts as intelligently as human being, then it is as intelligent as a human being.*

Human intelligence vs. intelligence in general

One criticism of the Turing test is that it is explicitly anthropomorphic. If our ultimate goal is to create machines that are *more* intelligent than people, why should we insist that our machines must closely *resemble* people? Russell and Norvig write that "aeronautical engineering texts do not define the goal of their field as 'making machines that fly so exactly like pigeons that they can fool other pigeons.'" Recent AI research defines intelligence in terms of rational agents or intelligent agents. An "agent" is something which perceives and acts in an environment. A "performance measure" defines what counts as success for the agent.

- *If an agent acts so as maximise the expected value of a performance measure based on past experience and knowledge then it is intelligent.*

Definitions like this one try to capture the essence of intelligence. They have the advantage that, unlike the Turing test, they don't also test for human traits that we may not want to consider intelligent, like the ability to be insulted or the temptation to lie. They have the disadvantage that they fail to make the commonsense differentiation between "things that think" and "things that don't". By this definition, even a thermostat has a rudimentary intelligence.

Arguments that a Machine can Display General Intelligence

The brain can be simulated

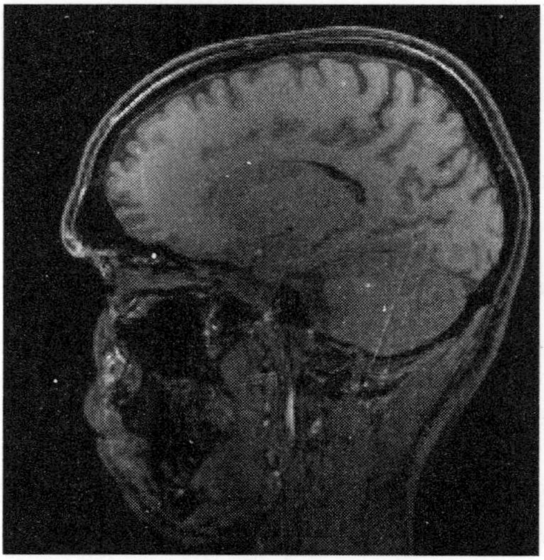

An MRI scan of a normal adult human brain

Marvin Minsky writes that "if the nervous system obeys the laws of physics and chemistry, which we have every reason to suppose it does, then .... we ... ought to be able to reproduce the behaviour of the nervous system with some physical device." This argument, first introduced as early as 1943 and vividly described by Hans Moravec in 1988, is now associated with futurist Ray Kurzweil, who estimates that computer power will be sufficient for a complete brain simulation by the year 2029.

Few disagree that a brain simulation is possible in theory, even critics of AI such as Hubert Dreyfus and John Searle. However, Searle points out that, in principle, *anything* can be simulated by a computer, and so any process at all can be considered "computation", if you're willing to stretch the definition to the breaking point. "What we wanted to know is what distinguishes the mind from thermostats and livers," he writes. Any argument that involves simply copying a brain is an argument that admits that we know nothing about how intelligence works. "If we had to know how the brain worked to do AI, we wouldn't bother with AI."

Human Thinking is Symbol Processing

In 1963, Alan Newell and Herbert Simon proposed that "symbol manipulation" was the essence of both human and machine intelligence. They wrote:

- *A physical symbol system has the necessary and sufficient means of general intelligent action.*

This claim is very strong: it implies both that human thinking is a kind of symbol manipulation (because a symbol system is *necessary* for intelligence) and that machines can be intelligent (because a symbol system is *sufficient* for intelligence). Another version of this position was described by philosopher Hubert Dreyfus, who called it "the psychological assumption":

- *The mind can be viewed as a device operating on bits of information according to formal rules.*

A distinction is usually made between the kind of high level symbols that directly correspond with objects in the world, such as <dog> and <tail> and the more complex "symbols" that are present in a machine like a neural network. Early research into AI, called "good old fashioned artificial intelligence" (GOFAI) by John Haugeland, focussed on these kind of high level symbols.

Arguments Against Symbol Processing

These arguments show that human thinking does not consist (solely) of high level symbol manipulation. They do *not* show that artificial intelligence is impossible, only that more than symbol processing is required.

Lucas, Penrose and Gödel

In 1931 Kurt Gödel proved that it is always possible to create statements that a formal system (such as an AI programme) could not prove. A human being, however, can (with some thought) see the truth of these "Gödel statements". This proved to philosopher John Lucas that human reason would always be superior to machines. He wrote "Gödel's theorem seems to me to prove that mechanism is false, that is, that minds cannot be explained as machines." Roger Penrose expanded on this argument in his 1989 book The Emperor's New Mind, where he speculated that quantum mechanical processes inside individual neurons gave humans this special advantage over machines.

Douglas Hofstadter, in his Pulitzer prize winning book *Gödel, Escher, Bach: An Eternal Golden Braid,* explains that these "Gödel-statements" always refer to the system itself, similar to the way the Epimenides paradox uses statements that refer to themselves, such as "this statement is false" or "I am lying". But, of course, the Epimenides paradox applies to anything that makes statements, whether they are machines *or* humans, even Lucas himself. Consider:

- *Lucas can't assert the truth of this statement.*

This statement is true but can't be asserted by Lucas. This shows that Lucas himself is subject to the same limits that he describes for machines, as are all people, and so Lucas's argument is pointless.

Further, Russell and Norvig note that Gödel's argument only applies to what can theoretically be proved, given an infinite amount of memory and time. In practice, real machines (including humans) have finite resources and will have difficulty proving many theorems. It is not necessary to prove everything in order to be intelligent.

Dreyfus: the primacy of unconscious skills

Hubert Dreyfus argued that human intelligence and expertise depended primarily on unconscious instincts rather than conscious symbolic manipulation, and argued that these unconscious skills would never be captured in formal rules.

Dreyfus's argument had been anticipated by Turing in his 1950 paper Computing machinery and intelligence, where he had classified this as the "argument from the informality of behaviour." Turing argued in response that, just because we don't know the rules that govern a complex behaviour, this does not mean that no such rules exist. He wrote: "we cannot so easily convince ourselves of the absence of complete laws of behaviour ... The only way we know of for finding such laws is scientific observation, and we certainly know of no circumstances under which we could say, 'We have searched enough. There are no such laws.'"

Russell and Norvig point out that, in the years since Dreyfus published his critique, progress has been made towards discovering the "rules" that govern unconscious reasoning. The situated movement in robotics research attempts to capture our unconscious skills at perception and attention. Computational intelligence paradigms, such as neural nets, evolutionary algorithms and so on are mostly directed at simulated unconscious reasoning and learning. Research into commonsense knowledge has focussed on reproducing the "background" or context of knowledge. In fact, AI research in general has moved away from high level symbol manipulation or "GOFAI", towards new models that are intended to capture more of our *unconscious* reasoning. Historian and AI researcher Daniel Crevier wrote that "time has proven the accuracy and perceptiveness of some of Dreyfus's comments. Had he formulated them less aggressively, constructive actions they suggested might have been taken much earlier."

Can a Machine have a Mind, Consciousness and Mental States?

This is a philosophical question, related to the problem of other minds and the hard problem of consciousness. The question revolves around a position defined by John Searle as "strong AI":

- *A physical symbol system can have a mind and mental states.*

Searle distinguished this position from what he called "weak AI":

- *A physical symbol system can act intelligently.*

Searle introduced the terms to isolate strong AI from weak AI so he could focus on what he thought was the more interesting and debatable issue. He argued that *even if we assume* that we had a computer programme that acted exactly like a human mind, there would still be a difficult philosophical question that needed to be answered.

Neither of Searle's two positions are of great concern to AI research, since they do not directly answer the question "can a machine display general intelligence?" (unless it can also be shown that consciousness is *necessary* for intelligence). Turing wrote "I do not wish to give the impression that I think there is no mystery about consciousness ... [b]ut I do not think these mysteries necessarily need to be solved before we can answer the question [of whether machines can think]." Russell and Norvig agree: "Most AI researchers take the weak AI hypothesis for granted, and don't care about the strong AI hypothesis."

Before we can answer this question, we must be clear what we mean by "minds", "mental states" and "consciousness".

Consciousness, Minds, Mental States, Meaning

The words "mind" and "consciousness" are used by different communities in different ways. Some new age thinkers, for example, use the word "consciousness" to describe something similar to Bergson's "élan vital": an invisible, energetic fluid that permeates life and especially the mind. Science fiction writers use the word to describe some essential property that makes us human: a machine or alien that is "conscious" will be presented as a fully human character, with intelligence, desires, will, insight, pride and so on. (Science fiction writers also use the words "sentience", "sapience," "self-awareness" or "ghost" (as in the *Ghost in the Shell* manga and anime series) to describe this essential human property.) For others, the words "mind" or "consciousness" are used as a kind of secular synonym for the soul.

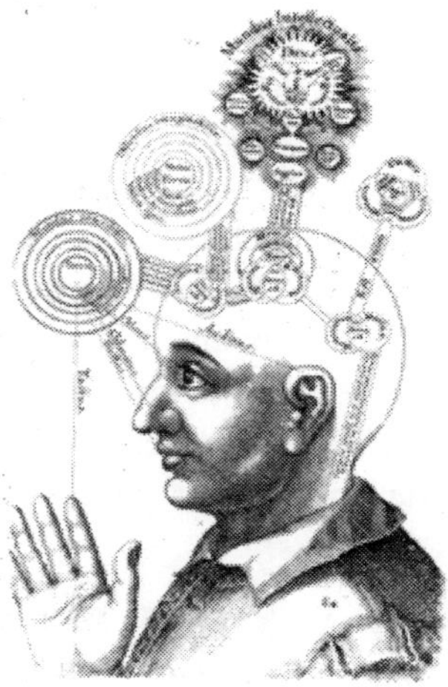

Representation of consciousness from the 17th century.

For philosophers, neuroscientists and cognitive scientists, the words are used in a way that is both more precise and more mundane: they refer to the familiar, everyday experience of having a "thought in your head", like a perception, a dream, an intention or a plan, and to the way we *know* something, or *mean* something or *understand* something. "It's not hard to give a commonsense definition of consciousness" observes philosopher John Searle. What is mysterious and fascinating is not so much *what* it is but *how* it is: how does a lump of fatty tissue and electricity give rise to this (familiar) experience of perceiving, meaning or thinking?

Philosophers call this the hard problem of consciousness. It is the latest version of a classic problem in the philosophy of mind called the "mind-body problem." A related problem is the problem of *meaning* or *understanding* (which philosophers call "intentionality"): what is the connection between our *thoughts* (i.e. patterns of neurons) and *what we are thinking about* (i.e. objects and situations out in the world)? A third issue is the problem of *experience* (or "phenomenology"): If two people see the same thing, do they have the same experience? Or are there things "inside their head" (called "qualia") that can be different from person to person?

Neurobiologists believe all these problems will be solved as we begin to identify the neural correlates of consciousness: the actual machinery in our heads that creates the mind, experience and understanding. Even the harshest critics of artificial intelligence agree that the brain is just a machine, and that consciousness and intelligence are the result of a physical processes in the brain. The difficult philosophical question is this: can a computer programme, running on a digital machine that shuffles the binary digits of zero and one, duplicate the ability of the neurons to create minds, with mental states (like understanding or perceiving), and ultimately, the experience of consciousness?

ARGUMENTS THAT A COMPUTER CAN'T HAVE A MIND AND MENTAL STATES

Searle's Chinese Room

John Searle asks us to consider a thought experiment: suppose we have written a computer programme that passes the Turing Test and demonstrates "general intelligent action." Suppose, specifically that the programme can converse in fluent Chinese. Write the programme on 3x5 cards and give them to an ordinary person. Lock the person into a room and have him follow the instructions on the cards. He will copy out Chinese characters and pass them in and out of the room through a slot. From the outside, it will appear that the Chinese room contains a fully intelligent person who speaks Chinese. The question is this: is there anyone (or anything) in the room that understands Chinese? That is, is there anything that has the mental state of understanding, or which has conscious awareness of what is being discussed in Chinese? The man is clearly not aware. The room can't be aware. The *cards* certainly aren't aware. Searle concludes that the Chinese room, or *any* other physical symbol system, cannot have a mind.

Searle goes on to argue that actual mental states and consciousness require (yet to be described) "actual physical-chemical properties of actual human brains." He argues there are special "causal properties" of brains and neurons that gives rise to minds: in his words "brains cause minds."

Related arguments: Leibniz' mill, Block's telephone exchange and blockhead

Gottfried Leibniz made essentially the same argument as Searle in 1714, using the thought experiment of expanding the brain until it was the size of a mill. In 1974, Lawrence Davis imagined duplicating the brain using telephone lines and offices staffed by people, and in 1978 Ned Block envisioned the entire population of China involved in such a brain simulation. This thought experiment is called "the Chinese Nation" or "the Chinese Gym". Ned Block also proposed his "blockhead" argument, which is a version of the Chinese room in which the programme has been re-factored into a simple set of rules of the form "see this, do that", removing all mystery from the programme.

Responses to the Chinese Room

Responses to the Chinese room emphasize several different points.

1. **The systems reply and the virtual mind reply:** This reply argues that *the system*, including the man, the programme, the room, and the cards, is what understands Chinese. Searle claims that the man in the room is the only thing which could possibly "have a mind" or "understand", but others disagree, arguing that it is possible for there to be *two* minds in the same physical place, similar to the way a computer can simultaneously "be" two machines at once: one physical (like a Macintosh) and one "virtual" (like a word processor).
2. **Speed, power and complexity replies:** Several critics point out that the man in the room would probably take millions

of years to respond to a simple question, and would require "filing cabinets" of astronomical proportions. This brings the clarity of Searle's intuition into doubt.

3. **Robot reply:** To truly understand, some believe the Chinese Room needs eyes and hands. Hans Moravec writes: 'If we could graft a robot to a reasoning programme, we wouldn't need a person to provide the meaning anymore: it would come from the physical world."
4. **Brain simulator reply:** What if the programme simulates the sequence of nerve firings at the synapses of an actual brain of an actual Chinese speaker? The man in the room would be simulating an actual brain. This is a variation on the "systems reply" that appears more plausible because "the system" now clearly operates like a human brain, which strengthens the intuition that there is something besides the man in the room that could understand Chinese.
5. **Other minds reply and the epiphenomena reply:** Several people have noted that Searle's argument is just a version of the problem of other minds, applied to machines. Since it's difficult to decide if people are "actually" thinking, we shouldn't be surprised that it's difficult to answer the same question about machines. A related idea is that Searle's "causal properties" of neurons are epiphenomenal: they have no effect on the real world. Why would natural selection create them in the first place, if they make no difference to behaviour?

Is Thinking a Kind of Computation?

This issue is of primary importance to cognitive scientists, who study the nature of human thinking and problem solving.

The computational theory of mind or "computationalism" claims that the relationship between mind and body is similar (if not identical to) the relationship between a *running programme* and a computer. The idea has philosophical roots in Hobbes (who claimed reasoning was "nothing more than reckoning"), Leibniz (who attempted to create a logical calculus of all human ideas), Hume (who thought perception could be reduced to "atomic impressions") and even Kant (who analysed all experience as controlled by formal rules). The latest version is associated with philosophers Hilary Putnam and Jerry Fodor.

This question bears on our earlier questions: if the human brain is a kind of computer then computers can be both intelligent and conscious, answering both the practical and philosophical questions of AI. In terms of the practical question of AI ("Can a machine display general intelligence?"), some versions of computationalism make the claim that (as Hobbes wrote):

- *Reasoning is nothing but reckoning*

In other words, our intelligence derives from a form of *calculation*, similar to arithmetic. This is the physical symbol system hypothesis discussed above, and it implies that artificial intelligence is possible. In terms of the philosophical question of AI ("Can a machine have mind, mental states and consciousness?"), most versions of computationalism claim that (as Stevan Harnad characterises it):

- *Mental states are just implementations of (the right) computer programmes*

This is John Searle's "strong AI" discussed above, and it is the real target of the Chinese Room argument (according to Harnad).

Other Related Questions

Alan Turing noted that there are many arguments of the form "a machine will never do X", where X can be many things, such as:

Be kind, resourceful, beautiful, friendly, have initiative, have a sense of humor, tell right from wrong, make mistakes, fall in love, enjoy strawberries and cream, make someone fall in love with it, learn from experience, use words properly, be the subject of its own thought, have as much diversity of behaviour as a man, do something really new.

Turing argues that these objections are often based on naive assumptions about the versatility of machines or are "disguised forms of the argument from consciousness". Writing a programme that exhibits one of these behaviours "will not make much of an impression." All of these arguments are tangential to the basic premise of AI, unless it can be shown that one of these traits is essential for general intelligence.

Can a Machine have Emotions?

Hans Moravec believes "I think robots in general will be quite emotional about being nice people" and describes emotions in terms of the behaviours they cause. Fear is a source of urgency. Empathy is a necessary component of good human computer interaction. He says robots "will try to please you in an apparently selfless manner because it will get a thrill out of this positive reinforcement. You can interpret this as a kind of love." Daniel Crevier writes "Moravec's point is that emotions are just devices for channeling behaviour in a direction beneficial to the survival of one's species."

The question of whether the machine *actually feels* an emotion, or whether it merely acts as if feeling an emotion is the philosophical question, "can a machine be conscious?" in another form.

Can a Machine be Self Aware?

"Self awareness", as noted above, is sometimes used by science fiction writers as a name for the essential human property that makes a character fully human. Turing strips away all other properties of human beings and reduces the question to "can a machine be the subject of its own thought?" Can it *think about itself?* Viewed in this way, it is obvious that a programme can be written that can report on its own internal states, such as a debugger.

Can a Machine be Original or Creative?

Turing reduces this to the question of whether a machine can "take us by surprise" and argues that this is obviously true, as any programmer can attest. He notes that, with enough storage capacity, a computer can behave in an astronomical number of different ways. It must be possible, even trivial, for a computer that can represent ideas to combine them in new ways. (Douglas Lenat's Automated Mathematician, as one example, combined ideas to discover new mathematical truths.)

Can a Machine have a Soul?

Finally, those who believe in the existence of a soul would argue that

- *Thinking is a function of man's immortal soul*

Alan Turing called this "the theological objection" and writes:

In attempting to construct such machines we should not be irreverently usurping His power of creating souls, any more than we are in the procreation of children: rather we are, in either case, instruments of His will providing mansions for the souls that he creates.

Natural Language Processing

Natural language processing (NLP) is a subfield of artificial intelligence and computational linguistics. It studies the problems of automated generation and understanding of natural human languages.

Natural-language-generation systems convert information from computer databases into normal-sounding human language. Natural-language-understanding systems convert samples of human language into more formal representations that are easier for computer programmes to manipulate.

EVALUATION OF NATURAL LANGUAGE PROCESSING

Objectives

The goal of NLP evaluation is to measure one or more *qualities* of an algorithm or a system, in order to determine if (or to what extent) the system answers the goals of its designers, or the needs of its users. Research in NLP evaluation has received considerable attention, because the definition of proper evaluation criteria is one way to specify precisely an NLP problem, going thus beyond the vagueness of tasks defined only as *language understanding* or *language generation.* A precise set of evaluation criteria, which includes mainly evaluation data and evaluation metrics, enables several teams to compare their solutions to a given NLP problem.

Short History of Evaluation in NLP

The first evaluation campaign on written texts seems to be a campaign dedicated to message understanding in 1987 (Pallet 1998). Then, the Parseval/GEIG project compared phrase-structure grammars (Black 1991). A series of campaigns within Tipster project were realised on tasks like summarisation, translation and searching (Hirshman 1998). In 1994, in Germany, the Morpholympics compared German taggers. Then, the Senseval and Romanseval campaigns were conducted with the objectives of semantic disambiguation. In 1996, the Sparkle campaign compared syntactic parsers in four different languages (English, French, German and Italian). In France, the Grace project compared a set of 21 taggers for French in 1997 (Adda 1999). In 2004, during the Technolangue/Easy project, 13 parsers for French were compared. Large-scale evaluation of dependency parsers were performed in the context of the CoNLL shared tasks in 2006 and 2007. In Italy, the evalita campaign was conducted in 2007 to compare various tools for Italian evalita web site. In France, within the ANR-Passage project (end of 2007), 10 parsers for French were compared passage web site.Robotics Robotics is the science and technology of robots, their design, manufacture, and application. Robotics requires a working knowledge of electronics, mechanics and software, and is usually accompanied by a large working knowledge of many subjects. A person working in the field is a roboticist.

Kismet, a robot with rudimentary social skills.

The structure of a robot is usually mostly mechanical and can be called a kinematic chain (its functionality being similar to the skeleton of the human body). The chain is formed of links (its bones), actuators (its muscles) and joints which can allow one or more degrees of freedom. Most contemporary robots use open serial chains in which each link connects the one before to the one after it. These robots are called serial robots and often resemble the human arm. Some robots, such as the Stewart platform, use closed parallel chains. Other structures, such as those that mimic the mechanical structure of humans, various animals and insects, are comparatively rare. However, the development and use of such structures in robots is an active area of research (e.g. biomechanics). Robots used as manipulators have an end effector mounted on the last link. This end effector can be anything from a welding device to a mechanical hand used to manipulate the environment. ISO 10248 defines a robotic application on the industrial field.

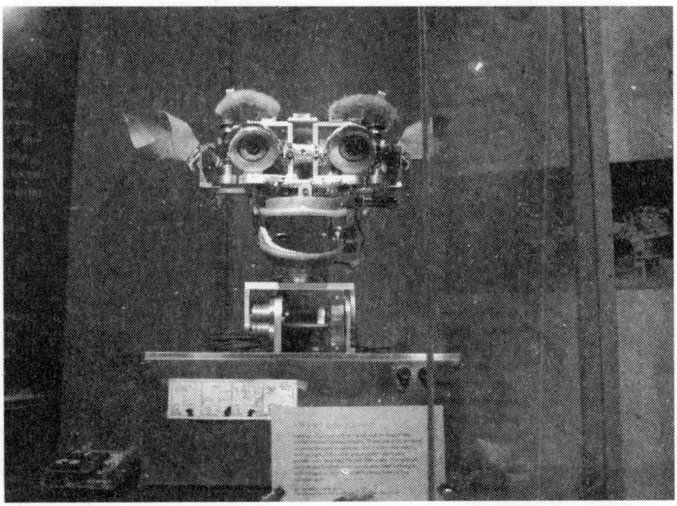

The field of robotics is closely related to AI. Intelligence is required for robots to be able to handle such tasks as object manipulation and navigation, with sub-problems of localisation (knowing where you are), mapping (learning what is around you) and motion planning (figuring out how to get there).

ASIMO uses sensors and intelligent algorithms to avoid obstacles and navigate stairs.

Speech recognition

Speech recognition (also known as automatic speech recognition or computer speech recognition) converts spoken words to machine-readable input (for example, to keypresses, using the binary code for a string of character codes). The term voice recognition may also be used to refer to speech recognition, but more precisely refers to speaker recognition, which attempts to identify the person speaking, as opposed to what is being said.

Speech recognition applications include voice dialing (e.g., "Call home"), call routing (e.g., "I would like to make a collect call"), domotic appliance control and content-based spoken audio search (e.g., find a podcast where particular words were spoken), simple data entry (e.g., entering a credit card number), preparation of structured documents (e.g., a radiology report), speech-to-text processing (e.g., word processors or emails), and in aircraft cockpits (usually termed Direct Voice Input).

Popular speech recognition conferences held each year or two include ICASSP, Eurospeech/ICSLP (now named Interspeech) and the IEEE ASRU. Conferences in the field of Natural Language Processing, such as ACL, NAACL, EMNLP, and HLT, are beginning to include papers on speech processing. Important journals include the IEEE Transactions on Speech and Audio Processing (now named IEEE Transactions on Audio, Speech and Language Processing), Computer Speech and Language, and Speech Communication. Books like "Fundamentals of Speech Recognition" by Lawrence Rabiner can be useful to acquire basic knowledge but may not be fully up to date (1993). Another good source can be "Statistical Methods for Speech Recognition" by Frederick Jelinek which is a more up to date book (1998). Even more up to date is "Computer Speech", by Manfred R. Schroeder, second edition published in 2004. A good insight into the techniques used in the best modern systems can be gained by paying attention to government sponsored evaluations such as those organised by DARPA (the largest speech recognition-related project ongoing as of 2007 is the GALE project, which involves both speech recognition and translation components).

In terms of freely available resources, the HTK book (and the accompanying HTK toolkit) is one place to start to both learn about speech recognition and to start experimenting. Another such resource is Carnegie Mellon University's SPHINX toolkit. The AT&T libraries FSM Library, GRM library, and DCD library are also general software libraries for large-vocabulary speech recognition.

Strong AI

Strong AI is artificial intelligence that matches or exceeds human intelligence—the intelligence of a machine that can successfully perform any intellectual task that a human being can. It is a primary goal of artificial intelligence research and an important topic for anyone interested in the future, such as science fiction writers and futurists. Strong AI is also referred to as "artificial general intelligence" or as the ability to perform "general intelligent action". Strong AI is also closely related to such traits as sentience, sapience, self-awareness and consciousness.

Some references emphasize a distinction between strong AI and "applied AI" (also called "narrow AI" or "weak AI"): the use of software to study or accomplish specific problem solving or reasoning tasks that do not encompass (or in some cases are completely outside of) the full range of human cognitive abilities.

Requirements of strong AI

Many different definitions of intelligence have been proposed (such as being able to pass the Turing test) but there is to date no definition that satisfies everyone. However, there *is* wide agreement among artificial intelligence researchers that an intelligent machine must at least have the ability to:

- reason, use strategy, solve puzzles, and make judgements under uncertainty;
- represent knowledge, including commonsense knowledge;
- plan;
- learn;
- communicate in natural language;
- perceive, and especially see;
- have social intelligence;
- be able to move and manipulate objects (robotics);
- and the ability to integrate all these skills towards common goals.

Together these skills provide a working definition of what intelligence is, and work is underway to design machines that have these abilities. **Strong AI** is, at the very least, a system that can perform all these tasks as well as humans do or better.

There are other aspects of the human mind besides intelligence that also bear on the concept of strong AI:

- consciousness: To say there is something it would "be like" to have strong AI.
- self-awareness: To be aware of oneself as a separate individual, especially to be aware of one's own thoughts.
- sentience: The ability to "*feel.*"
- sapience: the capacity for wisdom.

It is not clear whether any of these are necessary for strong AI—for example, it is not clear if consciousness is necessary for a machine to reason as well as human beings can. It is also not clear whether any of these traits are sufficient for intelligence: if a machine is built with a device that simulates the neural correlates of consciousness, would it automatically have the ability to represent knowledge or use natural language?

It is also possible that some of these properties, such as sentience, naturally emerge from a fully intelligent machine, or that it becomes natural to *ascribe* these properties to machines once they begin to act in a way that is clearly intelligent. For example, intelligent action may be sufficient for sentience, rather than the other way around.

Research Approaches

Modern AI research began in the middle 50s. The first generation of AI researchers were convinced that strong AI was possible and that it would exist in just a few decades. As AI pioneer Herbert Simon wrote in 1965: "machines will be capable, within twenty years, of doing any work a man can do." Their predictions were the inspiration for Stanley Kubrick and Arthur C. Clarke's character HAL 9000, who accurately embodied what AI researchers believed they could create by the year 2001. Of note is the fact that AI pioneer Marvin Minsky was a consultant on the project of making HAL 9000 as realistic as possible according to the consensus predictions of the time, having himself said on the subject in 1967, "Within a generation...the problem of creating 'artificial intelligence' will substantially be solved."

However, in the early 70s, it became obvious that researchers had grossly underestimated the difficulty of the project. The agencies that funded AI became skeptical of strong AI and put researchers under increasing pressure to produce useful technology, or "applied AI". As the eighties began, Japan's fifth generation computer project revived interest in strong AI, setting out a ten year timeline that included strong AI goals like "carry on a casual conversation". In response to this and the success of expert systems, both industry and government pumped money back into the field. However, the market for AI spectacularly collapsed in the late 80s and the goals of the fifth generation computer project were never fulfilled. For the second time in 20 years, AI researchers who had predicted the imminent arrival of strong AI had been shown to be fundamentally mistaken about what they could accomplish.

By the 1990s, AI researchers had gained a reputation for making promises they could not keep. AI researchers became reluctant to make any kind of prediction at all and avoid any mention of "human level" artificial intelligence, for fear of being labeled a "wild-eyed dreamer." This is an unfortunate consequence of developing nascent technologies.

Mainstream AI Research

For the most part, researchers today choose to focus on specific sub-problems where they can produce verifiable results and commercial applications, such as neural nets, computer vision or data mining.

Most mainstream AI researchers hope that strong AI can be developed by combining the programmes that solve various subproblems using an integrated agent architecture, cognitive architecture or subsumption architecture. Hans Moravec wrote in 1988 "I am confident that this bottom-up route to artificial intelligence will one day meet the traditional top-down route more than half way, ready to provide the real world competence and the commonsense knowledge that has been so frustratingly elusive in reasoning programmes. Fully intelligent machines will result when the metaphorical golden spike is driven uniting the two efforts."

Artificial General Intelligence

Artificial General Intelligence research aims to create AI that can replicate human-level intelligence completely, often called an Artificial General Intelligence (AGI) to distinguish from less ambitious AI projects. (The concept is derived from the psychometric notion of *natural* general intelligence (often denoted "*g*"), though no adherence to any particular theory of *g* is implied.) As yet, researchers have devoted little attention to AGI, with some claiming that intelligence is too complex to be completely replicated in the near term. Some small groups of computer scientists are doing AGI research, however. Organisations pursuing AGI include the Adaptive AI, Artificial General Intelligence Research Institute (AGIRI), Singularity Institute for Artificial Intelligence and Texai. One recent addition is Numenta, a project based on the theories of Jeff Hawkins, the creator of the Palm Pilot. While Numenta takes a computational approach to general intelligence, Hawkins is also the founder of the RedWood Neuroscience Institute, which explores conscious thought from a biological perspective.

Simulated Human Brain Model

Simulated human brain model is one of the quickest means of achieving strong AI, as it doesn't require complete understanding of how intelligence works. Basically, a very powerful computer would simulate a human brain, often in the form of a network of neurons. For example, given a map of all (or most) of the neurons in a functional human brain, and a good understanding of how a single neuron works, it is theoretically possible for a computer programme to simulate the working brain over time. Given some method of communication, this simulated brain might then be shown to be fully intelligent. The exact form of the simulation varies: instead of neurons, a simulation might use groups of neurons, or alternatively, individual molecules might be simulated. It's also unclear which portions of the human brain would need to be modeled: humans can still function while missing portions of their brains, and areas of the brain are associated with activities (such as breathing) that might not be necessary to think.

This approach would require three things:

The RIKEN MDGRAPE-3 Supercomputer

- *Hardware.* An extremely powerful computer would be required for such a model. Futurist Ray Kurzweil estimates 10 million MIPS, or ten petaflops. At least one special-purpose petaflops computer has already been built (the Riken MDGRAPE-3) and there are nine current computing projects (such as BlueGene/P) to build more general purpose petaflops computers all of which should be completed by 2008, if not sooner. Most other attempted estimates of the brain's computational power equivalent have been rather higher, ranging from 100 million MIPS (100 petaflops) to 100 billion MIPS (100,000 petaflops). Using accurate Top500 projections, it might be estimated that such levels of computing power might be reached using the top-performing CPU-based supercomputers to be by ~2015 (for 100 petaflops), up to a more conservative estimate of ~2025 (for 100,000 petaflops). However, considering that GPU processing and Stream Processing power appears to double every year, these estimates will be reached much sooner using GPGPU processing as high-end GPU's set to arrive in early 2008 are already going to be able to process over 1 teraflop, which is 20x more powerful than a standard quad-core CPU. It should also be noted, however, that the overhead introduced by the modeling of the biological, chemical, and physical details of neural behaviour (especially on a molecular scale) might require a simulator to have access to computational power much greater than that of the brain itself and that current simulations and estimates do not account for the importance of Glial cells which outnumber neurons 10:1.

- *Software.* Software to simulate the function of a brain would be required. This assumes that the human mind is the central nervous system and is governed by physical laws. Constructing the simulation would require a great deal of knowledge about the physical and functional operation of the human brain, and might require detailed information about a particular human brain's structure. Information would be required both of the function of different types of neurons, and of how they are connected. Note that the particular form of the software dictates the hardware necessary to run it. For example, an extremely detailed simulation including molecules or small groups of molecules would require enormously more processing power than a simulation that models neurons using a simple equation, and a more accurate model of a neuron would be expected to be much more expensive computationally than a simple model. The more neurons in the simulation, the more processing power it would require.
- *Understanding.* Finally, it requires sufficient understanding thereof to be able to model it mathematically. This could be done either by understanding the central nervous system, or by mapping and copying it. Neuroimaging technologies are improving rapidly, and Kurzweil predicts that a map of sufficient quality will become available on a similar timescale to the required computing power. However, the simulation

would also have to capture the detailed cellular behaviour of neurons and glial cells, presently only understood in the broadest of outlines.

Once such a model is built, it will be easily altered and thus open to trial-and-error experimentation. This is likely to lead to huge advances in understanding, allowing the model's intelligence to be improved/motivations altered.

The Blue Brain project aims to use one of the fastest supercomputer architectures in the world, IBM's Blue Gene platform, to simulate a single neocortical column consisting of approximately 60,000 neurons and 5km of interconnecting synapses. The eventual goal of the project is to use supercomputers to replicate an entire brain.

The brain gets its power from performing many parallel operations, a standard computer from performing operations very quickly. It should be noted, however, that supercomputers also perform many operations in parallel. Good examples of this are the Cray and NEC vector computers which operate as a single machine but perform many calculations at once. Another example is any form of cluster computing, where multiple single computers operate as one.

The human brain has roughly 100 billion neurons operating simultaneously, connected by roughly 100 trillion synapses. By comparison, a modern computer microprocessor uses only 1.7 billion transistors. Although estimates of the brain's processing power put it at around 10^{14} neuron updates per second, it is expected that the first unoptimised simulations of a human brain will require a computer capable of 10^{18} FLOPS. By comparison a general purpose CPU (circa 2006) operates at a few GFLOPS (10^{9} FLOPS). (each FLOP may require as many as 20,000 logic operations).

However, a neuron is estimated to spike 200 times per second (this giving an upper limit on the number of operations). Signals between them are transmitted at a maximum speed of 150 meters per second. A modern 2GHz processor operates at 2 billion cycles per second, or 10,000,000 times faster than a human neuron, and signals in electronic computers travel at roughly half the speed of light; faster than signals in humans by a factor of 1,000,000. The brain consumes about 20W of power whereas supercomputers may use as much as 1MW or an order of 100,000 more (note: Landauer limit is 3.5×10^{20} op/sec/watt at room temperature).

Neuro-silicon interfaces have also been proposed.

Critics of this approach believe that it is possible to achieve AI directly without imitating nature and often have used the analogy that early attempts to construct flying machines modeled them after birds, but that modern aircraft do not look like birds. The direct approach is used in AI—What is this, where it is shown that if we have a formal definition of AI, it can be found by enumerating all possible programmes and then testing each of them to see whether it has produced Artificial Intelligence, or has not.

Artificial Consciousness Research

Artificial consciousness research aims to create and study artificially conscious systems. Professor Igor Aleksander argues that the principles for creating a conscious machine already existed but that it would take forty years to train such a machine to understand language.

Franklin's Intelligent Distribution Agent

Stan Franklin (1995, 2003) defines an autonomous agent as possessing functional consciousness when it is capable of several of the functions of consciousness as identified by Bernard Baars' *Global Workspace Theory* (Baars 1988), (Baars 1997). His brain child IDA (Intelligent Distribution Agent) is a software implementation of GWT, which makes it functionally conscious by definition. IDA's task is to negotiate new assignments for sailors in the US Navy after they end a tour of duty, by matching each individual's skills and preferences with the Navy's needs. IDA interacts with Navy databases and communicates with the sailors via natural language email dialog while obeying a large set of Navy policies. The IDA computational model was developed during 1996-2001 at Stan Franklin's "Conscious" Software Research Group at the University of Memphis. It "consists of approximately a quarter-million lines of Java code, and almost completely consumes the resources of a 2001 high-end workstation." It relies heavily on *codelets*, which are "special purpose, relatively independent, mini-agent[s] typically implemented as a small piece of code running as a separate thread." In IDA's top-down architecture, high-level cognitive functions are explicitly modeled; see Franklin (1995) and Franklin (2003) for details. While IDA is functionally conscious by definition, Franklin does "not attribute phenomenal consciousness to [his] own 'conscious' software agent, IDA, in spite of her many human-like behaviours. This in spite of watching several US Navy detailers repeatedly nodding their heads saying 'Yes, that's how I do it' while watching IDA's internal and external actions as she performs her task."

Ron Sun's cognitive Architecture CLARION

CLARION posits a two-level representation that explains the distinction between conscious and unconscious mental processes.

CLARION has been successful in accounting for a variety of psychological data. A number of well-known skill learning tasks have been simulated using CLARION that span the spectrum ranging from simple reactive skills to complex cognitive skills. The tasks include serial reaction time (SRT) tasks, artificial grammar learning (AGL) tasks, process control (PC) tasks, the categorical inference (CI) task, the alphabetical arithmetic (AA) task, and the Tower of Hanoi (TOH) task *(Sun 2002)*. Among them, SRT, AGL, and PC are typical implicit learning tasks, very much relevant to the issue of consciousness as they operationalised the notion of consciousness in the context of psychological experiments .

The simulations using CLARION provide detailed, process-based interpretations of experimental data related to consciousness, in the context of a broadly scoped cognitive architecture and a unified theory of cognition. Such interpretations are important for a precise, process-based understanding of consciousness and other aspects of cognition, leading up to better appreciations of the role of consciousness in human cognition *(Sun 1999)*. CLARION also makes quantitative and qualitative predictions regarding cognition in the areas of memory, learning, motivation, meta-cognition, and so on. These predictions either have been experimentally tested already or are in the process of being tested.

Haikonen's Cognitive Architecture

Pentti Haikonen (2003) considers classical rule-based computing inadequate for achieving AC: "the brain is definitely not a computer. Thinking is not an execution of programmed strings of commands. The brain is not a numerical calculator either. We do not think by numbers." Rather than trying to achieve mind and consciousness by identifying and implementing their underlying computational rules, Haikonen proposes "a special cognitive architecture to reproduce the processes of perception, inner imagery, inner speech, pain, pleasure, emotions and the cognitive functions behind these. This bottom-up architecture would produce higher-level functions by the power of the elementary processing units, the artificial neurons, without algorithms or programmes". Haikonen believes that, when implemented with sufficient complexity, this architecture will develop consciousness, which he considers to be "a style and way of operation, characterised by distributed signal representation, perception process, cross-modality reporting and availability for retrospection." Haikonen is not alone in this process view of consciousness, or the view that AC will spontaneously emerge in autonomous agents that have a suitable neuro-inspired architecture of complexity; these are shared by many, e.g. Freeman (1999) and Cotterill (2003). A low-complexity implementation of the architecture proposed by Haikonen (2004) was reportedly not capable of AC, but did exhibit emotions as expected.

Self-awareness Research

Self-awareness in robots is being investigated by Junichi Takeno at Meiji University in Japan. Takeno is asserting that he has developed a robot capable of discriminating between a self-image in a mirror and any other having an identical image to it, and this claim has been already reviewed. *(Takeno, Inaba & Suzuki 2005)*

Emergence

Some have suggested that intelligence can arise as an emergent quality from the convergence of random, man-made technologies. Human sentience — or any other biological and naturally occurring intelligence — arises out of the natural process of species evolution and an individual's experiences. Discussion of this eventuality is currently limited to fiction and theory.

Origin of the Term: John Searle's Strong AI

The term "strong AI" was adopted from the name of an argument in the philosophy of artificial intelligence first identified by John Searle as part of his Chinese room argument in 1980. He wanted to distinguish between two different hypotheses about artificial intelligence:

- An artificial intelligence system can *think* and have a *mind.*
- An artificial intelligence system can (only) *act like* it thinks and has a mind.

The first one is called "the *strong* AI hypothesis" and the second is "the *weak* AI hypothesis" because the first one makes the *stronger* statement: it assumes something special has happened to the machine that goes beyond all its abilities that we can test. Searle referred to the "strong AI hypothesis" as "strong AI". This usage, which is fundamentally different than the subject of this article, is common in academic AI research and textbooks.

The term "strong AI" is now used to describe any artificial intelligence system that acts like it has a mind, regardless of whether a philosopher would be able to determine if it *actually* has a mind or not. As Russell and Norvig write: "Most AI researchers take the weak AI hypothesis for granted, and don't care about the strong AI hypothesis." AI researchers *are* interested in a related statement (that some sources confusingly call "the strong AI hypothesis"):

- An artificial intelligence system can think (*or* act like it thinks) *as well or better than people do.*

This assertion, which hinges on the breadth and power of machine intelligence, *is* the subject of this article.

The New Neats

In the 1990s, AI researchers developed sophisticated mathematical tools to solve specific subproblems. These tools are truly scientific, in the sense that their results are both measurable and verifiable, and they have been responsible for many of AI's recent successes. The shared mathematical language has also permitted a high level of collaboration with more established fields (like mathematics, economics or operations research). Russell & Norvig (2003) describe this movement as nothing less than a "revolution" and "the victory of the neats."

Applications of Artificial Intelligence

Artificial intelligence has been used in a wide range of fields including medical diagnosis, stock trading, robot control, law, scientific discovery and toys.

Many practical applications are dependent on artificial neural networks, networks that pattern their organisation in mimicry of a brain's neurons, which have been found to excel in pattern recognition.

Business

Banks use artificial intelligence systems to organise operations, invest in stocks, and manage properties. In August 2001, robots beat humans in a simulated financial trading competition.

Financial institutions have long used artificial neural network systems to detect charges or claims outside of the norm, flagging these for human investigation.

Medical Clinics

A medical clinic can use artificial intelligence systems to organise bed schedules, make a staff rotation, and provide medical information.

They may also be used for medical diagnosis.

Artificial neural networks are used for medical diagnosis (such as in Concept Processing technology in EMR software), functioning as machine differential diagnosis.

Heavy Industry

Robots have become common in many industries. They are often given jobs that are considered dangerous to humans. Robots have proven effective in jobs that are very repetitive which may lead to mistakes or accidents due to a lapse in concentration and other jobs which humans may find degrading. General Motors uses around 16,000 robots for tasks such as painting, welding, and assembly. Japan is the leader in using and producing robots in the world. In 1995, 700,000 robots were in use worldwide; over 500,000 of which were from Japan.

Toys and Games

The 1990s saw some of the first attempts to mass-produce domestically aimed types of basic Artificial Intelligence for education, or leisure. This prospered greatly with the Digital Revolution, and helped introduce people, especially children, to a life of dealing with various types of AI, specifically in the form of Tamagotchis and Giga Pets, the Internet (example: basic search engine interfaces are one simple form), and the first widely released robot, Furby. A mere year later an improved type of domestic robot was released in the form of Aibo, a robotic dog with intelligent features and autonomy.

Aviation

The Air Operations Division, AOD, uses for the rule based expert systems. The AOD has use for artificial intelligence for surrogate operators for combat and training simulators, mission management aids, support systems for tactical decision making, and post processing of the simulator data into symbolic summaries.

The use of artificial intelligence in simulators is proving to be very useful for the AOD. Airplane simulators are using artificial intelligence in order to process the data taken from simulated flights. Other than simulated flying, there is also simulated aircraft warfare. The computers are able to come up with the best success scenarios in these situations. The computers can also create strategies based on the placement, size, speed, and strength of the forces and counter forces. Pilots may be given assistance in the air curing combat by computers. The artificial intelligent programmes can sort the information and provide the pilot with the best possible maneuvers, not to mention getting rid of certain maneuvers that would be impossible for a sentient being to perform. Multiple aircraft are needed to get good approximations for some calculations so computer simulated pilots are used to gather data. These computer simulated pilots are also used to train future air traffic controllers.

The system used by the AOD in order to measure performance was the Interactive Fault Diagnosis and Isolation System, or IFDIS. It is a rule based expert system put together by collecting information from TF-30 documents and the expert advice from mechanics that work on the TF-30. This system was designed to be used to for the development of the TF-30 for the RAAF F-111C. The performance system was also used to replace specialised workers. The system allowed the regular workers to communicate with the system and avoid mistakes, miscalculations, or having to speak to one of the specialised workers.

The AOD also uses artificial intelligence in speech recognition software. The air traffic controllers are giving directions to the artificial pilots and the AOD wants to the pilots to respond to the ATC's with simple responses. The programmes that incorporate the speech software must be trained, which means they use neural networks. The programme used, the Verbex 7000, is still a very early programme that has plenty of room for improvement. The improvements are imperative because ATCs use very specific dialog and the software needs to be able to communicate correctly and promptly every time.

The Artificial Intelligence supported Design of Aircraft, or AIDA, is used to help designers in the process of creating conceptual designs of aircraft. This programme allows the designers to focus more on the design itself and less on the design process. The software also allows the user to focus less on the software tools. The AIDA uses rule based systems to compute its data. This is a diagram of the arrangement of the AIDA modules. Although simple, the programme is proving effective.

In 2003, NASA's Dryden Flight Research Center, and many other companies, created software that could enable a damaged aircraft to continue flight until a safe landing zone can be reached. The Intelligent Flight Control System was tested on an F-15, which was heavily modified by NASA. The software compensates for all the damaged components by relying on the undamaged components. The neural network used in the software proved to be effective and marked a triumph for artificial intelligence.

The Integrated Vehicle Health Management system, also used by NASA, on board an aircraft must process and interpret data taken from the various sensors on the aircraft. The system needs to be able to determine the structural integrity of the aircraft. The system also needs to implement protocols in case of any damage taken the vehicle.

Computer Science

AI researchers have created many tools to solve the most difficult problems in computer science. Many of their inventions have been adopted by mainstream computer science and are no longer considered a part of AI. According to Russell & Norvig (2003), all of the following were originally developed in AI laboratories:

- Time sharing
- Interactive interpreters

- Graphical user interfaces and the computer mouse
- Rapid development environments
- The linked list data type
- Automatic storage management
- Symbolic programming
- Functional programming
- Dynamic programming
- Object-oriented programming

Other

Neural networks are also being widely deployed in homeland security, speech and text recognition, data mining, and e-mail spam filtering.

List of Applications

Typical problems to which AI methods are applied

- Pattern recognition
  - o Optical character recognition
  - o Handwriting recognition
  - o Speech recognition
  - o Face recognition
- Artificial Creativity
- Computer vision, Virtual reality and Image processing
- Diagnosis (artificial intelligence)
- Game theory and Strategic planning
- Game artificial intelligence and Computer game bot
- Natural language processing, Translation and Chatterbots
- Nonlinear control and Robotics

Other fields in which AI methods are implemented

- Artificial life
- Automated reasoning
- Automation

- Biologically-inspired computing
- Colloquis
- Concept mining
- Data mining
- Knowledge representation
- Semantic Web
- E-mail spam filtering
- Robotics
  - o Behaviour-based roboticso
  - o Cognitiveo
  - o Cybernetics
  - o Developmental robotics
  - o Epigenetic robotics
  - o Evolutionary robotics
- Hybrid intelligent system
- Intelligent agent
- Intelligent control
- Litigation

Progress in Artificial Intelligence

Artificial intelligence can be evaluated on constrained and well-defined problems that allow comparison with human performance. Such tests have been termed subject matter expert Turing tests. Smaller problems provide more achievable goals and there are an ever-increasing number of positive results.

Performance Evaluation

The broad classes of outcome for an AI test are:

- **optimal**: it is not possible to perform better
- **strong super-human**: performs better than all humans
- **super-human**: performs better than most humans
- **sub-human**: performs worse than most humans

Optimal

- Checkers

Computer Players

The first computer English draughts programme was written by C.S. Strachey, M.A., National Research Development Corporation, London, in the early 1950s.

The second computer programme was written in 1956 by Arthur Samuel, a researcher from IBM. Other than it being one of the most complicated game playing programmes written at the time, it is also well known for being one of the first adaptive programmes. It learned by playing games against modified versions of itself, with the victorious versions surviving. Samuel's programme was far from mastering the game, although one win against a blind checkers master gave the general public the impression that it was very good.

In the 1990s, the strongest programme was *Chinook*, written in 1989 by a team from the University of Alberta led by Jonathan Schaeffer. Marion Tinsley, world champion from 1955-1962 and from 1975-1991, won a match against the machine in 1992. In 1994, Tinsley had to resign in the middle of an even match for health reasons; he died shortly thereafter. In 1995, Chinook defended its man-machine title against Don Lafferty in a 32 game match where each had 1 win and 1 loss, and a record setting 30 draws. In 1996 Chinook won in the USA National Tournament by the widest margin ever, and was retired from play after that event. The man-machine title has not been contested since.

On July 2007, in an article published in Science Magazine, Chinook's developers announced that the programme had been improved to the point where it could not lose a game. If no mistakes were made by either player, the game would always end in a draw. After eighteen years, they have mathematically proven a weak solution to the game of Checkers. Using between 200 desktop computers at the peak of the project down to around 50 later on, the team made just 10^{14} calculations to search from the initial position to a database of positions with at most 10 pieces.

When both players are no longer able to move any pieces, the game is termed a Bildago and ends in a tie.

Computational Complexity

The number of legal positions in English draughts is estimated to be 10^{20}, and it has a game-tree complexity of approximately 10^{31}. By comparison, chess is estimated to have 10^{40} legal positions.

When draughts is generalised so that it can be played on an *n*-by-*n* board, the problem of determining if the first player has a win in a given position is EXPTIME-complete.

The July 2007 announcement by Chinook's team stating that the game had been solved must be understood in the sense that, with perfect play on both sides, the game will always finish with a draw. Yet, not all positions that could result from imperfect play have been analysed.

Super-human

- Backgammon: strong super-human
- Bridge: nearing strong super-human
- Chess: nearing strong super-human
- Reversi: strong super-human
- Scrabble: strong super-human

Sub-human

- Go
- Machine translation
- Most everyday tasks performed by humans.

Artificial Life

Artificial life (commonly Alife or alife) is a field of study and an associated art form which examine systems related to life, its processes, and its evolution through simulations using computer models, robotics, and biochemistry. There are three main kinds of alife, named for their approaches: *soft*, from software; *hard*, from hardware; and *wet*, from biochemistry. Artificial life imitates traditional biology by trying to *recreate* biological phenomena. The term "artificial life" is often used to specifically refer to soft alife.

Artificial life studies the logic of living systems in artificial environments. The goal is to study the phenomena of living systems in order to come to an understanding of the complex information processing that defines such systems.

Also sometimes included in the umbrella term Artificial Life are agent based systems which are used to study the emergent properties of societies of agents.

On the ecological front, research regarding the evolution of animal cooperative behaviour (started by W. D. Hamilton in the 60s resulting in theories of kin selection, reciprocity, multilevel selection and cultural group selection) was re-introduced via artificial life by Peter Turchin and Mikhail Burtsev in 2006. Previously, game theory has been utilised in similar investigation, however, that approach was deemed to be rather limiting in its amount of possible strategies and debatable set of payoff rules. The alife model designed here, instead, is based upon Conway's Game of Life but with much added complexity (there are over 10^{1000} strategies that can potentially emerge). Most significantly, the interacting agents are characterised by external phenotype markers which allows for recognition amongst in-group members. In effect, it is shown that given the capacity to perceive these markers, agents within the system are then able to evolve new group behaviours under minimalistic assumptions. On top of the already known strategies of the bourgeois-hawk-dove game, here two novel modes of cooperative attack and defense arise from the simulation.

For the setup, this two-dimensional artificial world is divided into cells, each containing either a resource bundle or is empty. An empty cell can acquire a resource bundle with a certain probability per unit of time and lose it when an agent consumes the resource.

Each agent is plainly constructed with a set of receptors, effectors (the components that govern the agents' behaviour), and neural net which connect the two. In response to the environment, an agent may rest, eat, reproduce by division, move, turn and attack. All actions expend energy taken from its internal energy storage which, once depleted, leads to the agent's death. Consumption of resource, as well as other agents after defeating it, yields an increase in the energy storage. Reproduction is modeled as being asexual while the offspring receive half the parental energy. Agents are also equipped with sensory inputs that allow them to detect resources or other members within a parameter in addition to its own level of vitality. As regard to the phenotype markers, they do not influence behaviour but solely function as indicator of 'genetic' similarity. Heredity is achieved by having the relevant information be inherited by the offspring and subjected to a set rate of mutation.

The objective of the investigation is to study how the presence of phenotype markers affects the model's range of evolving cooperative strategies. In addition, as the resource available in this 2D environment is capped, the simulation also serves to determine the effect of environmental carrying capacity on their emergence.

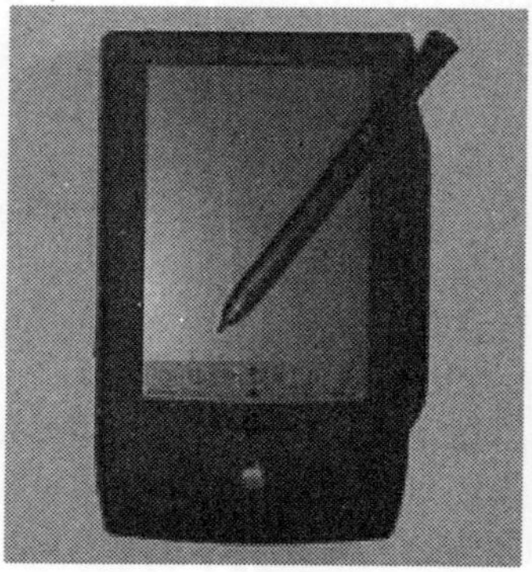

PDA from Apple (Newton)

First "PDA": EO Personal Communicator (440) from AT&T

One previously unseen strategy is termed the "raven". Here, agents left cells with in-group members, thus avoiding intra-specific competition, and attack out-group members voluntarily. Another strategy name the 'starling' involves the agent sharing cells with in-group members. Despite individuals having smaller energy storage due to resource partitioning, this strategy permits highly effective defense against large invader via the advantage in numbers. Ecologically speaking, this resembles the mobbing behaviour that characterises many species of small birds when they collectively defend against the predator.

In conclusion, the research claims that the simulated results have important implications for the evolution of territoriality (ethology) by showing that within the alife framework it's possible to "model not only how one strategy displaces another, but also the very process by which new strategies emerge out of a large quantity of possibilities".

Work is also underway to create cellular models of artificial life. Initial work on building a complete biochemical model of cellular behaviour is underway as part of a number of different research projects, namely BlueGene which seeks to understand the mechanisms behind protein folding.

7

PERSONAL DIGITAL ASSISTANT

A personal digital assistant (PDA) is a handheld computer, also known as small or palmtop computers. Newer PDAs also have both colour screens and audio capabilities, enabling them to be used as mobile phones (smartphones), web browsers, or portable media players. Many PDAs can access the Internet, intranets or extranets via Wi-Fi, or Wireless Wide-Area Networks (WWANs). Many PDAs employ touch screen technology.

The first PDA is considered to be the CASIO PF-3000 released in May 1983. GO Corp. was also pioneering in the field. The term was first used on January 7, 1992 by Apple Computer CEO John Sculley at the Consumer Electronics Show in Las Vegas, Nevada, referring to the Apple Newton. PDAs are sometimes referred to as "Palms", "Palm Pilot", or "Palm Tops".

Typical Features

Currently, a typical PDA has a touch screen for entering data, a memory card slot for data storage and at least one of the following for connectivity: IrDA, Bluetooth and/or WiFi. However, many PDAs (typically those used primarily as telephones) may not have a touch screen, using softkeys, a directional pad and either the numeric keypad or a thumb keyboard for input.

Software typically required to be a PDA includes an appointment calendar, a to-do list, an address book for contacts and some sort of note programme. Connected PDAs also typically include E-mail and Web support.

Touch Screen

Many original PDAs, such as the Apple Newton and the Palm Pilot, featured touch screens for user interaction, having only a few buttons usually reserved for shortcuts to often used programmes. Touch screen PDAs, including Windows Pocket PC devices, usually have a detachable stylus that can be used on the touch screen. Interaction is then done by tapping the screen to activate buttons or menu choices, and dragging the stylus to, for example, highlight. Text input is usually done in one of four ways:

- Using a virtual keyboard, where a keyboard is shown on the touch screen. Input is done by tapping letters on the screen.
- Using external keyboard or chorded keyboard connected by USB, IR or Bluetooth.

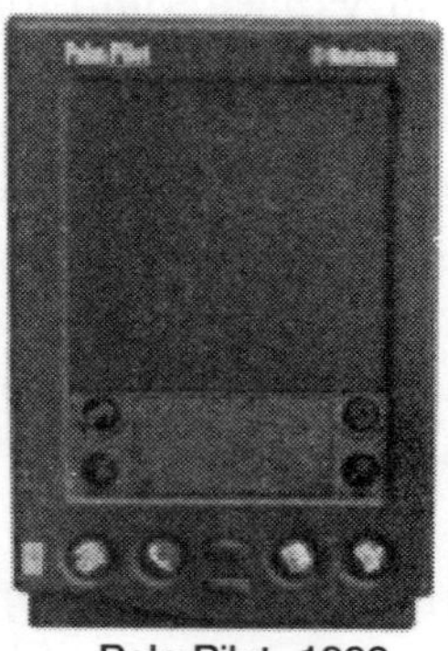

PalmPilot, 1998

- Using letter or word recognition, where letters or words are written on the touch screen, and then "translated" to letters in the currently activated text field. Despite rigorous research and development projects, end-users experience mixed results with this input method, with some finding it frustrating and inaccurate, while others are satisfied with the quality. Recognition and computation of handwritten horizontal and vertical formulas such as "1 + 2 =" was also under development.

- Stroke recognition (termed Graffiti by Palm). In this system a predefined set of strokes represents the various characters needed. The user learns to draw these strokes on the screen or in an input area. The strokes are often simplified character shapes to make them easier to remember.

PDAs for business use, including the BlackBerry and Treo, have full keyboards and scroll wheels or thumb wheels to facilitate data entry and navigation, in addition to supporting touch-screen input. There are also full-size foldable keyboards available that plug directly, or use wireless technology to interface with the PDA and allow for normal typing. BlackBerry has additional functionality, such as push-based email and applications.

Newer PDAs, such as the Apple iPhone and iPod touch include new user interfaces using other means of input. The iPhone and iPod touch uses a technology called Multi-touch.

Memory Cards

Although many early PDAs did not have memory card slots, now most have either an SD (Secure Digital) and/or a Compact Flash slot. Although originally designed for memory, SDIO and Compact Flash cards are available for such things as Wi-Fi and Webcams. Some PDAs also have a USB port, mainly for USB flash drives.

As more PDAs include telephone support, to keep the size down, many now offer miniSD or microSD slots instead of full-sized SD slots.

Wired Connectivity

While many earlier PDAs connected via serial ports or other proprietary format, many today connect via USB cable. This served primarily to connect to a computer, and few, if any PDAs were able to connect to *each other* out of the box using cables, as USB requires one machine to act as a host—functionality which was not often planned. Some PDAs were able to connect to the internet, either by means of one of these cables, or by using an extension card with an ethernet port/RJ-45 adaptor.

Wireless Connectivity

Most modern PDAs have Bluetooth wireless connectivity, an increasingly popular tool for mobile devices. It can be used to connect keyboards, headsets, GPS and many other accessories, as well as sending files between PDAs. Many mid-range and superior PDAs have Wi-Fi/WLAN/802.11-connectivity, used for connecting to Wi-Fi hotspots or wireless networks. Older PDAs predominantly have an IrDA (infrared) port; however fewer current models have the technology, as it is slowly being phased out due to support for Bluetooth and Wi-Fi. IrDA allows communication between two PDAs: a PDA and any device with an IrDA port or adapter. Most universal PDA keyboards use infrared technology because many older PDAs have it, and infrared technology is low-cost and has the advantage of being permitted aboard aircraft.

Synchronisation

An important function of PDAs is synchronising data with a PC. This allows up-to-date contact information stored on software such as Microsoft Outlook or ACT! to update the database on the PDA. The data synchronisation ensures that the PDA has an accurate list of contacts, appointments and e-mail, allowing users to access the same information on the PDA as the host computer.

The synchronising also prevents the loss of information stored on the device in case it is lost, stolen, or destroyed. Another advantage is that data input is usually a lot quicker on a PC, since text input via a touch screen is still not quite optimal. Transferring data to a PDA via the computer is therefore a lot quicker than having to manually input all data on the handheld device.

Most PDAs come with the ability to synchronize to a PC. This is done through synchronisation software provided with the handheld, such as HotSync Manager, which comes with Palm OS handhelds, Microsoft ActiveSync for older versions of Windows or Windows Mobile Device Center on Windows Vista, which comes with Windows Mobile handhelds.

These programmes allow the PDA to be synchronised with a Personal information manager. This personal information manager may be an outside programme or a proprietary programme. For example, the BlackBerry PDA comes with the Desktop Manager programme which can synchronize to both Microsoft Outlook and ACT!. Other PDAs come only with their own proprietary software. For example, some early Palm OS PDAs came only with Palm Desktop while later Palms such as the Treo 650 has the built-in ability to sync to Palm Desktop and/or Microsoft Outlook, while Microsoft's ActiveSync and Windows Mobile Device Center only synchronize with Microsoft Outlook or a Microsoft Exchange server.

Third-party synchronisation software is also available for many PDAs from companies like Intellisync and CompanionLink. This software synchronises these handhelds to other personal information managers which are not supported by the PDA manufacturers, such as GoldMine and Lotus Notes.

CUSTOMISATION

Uses

PDAs are used to store information that can be accessed at any time and anywhere.

Automobile Navigation

Many PDAs are used in car kits and are fitted with differential Global Positioning System (GPS) receivers to provide realtime automobile navigation. PDAs are increasingly being fitted as standard on new cars.

Many systems can also display traffic conditions, dynamic routing and roadside mobile radar guns. Popular software in Europe and in America for this functionality are TomTom, Garmin, iGO etc. showing road conditions and 2D or 3D environments.

Ruggedized PDAs

For many years businesses and government organisations have relied upon rugged PDAs also known as enterprise digital assistants (EDAs) for mobile data applications. Typical applications include supply chain management in warehouses, package delivery, route accounting, medical treatment and record keeping in hospitals, facilities maintenance and management, parking enforcement, access control and security, capital asset maintenance, meter reading by utilities, and "wireless waitress" applications in restaurants and hospitality venues. A common feature of EDAs are the integration of Data Capture devices like Bar Code, RFID and Smart Card Readers.

Medical and Scientific Uses

In medicine, PDAs have been shown to aid diagnosis and drug selection and some studies have concluded that their use by patients to record symptoms improves the effectiveness of communication with hospitals during follow-up. The first landmark study in testing the effectiveness of PDAs in a medical setting was conducted at the Brigham & Women's Hospital and Massachusetts General Hospitals in affiliation with Harvard Medical School. Led by the team of Steven Labkoff, MD and Sandeep Shah, the Constellation project used Apple's Newton (first PDA in the market) to cater to the demands of the medical professionals. Constellation's objective was to test how clinicians in various medical environments (wired vs un wired) would use medical reference books on a hand-held device. The study validated the hypothesis that PDAs with medical content would be used to a greater degree (>40% more often) in unwired environments. Today, the company evolved from the effort Skyscape offers a wide range of resources including drug information, treatment options, guidelines, evidence based information and journal summaries including the drug & safety alerts. Other entrants include Epocrates and ABX guide, which supply drug databases, treatment information and relevant news in formats specific to mobile devices and services such as AvantGo translate medical journals into readable formats and provide updates from journals. WardWatch organises medical records to remind doctors making ward rounds of information such as the treatment regimens of patients and programmes. Finally, Pendragon and Syware provide tools for conducting research with mobile devices, and connecting to a central server allowing the user to enter data into a centralised database using their PDA. Additionally, Microsoft Visual Studio and Sun Java provide programming tools for developing survey instruments on the handheld. These development tools allow for integration with SQL databases that are stored on the handheld and can be synchronised with a desktop/server based database.

Recently the development of Sensor Web technology has led to discussion of using wearable bodily sensors to monitor ongoing conditions like diabetes and epilepsy and alerting medical staff or the patient themselves to the treatment required via communication between the web and PDAs.

Educational Uses

As mobile technology has become very common, it is no surprise that personal computing has become a vital learning tool by this time. Educational institutes have commenced a trend of integrating PDAs into their teaching practices (mobile learning). With the capabilities of PDAs, teachers are now able to provide a collaborative learning experience for their students. They are also preparing their students for possible practical uses of mobile computing upon their graduation.

PDAs and handheld devices have recently allowed for digital note taking. This has increased student's productivity by allowing individuals to quickly spell-check, modify, and amend their class notes or e-notes. Educators are currently able to distribute course material through the use of the internet connectivity or infrared file sharing functions of the PDA. With concerns to class material, textbook publishers have begun to release e-books, or electronic textbooks, which can be uploaded directly to a PDA. This then lessens the effort of carrying multiple textbooks at one time.

To meet the instructive needs sought by educational institutes, software companies have developed programmes with the learning aspects in mind. Simple programmes such as dictionaries, thesauri, and word processing software are important to the digital note taking process. In addition to these simple programmes, encyclopedias and digital planning lessons have created added functionality for users.

With the increase in mobility of PDAs, school boards and educational institutes have now encountered issues with these devices. School boards are now concerned with students utilising the internet connectivity to share test answers or to gossip during class time, which creates disruptions. Many school boards have modernised their computer policies to address these new concerns. Software companies such as Scantron Corp. have now created a programme for distributing digital quizzes. The quiz software disables the infrared function on PDAs, which eliminates the element of information sharing among individuals during the examination. Many colleges encourage the use of PDAs.

Sporting Uses

PDAs are used by glider pilots for pre-flight planning and to assist navigation in cross-country competitions. They are linked to a GPS to produce moving-map displays showing the tracks to turn-points, airspace hazards and other tactical information.

PDA's may also be used by music enthusiasts. They can be used to play a variety of file formats (unlike most MP3 Players) which may be played during physical exercise (eg running). This, unlike certain other devices as laptops.

PDAs can be used by road rally enthusiasts. PDA software can be used for calculating distance, speed, time, and GPS navigation as well as unassisted navigation.

PDA for People with Disabilities

PDAs offer varying degrees of accessibility for people with differing abilities, based on the particular device and service. People with vision, hearing, mobility, and speech impairments may be able to use PDAs on a limited basis, and this may be enhanced by the addition of accessibility software (e.g. speech recognition for verbal input instead of manual input). Universal design is relevant to PDAs as well as other technology, and a viable solution for many user-access issues, though it has yet to be consistently integrated into the design of popular consumer PDA devices.

PDAs have recently become quite useful in the Traumatic Brain Injury/Posttraumatic Stress Disorder population, especially seen in troops returning home from Operation Iraqi Freedom(OIF)/ Operation Enduring Freedom(OEF). PDAs address memory issues and help these men and women out with daily life organisation and reminders. As of quite recently, the Department of Veterans' Affairs (VA) has begun issuing thousands of PDAs to troops who present the need for them. Occupational therapists have taken on a crucial role within this population helping these veterans return to the normalcy of life they once had.

TECHNICAL DETAILS

Architecture

Many PDAs run using a variation of the ARM architecture (usually denoted by the Intel XScale trademark). This encompasses a class of RISC microprocessors that are widely used in mobile devices and embedded systems, and its design was influenced strongly by a popular 1970s/1980s CPU; the MOS Technology 6502.

OS

The currently major PDA operating systems are:

- Palm OS—owned by PalmSource
- Windows Mobile Professional and Classic for use on Pocket PCs, (based on the Windows CE kernel)—owned by Microsoft
- iPhone OS—owned by Apple Inc.
- BlackBerry OS—owned by Research In Motion

- Many operating systems based on the Linux kernel—free (not owned by any company) These include
  - o Familiar (comes in three flavours: GPE, Opie and barebone)
  - o OpenZaurus (for Zaurus PDAs)
  - o Ångström, a descendent of OpenZaurus
  - o Intimate (for PDAs with an exceedingly large amount of memory)
- Symbian OS (formerly EPOC) owned by Motorola, Panasonic, Nokia, Samsung, Siemens and Sony Ericsson

---

List of Mobile Operating Systems

BREW[m]

Symbian OS[m n s]

Windows Mobile[m n]

BlackBerry OS[m]

iPhone OS[n]

Palm OS (Garnet OS)[n]

Mobilinux[l]

LiMo Foundation[l]

- Access Linux Platform[l n s]
- LiMo Platform[l m n]
  - o MotoMagx[j l]

Android[l m]

Maemo[l]

- Internet Tablet OS[l n]
- Moblin project[l] o Ubuntu Mobile[l m]
  - o Red Flag MIDINUX[l]

Openmoko Linux[l n]

Qtopia[l m n]

DoJa[j]

JavaFX Mobile[j]

SavaJe[j]

[j] = Java based

[l] = Linux based

[m] = Managed code support

[n] = Native code permitted

[s] = Capability-based security

Decline of Stand-alone PDAs vs Phones

Stand-alone PDA sales fell 43.5% from 2006 to 2007. Approximately 4 million PDAs are sold per year. However, with smartphone sales increasing from levels of approximately 60 million per year, more telephones are being used as PDAs with phone capability.

According to a Gartner market study, the overall market for PDAs grew by 20.7% in the third quarter (Q3) of 2005, compared to Q3 2004, with marketshare resolving as follows (by operating system):

- Palm OS for Palm, Inc. PDAs and some other licensees-14.9% (declining)
- Windows Mobile for PDAs that comply with the Microsoft's Pocket PC specifications—49.2% (increasing)
- RIM BlackBerry (produced by Research In Motion)—25.0% (increasing)
- Symbian OS—5.8% (increasing)
- Various operating systems based on the Linux kernel for various special designed PDAs (many other supported)—0.7% (stable)
- Other—4.4% (stable)

Popular Consumer PDAs

- E-TEN
- Abacus PDA Watch
- Acer N Series
- AlphaSmart

- Amida Simputer
- BlackBerry
- Fujitsu Siemens Loox
- HP iPAQ
- High Tech Computer Corporation(Dopod,Qtek)'s series of Windows Mobile PDA/phones (HTC)
- iPod Touch
- iPhone
- Palm, Inc. (Tungsten E2, TX, Treo and Zire)
- PocketMail (email PDA with inbuilt acoustic coupler)
- Psion
- Sharp Wizard and Sharp Zaurus
- Sidekick
- Royal

HP Compaq tablet PC with rotating/removable keyboard

Discontinued

- Apple Newton
- Dell Axim

- GMate Yopy
- hp Jornada Pocket PC (phased out/merged with iPAQ line in 2002)
- LifeDrive
- NEC MobilePro
- Casio Pocket Viewer
- Sony CLIÉ
- Tapwave Zodiac

Rugged PDAs

- Hand Held Products (HHP)
- Intermec
- Psion Teklogix
- Symbol Technologies
- MobileCompia (M3)

8

TABLET PC

A Tablet PC is a notebook or slate-shaped mobile computer, equipped with a touchscreen or graphics tablet/screen hybrid technology which allows the user to operate the computer with a stylus or digital pen, or a fingertip, instead of a keyboard or mouse.

The form factor offers a more mobile way to interact with a computer. Tablet PCs are often used where normal notebooks are impractical or unwieldy, or do not provide the needed functionality.

FORMS

Slates

Slates, which resemble writing slates, are tablet PCs without a dedicated keyboard. Keyboards can usually be attached via a wireless or USB connection.

These tablet PCs typically incorporate small (8.4-14.1 inches/ 21–36 cm) LCD screens and have been popular for quite some time in vertical markets such as health care, education, and field work.

Slate models are often designed with a focus on pure mobility, that is, the less to carry, the better.

Rugged tablet PC models are usually in the slate form factor; without a keyboard, there are fewer moving parts to break.

Thin-client Slates

Thin-client slates consist of a touchscreen and an integrated wireless connection device. These units by design have limited processing power which is chiefly involved with Input/Output data processing such as video display, network communications, audio encoding/decoding, and input capture (touchscreen input, bar code reading, magnetic stripe reading (credit card swipe). The unit transmits data via a secured wireless connection to a remote server for processing.

Thin-client slates have the design advantages of a very lightweight form factor, more secure data (no data storage on the slate computer), long battery life (no processor to power). The Panasonic Toughbook 08 is representative of the application of thin-client computing to tablet PCs.

Convertibles

Convertible notebooks have a base body with an attached keyboard. They more closely resemble modern notebooks/laptops, and are usually heavier and larger than slates.

Typically, the base of a convertible attaches to the display at a single joint called a swivel hinge or rotating hinge. The joint allows the screen to rotate around 180° and fold down on top of the keyboard to provide a flat writing surface. This design, although the most common, creates a physical point of weakness on the notebook.

Some manufacturers, however, have attempted to overcome these weak points. The Panasonic Toughbook 19, for example, is advertised as a more durable convertible notebook. One model by Acer has a sliding design in which the screen slides up from the slate-like position and locks into place to provide the laptop mode.

Convertibles are by far the most popular form factor of tablet PCs, because for people who are unsure about the practicality of using the pen as the primary method of input, the convertibles still offer the keyboard and pointing device of traditional notebooks as a backup plan.

Hybrids

Hybrids, coined by users of the HP/Compaq TC1000 and TC1100 series, share the features of the slate and convertible by using a detachable keyboard which operates in a similar fashion to a convertible when attached.

This is not to be confused with slate models that have a detachable keyboard—detachable keyboards for pure slate models do not rotate around to allow the tablet to rest on it like a convertible.

Despite a loyal following of users, the hybrid form factor has not received any recent updates after the TC1100 was discontinued.

History

- **Late 1960s**
  - Alan Kay of Xerox PARC proposed a notebook using pen input called Dynabook.
- **1989**
  - The first commercially available tablet-type computer was the GRiDPad from GRiD Systems, released in September. Its operating system was based on MS-DOS.
- **1991**
  - The Momenta Pentop was released.
  - GO Corp announced a dedicated operating system, called PenPoint OS.
  - NCR released model 3125 pen computer running MS-DOS, Penpoint or Pen Windows.
  - The Apple Newton entered development; although it ultimately became a PDA, its original concept (which called for a larger screen and greater sketching capabilities) resembled that of a tablet PC.
- **1992**
  - GO Corp shipped PenPoint and IBM announced IBM 2125 pen computer (the first IBM model named "ThinkPad") in April.

  - o Microsoft released Windows for Pen Computing.
- **1993**
  - o The first commercialised tablet computer systems available to the consumer market were the IBM ThinkPad 750P and 360P introduced in 1993.
  - o AT&T introduced the EO Personal Communicator combining PenPoint with wireless communications.
- **1999**
  - o The "QBE" Tablet PC created by Aqcess Technologies wins Comdex Best of Show.
- **2000**
  - o The "QBE Vivo" Tablet PC created by Aqcess Technologies ties for Comdex Best of Show.
- **2002**
  - o Tablet PCs were made further available with the introduction of Microsoft's Windows XP Tablet PC Edition.
  - § Microsoft's operating system for the tablet PCs had the advantage of the standardisation in the PC market with Microsoft's operating systems.
- **2002-Present**
  - o Recent advances in computer technology and lowering of manufacturing costs allowed for tablet PCs to become more affordable and widespread.
- **Present**
  - o Windows Vista is released to the public. Many of the different editions include the same Tablet PC support found in Windows XP Tablet PC edition.

SYSTEM SOFTWARE

Microsoft

The operating system on which most tablet PCs run is Windows XP Tablet PC Edition. Tablet PC Edition is a superset of Windows

XP Professional, the difference being tablet functionality, including alternate text input (Tablet PC Input Panel) and basic drivers for support of tablet PC specific hardware. Requirements to install Tablet PC Edition include a tablet digitizer or touchscreen device, and hardware control buttons including a Ctrl-Alt-Delete shortcut button, scrolling buttons, and at least one user-configurable application button.

Service Pack 2 for Windows XP includes Tablet PC Edition 2005 and is a free upgrade. This version brought improved handwriting recognition and improved the Input Panel, allowing it to be used in almost every application. The Input Panel was also revised to extend speech recognition services (input and correction) to other applications.

With Windows Vista, the Tablet PC functionality no longer requires a separate edition. Tablet PC support is built into all editions of Windows Vista with the exception of Home Basic. This extends the handwriting recognition, ink collection, and additional input methods to any computer running Vista even if the input device is an external digitizer, a touch screen, or even a regular mouse.

Windows Applications

There are quite a lot of operating systems in use on devices marketed as tablets. Note that most tablet PC software is targeted particularly for the Microsoft Tablet PC API, and will not run on devices without Windows XP Tablet PC Edition. Care should be taken when researching a tablet system or any device or software that claims to be designed for tablet PCs, as the phrase does not guarantee compatibility.

Applications developed for the tablet PC cater to the form factor and functionality available on the platform. Many forms of applications incorporate a pen-friendly user interface and/or the ability to handwrite directly in the document or interface.

A brief description of the applications included follows:

Experience Pack

- Ink Desktop: an Active Desktop control designed to run in the background and allow the user to write directly on the desktop.
- Snipping Tool: a screen capture application which allows the tablet pen to be used to select a portion of the screen and then annotate it and save as a file or send in an email.
- Ink Art: a painting application developed by Ambient Design originally as ArtRage, licensed to Microsoft for release to Tablet PC users.
- Ink Crossword: a crossword application developed to mirror the experience of a paper crossword puzzle on a tablet PC.
- Media Transfer: a synchronisation utility designed to download music, pictures, and videos off of computers in the same network.

Education Pack

- Ink Flash Cards: an application designed to assist memorisation by using a flash card approach, enabling the user to handwrite their own flash cards and display them back in a slideshow.
- Equation Writer: a recognition tool specialising in converting handwritten mathematical equations to a computer-generated image for pasting into other documents.
- GoBinder Lite: an organisation and note-taking application developed by Agilix Labs.
- Hexic Deluxe: a game with a tablet PC specific gesture enabled for easier use with the tablet

GNU/Linux

Running Linux on tablet PCs is as practical as on conventional notebooks. More recently, tablet PCs may also be configured with Linux pre-installed.

One early implementation of a Linux tablet was the ProGear by FrontPath. The ProGear used a Transmeta chip and a resistive digitizer. The ProGear initially came with a version of Slackware Linux, but could later be bought with Windows 98. Because these computers are general purpose IBM PC compatible machines, they can run many different operating systems.

Xorg now supports screen rotation and tablet input through Wacom drivers, and handwriting recognition software from both the Qt-based Qtopia and GTK+-based Internet Tablet OS provide promising free and open source systems for future development.

Another handwriting recognition software for GNU/Linux is CellWriter; a note-taking application for GNU/Linux and FreeBSD is Xournal

However, little mature desktop-oriented software of the sort has arisen, leading many users to rely on on-screen keyboards and alternative text input methods like Dasher.

TabletKiosk currently offers a hybrid digitizer / touch device running SUSE Linux. It is the first device with this feature to support Linux.

Apple

The aftermarketer Axiotron has introduced aftermarket, heavily modified Apple MacBooks called Modbooks, a Mac OS X-based tablet computer. It uses Apple's Inkwell for handwriting and gesture recognition and bundles additional digitisation software from Wacom.

While Apple Inc. doesn't sanction running their operating system Mac OS X on non-Apple hardware, there are a large number of computer enthusiasts who are running hacked copies of Mac OS X on various x86 architecture PC models, among them Tablet PC computers. To get Mac OS X to talk to the digitizer on Tablet PC systems they use a free open source driver originally written to support serial tablets for which Wacom no longer supplies Mac drivers.

Tablets vs. Traditional Notebooks

The advantages and disadvantages of tablet PCs are highly subjective measures. What appeals to one user may be exactly what disappoints another. The following are commonly cited opinions of the tablet PC platform:

Advantages

- More natural form of input—sketching and handwriting are a much more familiar form of input than a keyboard and mouse, especially for people who are new to computers.
- Gesture recognition—gestures (moving the stylus in special patterns over the screen) are powerful ways to increase efficiency. Many applications, or the operating system itself, can be programmed to respond in different ways to certain gestures created by the pen.
- Note-taking—taking handwritten notes and drawing diagrams at a class or conference increases productivity and retention of information. The notes can also be searched automatically if handwriting recognition is implemented.
- Accessibility—those who are physically unable to type can utilise the additional features of a tablet PC to be able to interact with the electronic world.
- Digital art—tablets are often necessary for professional digital artist work. For many, mouse movement is too jerky to be used as a precision tool.
- Portability—slate tablets and hybrids without keyboards are very slim and light compared to typical laptops and can easily be tucked under the arm like a book.
- Horizontal orientation—most tablet PCs do not interrupt line of sight since they lie flat on the table or in one's arms. This allows for better interaction in business meetings and conferences and also makes it easy for digital artists who wish to draw on a horizontal medium.

Disadvantages

- Higher cost—convertible tablet PCs can cost significantly more than their non-tablet counterparts although this premium has been predicted to fall.
- Screen size—the size of tablet PC screens peaks at around 14.1 inches although some models make up for this with higher resolution (pixel density per unit area).
- Input speed—handwriting can be significantly slower than peak typing speeds which can be as high as 50-150 WPM.
- Screen damage risk—Tablet PC's are handled more than conventional laptops yet built on the same frames and since their screens also serve as input devices (like PDAs) they run a higher risk of screen damage.
- No built in optical drive (in many Tablet PCs) — in order to reduce weight and thickness.

Designing around Disadvantages

Manufacturers can design additional durability into the displays of tablets to effectively reduce screen damage risk, hinge failure, and screen size limitations. As an example, Panasonic Computer Solutions Company designed the Toughbook 19 specifically to overcome the screen damage issue potential. The use of scissor shock absorbers mounted to the screen, flexible connectors for data cables, molded magnesium alloy screen casing, durable and replaceable screen overlayments, and purpose built convertible hinges impact reliability. However, handheld models of computer such as the OQO Model 2 have a retractable keyboard that slides out sideways as a measure against having weak hinges and that the clamps for the sideway retracting keyboard are stronger if you put it into proportion to the robustness.

Features

New Tablet PCs includes:

- Capacitive technology, which senses touch of finger with no pressure required for system to recognise input.

- Digital palm recognition technology prevents inadvertant contact from disrupting pen input.
- Multi-touch is the ability to touch the screen in more than one place at the same time and do things.
- Sunlight readable displays (800 nit display), so you can clearly read it even in bright and direct sunlight.

Popular Models

Major tablet PC Manufacturers include Acer, Asus, Bosanova, Fujitsu, Gateway, Inc., Hewlett-Packard, IBM, Lenovo Group, LG Electronics, NEC, TabletKiosk, Motion Computing, Panasonic and Toshiba.

Popular models include:

Slate

- PaceBlade SlimBook 200
- Fujitsu Stylistic ST5010
- Electrovaya Scribbler SC4000 series (older: SC2000, SC3000, SC3100)
- MobileDemand xTablet T8600 Rugged Tablet PC
- Motion M1200, M1300, M1400, LE-Series, C5, LS800, LE 1700 and C5 which is targeted towards the healthcare industry
- JLT8404 Field Tablet PC
- Panasonic Toughbook 08
- TabletKiosk Sahara i400 series
- Samsung Q1 (Q1 Ultra)
- Xplore Technologies
- COWON Q5W
- Axiotron Modbook
- Nokia N800/N810

Convertible

- Acer TravelMate C100/C300/C310

- Asus R1F
- Asus R1E
- Averatec C3500 Series
- Dialogue Flybook V5
- Dell Latitude XT
- Fujitsu LifeBook P1610(Slim, Ultra-portable, Small)/T4020, /T4210, /T4220 /T2010 (Latest)
- Gateway C-140X (aka S-7235/E-295C)
- Gateway C-120X (aka S-7125C/E-155C)
- HP Compaq TC4200/TC4400
- HP Compaq 2710p
- HP Pavilion tx1000 Entertainment PC
- HP Pavilion tx2000
- HP Pavilion tx2500z
- Lenovo ThinkPad X41 Tablet
- Lenovo ThinkPad X60 Tablet (known popularly as "X60t")
- Lenovo ThinkPad X61 Tablet
- LG XNote C1
- LG LT-20-47CE
- Panasonic Toughbook 19
- Toshiba Portégé 3500/3505
- Toshiba Portégé M200
- Toshiba Portégé M400/405/700
- Toshiba Portégé R400/405
- Toshiba Satellite R10/R15/R20/R25
- Toshiba Tecra M4/M7

Hybrid

- Compaq TC1000
- HP Compaq TC1100
- Tatung Tangy

Programmes

- Microsoft Office OneNote
- Einstein Technologies Tablet Enhancements for Outlook
- GO Corporation
- Agilix GoBinder
- Mobilis—Protectis Range
- EverNote
- IHMC CmapTools—a free concept mapping application
- Xournal—a linux notetaking application
- Ergo from Invu—a search, clustering, visualisation and annotation application from YourErgo
- OnSite Companion Construction Software for Tablet PC
- MusicReader—Electronic Music Stand—sheet music display on Tablet PC.

9

IEEE 802.11

IEEE 802.11

IEEE 802.11 is a set of standards for wireless local area network (WLAN) computer communication, developed by the IEEE LAN/MAN Standards Committee (IEEE 802) in the 5 GHz and 2.4 GHz public spectrum bands.

Although the terms 802.11 and Wi-Fi are often used interchangeably, the Wi-Fi Alliance uses the term "Wi-Fi" to define a slightly different set of overlapping standards. In some cases, market demand has led the Wi-Fi Alliance to begin certifying products before amendments to the 802.11 standard are completed.

A Linksys Residential gateway with an 802.11b radio and a 4-port ethernet switch.

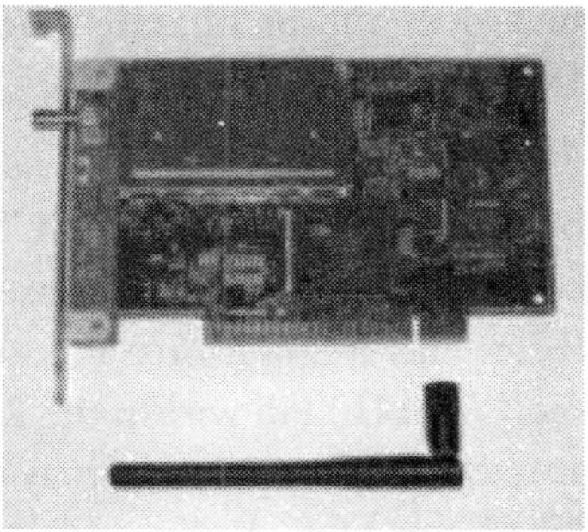

A Compaq 802.11b PCI card

The 802.11 family includes over-the-air modulation techniques that use the same basic protocol. The most popular are those defined by the 802.11b and 802.11g protocols, and are amendments to the original standard. 802.11a was the first wireless networking standard, but 802.11b was the first widely accepted one, followed by 802.11g and 802.11n. Security was originally purposefully weak due to export requirements of some governments, and was later enhanced via the 802.11i amendment after governmental and legislative changes. 802.11n is a new multi-streaming modulation technique that is still under draft development, but products based on its proprietary pre-draft versions are being sold. Other standards in the family (c–f, h, j) are service amendments and extensions or corrections to previous specifications.

802.11b and 802.11g use the 2.4 GHz ISM band, operating in the United States under Part 15 of the US Federal Communications Commission Rules and Regulations. Because of this choice of frequency band, 802.11b and g equipment may occasionally suffer interference from microwave ovens and cordless telephones. Bluetooth devices, while operating in the same band, in theory do not interfere with 802.11b/g because they use a frequency hopping spread spectrum signaling method (FHSS) while 802.11b/g uses a direct sequence spread spectrum signaling method (DSSS). 802.11a uses the 5 GHz U-NII band, which offers 8 non-overlapping channels rather than the 3 offered in the 2.4GHz ISM frequency band.

The segment of the radio frequency spectrum used varies between countries. In the US, 802.11a and 802.11g devices may be operated without a license, as explained in Part 15 of the FCC Rules and Regulations. Frequencies used by channels one through six (802.11b) fall within the 2.4 GHz amateur radio band. Licensed amateur radio operators may operate 802.11b/g devices under Part 97 of the FCC Rules and Regulations, allowing increased power output but not commercial content or encryption.

Protocols Summary

Wireless networking standards

802.11 Protocol	Release[3]	Freq. (GHz)	Thru. (Mbit/s)	Data (Mbit/s)	Mod.	$r_{in.}$ (m)	$r_{out.}$ (m)
–	1997	2.4	0.9	2		~20	~100
a	1999	5	23	54	OFDM	~35	~120
b	1999	2.4	4.3	11	DSSS	~38	~140
g	2003	2.4	19	54	OFDM	~38	~140
n	2009	2.4, 5	74	248		~70	~250[4]
y	2008	3.7	23	54		~50	~5000

802.11-1997 (802.11 legacy)

The original version of the standard IEEE 802.11, released in 1997 and clarified in 1999, specified two raw data rates of 1 and 2 megabits per second (Mbit/s) to be transmitted in Industrial Scientific Medical frequency band at 2.4 GHz.

Legacy 802.11 was rapidly supplemented (and popularized) by 802.11b.

802.11a

Release Date	Op. Frequency	Data Rate (Typ)	Data Rate (Max)	Range (Indoor)
October 1999	5 GHz	23 Mbit/s	54 Mbit/s	~35 m

The 802.11a standard uses the same core protocol as the original standard, operates in 5 GHz band with a maximum raw data rate of 54 Mbit/s, which yields realistic net achievable throughput in the mid-20 Mbit/s.

Since the 2.4 GHz band is heavily used to the point of being crowded, using the relatively un-used 5 GHz band gives 802.11a a significant advantage. However, this high carrier frequency also brings a slight disadvantage: The effective overall range of 802.11a is slightly less than that of 802.11b/g; 802.11a signals cannot penetrate as far as those for 802.11b because they are absorbed more readily by walls and other solid objects in their path.

802.11b

Release Date	Op. Frequency	Data Rate (Typ)	Data Rate (Max)	Range (Indoor)
October 1999	2.4 GHz	4.5 Mbit/s	11 Mbit/s	~35 m

802.11b has a maximum raw data rate of 11 Mbit/s and uses the same media access method defined in the original standard. 802.11b products appeared on the market in early 2000, since 802.11b is a direct extension of the modulation technique defined in the original standard. The dramatic increase in throughput of 802.11b (compared to the original standard) along with simultaneous substantial price reductions led to the rapid acceptance of 802.11b as the definitive wireless LAN technology.

802.11b devices suffer interference from other products operating in the 2.4 GHz band. Devices operating in the 2.4 GHz range include: microwave ovens, Bluetooth devices, baby monitors and cordless telephones.

802.11g

Release Date	Op. Frequency	Data Rate (Typ)	Data Rate (Max)	Range (Indoor)
June 2003	2.4 GHz	23 Mbit/s	54 Mbit/s	~35 m

In June 2003, a third modulation standard was ratified: 802.11g. This works in the 2.4 GHz band (like 802.11b) but operates at a maximum raw data rate of 54 Mbit/s, or about 19 Mbit/s net throughput. 802.11g hardware is fully backwards compatible with 802.11b hardware.

The then-proposed 802.11g standard was rapidly adopted by consumers starting in January 2003, well before ratification, due to the desire for higher speeds, and reductions in manufacturing costs. By summer 2003, most dual-band 802.11a/b products became dual-band/tri-mode, supporting a and b/g in a single mobile adapter card or access point. Details of making b and g work well together occupied much of the lingering technical process; in an 802.11g network, however, activity by a 802.11b participant will reduce the speed of the overall 802.11g network.

Like 802.11b, 802.11g devices suffer interference from other products operating in the 2.4 GHz band. Devices operating in the 2.4 GHz range include: microwave ovens, Bluetooth devices, baby monitors and cordless telephones.

802.11-2007

In 2003, task group TGma was authorised to "roll up" many of the amendments to the 1999 version of the 802.11 standard. REVma or 802.11ma, as it was called, created a single document that merged 8 amendments (802.11a,b,d,e,g,h,i,j) with the base standard. Upon approval on March 08, 2007, 802.11REVma was renamed to the current standard **IEEE 802.11-2007**. This is the single most modern 802.11 document available that contains cumulative changes from multiple sub-letter task groups.

802.11n

Release Date	Op. Frequency	Data Rate (Typ)	Data Rate (Max)	Range (Indoor)
Pending	5 GHz and/or 2.4 GHz	74 Mbit/s	300 Mbit/s (2 streams)	~70 m

802.11n is a proposed amendment which improves upon the previous 802.11 standards by adding multiple-input multiple-output (MIMO) and many other newer features. Though there are already many products on the market based on Draft 2.0 of this proposal, the TGn workgroup is not expected to finalise the amendment until December 2009.

Standard and Amendments

Within the IEEE 802.11 Working Group, the following IEEE Standards Association Standard and Amendments exist:

- IEEE 802.11—THE WLAN STANDARD was original 1 Mbit/s and 2 Mbit/s, 2.4 GHz RF and IR standard (1997), all the others listed below are Amendments to this standard, except for Recommended Practices 802.11F and 802.11T.
- IEEE 802.11a—54 Mbit/s, 5 GHz standard (1999, shipping products in 2001)
- IEEE 802.11b—Enhancements to 802.11 to support 5.5 and 11 Mbit/s (1999)
- IEEE 802.11c—Bridge operation procedures; included in the IEEE 802.1D standard (2001)
- IEEE 802.11d—International (country-to-country) roaming extensions (2001)
- IEEE 802.11e—Enhancements: QoS, including packet bursting (2005)
- *IEEE 802.11F—Inter-Access Point Protocol (2003) Withdrawn February 2006*
- IEEE 802.11g—54 Mbit/s, 2.4 GHz standard (backwards compatible with b) (2003)
- IEEE 802.11h—Spectrum Managed 802.11a (5 GHz) for European compatibility (2004)
- IEEE 802.11i—Enhanced security (2004)
- IEEE 802.11j—Extensions for Japan (2004)
- IEEE 802.11-2007—A new release of the standard that includes amendments a, b, d, e, g, h, i & j. (July 2007)
- IEEE 802.11k—Radio resource measurement enhancements (proposed—2007?)

- IEEE 802.11l—(reserved and will not be used)
- IEEE 802.11m—Maintenance of the standard. Recent edits became 802.11-2007. (ongoing)
- IEEE 802.11n—Higher throughput improvements using MIMO (multiple input, multiple output antennas) (September 2008)
- IEEE 802.11o—(reserved and will not be used)
- IEEE 802.11p—WAVE—Wireless Access for the Vehicular Environment (such as ambulances and passenger cars) (working—2009?)
- IEEE 802.11q—(reserved and will not be used, can be confused with 802.1Q VLAN trunking)
- IEEE 802.11r—Fast roaming Working "Task Group r"—2007?
- IEEE 802.11s—ESS Extended Service Set Mesh Networking (working—2008?)
- IEEE 802.11T—Wireless Performance Prediction (WPP)—test methods and metrics Recommendation (working—2008?)
- IEEE 802.11u—Interworking with non-802 networks (for example, cellular) (proposal evaluation—?)
- IEEE 802.11v—Wireless network management (early proposal stages—?)
- IEEE 802.11w—Protected Management Frames (early proposal stages—2008?)
- IEEE 802.11x—(reserved and will not be used, can be confused with 802.1x Network Access Control)
- IEEE 802.11y—3650-3700 MHz Operation in the U.S. (March 2008?)
- IEEE 802.11z—Extensions to Direct Link Setup (DLS) (Aug. 2007—Dec. 2011)

There is no standard or task group named "802.11x". Rather, this term is used informally to denote any current or future 802.11 amendment, in cases where further precision is not necessary. (The IEEE 802.1x standard for port-based network access control is often mistakenly called "802.11x" when used in the context of wireless networks.)

802.11F and 802.11T are recommended practices rather than standards, and are capitalised as such.

Standard or Amendment?

Both the terms "standard" and "amendment" are used when referring to the different variants of **IEEE 802.11**.

As far as the IEEE Standards Association is concerned, there is only one current standard, it is denoted by- IEEE 802.11 followed by the date that it was published. IEEE 802.11-2007 is the only version currently in publication. The standard is updated by means of amendments. Amendments are created by task groups (TG). Both the task group and their finished document are denoted by 802.11 followed by a non-capitalised letter. For example IEEE 802.11a and IEEE 802.11b. Updating 802.11 is the responsibility of task group m. In order to create a new version, TGm combines the previous version of the standard and all published amendments. TGm also provides clarification and interpretation to industry on published documents. New versions of the IEEE 802.11 were published in 1999 and 2007.

The working title of 802.11-2007 was 802.11-REVma. This denotes a third type of document, a "revision". The complexity of combining 802.11-1999 with 8 amendments made it necessary to revise already agreed upon text. As a result, additional guidelines associated with a revision had to be followed.

Security

In 2001, a group from the University of California, Berkeley presented a paper describing weaknesses in the 802.11 Wired Equivalent Privacy (WEP) security mechanism defined in the original standard; they were followed by Fluhrer, Mantin, and Shamir's paper entitled "Weaknesses in the Key Scheduling Algorithm of RC4". Not long after, Adam Stubblefield and AT&T publicly announced the first verification of the attack. In the attack they were able to intercept transmissions and gain unauthorised access to wireless networks.

The IEEE set up a dedicated task group to create a replacement security solution, 802.11i (previously this work was handled as part of a broader 802.11e effort to enhance the MAC layer). The Wi-Fi Alliance announced an interim specification called Wi-Fi Protected Access (WPA) based on a subset of the then current IEEE 802.11i draft. These started to appear in products in mid-2003. IEEE 802.11i (also known as WPA2) itself was ratified in June 2004, and uses government strength encryption in the Advanced Encryption Standard AES, instead of RC4, which was used in WEP. The modern recommended encryption for the home/consumer space is WPA2 (AES PreShared Key) and for the Enterprise space is WPA2 along with a radius server the strongest is EAP-TLS.

In January 2005, IEEE set up yet another task group TGw to protect management and broadcast frames, which previously were sent unsecured.

10

BLUETOOTH

Bluetooth is a wireless protocol utilising short-range communications technology facilitating data transmissions over short distances from fixed and/or mobile devices, creating wireless personal area networks (PANs). The intent behind the development of Bluetooth was the creation of a single digital wireless protocol, capable of connecting multiple devices and overcoming issues arising from synchronisation of these devices. Bluetooth provides a way to connect and exchange information between devices such as mobile phones, telephones, laptops, personal computers, printers, GPS receivers, digital cameras, and video game consoles over a secure, globally unlicensed Industrial, Scientific, and Medical (ISM) 2.4 GHz short-range radio frequency bandwidth. The Bluetooth specifications are developed and licensed by the Bluetooth Special Interest Group (SIG). The Bluetooth SIG consists of companies in the areas of telecommunication, computing, networking, and consumer electronics.

Uses

Bluetooth is a standard and communications protocol primarily designed for low power consumption, with a short range (power-class-dependent: 1 meter, 10 meters, 100 meters) based on low-cost transceiver microchips in each device. Bluetooth enables these devices to communicate with each other when they are in range. The devices use a radio communications system, so they do not have to be in line of sight of each other, and can even be in other rooms, as long as the received transmission is powerful enough. Bluetooth device class indicates the type of device and the supported services of which the information is transmitted during the discovery process.

Class	Maximum Permitted	Range (approximate) PowermW(dBm)
Class 1	100 mW (20 dBm)	~100 meters
Class 2	2.5 mW (4 dBm)	~10 meters
Class 3	1 mW (0 dBm)	~1 meter

In most cases the effective range of class 2 devices is extended if they connect to a class 1 transceiver, compared to pure class 2 network. This is accomplished by the higher sensitivity and transmission power of Class 1 devices.

Version	Data Rate
Version 1.2	1 Mbit/s
Version 2.0 + EDR	3 Mbit/s
WiMedia Alliance (proposed)	53—480 Mbit/s

Bluetooth Profiles

In order to use Bluetooth, a device must be compatible with certain Bluetooth profiles. These define the possible applications and uses of the technology.

List of Applications

More prevalent applications of Bluetooth include:

- Wireless control of and communication between a mobile phone and a hands-free headset. This was one of the earliest applications to become popular.
- Wireless networking between PCs in a confined space and where little bandwidth is required.

- Wireless communications with PC input and output devices, the most common being the mouse, keyboard and printer.
- Transfer of files between devices with OBEX.
- Transfer of contact details, calendar appointments, and reminders between devices with OBEX.
- Replacement of traditional wired serial communications in test equipment, GPS receivers, medical equipment, bar code scanners, and traffic control devices.
- For controls where infrared was traditionally used.
- Sending small advertisements from Bluetooth enabled advertising hoardings to other, discoverable, Bluetooth devices.
- Two seventh-generation game consoles, Nintendo's Wii and Sony's PlayStation 3 use Bluetooth for their respective wireless controllers.
- Dial-up internet access on personal computer or PDA using a data-capable mobile phone as a modem.

Bluetooth vs. Wi-Fi in Networking

Bluetooth and Wi-Fi have different applications in today's offices, homes, and on the move: setting up networks, printing, or transferring presentations and files from PDAs to computers. Both are versions of unlicensed wireless technology. Wi-fi differs from

A typical Bluetooth mobile phone headset

bluetooth in that it provides higher throughput and covers greater distances, but requires more expensive hardware and higher power consumption.

They use the same frequency range, but employ different modulation techniques. While Bluetooth is a replacement for cabling in a variety of applications, Wi-Fi is a replacement for cabling for general local area network access. Bluetooth can be taken as replacement for USB or any other serial cable link, whereas Wi-Fi is wireless Ethernet communications according to the protocol architectures of IEEE 802.3 with TCP/IP. Both standards are operating at a specified bandwidth not identical with that of other networking standards. Generally a wireless system is not suited for identical replacement of a cable networking systems, a re-arrangement of resources must be foreseen. However, the mechanical plug compatibility problem known with cables is replaced by the compatibility requirement for an air interface and an protocol stack.

Bluetooth Devices

Bluetooth exists in many products, such as telephones, printers, modems and headsets. The technology is useful when transferring information between two or more devices that are near each other in low-bandwidth situations. Bluetooth is commonly used to transfer sound data with telephones (i.e. with a Bluetooth headset) or byte data with hand-held computers (transferring files).

A typical Bluetooth USB dongle

An internal notebook Bluetooth card (14x36x4mm)

Bluetooth protocols simplify the discovery and setup of services between devices. Bluetooth devices advertise all of the services they provide. Any Bluetooth device can, in theory, host any other Bluetooth device. This makes using services easier because there is no longer a need to set up network addresses or permissions as in many other network.

Wi-Fi

Wi-Fi is more like a traditional Ethernet network, and requires configuration to set up shared resources, transmit files, and to set up audio links (for example, headsets and hands-free devices). It uses the same radio frequencies as Bluetooth, but with higher power resulting in a stronger connection. Wi-Fi is sometimes called "wireless Ethernet." This description is accurate as it also provides an indication of its relative strengths and weaknesses. Wi-Fi requires more setup, but is better suited for operating full-scale networks because it enables a faster connection, better range from the base station, and better security than Bluetooths.

Computer Requirements

A personal computer must have a Bluetooth adapter in order to be able to communicate with other Bluetooth devices (such as mobile phones, mice and keyboards). While some desktop computers and most recent laptops come with a built-in Bluetooth adapter, others will require an external one in the form of a dongle.

Unlike its predecessor, IrDA, which requires a separate adapter for each device, Bluetooth allows multiple devices to communicate with a computer over a single adapter.

Operating System Support

Apple has supported Bluetooth since Mac OS X v10.2 which was released in 2002.

For Microsoft platforms, Windows XP Service Pack 2 and later releases have native support for Bluetooth. Previous versions required users to install their Bluetooth adapter's own drivers, which were not directly supported by Microsoft. Microsoft's own Bluetooth dongles (packaged with their Bluetooth computer devices) have no external drivers and thus require at least Windows XP Service Pack 2.

Linux has two popular Bluetooth stacks, BlueZ and Affix. The BlueZ stack is included with most Linux kernels and it was originally developed by Qualcomm. The Affix stack was developed by Nokia. FreeBSD features Bluetooth support since its 5.0 release. NetBSD features Bluetooth support since its 4.0 release. Its Bluetooth stack has been ported to Open BSD as well.

Specifications and Features

The Bluetooth specification was developed in 1994 by Jaap Haartsen and Sven Mattisson, who were working for Ericsson Mobile Platforms in Lund, Sweden. The specification is based on frequency-hopping spread spectrum technology.

The specifications were formalised by the Bluetooth Special Interest Group (SIG). The SIG was formally announced on May 20, 1998. Today it has a membership of over 7000 companies worldwide. It was established by Ericsson, IBM, Intel, Toshiba, and Nokia, and later joined by many other companies.

Bluetooth 1.0 and 1.0B

Versions 1.0 and 1.0B had many problems, and manufacturers had difficulty making their products interoperable. Versions 1.0

and 1.0B also included mandatory Bluetooth hardware device address (BD_ADDR) transmission in the Connecting process (rendering anonymity impossible at the protocol level), which was a major setback for certain services planned for use in Bluetooth environments.

Bluetooth 1.1

- Ratified as IEEE Standard 802.15.1-2002.
- Many errors found in the 1.0B specifications were fixed.
- Added support for non-encrypted channels.
- Received Signal Strength Indicator (RSSI).

Bluetooth 1.2

This version is backward-compatible with 1.1 and the major enhancements include the following:

- Faster Connection and Discovery
- *Adaptive frequency-hopping spread spectrum (AFH)*, which improves resistance to radio frequency interference by avoiding the use of crowded frequencies in the hopping sequence.
- Higher transmission speeds in practice, up to 721 kbit/s, as in 1.1.
- Extended Synchronous Connections (eSCO), which improve voice quality of audio links by allowing retransmissions of corrupted packets, and may optionally increase audio latency to provide better support for concurrent data transfer.
- Host Controller Interface (HCI) support for three-wire UART.
- Ratified as IEEE Standard 802.15.1-2005.

Bluetooth 2.0

This version, specified on November 10, 2004, is backward-compatible with 1.1. The main enhancement is the introduction of an Enhanced Data Rate (EDR) for both data (ACL) and voice (eSCO) packets. The nominal signalling rate of EDR is about 3 megabits per second, although the practical data transfer rate is 2.1 megabits per second. This additional throughput is obtained by using a different modulation scheme for radio transmission of the data payload. Standard or Basic Rate transmission uses the Gaussian Frequency Shift Keying (GFSK) method, while EDR uses a combination of GFSK and Phase Shift Keying (PSK).

According to the 2.0 specification, EDR provides the following benefits:

- Three times faster transmission speed—up to 10 times in certain cases (up to 2.1 Mbit/s).
- Lower power consumption through a reduced duty cycle.
- Simplification of multi-link scenarios due to more available bandwidth.

The Bluetooth Special Interest Group (SIG) published the specification as "Bluetooth 2.0 + EDR" which implies that EDR is an optional feature. In some cases it is not clear whether a product claiming to support "Bluetooth 2.0" actually supports the EDR higher transfer rate. At least one commercial device, the HTC TyTN pocket PC phone, states "Bluetooth 2.0 without EDR" on its data sheet.

Bluetooth 2.1

Bluetooth Core Specification Version 2.1 is fully backward-compatible with 1.1, and was adopted by the Bluetooth SIG on July 26, 2007. This specification includes the following features:

- **Extended inquiry response**: provides more information during the inquiry procedure to allow better filtering of devices before connection. This information includes the name of the device, a list of services the device supports, as well as other information like the time of day, and pairing information.
- **Sniff subrating**: reduces the power consumption when devices are in the sniff low-power mode, especially on links

with asymmetric data flows. Human interface devices (HID) are expected to benefit the most, with mouse and keyboard devices increasing the battery life by a factor of 3 to 10. It lets devices decide how long they will wait before sending keepalive messages to one another. Previous Bluetooth implementations featured keep alive message frequencies of up to several times per second. In contrast, the 2.1 specification allows pairs of devices to negotiate this value between them to as infrequently as once every 5 or 10 seconds.

- **Encryption Pause Resume:** enables an encryption key to be refreshed, enabling much stronger encryption for connections that stay up for longer than 23.3 hours (one Bluetooth day).
- **Secure Simple Pairing:** radically improves the pairing experience for Bluetooth devices, while increasing the use and strength of security. It is expected that this feature will significantly increase the use of Bluetooth.
- Near Field Communication (NFC) cooperation: automatic creation of secure Bluetooth connections when NFC radio interface is also available. For example, a headset should be paired with a Bluetooth 2.1 phone including NFC just by bringing the two devices close to each other (a few centimeters). Another example is automatic uploading of photos from a mobile phone or camera to a digital picture frame just by bringing the phone or camera close to the frame.

Future of Bluetooth

- **Broadcast Channel:** enables Bluetooth information points. This will drive the adoption of Bluetooth into mobile phones, and enable advertising models based around users pulling information from the information points, and not based around the object push model that is used in a limited way today.

- **Topology Management:** enables the automatic configuration of the piconet topologies especially in scatternet situations that are becoming more common today. This should all be invisible to the users of the technology, while also making the technology just work.
- **Alternate MAC PHY:** enables the use of alternative MAC and PHY's for transporting Bluetooth profile data. The Bluetooth Radio will still be used for device discovery, initial connection and profile configuration, however when lots of data needs to be sent, the high speed alternate MAC PHY's will be used to transport the data. This means that the proven low power connection models of Bluetooth are used when the system is idle, and the low power per bit radios are used when lots of data needs to be sent.
- QoS improvements: enable audio and video data to be transmitted at a higher quality, especially when best effort traffic is being transmitted in the same piconet.

High-speed Bluetooth

On 28 March 2006, the Bluetooth Special Interest Group announced its selection of the WiMedia Alliance Multi-Band Orthogonal Frequency Division Multiplexing (MB-OFDM) version of UWB for integration with current Bluetooth wireless technology.

UWB integration will create a version of Bluetooth wireless technology with a high-speed/high-data-rate option. This new version of Bluetooth technology will meet the high-speed demands of synchronising and transferring large amounts of data, as well as enabling high-quality video and audio applications for portable devices, multi-media projectors and television sets, and wireless VOIP.

At the same time, Bluetooth technology will continue catering to the needs of very low power applications such as mouse, keyboards, and mono headsets, enabling devices to select the most appropriate physical radio for the application requirements, thereby offering the best of both worlds.

Bluetooth 3.0

The next version of Bluetooth after v2.1, code-named Seattle (the version number of which is TBD) has many of the same features, but is most notable for plans to adopt ultra-wideband (UWB) radio technology. This will allow Bluetooth use over UWB radio, enabling very fast data transfers of up to 480 Mbit/s, while building on the very low-power idle modes of Bluetooth.

Bluetooth Low Energy

On June 12, 2007, Nokia and Bluetooth SIG announced that Wibree will be a part of the Bluetooth specification as an ultra-low power Bluetooth technology. Expected use cases include watches displaying Caller ID information, sports sensors monitoring your heart rate during exercise, as well as medical devices. The Medical Devices Working Group is also creating a medical devices profile and associated protocols to enable this market. Battery life for devices using Bluetooth low energy technology is designed to be up to one year.

TECHNICAL INFORMATION

Bluetooth Protocol Stack

"Bluetooth is defined as a layer protocol architecture consisting of core protocols, cable replacement protocols, telephony control protocols, and adopted protocols".

Core Protocols

Bluetooth's core protocols form a five-layer stack, consisting of the following:

Bluetooth Radio–specifics details of the air interface, including frequency, frequency hopping, modulation scheme, and transmission power.

Baseband–concerned with connection establishment within a piconet, addressing, packet format, timing, and power control.

Link Manager Protocol (LMP)–establishes the link setup between Bluetooth devices and manages ongoing links, including security aspects (e.g. authentication and encryption), and control and negotiation of baseband packet size

Logical Link Control and Adaptation Protocol (L2CAP)–adapts the upper-layer protocols to the baseband layer, providing both connectionless and connection-oriented services.

Service Discovery Protocol (SDP)–handles device information, services, and queries for service characteristics between two or more Bluetooth devices.

Cable Replacement Protocol

Radio frequency communications (RFCOMM) is the cable replacement protocol used to create a virtual serial port used to make replacement of cable technologies transparent through minimal modification of existing devices. RFCOMM provides for binary data transport and emulates EIA-232 (formerly RS-232) control signals over the Bluetooth baseband layer.

Telephony Control Protocol

Telephony control protocol-binary (TCS BIN) is the bit-oriented protocol that defines the call control signaling for the establishment of voice and data calls between Bluetooth devices. Additionally, "TCS BIN defines mobility management procedures for handling groups of Bluetooth TCS devices"

Adopted Protocols

Adapted protocols are defined by other standards-making organisations and incorporated into Bluetooth's protocol stack., allowing Bluetooth to create protocols only when necessary. The adopted protocols include:

Point-to-Point Protocol (PPP)–Internet standard protocol for transporting IP datagrams over a point-to-point link

TCP/IP/UDP–Foundation Protocols for TCP/IP protocol suite

Object Exchange Protocol (OBEX)–Session-layer protocol for the exchange of objects, providing a model for object and operation representation

Wireless Application Environment/Wireless Application Protocol (WAE/WAP)–WAE specifies an application framework for wireless devices and WAP is an open standard to provide mobile users access to telephony and information services.

Communication and Connection

A master Bluetooth device can communicate with up to seven devices. This network group of up to eight devices is called a piconet.

A piconet is an ad-hoc computer network, using Bluetooth technology protocols to allow one master device to interconnect with up to seven active devices. Up to 255 further devices can be inactive, or parked, which the master device can bring into active status at any time.

At any given time, data can be transferred between the master and one other device, however, the devices can switch roles and the slave can become the master at any time. The master switches rapidly from one device to another in a round-robin fashion. (Simultaneous transmission from the master to multiple other devices is possible, but not used much.)

Bluetooth specification allows connecting two or more piconets together to form a scatternet, with some devices acting as a bridge by simultaneously playing the master role and the slave role in one piconet.

Many USB Bluetooth adapters are available, some of which also include an IrDA adapter. Older (pre-2003) Bluetooth adapters, however, have limited services, offering only the Bluetooth Enumerator and a less-powerful Bluetooth Radio incarnation. Such devices can link computers with Bluetooth, but they do not offer much in the way of services that modern adapters do.

Setting up Connections

Any Bluetooth device will transmit the following information on demand:

- Device name.
- Device class.
- List of services.
- Technical information, for example, device features, manufacturer, Bluetooth specification used, clock offset.

Any device may perform an inquiry to find other devices to connect to, and any device can be configured to respond to such inquiries. However, if the device trying to connect knows the address of the device, it always responds to direct connection requests and transmits the information shown in the list above if requested. Use of device services may require pairing or acceptance by its owner, but the connection itself can be initiated by any device and held until it goes out of range. Some devices can be connected to only one device at a time, and connecting to them prevents them from connecting to other devices and appearing in inquiries until they disconnect from the other device.

Every device has a unique 48-bit address. However these addresses are generally not shown in inquiries. Instead, friendly Bluetooth names are used, which can be set by the user. This name appears when another user scans for devices and in lists of paired devices.

Most phones have the Bluetooth name set to the manufacturer and model of the phone by default. Most phones and laptops show only the Bluetooth names and special programmes that are required to get additional information about remote devices. This can be confusing as, for example, there could be several phones in range named T610.

Pairing

Pairs of devices may establish a trusted relationship by learning (by user input) a shared secret known as a *passkey*. A device that wants to communicate only with a trusted device can cryptographically authenticate the identity of the other device. Trusted devices may also encrypt the data that they exchange over the airwaves so that no one can listen in. The encryption can, however, be turned off, and passkeys are stored on the device file system, not on the Bluetooth chip itself. Since the Bluetooth address is permanent, a pairing is preserved, even if the Bluetooth name is changed. Pairs can be deleted at any time by either device. Devices generally require pairing or prompt the owner before they allow a remote device to use any or most of their services. Some devices, such as mobile phones, usually accept OBEX business cards and notes without any pairing or prompts.

Certain printers and access points allow any device to use its services by default, much like unsecured Wi-Fi networks. Pairing algorithms are sometimes manufacturer-specific for transmitters and receivers used in applications such as music and entertainment.

Bluetooth 2.1 has an optional "touch-to-pair" feature based on NFC. By simply bringing two devices into close range (around 10cm), pairing can securely take place without entering a passkey or manual configuration.

Air Interface

The protocol operates in the license-free ISM band at 2.4-2.4835 GHz. To avoid interfering with other protocols that use the 2.45 GHz band, the Bluetooth protocol divides the band into 79 channels (each 1 MHz wide) and changes channels up to 1600 times per second. Implementations with versions 1.1 and 1.2 reach speeds of 723.1 kbit/s. Version 2.0 implementations feature Bluetooth Enhanced Data Rate (EDR) and reach 2.1 Mbit/s. Technically, version 2.0 devices have a higher power consumption, but the three times faster rate reduces the transmission times, effectively reducing power consumption to half that of 1.x devices (assuming equal traffic load)

Security

Bluetooth implements confidentiality, authentication and key derivation with custom algorithms based on the SAFER+ block cipher. In Bluetooth, key generation is generally based on a

Bluetooth PIN, which must be entered into both devices. This procedure might be modified if one of the devices has a fixed PIN, e.g. for headsets or similar devices with a restricted user interface. During pairing, an initialisation key or master key is generated, using the E22 algorithm. The E0 stream cipher is used for encrypting packets, granting confidentiality and is based on a shared cryptographic secret, namely a previously generated link key or master key. Those keys, used for subsequent encryption of data sent via the air interface, rely on the Bluetooth PIN, which has been entered into one or both devices.

An overview of Bluetooth vulnerabilities exploits has been published by Andreas Becker.

Bluejacking

Bluejacking is the sending of either a picture or a message from one user to an unsuspecting user through Bluetooth wireless technology. Common applications are short messages (e.g. "You've just been bluejacked!"), advertisements (e.g. "Eat at Joe's"). and business information. Bluejacking does not involve the removal or alteration of any data from the device. These business cards often have a clever or flirtatious message rather than the typical name and phone number. Bluejackers often look for the receiving phone to ping or the user to react. They then send another, more personal message to that device. Once again, in order to carry out a bluejacking, the sending and receiving devices must be within range of each other, which is typically 10 meters for most mobile devices. Devices that are set in non-discoverable mode are not susceptible to bluejacking. However, the Linux application Redfang claims to find non-discoverable Bluetooth devices.

HISTORY OF SECURITY CONCERNS

2003

In November 2003, Ben and Adam Laurie from A.L. Digital Ltd. discovered that serious flaws in Bluetooth security may lead to disclosure of personal data. It should be noted, however, that the reported security problems concerned some poor implementations of Bluetooth, rather than the protocol itself.

In a subsequent experiment, Martin Herfurt from the trifinite.group was able to do a field-trial at the CeBIT fairgrounds, showing the importance of the problem to the world. A new attack called BlueBug was used for this experiment. This is one of a number of concerns that have been raised over the security of Bluetooth communications.

2004

In 2004 the first purported virus using Bluetooth to spread itself among mobile phones appeared on the Symbian OS. The virus was first described by Kaspersky Lab and requires users to confirm the installation of unknown software before it can propagate. The virus was written as a proof-of-concept by a group of virus writers known as "29A" and sent to anti-virus groups. Thus, it should be regarded as a potential (but not real) security threat to Bluetooth or Symbian OS since the virus has never spread in the wild.

In August 2004, a world-record-setting experiment (see also Bluetooth sniping) showed that the range of Class 2 Bluetooth radios could be extended to 1.78 km (1.08 mile) with directional antennas and signal amplifiers. This poses a potential security threat because it enables attackers to access vulnerable Bluetooth-devices from a distance beyond expectation. The attacker must also be able to receive information from the victim to set up a connection. No attack can be made against a Bluetooth device unless the attacker knows its Bluetooth address and which channels to transmit on.

2005

In January 2005, a mobile malware worm known as Lasco.A began targeting mobile phones using Symbian OS (Series 60 platform) using Bluetooth-enabled devices to replicate itself and spread to other devices. The worm is self-installing and begins once the mobile user approves the transfer of the file (velasco.sis) from another device. Once installed, the worm begins looking for other Bluetooth-enabled devices to infect. Additionally, the worm infects other .SIS files on the device, allowing replication to another device through use of removable media (SanDisk, Compact Flash, etc.). The worm can render the mobile device unstable.

In April 2005, Cambridge University security researchers published results of their actual implementation of passive attacks against the PIN-based pairing between commercial Bluetooth devices, confirming the attacks to be practicably fast and the Bluetooth symmetric key establishment method to be vulnerable. To rectify this vulnerability, they carried out an implementation which showed that stronger, asymmetric key establishment is feasible for certain classes of devices, such as mobile phones.

In June 2005, Yaniv Shaked and Avishai Wool published a paper describing both passive and active methods for obtaining the PIN for a Bluetooth link. The passive attack allows a suitably equipped attacker to eavesdrop on communications and spoof, if the attacker was present at the time of initial pairing. The active method makes use of a specially constructed message that must be inserted at a specific point in the protocol, to make the master and slave repeat the pairing process. After that, the first method can be used to crack the PIN. This attack's major weakness is that it requires the user of the devices under attack to re-enter the PIN during the attack when the device prompts them to. Also, this active attack probably requires custom hardware, since most commercially available Bluetooth devices are not capable of the timing necessary.

In August 2005, police in Cambridgeshire, England, issued warnings about thieves using Bluetooth-enabled phones to track other devices left in cars. Police are advising users to ensure that any mobile networking connections are de-activated if laptops and other devices are left in this way.

2006

In April 2006, researchers from Secure Network and F-Secure published a report that warns of the large number of devices left in a visible state, and issued statistics on the spread of various Bluetooth services and the ease of spread of an eventual Bluetooth worm.

In October 2007, at the Luxemburgish Hack.lu Security Conference, Kevin Finistere and Thierry Zoller demonstrated and released a remote root shell via Bluetooth on Mac OS X v10.3.9 and v10.4. They also demonstrated the first Bluetooth PIN and Linkkeys cracker, which is based on the research of Wool and Shaked.

Health Concerns

Bluetooth uses the microwave radio frequency spectrum in the 2.4 GHz to 2.4835 GHz range. Maximum power output from a Bluetooth radio is 100 mW, 2.5 mW, and 1 mW for Class 1, Class 2, and Class 3 devices respectively, which puts Class 1 at roughly the same level as mobile phones, and the other two classes much lower. Accordingly, Class 2 and Class 3 Bluetooth devices are considered less of a potential hazard than mobile phones, and Class 1 may be comparable to that of mobile phones.

Origin of the Name and the Logo

Bluetooth was named after a tenth-century king, Harald Bluetooth, King of Denmark and Norway. Bluetooth is an anglicised version of Harald Blaatand, who was known for his unification of previously warring tribes from Denmark (including now Swedish Scania, where the Bluetooth technology was invented), and Norway. Bluetooth likewise was intended to unify different technologies, such as personal computers and mobile phones.

The name may have been inspired less by the historical Harald than the loose interpretation of him in *The Long Ships* by Frans Gunnar Bengtsson, a Swedish Viking-inspired novel.

The Bluetooth logo merges the Germanic runes analogous to the modern Latin letter H and B: (for *H*arald *B*luetooth) ᚼ(Hagall) and ᛒ(Berkanan) merged together, forming a bind rune.

Bluetooth Special Interest Group

Initially (circa 1996-1997) the technology later known as Bluetooth was an Ericsson-internal project named *multi-communicator link* or short *MC link.* Cooperation with Intel was initiated in 1997.

In 1998, Ericsson, IBM, Intel, Toshiba, and Nokia, formed a consortium and adopted the code name Bluetooth for their proposed open specification. In December 1999, 3Com, Lucent Technologies, Microsoft, and Motorola joined the initial founders as the promoter of Bluetooth Special Interest Group (SIG). Since that time, Lucent Technologies transferred their membership to their spinoff Agere Systems, and 3Com has left the promoter group. Agere Systems was later merged with LSI Corporation and left the Bluetooth promoters group in August 2007.

The Bluetooth Special Interest Group (SIG) is a privately held, not-for-profit trade association with headquarters in Bellevue, Washington. As of January 2008, the SIG is composed of over 10,000 member companies that are leaders in the telecommunications, computing, automotive, music, apparel, industrial automation, and network industries, and a small group of dedicated staff in Hong Kong, Sweden, and the USA. SIG members drive the development of Bluetooth wireless technology, and implement and market the technology in their products varying from mobile phones to printers. The Bluetooth SIG itself does not make, manufacture, or sell Bluetooth enabled products. The executive director of the Bluetooth SIG is Michael W. Foley.

High Speed Packet Access

High Speed Packet Access (HSPA) is a collection of mobile telephony protocols that extend and improve the performance of existing UMTS protocols. Two standards, HSDPA and HSUPA, have been established and a further standard, HSPA+, is soon to be released. The two existing standards (HSDPA and HSUPA) in the family provide increased performance by using improved modulation schemes and by refining the protocols by which handsets and base stations communicate. These improvements lead to a better utilisation of the existing radio bandwidth provided by UMTS.

The number of commercial 3.5G networks—also known as High-Speed Downlink Packet Access, or HSDPA, networks—launched worldwide grew by 69 per cent in 2007. There are now 174 commercial HSDPA networks in 76 countries. An additional 38 networks are committed to rollouts, which will bump the total to 211 HSDPA networks in 90 countries. Commercial HSDPA networks are widely available in Western Europe (61 networks), Southeast Asia (35), Eastern Europe (34), the Middle East and Africa (20), and the Americas and the Caribbean (16). Almost two-thirds (62 per cent) of existing commercial HSDPA networks support downlink speeds of 3.6 Mbit/s or more, while more than a fifth (21 per cent) support the peak downlink speed of 7.2 Mbit/s.

Many HSPA rollouts can be achieved by a software upgrade to existing 3G networks, giving 3.5G a headstart over WiMax, which requires dedicated network infrastructure. Rising sales of HSPA-enabled mobiles—aided by more-generous-than-expected operator subsidies of the hardware—are helping to drive the 3.5G market.

High Speed Downlink Packet Access (HSDPA)

HSDPA provides improved theoretical down-link performance of up to 14.4 Mbit/s. Existing deployments provide up to 7.2 Mbit/s in down-link. Up-link performance is a maximum of 384 kbit/s. The [Round-trip delay time] is around 150 ms.

For operational reasons, service providers may cap this rate to lower rates than the maximum 3.6 Mbit/s that most HSDPA handsets support. Voice calls are usually prioritised over data transfer. The Croatian VIPnet network supports the speed of 7.2 Mbit/s in down-link as does Rogers Wireless in Canada. In South Korea, a nationwide 7.2Mbit/s coverage is now established by SK Telecom and KTF. In Hong Kong, PCCW also provide 7.6Mbit/s coverage.

High Speed Uplink Packet Access (HSUPA)

HSUPA provides improved up-link performance of up to 5.76 Mbit/s theoretically. In Singapore, Starhub announced a 1.9 Mbit/s HSUPA Service as part of its new MaxMobile plan in 1 Aug 2007. In Finland, Elisa announced on 30.8.2007 1.4 Mbit/s HSUPA to most large cities with plans to add the service to its whole 3G network within months. 3 Italia and Ericsson announced on 16.07.2008 the successful tests of HSUPA 5.8 Mbps in the live network of 3 Italia .

Evolved High Speed Packet Access (HSPA+)

HSPA+ is defined in 3GPP release 7. It introduces simpler IP centric architecture for the mobile network bypassing most of the legacy equipment. HSPA+ boosts peak data rates to 42 Mbit/s on the downlink and 22 Mbit/s on the uplink.

Mobile Internet Device (Intel)

A **Mobile Internet Device** (**MID**) is an initiative raised by Intel for consumers and prosumers. Intel came up with the term and announced a prototype at the Intel Developer Forum in spring

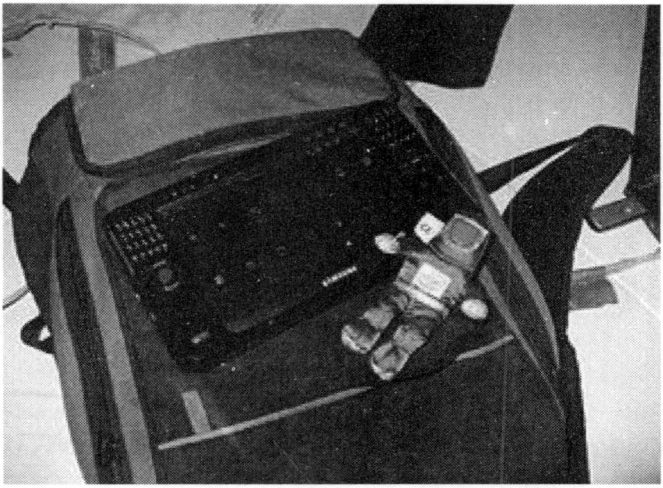

Samsung Q1 loaded with early Ubuntu Mobile and Embedded Edition.

2007 in Beijing. The product and specifications were announced at the conference. There are ongoing controversies regarding the use of ARM or Intel architectures in mobile internet devices. An MID development kit by Sophia Systems using Intel Centrino Atom was announced in April 2008.

Hardware

The device contains a processor and chipset produced by Intel that consume less power than most of the x86 derivatives and are an extension of the Centrino mobile platform. As of today, several platforms have been announced, as listed below:

McCaslin platform (2007)

This platform contains an Intel A100/A110 processor (code-named Stealey) 90 nm running at 600-800 MHz respectively.

Menlow platform (2008)

This platform contains an Intel Atom processor (code-named Silverthorne) 45 nm running up to 1.86 GHz.

Moorestown platform (2009)

This platform contains an Intel Atom processor (code-named Lincroft) 45 nm.

Operating system

The MID will run an embedded version of Linux with a *finger friendly* user interface modified by Intel instead of a Microsoft Windows operating system like other UMPCs. However, with the dual-core processor, the device is capable of running Windows XP and Windows Vista.

Intel said it would demo the version of Linux, based on China's Red Flag Linux known as Red Flag MIDINUX, in May.

Later, Intel announced collaboration with Ubuntu to create Ubuntu for Mobile Internet Devices distribution. Ubuntu's website says the new distribution "will provide a rich Internet experience for users of Intel's 2008 Mobile Internet Device (MID) platform."

11

THINKPAD

ThinkPad is a brand of portable laptop and notebook personal computers originally designed, manufactured and sold by IBM. Since early 2005, the ThinkPad range has been manufactured and marketed by Lenovo, which purchased the IBM PC division.

IBM introduced the first three ThinkPad models, the 700, 700C, 700T, in October 1992. The 700C used the Microsoft Windows 3.1 operating system, 25 MHz 486SLC processor, 120 MB hard disk drive, the industry's first 10.4" TFT colour display, 2.2" x 11.7" x 8.3" dimension (56 x 297 x 210 mm), and 3 kg (6.5 lb) weight, cost US$ 4,350. The design of the commercial versions differed significantly from the prototype's keyboard-less tablet design. The bright red TrackPoint, embedded in the keyboard, enabled the notebook to be used on an airline tray table without a mouse. An IBM researcher conceived the title "ThinkPad" from a corporate-issued leather-bound pocket notebook with the corporate motto 'Think' embossed on the cover. The name met disagreements from the IBM corporate naming committee because the nomenclature system for the IBM computers was then numerical; however, the brand name "ThinkPad" was kept as the press showed appreciation for the title. The first ThinkPads were very successful, and soon collected more than 300 awards for design and quality.

The ThinkPad 750 flew aboard the Space Shuttle Endeavour during a mission to repair the Hubble Space Telescope on December 2, 1993. The ThinkPad 750C's task was to run a NASA test programme which determined if radiation inherent in the space environment causes memory anomalies in the 750C or generates other unexpected problems. In 1995, the average number used was five, and in 1999 the average number was nine. Throughout 2006, a ThinkPad A31p was being used in the Service Module Central Post of the International Space Station and seven ThinkPad A31p laptops were in service in orbit aboard the International Space Station. ThinkPads have been praised for exceptional build quality, system reliability, and services throughout their decade and a half of presence in the consumer market. The original design was a collaboration between Tom Hardy, corporate manager of the IBM Design Programme, Italian-based designer Richard Sapper (noted then for the design of the Tizio lamp and later commissioned to design a ballpoint for Lamy) and Kazuhiko Yamazaki, lead notebook designer at IBM's Yamato Design Center in Japan. Sapper proposed a design inspired by the *Shôkadô bentô*, a traditional black-lacquered Japanese lunch box.

The fold-out butterfly keyboard, which appeared in the ThinkPad 701 series, is widely considered a design masterpiece and is on display at the Museum of Modern Art in New York. The ThinkPad 760 series also included an unusual keyboard design; the keyboard was elevated by two arms riding on small rails on the side of the screen, tilting the keyboard to achieve a more ergonomic design.

The 755CV featured another interesting design quirk: the screen could be separated from the lid, allowing it to be used to project the computer display using an overhead projector, before data projectors were commonplace.

Lenovo Purchase

In 2005 the Chinese manufacturer of ThinkPads, Lenovo, purchased the brand from IBM, in a multi-year deal whereby IBM still helps in the marketing and support of these products.

- Added Magnesium-alloy chassis roll cage to reduce motherboard flex caused by holding the laptop one handed on a corner.

- Added Carbon Fibre Reinforced Plastic to 15" ThinkPad Models.
- Reintroduced a line of Tablet PCs based on the X series.
- Moved the physical location of GPU to the edge of motherboard near hinge, further reduce the chance of solders come loose caused by motherboard flex.
- Introduced Widescreen displays with the Z series of ThinkPads and added the option of Widescreen to the T series models.
- Brought back a consumer friendly laptop under the Z series line of ThinkPads.
- Added rubber cushion to the hard drive tray to reduce vibration and to absorb shock.
- Added the Windows key to all models of the 60- and 61-series making all the Windows shortcuts possible. (Although possible before with the keyboard remapping utility)
- Added Magnesium-alloy lid roll cage for a sturdier lid while replacing the lid material from magnesium-alloy to plastic for better wireless signal reception.
- Official support for Linux.
- Added drain holes starting with the T60 series.
- Ported the ThinkPad keyboard into stand-alone keyboards for desktop PCs in PS/2 or USB flavor.
- Added user forum on its website where actual Thinkpad developers and engineers view and reply to posts.

Product Line

Executive	Everyday	Performance	Ultraportable	Tablet
ThinkPad Reserve Edition 12.1" with hand-sewn leather cover, uses Intel Core 2 Duo processors	**ThinkPad R Series** 14.1" or 15" with mainstream performance, uses 2 GHz Intel Core 2 Duo processors	**ThinkPad T Series** 14.1", 15" and 15.4" displays, uses Intel Core 2 Duo processors	**ThinkPad X Series** 12.1" display, light-weight ultra-portable with Intel Core 2 Duo processors	**ThinkPad X Series Tablet** 12.1" display for taking notes, uses Intel Core 2 Duo processors

Features

Traditionally black, ThinkPads have commonly featured magnesium, carbon fiber reinforced plastic or titanium composite cases. The ThinkPad has introduced many innovations, including the TrackPoint pointing device. ThinkLight, an LED keyboard light at the top of the LCD screen, Active Protection System, an accelerometer sensor which detects when a ThinkPad is falling and shuts the hard drive down to prevent damage, Roll-cage design to eliminate motherboard flex, Biometric fingerprint reader, Client Security Solution, which improves security using a built-in TPM and facilitates deployment in corporate environment and drain holes to help reduce damages to the keyboard and components from accidental spillage.

Model Information

Several ThinkPads in use aboard the International Space Station, including 760, 770, and A31p models.

ThinkPad S30 and S31

Japan & Taiwan-only Pentium III model with no CD drive, a 10-inch (250 mm) screen, 256MB Maximum RAM, PCMCIA slot, CF slot, 2 USB 1.1 ports, Firewire port, RJ11 and RJ45, and a keyboard with English and Japanese shared keys. Battery with built-in stand, long life 5 hr run. HDD 20 GB upgradeable to 160 GB tested. Some models have built-in WiFi. BIOS are interchangeable in S30 and S31 and tested to work. The latest known BIOS is 1.82.

ThinkPad 235

The Japan-only ThinkPad 235 (or Type 2607), is an interesting product because it is a progeny of the IBM/Ricoh RIOS project. Also known as Clavius or Chandra2, it contains unusual features like the presence of 3 PCMCIA slots and the use of dual camcorder batteries as a source of power. Features an Intel Pentium MMX 233 MHz CPU, support for up to 160 MB of EDO memory, and a built-in 2.5-inch (64 mm) hard drive with UDMA support. Hitachi markets Chandra2 as the Prius Note 210.

ThinkPad 240

The ultraportable ThinkPad 240 (X, Z) started with an Intel Celeron and went up to the 600 MHz Intel Pentium III. The RAM was expandable to 320 MB max with a bios update. With a 10.4-inch (260 mm) screen and an 18 mm key pitch (A standard key pitch is 19mm). They were also one of the first ThinkPad series to contain a built-in Mini PCI card slot (form factor 3b). The 240s have no optical drives and an external floppy drive. An optional extended battery sticks out the bottom like a bar and props up the back of the notebook. Weighing in at 2.9 pounds (1.3 kg) these were the smallest and lightest ThinkPads ever made.

ThinkPad 300 series

The 300 series (300, 310, 340, 350, 360, 365, 380, 385, 390 (all with various sub-series)) was a long-running value series starting at the 386SL/25 processor, all the way to the Pentium III 450. They were a bit large and slower than the more full-featured models but offered a less expensive ThinkPad.

ThinkPad 500 series

The 500 series (50C, 510, 560 (E, X, Z), 570 (E)) were the main line of the ultraportable ThinkPads. Starting with the 486SX2-50 Blue Lightning to the Pentium III 500, these machines had only a hard disk onboard. Any other drives were external (or in the 570's case in the ultrabase). They weighed in at around 4 pounds (1.8 kg) and because of their excellent design are still in use today.

ThinkPad 600 series

The 600 series (600, 600E and 600X) are the direct predecessors of the T series, and are legendary for their portability, comfortable keyboard, and sturdy construction. The 600 series packed a 12.1" SVGA or a 13.3" XGA TFT LCD, Pentium MMX, Pentium II or III processor, full-sized keyboard, and optical bay into a package weighing roughly 2.3 kg (5 lb). IBM was able to create this light, fully featured machine by using lightweight but strong carbon fibre composite plastics. The battery shipped with some 600 series models had a manufacturing defect that left it vulnerable to memory effect and resulted in poor battery life, but this problem can be avoided by use of a third-party battery.

ThinkPad 700 series

The 700 series (700, 701, 720, 730 (tablet), 750, 755, 760, 765, 770 (many with sub-models)) were the cutting-edge Intel-based ThinkPads. They featured the best screens, largest hard drives and fastest processors available at the time. This was the first successful ThinkPad introduced in 1992 (the first ThinkPad was a tablet PC without a keyboard and a mouse).

ThinkPad 800 series

The ThinkPad 800 series (800/820/821/822/823/850/851/860) were unique in that they were based on the PowerPC architecture, rather than the Intel x86 architecture. They all used the PowerPC 603e CPU, at speeds of 100 MHz, or 166 MHz in the 860 model. The 800 may have used a 603, and it is unclear if the 800 was experimental or not. All units used SCSI 2 instead of IDE hard disks. The units are believed to have all been extremely expensive, as the 850 cost upwards of $12,000. The 800 series can run Windows NT 3.5 (probably 4.0 as well), OS/2, AIX 4.14, Solaris Desktop 2.5.1 PowerPC Edition, and Linux.

ThinkPad TransNote

The ThinkPad TransNote was a pen-based PC in a notebook. Data could be entered through the keyboard, TrackPoint, paper notepad (with writing sensor below), or the screen via stylus. This ThinkPad expanded on IBM's previous pen based notebooks (360P(E), 730T(E), and 750(P)).

ThinkPad T20 series

Comprising the T20, T21, T22 and T23, these were Mobile Pentium III or Mobile Pentium III-M, sub-5 lb (2.3 kg) class machines. Contained processors ranging from 0.18 micrometre Mobile Pentium III 650 MHz to 0.13 micrometre Mobile Pentium III-M 1.20 GHz. Typically had 14.1-inch (360 mm) XGA screens, Ultrabay 2000 optical drives, S3 Savage/IX-MV graphics chip and Cirrus Logic CS 4614/22/24 sound chips; although variations along the line existed. Introduced the ThinkLight, a LED mounted inside the upper screen lip that illuminates the keyboard (activated with Fn-PgUp, the extreme diagonal keys); and titanium-reinforced and rubberised screen lids. Used MiniPCI form factor cards, which could be modem and/or Ethernet. With the T23, an internal WiFi antenna became available, so WiFi miniPCI cards could be used. These models did not contain the active hard drive protection or touchpad pointing device which appeared in later models. They were clad in black non-slip rubber with embedded glitter. The case lid had tabs along the edge that interlocked with depressions in the lower case when closed, to reduce case flexing. Comparatively more stylish, functional, and rugged machines; and easy to disassemble for repair or upgrades.

ThinkPad T30

Features include an Intel Mobile Pentium 4 processor ranging from 1.6 GHz to 2.4 GHz. A T30 may accommodate up to a 2.4 GHz processor with the latest BIOS and Embedded Controller upgrades. Graphics are provided by ATI Radeon Mobility 7500 hardware with 16 MB of discrete video memory, which supports external widescreen resolutions. Users have even reported success with output resolutions of 1920x1200 via DVI on the optional Port Replicator II docking station, although IBM claims a limit of 1280x1024 due to a weak TMDS transmitter. The T30 was available with a 14.1-inch (360 mm) screen, with resolutions of 1024 x 768 and 1400 x 1050. DVI video output is available with the optional Port Replicator II docking station, but resolution is officially limited to 1280x1024. Features available include the embedded security subsystem, UltraNav touchpad, 256 MB standard memory (1 GB maximum according to IBM manual, but it has been reported to accept 2 GB of RAM), a 20, 40 or 60 GB hard disk, Ultrabay Plus drive, wireless, and Bluetooth. The T30 also contains a miniPCI slot usable for a wireless card. The shell is titanium-reinforced composite. The whole package was a bit heavier and thicker than the T4x series.

ThinkPad R40 series

This line of notebooks comprised the R40 and the R40e. These had Mobile Celeron, Pentium 4-M or Pentium M processors, depending on sub-variant.

An ultraportable IBM X31 with an IBM T43 notebook

ThinkPad T40 series

Includes the T40, T41, T42, T43, and associated "p" series (for "performance"; e.g., T43p). A typical 14.1-inch (360 mm) T4x weighs 2.2 kg (4.9 lb), slightly less than the 600 series, and features an Intel Pentium M Processor (ranging from the Intel Pentium M at 1.3 GHz to the Intel Pentium M 770 at 2.13 GHz), a 14.1 or 15-inch (380 mm) LCD (XGA, SXGA+), an integrated GPU (Intel Graphics Media Adapter 900) or a discrete GPU (Radeon x300, 7500, 9000, Fire GL 9000, 9600, Fire GL T2, X300, and Fire GL V3200), and a hard drive ranging in size from 30 to 100 GB with the Active Protection System to protect the hard drive (T41 and later models). "p" (mobile workstation) models are also available with a 14-inch (360 mm) SXGA+ or a 15-inch (380 mm) SXGA+/UXGA FlexView display with wide viewing angle and high density IPS technology. These 15-inch (380 mm) display models weigh slightly more than their lesser brethren, with optical drive and battery, at 2.7 kg (5.9 lb). All T4x models use either 6-cell or 9-cell lithium-ion batteries, as well as an optional 4-cell Ultrabay Slim lithium-polymer battery. The 9-cell battery gives a runtime of 5+ hours and a crease allowing the notebook to lay flat on an airplane tray-table. Some T42 and T43 models feature a biometric security system with built-in fingerprint reader. Some types of the model also had the option to include Bluetooth support. The T40 was IBM's first ThinkPad to use the Pentium M "Banias" CPU. The T42 employed a Pentium M "Dothan" processor with a 400 MHz frontside bus, while the T43 used a later revision Dothan running a 533 MHz FSB.

ThinkPad R50 series

Based on the T40 series, this line of notebooks includes the R50, R50e, R50p, R51, R51e and R52. This series of notebooks is available with fingerprint-readers and uses many components also found in T40-series models, such as batteries, keyboards and planars (system boards). The R51e and the R52, both based on the T43 system board, are the first R-series notebook to utilise DDR2-memory and include a SATA-controller, however uses only PATA-harddrives.

ThinkPad T60 series

Includes the T60, T61; and associated "p" series (for "performance"; e.g. T60p); intended as the next generation of the

T4x Series ThinkPads; this is the first T Series ThinkPad to include the Intel Core Duo "Yonah" Technology, and later the Intel Core 2 Duo "Merom" Mobile technology; and the first T-series ThinkPads to come in widescreen resolution. This model has a VMX-enabled BIOS (although the lowest end Intel Core CPUs themselves do not support VMX, such as the T5500), meaning that running fully virtualised operating systems via Xen or VMware is possible. The T61, announced in May 2007, features a widescreen resolution as the default resolution, and incorporates the Intel Santa Rosa platform having a fully 64-bit chipset, and is the first T-series ThinkPad to have an integrated web camera (optional), smart card reader (optional), and media card reader (optional). Furthering innovation founded in the T60, the T61 also sports a top-cover roll cage, aside from the magnesium roll cage inside the main chassis. T61 extra features include a fingerprint reader (some models) and a new improved framing (all models).

ThinkPad X20 series

Pentium III Mobile, sub-4 lb machines. Contained Pentium III-M processors ranging from 500 MHz to 1.13 GHz. 12.1 inch XGA screens, and ATI Rage Mobility M1 (X20, X21) or Radeon Mobility M6 (X22, X23, X24) graphics chips. Used miniPCI form factor cards, which supports modem and/or Ethernet. With the X22 and later machines, provisions for wireless networking support are built into the chassis. Ultrabay 2000 optical drive support can be fitted via the Ultrabase portable docking station option, and extended batteries can give the series a 5-hour running time.

ThinkPad X30 series

Pentium III Mobile (X30), Pentium M Banias (X31) or Pentium M Dothan (X32), 12.1 inch XGA screens, dedicated Graphic Chip (ATI M6 with 16 MB, which means no shared memory is cut from the RAM), Bluetooth on some models (upgradable), WLAN (802.11b, b/g or even a/b/g), FireWire, CompactFlash card slot. No built-in optical drive. Lots of options like second battery, Medíaslice (for battery and UltraBay), port replicators, docking stations (some with a PCI slot).

ThinkPad X40 Series

An example of the lightweight X series, weighing in at 1.2 kg (2.7 lb), 25% lighter than its predecessor, the X31. The last variant of the X40 series, the X41 Tablet, was the first ThinkPad tablet PC since the original pen-based ThinkPad. It is the lightest 12" Tablet PC wi h a keyboard from any manufacturer. It was also the final released ThinkPad designed by IBM before the brand was purchased by Lenovo.

ThinkPad X60 series

Includes the X60 and X61, with their associated "s" and "Tablet" series. The X60 is first X Series ThinkPad to feature Intel chips using the Intel Core architecture. The Core Duo L2400 (Low Voltage) CPU on the X60s model achieves 7+ hours of battery life on standard benchmarks, and can reach around 10 hours under light use, when using the extended-life battery. Note this model lacks a built-in optical drive, unlike the larger T60. The X61, like the T61, also is the first X-series ThinkPad to use Intel's Santa Rosa platform.

ThinkPad Z60 series

This is the first ThinkPad to feature a widescreen (16:10 aspect ratio) display. The Z Series is also the first ThinkPad equipped with a titanium lid (on some models). Integrated WWAN and/or webcam also found on some configurations. The series includes, as of 2006, the Z60 and Z61; the latter of which is the first Z Series ThinkPad with Intel "Yonah" Dual Core Technology. The processor supports Intel VT; this is disabled in the BIOS but can be turned on thanks to a BIOS update. Running fully virtualised operating systems via Xen or VMware is therefore possible.

ThinkPad X300

Codenamed "Kodachi". Released February 26, 2008. Distinguished from other ultraportables by its usage of LED backlighting, removable battery, solid state drive, and integrated DVD burner, it is the flagship model for the X-series. It also integrates GPS, WWAN, and a webcam in the top lid. The thickest part of the notebook is 2.34 cm (0.92 inches)and the thinnest part is 1.85 cm (0.73 inches).

Reception

Both IBM and Lenovo-manufactured ThinkPads have been recognised by the press for their reliability. *Laptop Magazine* states that the ThinkPad has the highest-quality laptop computer keyboard available. The ThinkPad was ranked #1 in reliability and support according to PC Magazine's 2007 Survey. The Lenovo ThinkPad is the PC Magazine 2006 Reader's Choice for PC based laptops, and ranked number 1 in Support for PC based laptops. The ThinkPad Series is the first product line that has received PC World's Hall of Fame award. The ThinkPad X Tablet series is PC Magazine Editor's Choice for tablet PCs. The 3.5 lb (1.6 kg) ThinkPad X60s is ranked number 1 in ultraportable laptops by PC World. It lasted 8 hours and 21 minutes on a single charge with its 8 cell battery. The Lenovo ThinkPad X60s Series is on PC World's Top 100 Product of 2006. The 2005 PC World Reliability and Service survey ranked ThinkPad products ahead of all other brands for reliability. In the 2004 survey, they were ranked second (behind eMachines) Lenovo was named the most environment-friendly company in the electronics industry by Greenpeace in 2007. Lenovo ThinkPad T60p received the Editor's Choice award for Mobile Graphic Workstation from PC Magazine. Lenovo ThinkPad X60 is the PC Magazine Editor's Choice among ultra portable laptops.

Criticism

There have been concerns and complaints about the service, support, hardware, and security before and after Lenovo acquired the ThinkPad line. For example:

- IBM EasyServ has been outsourced to Solectron. The default depot repair is now handled by Solectron, and there have been complaints about unsatisfactory repairs and charges from users.
- Many who ordered T60s or T61s between May 9 and May 24, 2007, did not receive their orders when promised due to a variety of problems at Lenovo.
- Lenovo in Canada has a buggy ordering system that causes delayed delivery time and results in customer's frustration
- Many IBM ThinkPad models give a no-1802 error when trying to install "unauthorised" wireless cards. This prevents users from starting up their computers unless the wireless mini-PCI card is removed, or an IBM-authorised card is used. However, there are workaround patches.

12

WINDOWS XP EDITIONS

Windows XP has been released in several editions since its original release in 2001.

Windows XP is available in many languages. In addition, add-ons translating the user interface are also available for certain languages.

Home and Professional

The first two editions released by Microsoft are Windows XP Home Edition, designed for home users, and Windows XP Professional, designed for business and power-users.

Windows XP Professional offers a number of features unavailable in the Home Edition, including:

Original Windows XP cover boxes

Home Edition Professional

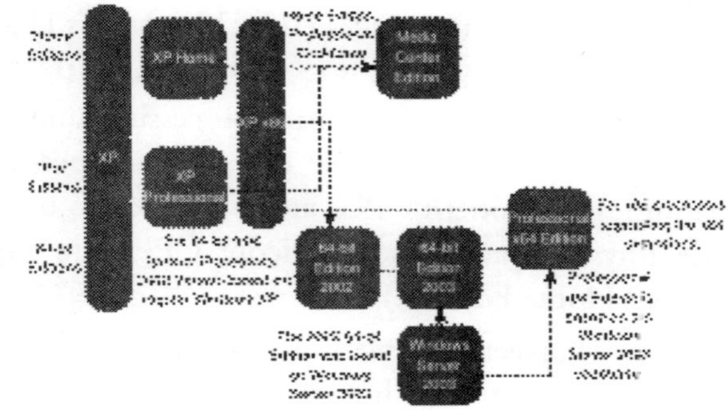

Diagram representing the main editions of Windows XP. It is based on the category of the edition (grey) and codebase (black arrow).

- The ability to become part of a Windows Server domain, a group of computers that are remotely managed by one or more central servers.
- A sophisticated access control scheme that allows specific permissions on files to be granted to specific users under normal circumstances. However, users can use tools other than Windows Explorer (like cacls or File Manager), or restart to Safe Mode to modify access control lists.
- Remote Desktop server, which allows a PC to be operated by another Windows XP user over a local area network or the Internet.
- Offline Files and Folders, which allow the PC to automatically store a copy of files from another networked computer and work with them while disconnected from the network.
- Encrypting File System, which encrypts files stored on the computer's hard drive so they cannot be read by another user, even with physical access to the storage medium.
- Centralised administration features, including Group Policies, Automatic Software Installation and Maintenance, Roaming User Profiles, and Remote Installation Service (RIS).

- Internet Information Services (IIS), Microsoft's HTTP and FTP Server.
- Support for two physical central processing units (CPU). (Because the number of CPU cores and Hyper-threading capabilities on modern CPUs are considered to be part of a single physical processor, multicore CPUs are supported using XP Home Edition.)
- Windows Management Instrumentation Console (WMIC): WMIC is a command-line tool designed to ease WMI information retrieval about a system by using simple keywords (aliases).

Windows XP Edition N

In March 2004, the European Commission fined Microsoft €497 million (£395 million or US$784 million) and ordered the company to provide a version of Windows without Windows Media Player. The Commission concluded that Microsoft "broke European Union competition law by leveraging its near monopoly in the market for PC operating systems onto the markets for work group server operating systems and for media players". After unsuccessful appeals in 2004 and 2005, Microsoft reached an agreement with the Commission where it would release a court-compliant version, Windows XP *Edition N*. This version does not include the company's Windows Media Player but instead encourages users to pick and download their own media player. Microsoft wanted to call this version *Reduced Media Edition*, but EU regulators objected and suggested the *Edition N* name, with the *N* signifying "not with Media Player" for both Home and Professional editions of Windows XP. Due to the fact that it is sold at the same price as the version with Windows Media Player included, Dell, Hewlett-Packard, Lenovo and Fujitsu Siemens have chosen not to stock the product. However, Dell did offer the operating system for a short time. Consumer interest has been low, with roughly 1,500 units shipped to OEMs, and no reported sales to consumers.

The N editions of Windows XP also do not include Windows Movie Maker, but Microsoft has made this available as a separate download.

Windows XP Edition K and KN

In December 2005, the Korean Fair Trade Commission ordered Microsoft to make available editions of Windows XP and Windows Server 2003 that do not contain Windows Media Player or Windows Messenger. Like the European Commission decision, this decision was based on the grounds that Microsoft had abused its dominant position in the market to push other products onto consumers. Unlike that decision, however, Microsoft was also forced to withdraw the non-compliant versions of Windows from the South Korean market.

The K and KN editions of Windows XP Home Edition and Professional Edition were released in August 2006, and are only available in the Korean language. Both editions contain links to third-party instant messenger and media player software, and the K editions continue to ship with media player and instant messaging capability, but the KN editions do not.

Starter Edition

Windows XP Starter Edition is a lower-cost version of Windows XP available in Thailand, Turkey, Malaysia, Indonesia, Russia, India, Colombia, Brazil, Argentina, Peru, Bolivia, Chile, Mexico, Ecuador, Uruguay and Venezuela. It is similar to Windows XP Home, but is limited to low-end hardware, can only run 3 programmes at a time, and has some other features either removed or disabled by default.

According to a Microsoft press release, Windows XP Starter Edition is "a low-cost introduction to the Microsoft Windows XP operating system designed for first-time desktop PC users in developing countries."

Specialisations

The Starter Edition includes some special features for certain markets where consumers may not be computer literate. Not found in the Home Edition, these include localised help features for those who may not speak English, a country-specific computer wallpaper and screensavers, and other default settings designed for easier use than typical Windows XP installations. The Malaysian version, for example, contains a desktop background of the Kuala Lumpur skyline.

In addition, the Starter Edition also has some unique limitations to prevent it from displacing more expensive versions of Windows XP. Only three applications can be run at once on the Starter Edition, and each application may open a maximum of three windows. The maximum screen resolution is 1024×768, and there is no support for workgroup networking or domains. In addition, the Starter Edition is licensed only for low-end processors like Intel's Celeron or AMD's Duron and Sempron. There is also a 512 MB limit on main memory and a 120 GB disk size limit (Microsoft has not made it clear, however, if this is for total disk space, per partition, or per disk). There are also fewer options for customising the themes, desktop, and taskbar.

Market Adoption

On October 9, 2006, Microsoft announced that they reached a milestone of 1,000,000 units of Windows XP Starter Edition sold. In the mass market, however, the Starter Edition has not had much success. Many markets where it is available have seen the uptake of cracked or pirated versions of higher end versions of Windows instead.

Media Center Edition

This edition is designed for media center PCs. Originally, it was only available bundled with one of these computers, and could not be purchased separately. In 2003 the Media Center Edition was updated as "Windows XP Media Center Edition 2003", which added additional features such as FM radio tuning. Another update was released in 2004, and again in 2005, which was the first edition available for System Builders. Many of the features of Windows XP Media Center Edition 2005 (including screen dancers, auto playlist DJ, and high end visual screen savers) were taken from the Windows XP Plus! packages. These were originally shipped as add ons to Windows XP to enhance the users experience of their Windows XP machine.

A typical Windows XP MCE 2005 Menu

Releases

There have been four releases of Windows XP Media Center Edition.

- **Windows XP Media Center Edition** (codename "Freestyle", Jan 2002), was only available from Tier 1 computer manufacturers (HP, Dell, Sony, Zitech, et al).
- **Windows XP Media Center Edition 2003** ("Freestyle", Oct 2002) added a number of features, including FM radio tuning.
- **Windows XP Media Center Edition 2004** ("Harmony", Nov 2003). Windows XP Service Pack 2 upgrades earlier versions of MCE to this one.
- **Windows XP Media Center Edition 2005** ("Symphony", Nov 2004) is the first edition of MCE available to non-Tier 1 system builders. Among other things it includes support for Media Center Extenders, and CD/DVD-Video burning support.

  2005 was the final release, but it was updated a number of times to incorporate new capabilities such as support for the Xbox 360 as a media center extender, DVB-T broadcasts, and support for two ATSC tuner cards.

After the 2005 release, Microsoft focused their efforts on building new media center features into Windows Vista's "Home Premium" and "Ultimate" editions, which, unlike the releases of Windows XP Media Center Edition, are available for retail purchase without the necessary hardware.

Features

The most notable feature unique to this edition is the Windows Media Center, which provides a large-font ("10-foot"), remotely accessible interface for television viewing on the computer as well as recording and playback, a TV guide, DVD playback, video playback, photo viewing, and music playback. Unlike competing commercial digital video recorder products, Microsoft does not charge a monthly subscription fee for its Media Center TV guide service.

Due to strict hardware requirements, Microsoft did not sell Media Center Edition in retail markets alongside the Home and Professional editions. Microsoft only distributes it to MSDN subscribers and OEM System Builders in certain countries. Consumers generally purchase Media Center preinstalled on a new computer, or from a reseller that sells OEM versions of Microsoft software.

Media Center Edition was the only consumer-oriented edition of Windows XP that was updated with new features on an annual basis during the five-year development of Windows Vista. The MCE 2005 release, for example, includes an update to Windows Movie Maker that supports burning DVDs, a new visual style called "Royale", support for Media Center Extenders, and SoundSpectrum's G-Force sound visualisations. Microsoft also released its own remote control, receiver and infrared blaster with MCE 2005. A new specially designed wireless computer keyboard for MCE 2005 was released September 2005.

Using Media Center Extenders or the Xbox 360, Media Center Edition is also able to connect and stream recorded TV, music and pictures, over a network connection.

Media Center Edition retains most of the features included Windows XP Professional, including Remote Desktop and the Encrypting File System. Earlier releases also included the ability to join an Active Directory domain. This capability was disabled in MCE 2005, but circumventions were later discovered; if the installation of MCE 2005 is an in-place upgrade from a previous version already joined to a domain, this ability is retained, unless a user uses a Windows Media Center Extender: in this case, such ability is lost and cannot be reverted back again. Presumably, Microsoft introduced this limit because Media Center Extender devices, introduced in this version, rely on the Fast User Switching component, but this component must be disabled in order to join a domain.

Hardware Requirements

Media Center has higher hardware requirements than other editions of Windows XP. MCE 2005 requires at least a 1.6 GHz processor, DirectX 9.0 hardware-accelerated GPU (ATI Radeon 9 series or nVidia GeForce FX Series or higher), and 256 MB of System RAM. Some functionality, such as Media Center Extender support, use of multiple tuners, or HDTV playback/recording carries higher system requirements.

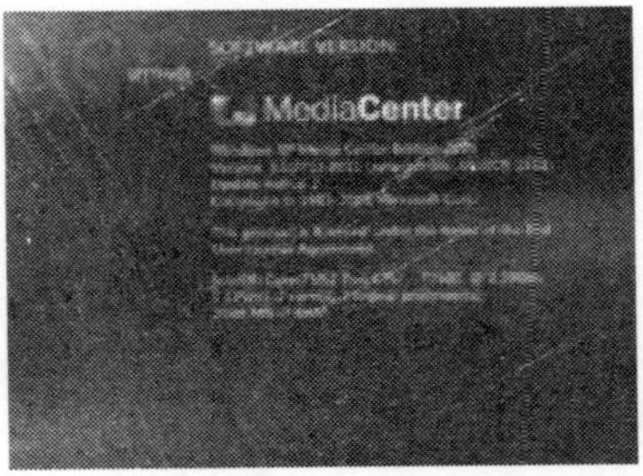

The Software Version screen showing MCE running on an Intel Core 2 Duo computer.

Media Center is much more restricted in the range of hardware that it supports than most other software DVR solutions. Media Center tuners must have a standardised driver interface, and they must have hardware MPEG-2 encoders, closed caption support, and a number of other features. Media Center remote controls are standardised in terms of button labels and functionality, and, to a degree, general layout.

In June 2007, the Media Center Components Database was set up as a resource for Media Center self builders to pool knowledge of which components play well with each other.

Hacks

There are a number of hacks that change the intended features of Windows XP Media Center Edition.

- **Windows Media Player 6.4**. Despite WMP 6.4 being removed from MCE 2005, it can be replaced by copying the executable from a Windows XP Home Edition or Professional installation. WMP 6.4 is not localised for non-English users: if the executable is used on non-English versions of MCE, it will retain its English GUI.
- **The viewing of Pay-Per-View using Media Center without an IR transmitter allows the recording of videos,** which can later be burned onto a DVD.

Windows XP Tablet PC Edition

This edition is intended for specially-designed notebook/laptop computers called tablet PCs. Windows XP Tablet PC Edition is compatible with a pen-sensitive screen, supporting handwritten notes and portrait-oriented screens. A retail version cannot be purchased separately from a tablet PC, but is available to Microsoft Developers Network (MSDN) subscribers. Unlike Windows XP Media Center Edition which is not available in a retail or volume license form, a volume license version is also available.

Tablet PC logo

There have been two releases:

- Windows XP Tablet PC Edition—The original version released in November 2002.
- Windows XP Tablet PC Edition 2005—The Tablet PC version released in August 2004 (codenamed *Lonestar*) as part of Windows XP Service Pack 2. The 2005 edition is available as a service pack upgrade, or as a new OEM version.

Included Software

Windows XP Tablet PC Edition is based on Windows XP Professional and includes all the software features provided in it. In addition, it includes some of the following components:

- Windows Journal
- Sticky Notes
- InkBall
- Energy Blue theme.

Tablet PC running Windows XP Tablet PC Edition and Energy Blue Theme

The following downloadable packs released by Microsoft add more functionality:

A Typical Tablet PC Screenshot, showing a docked TIP from Tablet PC Edition 2005 and Internet Explorer 6

- Microsoft Experience Pack
  - o Ink Art
  - o Ink Crossword
  - o Ink Desktop
  - o Media Transfer
  - o Snipping Tool 2.0
- Education Pack
  - o Ink Flash Cards
  - o Equation Writer
  - o GoBinder Lite
  - o Hexic Deluxe

Technology

Windows XP Tablet PC Edition utilises the Ink object as a means of data input and storage. This is a data type created as part of the Windows XP Tablet PC Edition API that allows users to manipulate and process handwritten data, including recognition results and, in some cases, the pressure information for each part of the stroke. Properties of Ink can be changed in much the same way as properties of other objects, and the data can be saved to allow future reference. Many applications referencing the Ink object also allow handwritten notes to be filtered and searched through, based on the recognition results stored when Ink is saved.

Integrated with the operating system is a Tablet PC Input Panel (TIP) which allows handwriting to be converted into text for use in most non-full-screen applications. The integrated handwriting recognition in Windows XP Tablet PC Edition 2005 can recognise print, cursive, or mixed writing. Accuracy can be increased by configuring the recognizer to expect left-handed writing or right-handed writing. Recognition in a variety of languages is available with the install of a recognizer pack. Unfortunately the handwriting engine cannot be trained to recognise a particular handwriting style so the user must modify their handwriting to be better recognised by the system in order to use this feature effectively.

Speech recognition functionality is also incorporated into the Tablet Input Panel. Compared to previous versions, a substantially improved speech recognition engine version 6 (which also ships with Office 2003) and a tutorial, microphone wizard and training modules are included. It is possible to dictate text using speech in certain supported applications and control the Windows GUI and applications using speech, although the accuracy improvements further made in Windows Vista surpass these features.

Subscription and Pre-paid Editions

In 2006, Microsoft made available two additional editions of Windows XP Home Edition for hardware manufacturers that wanted to provide subscription-based or pay as you go-based models for selling computers. These editions, named Windows XP Home Edition for Subscription Computers, and Windows XP Home Edition for Prepaid Computers respectively, are part of the "Microsoft FlexGo" initiative, described in a company-issued press release as, "[making] PCs more accessible by dramatically reducing the entry cost and enabling customers to pay for their computer as they use it, through the purchase of prepaid cards. Market trials are starting first in emerging markets where inadequate access to consumer credit, unpredictable income and high entry costs prevent many consumers from purchasing a computer." These editions were targeted towards emerging markets such as India, Brazil, Hungary and Vietnam.

Both editions contain additional components that enforce the subscription models via metering. The metering is typically enforced with a hardware component to prevent tampering. The installation of Windows operates in "normal mode", "Limited Access Mode", or "Hardware Locked Mode" depending on the state of the subscription. When a computer has a positive time balance, it operates in "normal mode" and functions as a regular Windows

XP Home Edition machine. When the time balance expires, the machine will then operate in "Limited Access Mode" for an amount of time set by the hardware manufacturer (five hours by default) before entering "Hardware Locked Mode". In Limited Access Mode, the screen uses high-contrast and low-resolution display settings, and in Hardware Locked Mode, the operating system is disabled entirely, and a message is displayed on boot-up with instructions on how to re-enable the machine.

64-bit editions

Two distinct editions of Windows XP were released to support 64-bit hardware.

Windows XP 64-bit Edition

Windows XP 64-bit Edition was designed to run on Intel Itanium family of microprocessors in their native IA-64 mode.

Two versions of Windows XP 64-bit Edition were released:

- Windows XP 64-bit Edition for Itanium systems, Version 2002 — Based on Windows XP codebase, which was released in 2001
- Windows XP 64-bit Edition, Version 2003 — Based on Windows Server 2003 codebase, which added support for the Itanium 2 processor, was released on March 28, 2003.

This edition was discontinued in early 2005, after Hewlett Packard, the last distributor of Itanium-based workstations, stopped selling Itanium systems marketed as 'workstations'. As of July 2005, Windows XP 64-bit Edition is no longer supported, and no further security updates were made available.

Windows XP 64-bit Edition wasn't marketed as the Itanium version of Microsoft's other Windows XP editions but was a separate edition made solely for the Itanium processor and its 64-bit instructions. It is mostly analogous to Windows XP Professional, but numerous older technologies such as DAO, Jet database, NTVDM and Windows on Windows are no longer present so support for MS-DOS and Win16 applications is absent. The original version also lacks most media applications such as Windows Media Player, NetMeeting, Windows Movie Maker, and integrated CD burning, although WMP and NetMeeting were added in the 2003 version.

Unlike previous alternate architecture ports of Windows (Windows NT 4.0 for PowerPC, MIPS R4x00, and Alpha) Windows XP 64-bit Edition could run standard x86 32-bit applications through its WOW64 (Windows on Windows) emulation layer. While the original Itanium processor contains an on-chip IA-32 decoder, it was deemed far too slow for serious use (running at about 400 MHz), so Microsoft and Intel wrote a software 32 to 64 bit translator dubbed the IA-32 Execution Layer. It allows real time translation of x86 32-bit instructions into IA-64 instructions, allowing 32-bit applications to run (albeit significantly more slowly than native code).

Windows XP Professional x64 Edition

This edition supports the x86-64 extension of the Intel IA-32 architecture. x86-64 is implemented by AMD as "AMD64", found in AMD's Opteron and Athlon 64 chips, and implemented by Intel as "Intel 64" (formerly known as IA-32e and EM64T), found in some of Intel's Pentium 4 and all of Intel's later chips.

Windows XP Professional x64 Edition uses version 5.2.3790.1830 of core files, the same version used by Windows XP 64-bit Edition 2003 and Windows Server 2003 SP1 as they were the latest versions during the operating system's development.

During the initial development phases (2003–2004), Windows XP Professional x64 Edition was named *Windows XP 64-bit Edition for x86 Extended systems* and later, *Windows XP 64-bit Edition for Extended systems*, as opposed to *64-bit Edition for Itanium systems*.

Known Issues

There are some common issues that arise with Windows XP Professional x64 Edition.

- Driver compatibility; Only 64-bit kernel mode drivers are supported. This means that devices for which there are no 64-bit Windows XP drivers available cannot be used. This includes a lot of common hardware.
- Any 32-bit Windows Explorer extension fails to work with 64-bit Windows Explorer. Explorer is a 64-bit programme, so it cannot load a 32-bit DLL. However, Windows XP x64 Edition also ships with the 32-bit explorer.exe, which can be used as the user's default shell with a registry change.
- Any 16-bit programmes will not run (32-bit software with 16-bit installers based on ACME Setup versions 2.6, 3.0, 3.01, and 3.1 and InstallShield versions 5.x will run correctly)
- Command prompts will not load in full-screen. This is also true of Windows Vista in both 32 and 64 bit editions.
- Some (typically older) programmes have 16-bit installers that will not install on the x64 Edition
- No native support for Type 1 fonts.
- Windows Media Player 11 for this version of Windows unusually runs as a 32-bit application. The only use for the specific release of Windows Media Player 11 is that the other applications such as Media Sharing do in fact, run 64-bit. Mini player mode on the taskbar is not available (except with the 32-bit explorer.exe).
- ID3 tag information from music files are not viewable in the Windows Explorer.
- Does not contain a Web Extender Client component for Web Folders (WebDAV).
- The Windows Live installer executable cannot be run, so one needs to find separate .msi installation files for each component (such as Windows Live Messenger, Windows Live Mail).

Service Packs

Because Windows XP Professional x64 Edition is derived from the Windows Server 2003 codebase, its service packs are also developed and released on the same timeline as the server product, instead of the other editions of Windows XP. For this reason, the RTM installation of Windows XP Professional x64 Edition identifies itself as "Service Pack 1".

Service Pack 2 (SP2) was released on March 12, 2007. This service pack is not equivalent to Service Pack 2 for 32-bit versions of Windows XP. Due to the earlier release date of the 32-bit version, the features introduced by Service Pack 2 for 32-bit (x86) editions of Windows XP were already present in the RTM version of its 64-bit (x86-64) counterpart.

Service Pack 3 (SP3) for Windows XP will not be compatible with Windows XP x64 Edition, and Microsoft has not announced any plans for another service pack for XP Professional x64 Edition.

Software compatibility

Windows XP Professional x64 Edition uses a technology named Windows-on-Windows 64-bit (WOW64), which permits the execution of 32-bit x86 applications. It was first employed in Windows XP 64-bit Edition (for the Itanium), but then reused for the "x64 Editions" of Windows XP and Windows Server 2003.

Since the X86-64 architecture includes hardware-level support for 32-bit instructions, WOW64 switches the process between 32- and 64-bit modes. As a result, X86-64 architecture microprocessors incur no performance loss when executing 32-bit Windows applications. On the Itanium architecture, WOW64 is required to translate 32-bit x86 instructions into their 64-bit Itanium equivalents—which in some cases were implemented in quite different ways—so that the processor could execute them. All 32-bit processes are shown with *32 in the task manager, while 64-bit processes have no extra text present.

Although 32-bit applications can be run transparently, the mixing of the two types of code within the same process is not allowed. A 64-bit application cannot link against a 32-bit library (DLL) and similarly a 32-bit application cannot link against a 64-bit library. This may lead to the need for library developers to provide both 32- and 64-bit binary versions of their libraries. Windows XP x64 Edition includes both 32- and 64-bit versions of Internet Explorer 6, in order to allow for the possibility that some third-party browser plugins or ActiveX controls may not yet be available in 64-bit versions.

Older 32-bit drivers and services are not supported by 64-bit Windows, but video and audio codecs such as XviD or OggDS (which are 32-bit DLLs), are supported as long as the media player that uses them is 32-bit as well.

64-bit Windows does not include NTVDM or Windows on Windows, so there is no native support for the execution of MS-DOS or 16-bit Windows applications, such as those written for Windows 3.1.

Advantages

The primary benefit of moving to 64-bit is the increase in the maximum allocable system memory (RAM). A single process on a 32-bit Windows operating system is limited to a total of 4 GB, which is typically equally divided between kernel and application usage. Windows XP x64 can support much more memory; although the theoretical memory limit a 64-bit computer can address is about 16 exabytes, Windows XP x64 is limited to 128 GB of physical memory and 16 terabytes of virtual memory.

64-bit processors calculate particular tasks (such as factorials of large figures) two times faster than working in 32-bit environments (given example is derived from comparison between 32-bit and 64-bit Calculator, noticeable for factorial of say 100 000). This gives a general feeling of theoretical possibilities of 64-bit optimised applications.

Windows XP Professional x64 Edition and Windows XP 64-bit Edition Version 2003 are the only releases of Windows XP to include Internet Information Services 6.0, which matches the version shipped with Windows Server 2003; other versions of XP include 5.1.

64-bit versions of Windows XP are also immune to certain types of 32-bit viruses such as root kits, as most system files are 64-bit. Spyware and other malware may still run on both 32-bit and 64-bit.

The extra registers of the x86-64 architecture can result in performance improvements in certain kinds of applications.

Embedded Editions

Microsoft has released three editions of Windows XP that are targeted towards developers of embedded devices, for use in specific consumer electronics, set-top boxes, kiosks/ATMs, medical devices, arcade video games, point-of-sale terminals, and Voice over Internet Protocol (VoIP) components.

Windows XP for Embedded Systems

Windows XP for Embedded Systems is an edition of Windows XP that contains the full feature set of Windows XP Professional, but has restrictions on licensing that require the resulting device to boot directly into the original equipment manufacturer's application.

As of April 2008, this edition is marketed as part of the "Windows Embedded Enterprise" brand, which includes both this release and its successor, Windows Vista for Embedded Systems.

Windows XP Embedded

Windows XP Embedded, commonly abbreviated "XPe", is a componentised version of the Professional edition of Windows XP. An original equipment manufacturer is free to choose only the components needed thereby reducing operating system footprint and also reducing attack area as compared with XP Professional. Unlike Windows CE, Microsoft's operating system for portable devices and consumer electronics, XP Embedded provides the full Windows API, and support for the full range of applications and device drivers written for Microsoft Windows. The system requirements state that XPe can run on devices with at least 32MB Compact Flash, 32MB RAM and a P-200 microprocessor. XPe was released on November 28, 2001. As of February 2007, the newest release is Windows XP Embedded SP2 Feature Pack 2007.

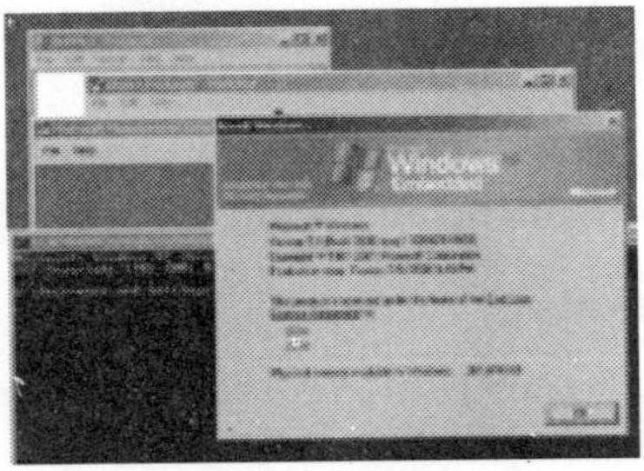

Screenshot of Windows XP Embedded Evaluation running several Windows components.

The devices targeted for XPe have included automatic teller machines, arcade games, slot machines, cash registers, industrial robotics, thin clients, set-top boxes, network attached storage (NAS), time clocks, navigation devices, etc. Custom versions of the OS can be deployed onto anything but a full-fledged PC; even though XPe supports the same hardware that XP Professional supports (x86 architecture), licensing restrictions prevent it from being deployed on to standard PCs. However, Microsoft has made at least one exception to this rule. Some Dell notebooks contain an embedded XP installation as part of the MediaDirect 2.0 feature. It is worth noting that all such laptops also have a standard OEM install of Windows in addition to the XP embedded installation.

Microsoft has announced that Windows Embedded Standard 2009 will succeed XPe by the end of 2008. Windows Embedded Standard 2009 is derived from Windows XP Embedded since Microsoft does not yet have a componentised version of Windows Vista. Windows Embedded Standard 2009 includes Silverlight,

.NET Framework 3.5, Internet Explorer 7, Windows Media Player 11, RDP 6.1 and Network Access Protection. Microsoft however *is* also developing a componentised version codenamed Windows Embedded 'Quebec', containing Windows Vista features such as Aero, SuperFetch, ReadyBoost, BitLocker Drive Encryption, Windows Firewall, Windows Defender, Address Space Layout Randomisation. It will be available in x86 and x64 versions and targeted for release in 2010. Reportedly, it will have a larger footprint (~ 300 MB) compared to 40 MB of XPe and will also require product activation.

FEATURES

Componentised OS

Write Filters

XPe includes feature components known as write filters, which can be used to filter out disk writes. The volumes can be marked as read-only using these filters and all writes to it can be redirected. Applications in user mode are unaware of this write filtering. XPe ships with two write filters:

A BT Internet payphone loading Windows XP Embedded.

Enhanced Write Filter (EWF)

EWF protects a system at volume level. It redirects all disk writes to a protected drive to memory or a separate disk. EWF is extremely useful when used in Thin Clients that have flash memory as their primary boot source.

File Based Write Filter (FBWF)

FBWF allows the configuration of individual files as read/write on a protected volume.

USB Boot

XPe adds a USB boot option to Windows. An XPe embedded device can be configured to boot from a USB drive.

CD Boot

An XPe device can be configured to boot from a CD-ROM. This allows the device to boot without the requirement of having a physical hard disk drive as well as provides a "fresh boot" every time the image is booted (a property inherited by the fact that the operating system is being booted from read-only media). One drawback to this technology is updating or servicing the image requires the complete process of setting up the runtime image to be completed once again from start to end.

Network Boot

An XPe device can be configured to boot from a properly configured network. Synonymous to CD Boot, Network Boot removes the requirement of having the physical hard drive as well as providing the "fresh boot" behaviour. One bonus to Network Boot though is the ability to service the already setup image. Once the image is updated the image is simply posted to the RIS Server and once clients are rebooted they will receive the updated image.

External Links

- Embedded Windows team blog

- Windows XP Embedded Home Page
- Windows XP Embedded discussion forum

Windows Embedded for Point of Service

Windows Embedded for Point of Service is a specialisation of Windows XP Embedded. It was released on May 25, 2005, and focuses on the point of sale device market, such as fuel pumps, self-checkout stations, automated teller machines and cash registers. Like other editions of XPe, it is not available for purchase directly from Microsoft, but is instead licensed to original equipment manufacturers.

Windows Fundamentals for Legacy PCs

In July 2006, Microsoft introduced a "thin-client" version of Windows XP called **Windows Fundamentals for Legacy PCs**, which targets older machines (as early as the original Pentium). It is only available to Software Assurance customers. It is intended for those who would like to upgrade to Windows XP to take advantage of its security and management capabilities, but can't afford to purchase new hardware. The status of WinFLP being an edition of Windows XP is arguable as it doesn't use the "Windows XP" marketing although it makes use of the Windows XP boot screen.

Mistaken to be an Edition of Windows XP

Windows Server 2003 is very similar to Windows XP, both visually and in the underlying system. However, it is not marketed as part of the XP lineup despite having a compatible kernel and a virtually identical interface.

Wearable Computer

Wearable computers are computers that are worn on the body. They have been applied to areas such as behavioural modeling, health monitoring systems, information technologies and media development. Government organisations, military, and health professionals have all incorporated wearable computers into their daily operations. Wearable computers are especially useful for applications that require computational support while the user's hands, voice, eyes or attention are actively engaged with the physical environment.

"Wearable computing" is an active topic of research, with areas of study including user interface design, augmented reality, pattern recognition, use of wearables for specific applications or disabilities, electronic textiles and fashion design. Many issues are common to the wearables, mobile computing, Pervasive computing, Ambient intelligence and ubiquitous computing research communities, including power management and heat dissipation, software architectures, wireless and personal area networks and sensor networks.

Evolution of Steve Mann's *WearComp* wearable computer from backpack based systems of the late 1970s and early 1980s to his current covert systems.

One of the main features of a wearable computer is consistency. There is a constant interaction between the computer and user, ie. there is no need to turn the device on or off. Another feature is the ability to multi-task. It is not necessary to stop what you are doing to use the device; it is augmented into all other actions. These devices can be incorporated by the user to act like a prosthetic. It can therefore be an extension of the user's mind and/or body.

Depending on how broadly one defines both wearable and computer, the first wearable computer could be as early as the 1500s with the invention of the pocket watch. The first device that would fit the modern-day image of a wearable computer was constructed in 1961 by the mathematician Edward O. Thorp, better known as the inventor of the theory of card-counting for blackjack, and Claude E. Shannon, who is best known as "the father of information theory." The system was a concealed cigarette-pack sized analog computer designed to predict roulette wheels. A data-taker would use microswitches hidden in his shoes to indicate the speed of the roulette wheel, and the computer would indicate an octant to bet on by sending musical tones via radio to a miniature speaker hidden in a collaborators ear canal. The system was successfully tested in Las Vegas in June 1961, but hardware issues with the speaker wires prevented them from using it beyond their test runs. Their wearable was kept secret until it was first mentioned in Thorp's book Beat the Dealer (revised ed.) in 1966 and later published in detail in 1969. The 1970s saw rise to similar roulette-prediction wearable computers using next-generation technology, in particular a group known as Eudaemonic Enterprises that used a CMOS 6502 microprocessor with 5K RAM to create a shoe-computer with inductive radio communications between a data-taker and better (Bass 1985).

Besides gambling aids, early wearable applications included two notable systems designed to help the disabled. In 1967, Hubert Upton developed an analogue wearable computer that included an eyeglass-mounted display to aid lip reading. Using high and low-pass filters, the system would determine if a spoken phoneme was a fricative, stop consonant, voiced-fricative, voiced stop consonant, or simply voiced. An LED mounted on ordinary eyeglasses illuminated to indicate the phoneme type. The LEDs were positioned to enable a simple form of augmented reality; for example, when a phoneme was voiced the LED at the bottom of the glass illuminated, making it seem as if the speaker's throat was glowing (Upton 1968). Another early wearable system was a camera-to-tactile vest for the blind, published by C.C. Collins in 1977, that converted images into a 1024-point, 10-inch square tactile grid on a vest (Collins 1977). On the consumer end, 1977 also saw the introduction of the HP-01 algebraic calculator watch by Hewlett-Packard (Marion 1977).

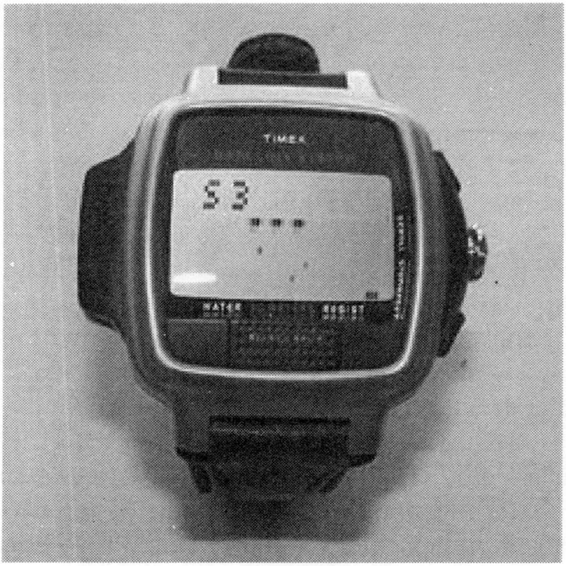

Datalink USB Dress edition with *Invasion* video game. (Three lives remaining). The watch crown *(icontrol)* can be used to move the defender left to right and the fire control is the Start/Split button on the lower side of the face of the watch at 6 o'clock.

The 1980s saw the rise of more general-purpose wearable computers. In 1981 Steve Mann designed and built a backpack-mounted 6502-based computer to control flash-bulbs, cameras and other photographic systems. Mann went on to be an early and active researcher in the wearables field, especially known for his 1994 creation of the Wearable Wireless Webcam. Though perhaps not technically "wearable," in 1986 Steve Roberts built Winnebiko-II, a recumbent bicycle with on-board computer and chording keyboard Winnebiko II was the first of Steve Roberts' forays into nomadic computing that allowed him to type while riding.

In 1989 Reflection Technology marketed the Private Eye head-mounted display, which scanned a vertical array of LEDs across the visual field using a vibrating mirror. This display gave rise to several hobbyist and research wearables, including Gerald "Chip" Maguire's IBM / Columbia University Student Electronic Notebook (Bade 1990), Doug Platt's Hip-PC and Carnegie Mellon University's VuMan 1 in 1991. The Student Electronic Notebook consisted of the Private Eye, Toshiba diskless AIX notebook computers (prototypes) and a stylus based input system plus virtual keyboard, and used direct-sequence spread spectrum radio links to provide all the usual TCP/IP based services, including NFS mounted file systems and X11, all running in the Andrew Project environment. The Hip-PC included an Agenda palmtop used as a chording keyboard attached to the belt and a 1.44 megabyte floppy drive. Later versions incorporated additional equipment from Park Engineering. The system debuted at "The Lap and Palmtop Expo" on April 16, 1991. VuMan 1 was developed as part of a Summer-term course at Carnegie Mellon's Engineering Design Research Center, and was intended for viewing house blueprints. Input was through a three-button unit worn on the belt, and output was through Reflection Tech's Private Eye. The CPU was an 8 MHz 80188 processor with 0.5 MB ROM. The project later turned into a full research project in wearable computing that remains strong today.

In 1993 the Private Eye was used in Thad Starner's wearable, based on Doug Platt's system and built from a kit from Park Enterprises, a Private Eye display on loan from Devon Sean McCullough, and the Twiddler chording keyboard made by Handykey. Many iterations later this system became the MIT "Tin Lizzy" wearable computer design, and Starner went on to become one of the founders of MIT's wearable computing project. 1993 also saw Columbia University's augmented-reality system known as KARMA: Knowledge-based Augmented Reality for Maintenance Assistance. Users would wear a Private Eye display over one eye, giving an overlay effect when the real world was viewed with both eyes open. KARMA would overlay wireframe schematics and maintenance instructions on top of whatever was being repaired. For example, graphical wireframes on top of a laser printer would explain how to change the paper tray. The system used sensors attached to objects in the physical world to determine their locations, and the entire system ran tethered from a desktop computer (Feiner 1993).

In 1994 Edgar Matias and Mike Ruicci of the University of Toronto, debuted the "wrist computer." Their system presented an alternative approach to the emerging head-up display plus chord keyboard wearable. The system was built from a modified HP 95LX palmtop computer and a Half-QWERTY one-handed keyboard. With the keyboard and display modules strapped to the operator's forearms, text could be entered by bringing the wrists together and typing (Matias 1994, 1996). The system debuted at ACM's Computer-Human Interaction 1994 conference in Boston, and is now being productised under the name "half keyboard". The same technology was used by IBM researchers to create the half-keyboard "belt computer." Also in 1994, Mik Lamming and Mike Flynnat Xerox EuroPARC demonstrated the Forget-Me-Not, a wearable device that would record interactions with people and devices and store this information in a database for later query. It interacted via wireless transmitters in rooms and with equipment in the area to remember who was there, who was being talked to on the telephone, and what objects were in the room, allowing queries like "Who came by my office while I was on the phone to Mark?" As with the Toronto system, Forget-Me-Not was not based on a head-mounted display.

Also in 1994, DARPA started the Smart Modules Programme to develop a modular, humionic approach to wearable and carryable computers, with the goal of producing a variety of products including computers, radios, navigation systems and human-computer interfaces that have both military and commercial use. In July 1996 DARPA went on to host the "Wearables in 2005" workshop, bringing together industrial, university and military visionaries to work on the common theme of delivering computing to the individual (DARPA 1996). A follow-up conference was hosted by Boeing in August 1996, where plans were finalised to create a new academic conference on wearable computing. In October 1997, Carnegie Mellon University, MIT, and Georgia Tech co-hosted the IEEE International Symposium on Wearables Computers in Cambridge, Massachusetts. The symposium was a full academic conference with published proceedings and papers ranging from sensors and new hardware to new applications for wearable computers, with 382 people registered for the event. The conference continues to be the primary academic conference for wearable computing today.

In 2002, as part of Kevin Warwick's Project Cyborg, Warwick's wife, Irena, wore a necklace which was electronically linked to Warwick's nervous system via an implanted electrode array. The colour of the necklace changed between red and blue dependent on the signals on Warwick's nervous system.

Commercialisation

The commercialisation of general-purpose wearable computers, as led by companies such as Xybernaut, CDI and ViA Inc, has thus far met with limited success. Publicly-traded Xybernaut tried forging alliances with companies such as IBM and Sony in order to make wearable computing widely available, but in 2005 their stock was delisted and the company filed for Chapter 11 bankruptcy protection amid financial scandal and federal investigation. Xybernaut emerged from bankruptcy protection in January, 2007. In 1998 Seiko marketed the Ruputer, a computer in a (fairly large) wristwatch, to mediocre returns. In 2001 IBM developed and publicly displayed two prototypes for a wristwatch computer running Linux, but the product never came to market. In 2002 Fossil, Inc. announced the Fossil Wrist PDA, which ran the Palm OS. Its release date was set for summer of 2003, but was delayed several times and was finally made available on January 5, 2005. Timex Datalink is another example of a practical wearable computer. Hitachi has lounched a wearable computer called poma in 2002.

Arcom Control Systems offers the the ZYPAD, a wrist wearable touch screen computer with GPS, Wi-Fi and Bluetooth connectivity and can run a number of custom applications.

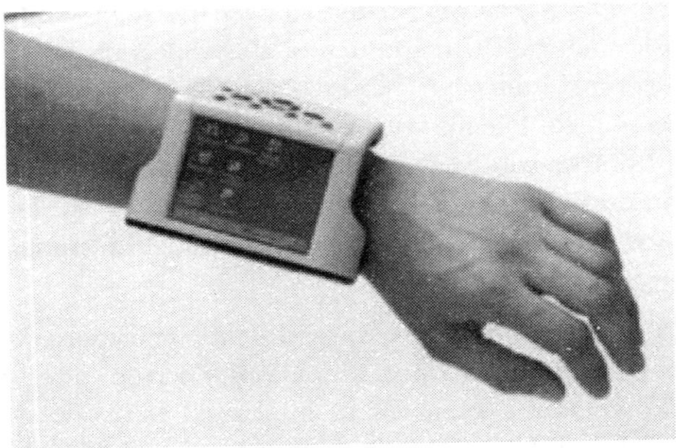

Image of the ZYPAD wrist wearable computer from Arcom Control Systems

Evidence of the allure of the wearable computer and the weak market acceptance is evident with market leading Panasonic Computer Solutions Company's failed product in this market. Panasonic has specialised in mobile computing with their Toughbook line for over 10 years and has extensive market research into the field of portable, wearable computing products. In 2002, Panasonic introduced a wearable brick computer coupled with a handheld or armworn touchscreen. The brick would communicate wirelessly to the screen, and concurrently the brick would communicate wirelessly out to the internet or other networks. The wearable brick was quietly pulled from the market in 2005, while the screen evolved to a thin client touchscreen used with a handstrap.

Microsoft Surface

Bill Gates will manage one of the highest-profile transitions in American business history and computer technology. Before stepping down as chairman of Microsoft (currently $300 billion company that he co-founded over 30 years ago) and moving on to philanthropy, Gates will head a few more high-tech projects and hopefully achieve his goal of bridging the physical and virtual worlds. A secret covert project code named Milan and is 5 years in the making was top secret until recently being unveiled to the public at the Wall Street Journal conference. The project involved transforming an ordinary tabletop into a brilliant, interactive surface with effortless interaction with digital content through natural gestures, touch, and physical objects. A revolutionary aspect of Microsoft Surface is its natural interaction with everyday objects and technologies with an intuitive touch-sensitive 30-inch tabletop with nothing but your fingers. No more computer mouse, keyboards, or wires. The multi-touch interface allows the user to have hands-on control of photos, music, maps, and more. The coolest feature I liked was the photo resizing and stacking that is similar to Macintosh's Apple iPhone's zoom gestures.

This idea is nothing new and is not the only company eyeing the new market, but it has never been more than a prototype until recently being exhibited at the All Things Digital conference.. Microsoft Surface made several appearances in movies like the futuristic movies Minority Report and The Island. This new technology, the brainchild of Stevie Bathiche and Andy Wilson, is breaking down the traditional barriers of people and technology by providing an effortless interaction with digital media. It is apart of Intel's vision of the near future where devices work seamlessly together. This innovative computer has price tags running $10,000 a unit. Microsoft however expects prices to plummet over the next three to five years to the point that it will be available for every home.

Key Attributes of Microsoft Surface

- Direct Interaction: Users can actually "grab" digital information with their hands and interact with content by touch and gestures, without the use of a mouse or keyboard.

- Multi-Touch Contact: Surface computing recognises many points of contact simultaneously, not just from one finger, as with a typical touch screen computer, but up to dozens and dozens of items at once.
- Mulit-User Experience: the horizontal form factor makes it easy for several people to gather around surface computers together, providing a collaborative, face-to-face computing experience

- Object-Recognition: Users can place physical objects on the surface to trigger different types of digital responses, including the transfer of digital content.

Microsoft Partners Get Latest Technology

The first people/companies to get their hands on these are partners T-Mobile USA, Starwood Hotels and Resorts, and Harrah's Entertainment. Hotels, retail stores, and restaurants will easily adapt to this technology and make use of this new technology.

T-Mobile plans to adapt the technology by allowing customers to place any cell phone(s) onto the surface and then view a detailed display of the product(s) information. This makes it easy and ideal to compare various phones at once and easily keep or remove your choices. Consider all your options for possible mobile telephones with all of the products information at hand. Harrah's is also exploring the idea of integrating further options for ordering food and beverages, and possibly gaming or game-related activities.

Starwood plans to make the machines available in public areas of select Sheraton properties, including in Seattle, starting later in 2007. Starwood is exploring the possibility of users being able to select music through their personal playlist, share photos, ordering food and adapting a virtual concierge idea.

Harrah's plans to start using the surface tables as a "virtual concierge" desk in conjunction with its Total Rewards loyalty programme at its eight Las Vegas properties, which include Caesars Palace and Bally's. People will be able to use the tables to access maps of the different properties, get details about events and venues and create itineraries for themselves.

New Computer with New Technology

The company launched "Alienware" new mobile computer "Area-51 m15x" The 15.4-inch screen and provides the Bmoasfath modern technical performance record distinctly suited to the realm of games, three-dimensional graphics in addition to segments of students and professional users. Relies on computer processor Intel Core 2 Extreme X9000 and unit address GeForce 8800M GTX graphics, also provides optical drive supports CD Bluegrass technical reading—opinion in addition to a hard drive capacity of 320 GB, as stated magazine digital world. The Altakinat modern and accessories included in the computer talk Area-51 m15x Bluetooth technology and technical Eluay Faye and the presence of 3 entrances USA me and the reader digital segments, in addition to the digital camera Racing 2.

13

COMPUTER RECYCLING

Computer recycling refers to recycling or reuse of a computer or electronic waste. This can include finding another use for the system (i. e. donated to charity), or having the system dismantled in a manner that allows for the safe extraction of the constituent materials for reuse in other products.

Reasons for Recycling

Obsolete computers are a valuable source for secondary raw materials, if treated properly, however if not treated properly they are a major source of toxins and carcinogens. Rapid technology change, low initial cost and even planned obsolescence have resulted in a fast growing problem around the globe. Technical solutions are available but in most cases a legal framework, a collection system, logistics and other services need to be implemented before a technical solution can be applied. Electronic waste represents 2 per cent of America's trash in landfills, but it equals 70 per cent of overall toxic waste. According to the U.S. Environmental Protection Agency, an estimated 30 to 40 million PCs will be ready for end-of-life management in each of the next few years. An estimated 251 million PCs were sold in 2007.

Many materials used in the construction of computer hardware can be recovered in the recycling process for use in future production. Reuse of tin, silicon, iron, aluminum, and a variety of plastics – all present in bulk in computers – can reduce the costs of constructing new systems. In addition, components frequently contain copper, gold, and other materials valuable enough to reclaim in their own right.

Computers being processed for recycling

Electronic devices, including audio-visual components (televisions, VCRs, stereo equipment), mobile phones and other hand-held devices, and computer components, contain valuable elements and substances suitable for reclamation, including lead, copper, and gold. They also contain a plethora of toxic substances, such as dioxins, PCBs, cadmium, chromium, radioactive isotopes, and mercury. Additionally, the processing required to reclaim the precious substances (including incineration and acid treatments) release, generate and synthesize further toxic by-products.

In the United States, an estimated 70% of heavy metals in landfills come from discarded electronics. Some regional governments are attempting to curtail the accumulation of electronics in landfills by passing laws obligating manufacturers and consumers to recycle these devices, but because in many cases safe dismantlement of these devices in accordance with first world safety standards is unprofitable, historically much of the electronic waste has been shipped to countries with lower or less rigorously-enforced safety protocols. Places like Guiyu, China, and Bangalore, India dismantle tons of electronics every year, profiting from the sale of precious metals, but at the cost of the local environment and the health of its residents.

Mining to produce the same metals, to meet demand for finished products in the west, also occurs in the same countries, and the United Nations Conference on Trade and Development (UNCTAD) has recommended that restrictions against recycling exports be balanced against the environmental costs of recovering those materials from mining. Hard rock mining in the USA produces 45% of all toxics produced by all USA industries.

REGULATIONS

Europe

In February 2003, the European Community signed into law the Waste Electrical and Electronic Equipment Directive 2002/96/EC (WEEE Directive). The directive imposes the responsibility for the disposal of waste electrical and electronic equipment (WEEE) on the manufacturers of such equipment. Those companies should establish an infrastructure for collecting WEEE, in such a way that "Users of electrical and electronic equipment from private households should have the possibility of returning WEEE at least free of charge". Also, the companies are compelled to use the collected waste in an ecological-friendly manner, either by ecological disposal or by reuse/refurbishment of the collected WEEE.

The Directive on the Restriction of the Use of Certain Hazardous Substances in Electrical and Electronic Equipment 2002/95/EC (commonly referred to as the Restriction of Hazardous Substances Directive or RoHS) was adopted in February 2003 by the European Union. The RoHS directive took effect on 1 July 2006, and is required to be enforced and become law in each member state. This directive restricts the use of six hazardous materials in the manufacture of various types of electronic and electrical equipment.

United States

Federal

There is a lack of federal regulation concerning computer and ewaste recycling, but for the stipulations concerning the lead in cathode ray tubes. CRTs fall under the RCRA, and must be disposed of accordingly, though state regulations may differ.

State

Many states have introduced legislation concerning recycling and reuse of computers or computer parts. Different strategies include:

- Arkansas–In 2001, Arkansas enacted the Arkansas Computer and Electronic Solid Waste Management Act, which requires that state agencies manage and sell surplus computer equipment, establishes a Computer and Electronics recycling fund, and authorises the Dept. of Environmental Quality to regulate and/or ban the disposal of computer and electronic equipment in Arkansas landfills.
- California–In 2003, California enacted the California Electronic Waste Recycling Act, which was amended in 2004. This act calls for an advance recovery fee on the sale of certain electronic products (including CRTs), which goes into a fund to manage recycling programmes.
- Maine–In 2004, Maine passed Maine Public Law 661, An Act to Protect Public Health and the Environment by Providing for a System of Shared Responsibility for the Safe Collection and Recycling of Electronic Waste. This extensive moniker describes how it necessitates that after 2006, computer manufacturers take responsibility for handling and recycling computer monitors, and pay the handling costs as well.

Process

Whole computers and pieces of electronic equipment are shredded into smaller pieces to be more manageable and facilitate the separation of the constituent components. Leaded glass from cathode ray tubes is sold to foundries for use as a fluxing agent in the processing of raw lead ore. Other valuable metals, such as copper, gold, palladium, silver and tin are sold to smelters for metal recycling. The hazardous smoke and gases generated by these processes are captured, contained, and treated to ensure that they do not become a threat to the environment. These methods allow for the safe reclamation of all the valuable materials used in computer construction.

Consumer Recycling

Most major computer manufacturers offer some form of recycling, often as a free replacement service when purchasing a new PC. At the user's request they may mail in their old computer, or arrange for pickup from the manufacturer. There are also a variety of donation options, including charities which may offer tax benefits. The United States Environmental Protection Agency maintains a list of electronic recycling and donation options for consumers in the US.

Computers being collected for recycling at a pickup event in Olympia, Washington, United States.

Individuals looking for environmentally-friendly ways in which to dispose of electronics can find corporate electronic take-back and recycling programmes across the country. Open to the public (in most cases), corporations nationwide have begun to offer low-cost to no-cost recycling, and have opened centers nationally and in some cases internationally. Such programmes frequently offer services to take-back and recycle electronics including mobile phones, laptop and desktop computers, digital cameras, and home and auto electronics. Companies such as Staples, Toshiba, and Gateway offer what are called "take-back" programmes that provide monetary incentives for recyclable and/or working technologies.

Though helpful to both citizens of the environment as well as the environment itself, there are some downsides to such programmes. Many corporations offer services for a variety of electronic items, however, their recycling centers are few in number. Recycling centers and take-back programmes are available in many parts of the country, but the type and number of equipment to be recycled tends to be limited. Some corporations, like Sony, only accept up to five recycled items per day and only if they are Sony products. Costco, which offers free shipping and handling for all recycled pieces of equipment, will only allow Costco club members to participate in their programmes. Hewlett Packard also offers free recycling, but of their three national recycling programmes, only one is available nationally, while the other two are restricted to either one or two specific states.

For more information on companies that work to support recycling and take-back programmes, reference this website.

Consumer Awareness Efforts

- Address the Mess is a Comedy Central pro-social campaign that seeks to increase awareness of the dangers of e-waste and to encourage recycling. Partners in the effort include Earth 911, ECO International, and the U.S. EPA. Many Comedy Central viewers are early adopters of new electronics, and produce a commensurate amount of waste that can be directed towards recycling efforts. The station is also taking steps to reduce its own environmental impact, in partnership with NativeEnergy, a company that specialises in renewable energy and carbon offsets.

- Electronic Take-Back Coalition, which is a campaign aimed at protecting human health, and environmental effects of where electronics are being produced, used and discarded. The main aim of the ETBC is to place responsibility of products on electronic manufacturers and brand owners. Responsibility includes not only the creation and use of the product, but also the disposal of the technology. This is primarily done through promotion through community groups and legal enforcement initiatives.
- Silicon Valley Toxics Coalition, (SVTC) is an organisation based from grassroots focused on various issues concerning our increasingly high-tech population and industry. The organisation focuses on promoting human health and addresses environmental justice problems resulting from toxins in technologies.
- Basel Action Network, (BAN) is a unique resource, as they are the only organisation in the world that is solely focused on addressing global environmental injustices and economic inefficiency of 'toxic trade' occurring around the world. The organisation confronts the human rights and the environment at the macro level, by preventing disproportionate dumping on the large scale. BAN is continually promoting sustainable solutions and working on banning waste trade.
- Staples Inc. offers free-of-charge recycling for any consumers who wish to bring electronic waste to any of their stores, regardless of where the products were initially purchased.
- The Sony Take Back Recycling Programme is a new initiative, in partnership with the Waste Management Inc. Recycle America programme to provide incentives for

consumers to recycle their old equipment. Not only they provide free recycling services, they also offer discounts and trade-up programmes for consumers who recycle.

Individual Efforts and Health Hazards

Only 10% of old Personal Computers are recycled properly. In order to *individually help make a difference*, you can choose one of many options. According to the Silicon Valley Toxics Coalition, consumers can follow a number of steps to help with the recycling of electronics:

- Send your old computing equipment back to the electronic company from which you bought it.
  - o Dell, HP, and Apple are all willing to take back your old products when you buy a new one.
  - o When researching computer companies before your computer purchase, find out if they offer such recycling services.
- Look into national programmes, such as the National Cristina Foundation, Tech Soup, and the National Technology Recycling Project. These organisations provide resources for people who are looking to recycle electronic goods.
- Look at the Silicon Valley Toxics Coalition, SVTC's, Responsible Recyclers List. These recyclers, who can be found all across the county, are committed to a clean and healthy recycling environment.

Find a Recycler in Your State

- Once you find a local recycling site, make sure that they process their waste products on site, thus avoiding the global e-waste crisis.
- Don't throw your electronics away in the trash.
- Educate yourself! Read, research, and gain some knowledge about the harmful effects of recycling as well as the recycling laws of your home-state.

Chemical Hazards

While there are several health hazards when it comes to dealing with computer recycling some of the substances you should be aware of:

- lead common in CRTs, older solder, some batteries and to some formulations of PVC. Can be harmful if not disposed of properly.
- Mercury in fluorescent tubes. With new technologies arising the elimination of mercury in many new model computers is taking place.
- Cadmium in some rechargeable batteries. It can be hazardous to your skin if exposed for too long. Although many people are exposed to it everyday it just depends on the amount of exposure.
- Liquid crystals are another health hazard that should be taken into consideration although they do not have the nearly the same effects as the other chemicals.

Corporate Recycling

Businesses seeking a cost-effective way to responsibly recycle large amounts of computer equipment face a more complicated process. They also have the option of contacting the manufacturers and arranging recycling options. However, in cases where the computer equipment comes from a wide variety of manufacturers, it may be more efficient to hire a third-party contractor to handle the recycling arrangements. There exist companies that specialise in corporate computer disposal services both offer disposal and recycling services in compliance with local laws and regulations. Such companies frequently also offer secure data elimination services.

Concerns

One of the major concerns about computer recycling programmes is export of waste to countries with lower environmental standards. Companies may find it cost effective in the short-term to sell outdated computers to less developed countries with lax regulations. The Basel Convention is an international treaty intended to restrict this sort of practice, but it has proven difficult to enforce and the United States has not yet ratified the agreement. Because the US has no domestic laws forbidding the export of toxic waste, the Basel Action Network estimates that about 80% of the e-waste directed to recycling in the US does not get recycled there at all but is put on container ships and sent to countries such as China. Due to lower environmental standards and working conditions in China, India, Kenya, and elsewhere, electronic waste is being sent to these countries for processing – in most cases illegally. Guiyu in Shantou region of China, and Delhi and Bangalore in India, all have electronic waste processing areas. Uncontrolled burning, disassembly, and disposal are causing environmental and health problems, including occupational safety and health effects among those directly involved, due to the methods of processing the waste.

Third-world countries, generally less concerned with worker safety or environmental issues, utilise methods that are not only more harmful, but also more wasteful. The most expedient and most prevalent method is to simply toss equipment onto an open fire, in order to melt plastics and burn away anything that's not valuable metal. This creates acrid smoke full of carcinogens and neurotoxins that linger in the air, shrouding regions in deadly smog. Any refuse left over from these bonfires are disposed of as quickly as possible, generally into a drainage ditch or waterway, where they will be swept into the ocean or local water supplies. Children are frequently employed in these dangerous recycling methods.

14

GREEN COMPUTING

Green computing is the study and practice of using computing resources efficiently. The primary objective of such a programme is to account for the triple bottom line, an expanded spectrum of values and criteria for measuring organisational (and societal) success. The goals are similar to green chemistry; reduce the use of hazardous materials, maximise energy efficiency during the product's lifetime, and promote recyclability or biodegradability of defunct products and factory waste.

Modern IT systems rely upon a complicated mix of people, networks and hardware; as such, a green computing initiative must be systemic in nature, and address increasingly sophisticated problems. Elements of such as solution may comprise items such as end user satisfaction, management restructuring, regulatory compliance, disposal of electronic waste, telecommuting, virtualisation of server resources, energy use, thin client solutions, and return on investment (ROI).

Origins

In 1992, the U.S. Environmental Protection Agency launched Energy Star, a voluntary labeling programme which is designed to promote and recognise energy-efficiency in monitors, climate control equipment, and other technologies. This resulted in the widespread adoption of sleep mode among consumer electronics. The term "green computing" was probably coined shortly after the

Energy Star programme began; there are several USENET posts dating back to 1992 which use the term in this manner. Concurrently, the Swedish organisation TCO Development launched the TCO Certification programme to promote low magnetic and electrical emissions from CRT-based computer displays; this programme was later expanded to include criteria on energy consumption, ergonomics, and the use of hazardous materials in construction.

Regulations and Industry Initiatives

Government

Many governmental agencies have continued to implement standards and regulations that encourage green computing. The Energy Star programme was revised in October 2006 to include stricter efficiency requirements for computer equipment, along with a tiered ranking system for approved products. The European Union's directives 2002/95/EC (RoHS), on the reduction of hazardous substances, and 2002/96/EC (WEEE) on waste electrical and electronic equipment required the substitution of heavy metals and flame retardants like PBBs and PBDEs in all electronic equipment put on the market starting on July 1, 2006. The directives placed responsibility on manufacturers for the gathering and recycling of old equipment (the Producer Responsibility model).

There are currently 26 US States that have established state-wide recycling programmes for obsolete computers and consumer electronics equipment. The statutes either impose a fee for each unit sold at retail (Advance Recovery Fee model), or require the manufacturers to reclaim the equipment at disposal (Producer Responsibility model).

In 2008, a report published in the UK by the Department for Communities and Local Government, quantified that the potential carbon savings from increasing the usage of online public service delivery were significantly in excess of the negative impact of extra IT server capacity.

Industry

- Climate Savers Computing Initiative (CSCI) is an effort to reduce the electric power consumption of PCs in active and inactive states. The CSCI provides a catalog of green products from its member organisations, and information for reducing PC power consumption. It was started on 2007-06-12. The name stems from the World Wildlife Fund's Climate Savers programme, which was launched in 1999. The WWF is also a member of the Computing Initiative.
- Green Computing Impact Organisation, Inc. (GCIO) is a non-profit organisation dedicated to assisting the end-users of computing products in being environmentally responsible. This mission is accomplished through educational events, cooperative programmes and subsidised auditing services. The heart of the group is based on the GCIO Cooperative, a community of environmentally concerned IT leaders who pool their time, resources, and buying power to educate, broaden the use, and improve the efficiency of, green computing products and services. Members work to increase the ROI of green computing products through a more thorough understanding of real measurable and sustainable savings incurred by peers; enforcing a greater drive toward efficiency of vendor products by keeping a community accounting of savings generated; and through group negotiation power.
- Green Electronics Council—The Green Electronics Council offers the Electronic Products Environmental Assessment Tool (EPEAT) to assist in the purchase of "green" computing systems. The Council evaluates computing equipment on

28 criteria that measure a product's efficiency and sustainability attributes. On 2007-01-24, President George W. Bush issued Executive Order 13423, which requires all United States Federal agencies to use EPEAT when purchasing computer systems.

- The Green Grid is a global consortium dedicated to advancing energy efficiency in data centers and business computing ecosystems. It was founded in February 2007 by several key companies in the industry – AMD, APC, Dell, HP, IBM, Intel, Microsoft, Rackable Systems, SprayCool, Sun Microsystems and VMware. The Green Grid has since grown to hundreds of members, including end users and government organisations, all focused on improving data center efficiency.

APPROACHES TO GREEN COMPUTING

Virtualisation

Computer virtualisation is the process of running two or more logical computer systems on one set of physical hardware. The concept originated with the IBM mainframe operating systems of the 1960s, but was commercialised for x86-compatible computers only in the 1990s. With virtualisation, a system administrator could combine several physical systems into virtual machines on one single, powerful system, thereby unplugging the original hardware and reducing power and cooling consumption. Several commercial companies and open-source projects now offer software packages to enable a transition to virtual computing. Intel Corporation and AMD have also built proprietary virtualisation enhancements to the x86 instruction set into each of their CPU product lines, in order to facilitate virtualised computing.

Power Management

The Advanced Configuration and Power Interface (ACPI), an open industry standard, allows an operating system to directly control the power saving aspects of its underlying hardware. This allows a system to automatically turn off components such as monitors and hard drives after set periods of inactivity. In addition, a system may hibernate, where most components (including the CPU and the system RAM) are turned off. ACPI is a successor to an earlier Intel-Microsoft standard called Advanced Power Management, which allows a computer's BIOS to control power management functions.

Some programmes allow the user to manually adjust the voltages supplied to the CPU, which reduces both the amount of heat produced and electricity consumed. This process is called undervolting. Some CPUs can automatically undervolt the processor depending on the workload; this technology is called "SpeedStep" on Intel processors, "PowerNow!"/"Cool'n'Quiet" on AMD chips, LongHaul on VIA CPUs, and LongRun with Transmeta processors.

Power Supply

Desktop computer power supplies (PSUs) are generally 70–75% efficient, dissipating the remaining energy as heat. An industry initiative called 80 PLUS certifies PSUs that are at least 80% efficient; typically these models are drop-in replacements for older, less efficient PSUs of the same form factor. As of July 20, 2007, all new Energy Star 4.0-certified desktop PSUs must be at least 80% efficient.

Storage

Smaller form factor (e.g. 2.5 inch) hard disk drives often consume less power than physically larger drives.

Unlike hard disk drives, solid-state drives store data in flash memory or DRAM. With no moving parts, power consumption may be reduced somewhat for low capacity flash based devices. Even at modest sizes, DRAM based SSDs may use more power than hard disks, (e.g., 4GB i-RAM uses more power and space than laptop drives). Flash based drives are generally slower for writing than hard disks. Flash based solid state drives generally allow far fewer write cycles than hard drives. Smaller storage capacity per dollar may further limit their usable lifetime. Shorter lifetimes may make SSDs less energy and material efficient in some applications.

Display

LCD monitors typically use a cold-cathode fluorescent bulb to provide light for the display. Some newer displays use an array of light-emitting diodes (LEDs) in place of the fluorescent bulb, which reduces the amount of electricity used by the display.

Materials Recycling

Computer systems that have outlived their particular function can be repurposed, or donated to various charities and non-profit organisations. However, many charities have recently imposed minimum system requirements for donated equipment. Additionally, parts from outdated systems may be salvaged and recycled through certain retail outlets and municipal or private recycling centers.

Recycling computing equipment can keep harmful materials such as lead, mercury, and hexavalent chromium out of landfills, but often computers gathered through recycling drives are shipped to developing countries where environmental standards are less strict than in North America and Europe. The Silicon Valley Toxics Coalition estimates that 80% of the post-consumer e-waste collected for recycling is shipped abroad to countries such as China, India, and Pakistan.

Computing supplies, such as printer cartridges, paper, and batteries may be recycled as well.

Telecommuting

Teleconferencing and telepresence technologies are often implemented in green computing initiatives. The advantages are many; increased worker satisfaction, reduction of greenhouse gas emissions related to travel, and increased profit margins as a result of lower overhead costs for office space, heat, lighting, etc. The savings are significant; the average annual energy consumption for U.S. office buildings is over 23 kilowatt hours per square foot, with heat, air conditioning and lighting accounting for 70% of all energy consumed. Other related initiatives, such as hotelling, reduce the square footage per employee as workers reserve space only when they need it. Many types of jobs—sales, consulting, field service—integrate well with this technique.

According to a report by the Consumer Electronics Association, there are 3.9 million workers telecommuting in the U.S. This translates into 9 to 14 billion kilowatt hours of electricity per year, says Doug Johnson who is senior director of technology policy for the CEA. That amount of electricity is enough to power 1 million U.S. households while saving the telecommuting family 840 million gallons of gasoline each year. Overall, the carbon emissions are being reduced by 14 million tons annually (equivalent to removing 2 million vehicles from the roads.)

Voice over IP (VoIP) reduces the telephony wiring infrastructure by sharing the existing Ethernet copper (a toxic metal). VoIP and phone extension mobility also made Hot desking and more practical.

Virtualisation

In computing, virtualisation is a broad term that refers to the abstraction of computer resources:

- Platform virtualisation, which separates an operating system from the underlying platform resources
    - o Full virtualisation
    - o Hardware-assisted virtualisation
    - o Partial virtualisation
    - o Paravirtualisation
    - o Operating system-level virtualisation
- Resource virtualisation, the virtualisation of specific system resources, such as storage volumes, name spaces, and network resources

- o Virtual memory, which allows uniform, contiguous addressing of physically separate and non-contiguous memory and disk areas
- o Redundant array of independent disks and logical volume management, combine many disks into one large logical disk.
- o Storage Virtualisation, the process of completely abstracting logical storage from physical storage
- o Channel bonding, the use multiple links combined to work as though they offered a single, higher-bandwidth link
- o Network virtualisation, creation of a virtualised network addressing space within or across network subnets
- o Computer clusters and grid computing, the combination of multiple discrete computers into larger metacomputers
- o partition (computing), is the splitting of a single resource (usually large), such as disk space or network bandwidth, into a number of smaller, more easily utilised resources of the same type
- o Encapsulation, the hiding of resource complexity by the creation of a simplified interface

- Application Virtualisation, the hosting of individual applications on alien hardware/software
  - o Portable application
  - o Cross-platform virtualisation
  - o Emulation or simulation
  - o Virtualisation Development, further work in this area
- Desktop virtualisation, the remote manipulation of a computer desktop.

TIMELINE OF VIRTUALISATION DEVELOPMENT

Note: This timeline is missing data for important historical systems, including: Atlas Computer (Manchester), GE 645, Burroughs B5000.

- **1964**
  - o IBM Cambridge Scientific Center begins development of CP-40.
- **1965**
  - o IBM M44/44X, experimental paging system, in use at Thomas J. Watson Research Center.
  - o IBM announces the IBM System/360-67, a 32-bit CPU with virtual memory hardware (August 1965).
- **1966**
  - o IBM ships the S/360-67 computer in June 1966
  - o IBM begins work on CP-67, a reimplementation of CP-40 for the S/360-67.
- **1967**
  - o CP-40 (January) and CP-67 (April) go into production time-sharing use.
- **1968**
  - o CP/CMS installed at eight initial customer sites.
  - o CP/CMS submitted to IBM Type-III Library by MIT's Lincoln Laboratory, making system available to all IBM S/360 customers at no charge in source code form.
  - o Resale of CP/CMS access begins at time-sharing vendor National CSS (becoming a distinct version, eventually renamed VP/CSS).
- **1970**
  - o IBM System/370 announced (June) – *without* virtual memory.
  - o Work begins on CP-370, a complete reimplementation of CP-67, for use on the System/370 series.
- **1971**
  - o First System/370 shipped: S/370-155 (January).

- 1972
    - o Announcement of virtual memory added to System/370 series.
    - o VM/370 announced – and running on announcement date. VM/370 includes the ability to run VM under VM (previously implemented both at IBM and at user sites under CP/CMS, but not made part of standard releases).
- 1973
    - o First shipment of announced virtual memory S/370 models (April: -158, May: -168).
- 1974-1998
    - o [ongoing history of VM family and VP/CSS.]
- 1985
    - o October 9, 1985: Announcement of the Intel 80286-based AT&T 6300+ with Simultask, a virtual machine monitor developed by Locus Computing Corporation in collaboration with AT&T, that enabled the direct execution of an Intel 8086 guest operating system under a host Unix System V Release 2 OS. Although the product was marketed with Microsoft MS-DOS as the guest OS, in fact the Virtual Machine could support any realmode operating system or standalone programme (such as Microsoft Flight Simulator) that was written using only valid 8086 instructions (not instructions introduced with the 80286). Locus subsequently developed this technology into their "Merge" product line.
- 1987
    - o January 1987: A "product evaluation" version of Merge/386 from Locus Computing Corporation was made available to OEMs. Merge/386 made use of the Virtual 8086 mode provided by the Intel 80386 processor, and supported multiple simultaneous virtual 8086 machines. The virtual machines supported unmodified guest operating systems and standalone programmes such as

Microsoft Flight Simulator; but in typical usage the guest was MS-DOS with a Locus proprietary redirector (also marketed for networked PCs as "PC-Interface") and a "network" driver that provided communication with a regular user-mode file server process running under the host operating system on the same machine.

- o October 1987: Retail Version 1.0 of Merge/386 began shipping, offered with Microport Unix System V Release 3.

- **1988**
  - o SoftPC 1.0 for Sun was introduced in 1988 by Insignia Solutions
  - o SoftPC appears in its first version for Apple Macintosh. These versions (Sun and Macintosh) have only support for DOS.
- **1997**
  - o First version of Virtual PC for Macintosh platform was released in June 1997 by Connectix
- **1998**
  - o October 26, 1998, VMware filed for a patent on their techniques, which is granted as U.S. Patent 6,397,242
- **1999**
  - o February 8, 1999, VMware introduced VMware Virtual Platform for the Intel IA-32 architecture.
- **2000**
  - o IBM announces z/VM, new version of VM for IBM's 64-bit z/Architecture
- **2001**
  - o June, Connectix launchs its first version of Virtual PC for Windows.
  - o July, VMWare created the first x86 server virtualisation product.

- **2003**
    - o February 18, 2003, Microsoft acquired virtualisation technologies (Virtual PC and unreleased product called "Virtual Server") from Connectix Corporation.
    - o Late 2003, EMC acquired VMware for $635 million.
    - o Late 2003, VERITAS acquired Ejascent for $59 million.
    - o November 10, 2003 Microsoft releases Microsoft Virtual PC, which is machine-level virtualisation technology, to ease the transition to Windows XP.
- **2005**
    - o HP releases Integrity Virtual Machines 1.0 and 1.2 which ran only HP-UX
    - o October 24, 2005 VMware releases VMware Player, a free player for virtual machines, to the masses.
- **2006**
    - o July 12, 2006 VMware releases VMware Server, a free machine-level virtualisation product for the server market.
    - o Microsoft Virtual PC 2006 is released as a free programme, also in July.
    - o July 17, 2006 Microsoft bought Softricity.
    - o August 16, 2006 VMware announces of the winners of the virtualisation appliance contest.
    - o September 26, 2006 moka5 delivers LivePC technology.
    - o HP releases Integrity Virtual Machines Version 2.0, which supports Windows Server 2003, CD and DVD burners, tape drives and VLAN.
    - o December 11, 2006 Virtual Iron releases Virtual Iron 3.1, a free bare metal virtualisation product for enterprise server virtualisation market.
- **2007**
    - o January 15, 2007 innoTek released VirtualBox Open Source Edition (OSE), the first professional PC

virtualisation solution released as open source under the GNU General Public License (GPL). It includes some code from the Qemu project.

- 2008
  - January 15, 2008 VMware, Inc. announced it has entered into a definitive agreement to acquire Thinstall, a privately-held application virtualisation software company.
  - February 12, 2008 Sun Microsystems announced that it had entered into a stock purchase agreement to acquire innotek, makers of VirtualBox.
  - In April, VMware releases VMware Workstation 6.5 beta, the first programme for Windows and Linux to enable DirectX 9 accelerated graphics on Windows XP guests.

Year 1960

In the mid 1960s, IBM's Cambridge Scientific Center developed CP-40, the first version of CP/CMS. It went into production use in January 1967. From its inception, CP-40 was intended to implement full virtualisation. Doing so required hardware and microcode customisation on a S/360-40, to provide the necessary address translation and other virtualisation features. Experience on the CP-40 project provided input to the development of the IBM System/360-67, announced in 1965 (along with its ill-starred operating system, TSS/360). CP-40 was reimplemented for the S/360-67 as CP-67, and by April 1967, both versions were in daily production use. CP/CMS was made generally available to IBM customers in source code form, as part of the unsupported IBM Type-III Library, in 1968.

Year 1970

IBM announced the System/370 in 1970. To the disappointment of CP/CMS users – as with the System/360 announcement – the series would not include virtual memory. In 1972, IBM changed direction, announcing that the option would be made available on all S/370 models, and also announcing several virtual storage operating systems, including VM/370. By the mid-1970s, CP/CMS, VM, and the maverick VP/CSS were running on a numerous large IBM mainframes. By the late 80s, there were reported to be more VM licenses than MVS licenses.

Year 1999

On February 8, 1999, VMware introduced the first x86 virtualisation product, *VMware Virtual Platform*, based on earlier research by its founders at Stanford University.

Year 2005

Free desktop virtualisation

Previously, a substantial licensing fee was required for the use of VMware's Workstation product. VMware decided to provide high quality virtualisation technology to everyone for free. They omitted the ability to create virtual machines and did not distribute the acceleration tools that come with VMware workstation. This early corporate play to encourage consumer applications of virtualisation went largely unnoticed.

Year 2006

This year Virtualisation has a new level of playing field in Application Virtualisation and Application Streaming.

Year 2008

VMware releases VMware Workstation 6.5 beta, the first programme for Windows and Linux to enable DirectX 9 accelerated graphics on Windows XP guests.

As an overview, there are three levels of virtualisation:

- At the hardware level, the VMs can run multiple guest OSes. This is best used for testing and training that require networking interoperability between more than one OSes, since not only the guest OS can be different than the host OS, it can run as many guest OS as long as there is enough CPU, RAM and HDD space. IBM introduced this around

1990 under the name logical partitioning (LPAR), at first only in the mainframe field.

- At the operating system level, it can only virtualise one OS: the guest OS is the host OS. This is similar to having many terminal server sessions without locking down the desktop. Thus, this is the best of both world, having the speed of a TS session with the benefit of a full access to the desktop as virtual machine, where the user can still control the **quotas** for CPU, RAM and HDD. Similar to the hardware level, this is still consider a **Server Virtualisation** where each guest OS has its own IP address, so it can be used for networking applications such as for web hosting.
- At the application level, it is running on the Host OS directly, without any guest OS, which can be in a locked down desktop, including in a terminal server session. This is called Application Virtualisation or Desktop Virtualisation, which virtualises the front-end, whereas Server Virtualisation virtualises the back-end. Now, Application Streaming refers to delivering applications directly onto the desktop and running them locally. Traditionally in terminal server computing, the applications are running on the server, not locally, and streaming the screenshots onto the desktop.

Application Virtualisation

Application Virtualisation solutions such as VMware ThinApp, Softricity, and Trigence attempt to separate application specific files and settings from the host operating system, thus allowing them to run in more-or-less isolated sandboxes without installation and without the memory and disk overhead of full machine virtualisation. Application Virtualisation is tightly tied to the host OS and thus does not translate to other operating systems or hardware. VMware ThinApp and Softricity are Intel Windows centric, while Trigence supports Linux and Solaris. Unlike machine virtualisation, Application virtualisation does not use code emulation or translation so CPU related benchmarks run with no changes, though fileystem benchmarks may experience some performance degradation. On Windows, VMware ThinApp and Softricity essentially work by intercepting filesystem and registry requests by an application and redirecting those requests to a preinstalled isolated sandbox, thus allowing the application to run without installation or changes to the local PC. Though VMware ThinApp and Softricity both began independent development around 1998, behind the scenes VMware ThinApp and Softricity are implemented using different techniques:

- VMware ThinApp works by packaging an application into a single "packaged" EXE which includes the runtime plus the application data files and registry. VMware ThinApp's runtime is loaded by Windows as a normal Windows application, from there the runtime replaces the Windows loader, filesystem, and registry for the target application and presents a merged image of the host PC as if the application had been previously installed. VMware ThinApp replaces all related API functions for the host application, for example the ReadFile API supplied to the application must pass through VMware ThinApp before it reaches the operating system. If the application is reading a virtual file, VMware ThinApp handles the request itself otherwise the request will be passed on to the operating system. Because VMware ThinApp is implemented in user-mode without device drivers and it does not have a client that is preinstalled, applications can run directly from USB Flash or network shares without previously needing elevated security privileges.
- Softricity (acquired by Microsoft) operates on a similar principle using device drivers to intercept file request in ring0 at a level closer to the operating system. Softricity installs a client in Administrator mode which can then be accessed by restricted users on the machine. An advantage of virtualising at the kernel level is the Windows Loader (responsible for loading EXE and DLL files) does not need to be reimplemented and greater application compatibility

can be achieved with less work (Softricity claims to support most major applications). A disadvantage for ring implementation is it requires elevated security privileges to be installed and crashes or security defects can occur system wide rather than being isolated to a specific application.

Because Application Virtualisation runs all application code natively, it can only provide security guarantees as strong as the host OS is able to provide. Unlike full machine virtualisation, Application virtualisation solutions currently do not work with device drivers and other code that runs at ring0 such as virus scanners. These special applications must be installed normally on the host PC in order to function.

Managed Runtimes

Another technique sometimes referred to as virtualisation, is portable byte code execution using a standard portable native runtime (aka Managed Runtimes). The two most popular solutions today include Java and .NET. These solutions both use a process called JIT (Just in time) compilation to translate code from a virtual portable machine language into the local processor's native code. This allows applications to be compiled for a single architecture and then run on many different machines. Beyond machine portable applications, an additional advantage to this technique includes strong security guarantees. Because all native application code is generated by the controlling environment, it can be checked for correctness (possible security exploits) prior to execution. Programmes must be originally designed for the environment in question or manually rewritten and recompiled to work for these new environments. For example, one cannot automatically convert or run a Windows / Linux native app on .NET or Java. Because portable runtimes try to present a common API for applications for a wide variety of hardware, applications are less able to take advantage of OS specific features. Portable application environments also have higher memory and CPU overheads than optimised native applications, but these overheads are much smaller compared with full machine virtualisation. Portable Byte Code environments such as Java have become very popular on the server where a wide variety of hardware exist and the set of OS-specific APIs required is standard across most Unix and Windows flavors. Another popular feature among managed runtimes is garbage collection, which automatically detects unused data and reclaims it without the developer having to explicitly invoke free operations.

Neutral View of Application Virtualisation

Given the industry-biased in the past, to be more neutral, there are also two other ways to look at the Application Level:

- The first type is application packagers (VMware ThinApp, Softricity) whereas the other is application compilers (Java and Dot Net). Because it is a packager, it can be used to stream applications without modifying the source code, whereas the latter can only be used to compile the source code.
- Another way to look at is through the Hypervisor point of view. The first one is "hypervisor" in user mode, whereas the other is "hypervisor" in runtime mode. The hypervisor was put in quotation, because both of them have similar behaviour in that it intercepts system calls in different mode: user mode and runtime mode. The user mode intercepts the system calls from the runtime mode before going to kernel mode. The real hypervisor only needs to intercept the system call using hypercall in kernel mode. Hopefully, once Windows have a Hypervisor, Virtual machine monitor, there may even be no need for JRE and CLR. Moreover, in Linux case, maybe the JRE can be modified to run on top of the Hypervisor as a loadable kernel module running in kernel mode, instead of the having the legacy runtime turtling around, running really slowly, in user mode. Now, if it were running on top of the Linux Hypervisor directly, then it should be called Java OS, not just another runtime mode JIT.

- Mendel Rosenblum called the runtime mode as High-level language virtual machines in August 2004. However, at that time, the first type, intercepting system calls in user mode, was irresponsible and unthinkable, so he didn't mention it on his article. Hence, Application Streaming was still mysterious in 2004. Now, when the JVM, no longer High-level language virtual machines, becomes Java OS running on Linux Hypervisor, then Java Applications will have a new level of playing field, just as Windows Applications already has with Softricity.
- In summary, the first one is virtualising the Binary Code so that it can be installed once and run anywhere, whereas the other is virtualising the Source Code using Byte code or Managed code so that it can be written once and run anywhere. Both of them are actually partial solution to portability problem: application portability and source code portability. Maybe it is time to combine the two problems into one complete solution at the hypervisor level in the kernel mode.

Further Development

However, the mysterious Application Streaming will soon become very popular, because Microsoft had just bought Softricity on July 17, 2006. Because of this, Traditional Rich Windows Applications will have a new level of playing field with the Web Applications and the Java Applications with respect to the ease of distributions (i.e. no more setup required, just click and run). Soon the frowned-upon will become the cheered-upon as every JRE and CLR will just be running virtually on the user mode without kernel mode drivers being installed and updated such that there can even be multiple versions of JRE and CLR in HDD as well as in RAM.

Nevertheless, this frowned and cheered-upon Rootkit technique such as filter driver maybe made obsolete once the Linux Hypervisor is integrated into the Linux Kernel and the Window Server

Virtualisation integrates the Windows Hypervisor with the Windows Kernel. This may take a while as the Linux Hypervisor are still waiting for the Xen Hypervisor and VMware Hypervisor to be fully compatible with each other as Oracle impatiently pounding at the door to let the Hypervisor come into the Linux Kernel so that it can full steam ahead with its Grid Computing life. Meanwhile, Microsoft have made their choice to be fully compatible with the Xen Hypervisor. IBM, of course, doesn't just sit idle as it is working with VMware for the x86 servers, and possibly helping Xen to move from x86 into IBM's POWER using the open source rHype. Now, to make the Hypervisor party to become a full house, Intel's Vanderpool and AMD's Pacifica are hoping to ease and speed up paravirtualisation so that guest OS can be run unmodified.

15

COMPUTER SECURITY

Computer security is a branch of technology known as information security as applied to computers. The objective of computer security varies and can include protection of information from theft or corruption, or the preservation of availability, as defined in the security policy.

Computer security imposes requirements on computers that are different from most system requirements because they often take the form of constraints on what computers are not supposed to do. This makes computer security particularly challenging because we find it hard enough just to make computer programmes do everything they are designed to do correctly. Furthermore, negative requirements are deceptively complicated to satisfy and require exhaustive testing to verify, which is impractical for most computer programmes. Computer security provides a technical strategy to convert negative requirements to positive enforceable rules. For this reason, computer security is often more technical and mathematical than some computer science fields.

Typical approaches to improving computer security (in approximate order of strength) can include the following:

- Physically limit access to computers to only those who will not compromise security.
- Hardware mechanisms that impose rules on computer programmes, thus avoiding depending on computer programmes for computer security.

- Operating system mechanisms that impose rules on programmes to avoid trusting computer programmes.
- Programming strategies to make computer programmes dependable and resist subversion.

Secure Operating Systems

One use of the term computer security refers to technology to implement a secure operating system. Much of this technology is based on science developed in the 1980s and used to produce what may be some of the most impenetrable operating systems ever. Though still valid, the technology is in limited use today, primarily because it imposes some changes to system management and also because it is not widely understood. Such ultra-strong secure operating systems are based on operating system kernel technology that can guarantee that certain security policies are absolutely enforced in an operating environment. An example of such a Computer security policy is the Bell-LaPadula model. The strategy is based on a coupling of special microprocessor hardware features, often involving the memory management unit, to a special correctly implemented operating system kernel. This forms the foundation for a secure operating system which, if certain critical parts are designed and implemented correctly, can ensure the absolute impossibility of penetration by hostile elements. This capability is enabled because the configuration not only imposes a security policy, but in theory completely protects itself from corruption. Ordinary operating systems, on the other hand, lack the features that assure this maximal level of security. The design methodology to produce such secure systems is precise, deterministic and logical.

Systems designed with such methodology represent the state of the art of computer security although products using such security are not widely known. In sharp contrast to most kinds of software, they meet specifications with verifiable certainty comparable to specifications for size, weight and power. Secure operating systems designed this way are used primarily to protect national security information, military secrets, and the data of international financial institutions. These are very powerful security tools and very few secure operating systems have been certified at the highest level (Orange Book A-1) to operate over the range of "Top Secret" to "unclassified" (including Honeywell SCOMP, USAF SACDIN, NSA Blacker and Boeing MLS LAN.) The assurance of security depends not only on the soundness of the design strategy, but also on the assurance of correctness of the implementation, and therefore there are degrees of security strength defined for COMPUSEC. The Common Criteria quantifies security strength of products in terms of two components, security functionality and assurance level (such as EAL levels), and these are specified in a Protection Profile for requirements and a Security Target for product descriptions. None of these ultra-high assurance secure general purpose operating systems have been produced for decades or certified under the Common Criteria.

Secure operating systems designed to meet medium robustness levels of security functionality and assurance have seen wider use within both government and commercial markets. Medium robust systems typically provide nearly all of the security features of the most advanced secure operating systems but do so at a lower assurance level (such as EAL4 or EAL5). These systems are found in use on web servers, guards, database servers, and management hosts and are used not only to protect the data stored on these systems but also to provide a high level of protection for network connections and routing services.

Security Architecture

Security Architecture can be defined as the design artifacts that describe how the security controls (security countermeasures) are positioned, and how they relate to the overall information technology architecture. These controls serve the purpose to maintain the system's quality attributes, among them confidentiality, integrity, availability, accountability and assurance. In simpler words, a security architecture is the plan that shows where security measures need to be placed. If the plan describes a specific solution then, prior to building such a plan, one would make a risk analysis. If the plan describes a generic high level design then (reference architecture) then the plan should be based on a threat analysis.

Security by Design

The technologies of computer security are based on logic. There is no universal standard notion of what secure behaviour is. "Security" is a concept that is unique to each situation. Security is extraneous to the function of a computer application, rather than ancillary to it, thus security necessarily imposes restrictions on the application's behaviour.

There are several approaches to security in computing, sometimes a combination of approaches is valid:

1. Trust all the software to abide by a security policy but the software is not trustworthy (this is computer insecurity).
2. Trust all the software to abide by a security policy and the software is validated as trustworthy (by tedious branch and path analysis for example).
3. Trust no software but enforce a security policy with mechanisms that are not trustworthy (again this is computer insecurity).
4. Trust no software but enforce a security policy with trustworthy mechanisms.

Many systems have unintentionally resulted in the first possibility. Since approach two is expensive and non-deterministic, its use is very limited. Approaches one and three lead to failure. Because approach number four is often based on hardware mechanisms and avoids abstractions and a multiplicity of degrees of freedom, it is more practical. Combinations of approaches two and four are often used in a layered architecture with thin layers of two and thick layers of four.

There are myriad strategies and techniques used to design security systems. There are few, if any, effective strategies to enhance security after design.

One technique enforces the principle of least privilege to great extent, where an entity has only the privileges that are needed for its function. That way even if an attacker gains access to one part of the system, fine-grained security ensures that it is just as difficult for them to access the rest.

Furthermore, by breaking the system up into smaller components, the complexity of individual components is reduced, opening up the possibility of using techniques such as automated theorem proving to prove the correctness of crucial software subsystems. This enables a closed form solution to security that works well when only a single well-characterised property can be isolated as critical, and that property is also assessable to math. Not surprisingly, it is impractical for generalised correctness, which probably cannot even be defined, much less proven. Where formal correctness proofs are not possible, rigorous use of code review and unit testing represent a best-effort approach to make modules secure.

The design should use "defense in depth", where more than one subsystem needs to be violated to compromise the integrity of the system and the information it holds. Defense in depth works when the breaching of one security measure does not provide a platform to facilitate subverting another. Also, the cascading principle acknowledges that several low hurdles does not make a high hurdle. So cascading several weak mechanisms does not provide the safety of a single stronger mechanism.

Subsystems should default to secure settings, and wherever possible should be designed to "fail secure" rather than "fail insecure". Ideally, a secure system should require a deliberate, conscious, knowledgeable and free decision on the part of legitimate authorities in order to make it insecure.

In addition, security should not be an all or nothing issue. The designers and operators of systems should assume that security breaches are inevitable. Full audit trails should be kept of system activity, so that when a security breach occurs, the mechanism and extent of the breach can be determined. Storing audit trails remotely, where they can only be appended to, can keep intruders from covering their tracks. Finally, full disclosure helps to ensure that when bugs are found the "window of vulnerability" is kept as short as possible.

Early history of Security by Design

The early Multics operating system was notable for its early emphasis on computer security by design, and Multics was possibly the very first operating system to be designed as a secure system from the ground up. In spite of this, Multics' security was broken, not once, but repeatedly. The strategy was known as 'penetrate and test' and has become widely known as a non-terminating process that fails to produce computer security. This led to further work on computer security that prefigured modern security engineering techniques producing closed form processes that terminate.

Secure Coding

If the operating environment is not based on a secure operating system capable of maintaining a domain for its own execution, and capable of protecting application code from malicious subversion, and capable of protecting the system from subverted code, then high degrees of security are understandably not possible. While such secure operating systems are possible and have been implemented, most commercial systems fall in a 'low security' category because they rely on features not supported by secure operating systems (like portability, et al.). In low security operating environments, applications must be relied on to participate in their own protection. There are 'best effort' secure coding practices that can be followed to make an application more resistant to malicious subversion.

In commercial environments, the majority of software subversion vulnerabilities result from a few known kinds of coding defects. Common software defects include buffer overflows, format string vulnerabilities, integer overflow, and code/command injection.

Some common languages such as C and C++ are vulnerable to all of these defects. Other languages, such as Java, are more resistant to some of these defects, but are still prone to code/command injection and other software defects which facilitate subversion.

Recently another bad coding practice has come under scrutiny; dangling pointers. The first known exploit for this particular problem was presented in July 2007. Before this publication the problem was known but considered to be academic and not practically exploitable.

In summary, 'secure coding' can provide significant payback in low security operating environments, and therefore worth the effort. Still there is no known way to provide a reliable degree of subversion resistance with any degree or combination of 'secure coding.'

Capabilities vs. ACLs

Within computer systems, the two fundamental means of enforcing privilege separation are access control lists (ACLs) and capabilities. The semantics of ACLs have been proven to be insecure in many situations (e.g., Confused deputy problem). It has also been shown that ACL's promise of giving access to an object to only one person can never be guaranteed in practice. Both of these problems are resolved by capabilities. This does not mean practical flaws exist in all ACL-based systems, but only that the designers of certain utilities must take responsibility to ensure that they do not introduce flaws.

Unfortunately, for various historical reasons, capabilities have been mostly restricted to research operating systems and commercial OSs still use ACLs. Capabilities can, however, also be implemented at the language level, leading to a style of programming that is essentially a refinement of standard object-oriented design. An open source project in the area is the E language.

First the Plessey System 250 and then Cambridge CAP computer demonstrated the use of capabilities, both in hardware and software, in the 1970s, so this technology is hardly new. A reason for the lack of adoption of capabilities may be that ACLs appeared to offer a 'quick fix' for security without pervasive redesign of the operating system and hardware.

The most secure computers are those not connected to the Internet and shielded from any interference. In the real world, the most security comes from operating systems where security is not an add-on, such as OS/400 from IBM. This almost never shows up in lists of vulnerabilities for good reason. Years may elapse between one problem needing remediation and the next.

A good example of a secure system is EROS. But see also the article on secure operating systems. TrustedBSD is an example of an open source project with a goal, among other things, of building capability functionality into the FreeBSD operating system. Much of the work is already done.

Applications

Computer security is critical in almost any technology-driven industry which operates on computer systems. The issues of computer based systems and addressing their countless vulnerabilities are an integral part of maintaining an operational industry.

In aviation

The aviation industry is especially important when analysing computer security because the involved risks include expensive equipment and cargo, transportation infrastructure, and human life. Security can be compromised by hardware and software malpractice, human error, and faulty operating environments. Threats that exploit computer vulnerabilities can stem from sabotage, espionage, industrial competition, terrorist attack, mechanical malfunction, and human error.

The consequences of a successful deliberate or inadvertent misuse of a computer system in the aviation industry range from loss of confidentiality to loss of system integrity, which may lead to more serious concerns such as data theft or loss, network and air traffic control outages, which in turn can lead to airport closures, loss of aircraft, loss of passenger life. Military systems that control munitions can pose an even greater risk.

A proper attack does not need to be very high tech or well funded for a power outage at an airport alone can cause repercussions worldwide. One of the easiest and, arguably, the most difficult to trace security vulnerabilities is achievable by transmitting unauthorised communications over specific radio frequencies. These transmissions may spoof air traffic controllers or simply disrupt communications altogether. These incidents are very common, having altered flight courses of commercial aircraft and caused panic and confusion in the past. Controlling aircraft over oceans is especially dangerous because radar surveillance only extends 175 to 225 miles offshore. Beyond the radar's sight controllers must rely on periodic radio communications with a third party.

Lightning, power fluctuations, surges, brown-outs, blown fuses, and various other power outages instantly disable all computer systems, since they are dependent on electrical source. Other accidental and intentional faults have caused significant disruption of safety critical systems throughout the last few decades and dependence on reliable communication and electrical power only jeopardises computer safety.

Notable System Accidents

In 1983, Korean Airlines Flight 007, a Boeing 747 was shot down by Soviet SU-15 jets after a navigation computer malfunction caused the aircraft to steer 185 miles off course into Soviet Union airspace. All 269 passengers were killed.

In 1994, over a hundred intrusions were made by unidentified hackers into the Rome Laboratory, the US Air Force's main command and research facility. Using trojan horse viruses, hackers were able to obtain unrestricted access to Rome's networking systems and remove traces of their activities. The intruders were able to obtain classified files, such as air tasking order systems data and furthermore able to penetrate connected networks of National Aeronautics and Space Administration's Goddard Space Flight Center, Wright-Patterson Air Force Base, some Defense contractors, and other private sector organisations, by posing as a trusted Rome center user.

Electromagnetic interference is another threat to computer safety and in 1989, a United States Air Force F-16 jet accidentally dropped a 230 kg bomb in West Georgia after unspecified interference caused the jet's computers to release it.

A similar telecommunications accident also happened in 1994, when two UH-60 Blackhawk helicopters were destroyed by F-15 aircraft in Iraq because the IFF system's encryption system malfunctioned.

Terminology

The following terms used in engineering secure systems are explained below.

- Firewalls can either be hardware devices or software programmes. They provide some protection from online intrusion, but since they allow some applications (e.g. web browsers) to connect to the Internet, they don't protect against some unpatched vulnerabilities in these applications (e.g. lists of known unpatched holes from Secunia and Security Focus).
- Automated theorem proving and other verification tools can enable critical algorithms and code used in secure systems to be mathematically proven to meet their specifications.
- Thus simple microkernels can be written so that we can be sure they don't contain any bugs: eg EROS and Coyotos.

A bigger OS, capable of providing a standard API like POSIX, can be built on a secure microkernel using small API servers running as normal programmes. If one of these API servers has a bug, the kernel and the other servers are not affected: e.g. Hurd or Minix 3.

- Cryptographic techniques can be used to defend data in transit between systems, reducing the probability that data exchanged between systems can be intercepted or modified.
- Strong authentication techniques can be used to ensure that communication end-points are who they say they are.

Secure cryptoprocessors can be used to leverage physical security techniques into protecting the security of the computer system.

- Chain of trust techniques can be used to attempt to ensure that all software loaded has been certified as authentic by the system's designers.
- Mandatory access control can be used to ensure that privileged access is withdrawn when privileges are revoked. For example, deleting a user account should also stop any processes that are running with that user's privileges.
- Capability and access control list techniques can be used to ensure privilege separation and mandatory access control. The next sections discuss their use.

Some of the following items may belong to the computer insecurity article:

- application with known security flaws should not be run. Either leave it turned off until it can be patched or otherwise fixed, or delete it and replace it with some other application. Publicly known flaws are the main entry used by worms to automatically break into a system and then spread to other systems connected to it. The security website Secunia provides a search tool for unpatched known flaws in popular products.

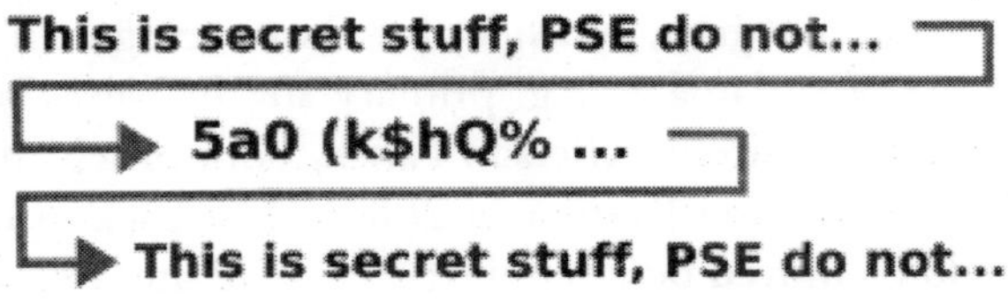

Cryptographic techniques involve transforming information, scrambling it so it becomes unreadable during transmission. The intended recipient can unscramble the message, but eavesdroppers cannot.

- Backups are a way of securing information; they are another copy of all the important computer files kept in another location. These files are kept on hard disks, CD-Rs, CD-RWs, and tapes. Suggested locations for backups are a fireproof, waterproof, and heat proof safe, or in a separate, offsite location than that in which the original files are contained. Some individuals and companies also keep their backups in safe deposit boxes inside bank vaults. There is also a fourth option, which involves using one of the file hosting services that backs up files over the Internet for both business and individuals.
  - o Backups are also important for reasons other than security. Natural disasters, such as earthquakes, hurricanes, or tornadoes, may strike the building where the computer is located. The building can be on fire, or an explosion may occur. There needs to be a recent backup at an alternate secure location, in case of such kind of disaster. Further, it is recommended that the alternate location be placed where the same disaster would not affect both locations. Examples of alternate disaster recovery sites being compromised by the same disaster that affects the primary site include having had a primary site in World Trade Center I and the recovery site in 7 World Trade Center, both of which were destroyed in the 9/11 attack, and having one's primary site and recovery site in the same coastal region, which leads to both being vulnerable to hurricane damage (e.g. primary site in New Orleans and recovery site in Jefferson Parish, both of which were hit by Hurricane Katrina in 2005). The backup media should be moved between the geographic sites in a secure manner, in order to prevent them from being stolen.

- Anti-virus software consists of computer programmes that attempt to identify, thwart and eliminate computer viruses and other malicious software (malware).
- Firewalls are systems which help protect computers and computer networks from attack and subsequent intrusion by restricting the network traffic which can pass through them, based on a set of system administrator defined rules.
- Access authorisation restricts access to a computer to group of users through the use of authentication systems. These systems can protect either the whole computer—such as through an interactive logon screen—or individual services, such as an FTP server. There are many methods for identifying and authenticating users, such as passwords, identification cards, and, more recently, smart cards and biometric systems.
- Encryption is used to protect the message from the eyes of others. It can be done in several ways by switching the characters around, replacing characters with others, and even removing characters from the message. These have to be used in combination to make the encryption secure enough, that is to say, sufficiently difficult to crack. Public key encryption is a refined and practical way of doing encryption. It allows for example anyone to write a message for a list of recipients, and only those recipients will be able to read that message.
- Intrusion-detection systems can scan a network for people that are on the network but who should not be there or are doing things that they should not be doing, for example trying a lot of passwords to gain access to the network.
- Pinging The ping application can be used by potential crackers to find if an IP address is reachable. If a cracker finds a computer they can try a port scan to detect and attack services on that computer.
- Social engineering awareness keeps employees aware of the dangers of social engineering and/or having a policy in

place to prevent social engineering can reduce successful breaches of the network and servers.

- Honey pots are computers that are either intentionally or unintentionally left vulnerable to attack by crackers. They can be used to catch crackers or fix vulnerabilities.

Bibliography

Abelson, H. and G. J. Sussman. *Structure and Interpretation of Computer Programs (2nd Edition)* (MIT Press, 1996).

Abercrombie, John R. *Computer Programs for Literary Analysis.* Philadelphia: University of Pennsylvania Press, 1984.

Abrahams, D. "Exception Safety in Generic Components," in M. Jazayeri, R. Loos, D. Musser (eds.), *Generic Programming: International Seminar on Generic Programming,* Dagstuhl Castle, Germany, April/May 1998, Selected Papers, Lecture Notes in Computer Science 1766 (Springer, 2001).

Alexandrescu, A. "Lock-Free Data Structures" (*C/C++ Users Journal,* 22(10), October 2004

Association for Computing Machinery. 1998, *ACM Computing Classification System.* 1998.

Austern, M.H. *Generic Programming and the STL* (Addison-Wesley, 1999).

Baker, Jason D. *Christian Cyberspace Companion. A Guide to the Internet and Christian Online Resources.* Grand Rapids, Mi.: Baker, 1995.

Barton, J. and L. Nackman. *Scientific and Engineering C++* (Addison-Wesley, 1994).

Bentley, J. *Programming Pearls (2nd Edition)* (Addison-Wesley, 2000).

Biermann, A.W., *Great Ideas in Computer Science: A Gentle Introduction* (2d ed. 1997).

Bolter, David J. *Turing's Man: Western Culture in the Computer Age* (1984 ed.). The University of North Carolina Press, Chapel Hill NC.

Butenhof, D. *Programming with POSIX Threads* (Addison-Wesley, 1997).

Campbell, Dave and Mary Campbell. *The Student's Guide to Doing Research on the Internet.* Reading, Massachusetts: Addison-Wesley, 1995.

Christos Papadimitriou (1993). *Computational Complexity* (1st ed.). Addison Wesley, Chapter 3: Computability, pp.57–70.

Cline, M., G. Lomow, and M. Girou. *C++ FAQs (2nd Edition)* (Addison-Wesley, 1999).

Cohen, D. I. A., *Introduction to Computer Theory* (2d ed. 1996).

Committee on the Fundamentals of Computer Science: Challenges and Opportunities, National Research Council (2004). *Computer Science: Reflections on the Field, Reflections from the Field.* National Academies Press.

Computer science is the study of information" New Jersey Institute of Technology, Gutenberg Information Technologies.

Constable, R.L. (March 2000) *Computer Science: Achievements and Challenges circa 2000.*

Cooper, S. Barry (2004). *Computability Theory* (1st ed.). Chapman & Hall/CRC.

Crowley, J. L.; Coutaz, J.; Bérard, F. Perceptual user interfaces: things that see. *Commun. ACM 2000*, 43 (3), 54–64.

Denning, P.J. (2000). "Computer Science: The Discipline". *Encyclopedia of Computer Science.*

Denning, Peter J. *Is computer science science?*, Communications of the ACM, April 2005.

Denning, Peter J., *Great principles in computing curricula*, Technical Symposium on Computer Science Education, 2004.

Dilson, Jesse. *The Abacus* ((1968,1994) ed.). St. Martin's Press, NY.

Fielding, R.; Gettys, J.; Mogul, J.; Frystyk, H.; Masinter, L.; Leach, P.; Berners-Lee, T. (June 1999). *Hypertext Transfer Protocol — HTTP/1.1.*

Hahne, Harry, "Computer Resources: Exploring the Options for Graduate Students." In *1996 Seminary and Graduate School Handbook: Spring Edition.* Evanston, IL: Berry Publishing Services, 1996.

Harel, David, Yishai A. Feldman, *Algorithmics: the spirit of computing,* Edition 3, Pearson Education, 2004.

Hockey, Susan. *A Guide to Computer Applications in the Humanities.* Baltimore: John Hopkins Univerisity Press, 1980.

Hodges, Andrew. *Alan Turing: The Enigma* ((1983) ed.). Simon and Schuster, New York.

Hsu, Jeffrey. *A Comprehensive Guide to Computer Bible Study. Up-to-Date Information on the Best Software and Techniques.* Dallas: Word, 1993.

Hughes, John J. *Bits, Bytes and Biblical Studies.* Grand Rapids, Mi.: Zondervan, 1987.

Hughes, John J., ed. *Bits and Bytes Review.* Whitefish, Montana, 59937: Bits and Bytes Computer Resources, 1986-1991.

IEEE Computer Society and the Association for Computing Machinery. *Computing Curricula* 2001: Computer Science. December 15, 2001.

Jan, T.; Piccardi, M.; Hintz, T. Automated Human Behaviour Classification using Modified Probabilistic Neural Network. In *Proc. Int. Conf. Computational Intelligence for Modelling, Control and Automation*; CIMCA 2003, Vienna, Austria, Feb. 12–14, 2003.

Jean-Luc Chabert, Évelyne Barbin, *A history of algorithms: from the pebble to the microchip*, Springer, 1999.

Kempf, Karl (1961). *Historical Monograph: Electronic Computers Within the Ordnance Corps.* Aberdeen Proving Ground (United States Army).

Knuth, Donald E. *Selected Papers on Computer Science,* CSLI Publications, Cambridge Univ. Press, 1996.

Kraft, Robert A. *Computer Assisted Tools for Septuagint Analysis*, 1986.

Lakos, J. *Large-Scale C++ Software Design* (Addison-Wesley, 1996).

Levy, Steven (1984). *Hackers: Heroes of the Computer Revolution.* Doubleday.

Maran, R., *Computers Simplified* (4th ed. 1998).

McCarty, Willard, ed. *Humanities Computing Yearbook.* Oxford: Clarendon Press, 1988-.

Miall, David S., ed. *Humanities and the Computer: New Directions.* Clarendon Press: Oxford, 1990.

Musser, D. R., G. J. Derge, and A. Saini. *STL Tutorial and Reference Guide, 2nd Edition* (Addison-Wesley, 2001).

Nash, S.G., *A History of Scientific Computing* (1990).

Neumann, Kenneth J. *The Authenticity of the Pauline Epistles in the Light of Stylostatistical Analysis.* SBLDS, no. 120. Atlanta: Scholars Press, 1990.

Norton, P., *Peter Norton's Introduction to Computers* (2d ed. 1996).

Oakman, R.L., *The Computer Triangle: Hardware, Software, People* (2d ed. 1997).

Parnas, David L. (1998). "Software Engineering Programmes are not Computer Science Programmes". *Annals of Software Engineering* 6: 19–37.

Poswick, Ferdinand R., ed. *Bible and Computer: Interpretation, Hermeneutics, Expertise.* Paris-Genéve: Champion-Slatkine, 1992

Poswick, Ferdinand R., ed. *Computers: Desk and Discipline, The Impact of Computers on Biblical Studies.* Geneva: Champion-Slatkine, 1995.

Rehmeyer, Julie J. 2007. Mapping a medusa: The Internet spreads its tentacles. Science News 171(June 23):387-388.

Sipser, Michael (1997). *Introduction to the Theory of Computation.* PWS Publishing, Chapters 3–6, pp.123–222.

Tanenbaum, A.S. and J. R. Goodman. *Structured Computer Organization* (4th ed. 1998).

Tout, Nigel (2006). "Calculator Timeline". *Vintage Calculator Web Museum.*

van Heijenoort, Jean. *From Frege to Gödel, A Source Book in Mathematical Logic, 1879–1931* ((1967) ed.). Harvard University Press, Cambridge, MA., 3rd edition 1976.

Willinger, Walter, Ramesh Govindan, Sugih Jamin, Vern Paxson, and Scott Shenker (2002). Scaling phenomena in the Internet, in *Proceedings of the National Academy of Sciences, 99*, suppl. 1, 2573–2580.

Index

A

Abelson, H. 443
Abercrombie, John R. 443
Abrahams, D. 443
Accounting machines 9
Advanced analog computers 10
Aiken, Howard 18
Alexandrescu, A. 443
Algorithms 54, 55, 57, 261, 272
Ames Research Center 2
Analog computing machines 12
  systems 11
Analytical Engine 18
Ancient Greece 4
Antikythera mechanism 4
Application packagers 426
  Virtualisation 423, 425, 426
Arithmetic tasks 4
Arithmometer, Thomas 5
Artificial Intelligence 254
Astronomical calculations 4, 8
  clock tower 4
  Computing Bureau 8
Austern, M.H. 443
Auto electronics 404
Automata theory 54
Automatic Sequence Controlled Calculator 18

B

Babbage, Charles 6
Baker, Jason D. 443
Barton, J. 443
Basel Action Network 405
Bentley, J. 443
Biermann, A.W. 443
Binary software techniques 74
Biometric fingerprinting 146
Blaise Pascal 5
Bluetooth 172, 194, 196, 197, 202, 296, 297, 299
  connectivity 394
  low energy 340
  protocol stack 340
  Radio 340
  wireless 205
Bolter, David J. 443

Broadband antenna 161
  modem 188, 214
Bush, Vannevar 12
Butenhof, D. 444

C

Calculating clock 5
Campbell, Dave 444
Card readers 154
CD Controller 174
Chemical hazards 407
Cline, M. 444
Cohen, D. I. A. 444
Columbia Supercomputer 2
Columbia University 8
Commercial aircraft 437
Compromise security 429
Computability theory 54
Computational complexity theory 54
  geometry 54
Computer Forensics 136
  Hardware 3
  Management 155
  networking 43, 46, 193, 229
  Online Forensic Evidence Extractor 136
  programming 8, 12, 55
  security 429, 430, 432, 434, 436
Computing Hardware 2
Constable, R.L. 444
Consumer Awareness Efforts 404
  Electronics Association 415
Cooper, S. Barry 444
Core protocols 340
Corporate recycling 407
Crowley, J. L. 444
Cryptographic techniques 439

D

Dangerous recycling methods 408
Data structures 54
Denning, Peter J. 444
Desktop calculators 9
  computer 43, 163, 208, 230, 335, 379, 442
  Virtualisation 422, 423
Dialup speeds 185
Digital 3D record 71
  audio players 115, 154
  audio recordings 56
  cameras 1, 133, 135, 154, 158, 192, 241, 246, 330, 404
  circuit 12, 17
  computers 2, 11, 12, 13
  devices 12
  electronic calculator 18
  information 163
  mechanical calculator 5
  music 21
Dilson, Jesse 444
Direct broadcast satellite 186
Disk enclosure 149

Management 155
DVD Controller 174
reader 154

E

Eckert, W.J. 8
Electrical analog computers 11
Engineering 12
equipment 402
power 437
voltages 11
Electro-mechanical computer 18
Electromagnetic interference 438
Electronic circuit elements 12
computers 1
devices 120, 215, 400
equipment 401
Products Environmental Assessment Tool 411
Embedded computer 1
Environmental impact 405
issues 408
Ethernet router 214
European Community 401
ExpressCard 159
External hard disk 145
External hard drive 152
External magnetic hard drives 154

F

Fielding, R. 444
Formal methods 59
Frystyk, H. 444
Future development 147, 315

G

German polymath 5
Goddard Space Flight Center 438
Graphing Calculators 156
Green computing 409, 410, 411, 412, 414
Electronics Council 411

H

Harvard mathematician 18
Hazardous materials 410
Health Hazards 406
High speed dialup 185
Hollerith, Herman 8
Hughes, John J. 445
Human error 436
life 436
Hurricane damage 440

I

IBM Zurich Research Laboratory 181
Industrial robots 1
Integrated circuits 1
Interactive Disassembler 80
Intermediate translation layer 159
Internal host adapter 152
Internet Service 184

Intra-city communication network 214

J

Jan, T. 445
Java Applications 427

K

Katrina, Hurricane 440
Kempf, Karl 445
Kepler, Johannes 5
Knuth, Donald E. 445
Kraft, Robert A. 445

L

Law enforcement 136
Levy, Steven 445
Link Manager Protocol 340
Linux Hypervisor 427
Logical Link Control 341
London Science Museum 7

M

Magnetic core memory 40
Managed runtimes 425
Masinter, L. 444
Materials recycling 414
Mathematical calculations 9
Mechanical analog computers 4
  calculators 5, 9, 10
  computing devices 4
  disk drive 129
Memory management unit 118
  strategies 118
Miall, David S. 446
Microcomputer 28
Microsoft Partners 397
  Surface 394, 396
  Windows 146, 154
  Windows systems 73
Minicomputer 28, 38
Mobile computing environments 46
Modern computers 1, 5, 13, 14, 32, 41, 44, 141, 183
  digital computers 11
  operating systems 128
  telecommunications 186
Music machine 6
  storage 137
Musser, D. R. 446

N

Napier, John 4
Nash, S.G. 446
National Aeronautics and Space Administration 438
  Cristina Foundation 406
  recycling programmes 404
  Technology Recycling Project 406
Natural Language Processing 272
Nervous system 393
Network protocols 153
Networking technologies 46
Neumann, Kenneth J. 446

Nieman, H.W. 12
Non-discoverable Bluetooth devices 345
Notable system accidents 437
Numerical algorithms 59

O

Operating system support 154
Operational industry 436

P

Panasonic Computer Solutions Company 394
Parnas, David L. 446
Partial virtualisation 415
Periodic radio communications 437
Peripheral device 26, 27, 45
Personal computer 1, 36, 43, 46, 129, 162, 207, 213, 238, 240, 255
Physical environment 388
  phenomena 11
Physicist 4
Portable flash memory devices 154
  Gaming systems 154
  media players 154
Post-World War II 8
Poswick, Ferdinand R. 446
Power management 412
  supply 413
Punched card system 6
Purchasing computer systems 412

Q

Quantum computing theory 54
  properties 54

R

Radio modems 164
Recycling centers 414
  environment 406
  services 406
Regional governments 400
Rehmeyer, Julie J. 446
Reliable communication 437
Reverse engineering 70
Rosenblum, Mendel 427
Runtime mode 426, 427

S

Schickard, Wilhelm 5
Scottish mathematician 4
Secure cryptoprocessors 439
Security architecture 431
  controls 431
  countermeasures 431
Semiconductor memory 40
Server Virtualisation 427
Service Discovery Protocol 341
Service-oriented modeling 89
Silicon Valley Toxics Coalition 405

Social engineering 441
Software programme 70, 438
Song Dynasty 4
Strong authentication techniques 439
Symbolic mathematics 59
System's designers 439

T

Tanenbaum, A.S. 446
Technical information 340
Telecommunications accident 438
Telephony control protocol 341
Theoretical maxima 166
Thinkpad developers 355
  keyboard 355
Thomas, Charles Xavier 5
Thomas J. Watson 8
Thomson, James 12
Tout, Nigel 446

U

United States 12, 14, 45, 73, 189, 210, 215, 246, 329, 406, 408, 409, 413, 418, 442
United States Census Bureau 8

V

Virtual memory 382, 416, 417, 418, 421
Virtualisation Development 416
von Neumann architecture 2, 3

W

Wearable computer 387
WEEE Directive 401
Wi-Fi 186, 191, 192, 193, 194, 195, 198, 202, 238, 296, 377, 379, 394
Willinger, Walter 446
Windows 98 154, 155, 315
  applications 136
  Fundamentals 387
  Hypervisor 428
  Vista ReadyBoost 137
  XP 145, 147, 201, 312, 313, 335, 352, 366, 367, 368, 369, 370, 371, 372, 373, 374, 375, 376, 377, 378, 379, 380, 381, 382, 383, 387
Wireless Application Environment 342
  Application Protocol 342
  communications 215, 312, 332
  community network 214
  networking 171, 192, 213, 215, 216, 217, 322, 349
World War II 11

Z

Zwinger Museum 5